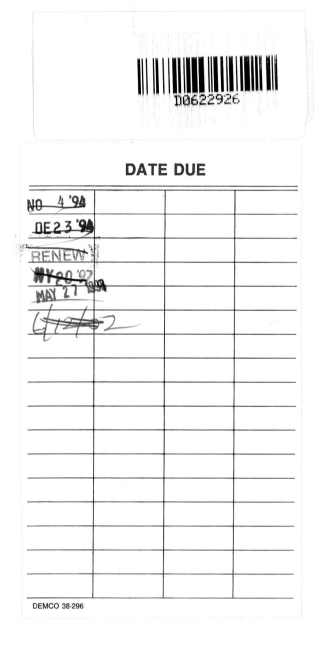

DATE DUE

NO 4 '94			
DE 23 '94			
RENEW			
MY 20 '97			
MAY 27			

A LIBRARY OF LITERARY CRITICISM

A Library
of Literary Criticism

THE
NEW
TESTAMENT *in*

Literary
Criticism

Compiled and edited by
LELAND RYKEN

Frederick Ungar Publishing Co., New York

Copyright © 1984 by Frederick Ungar Publishing Co., Inc.
Printed in the United States of America

Library of Congress Cataloging in Publication Data
Main entry under title:

The New Testament in literary criticism.

(A Library of literary criticism)
Includes bibliographical references and index.
1. Bible. N.T. Criticism, interpretation, etc.
I. Ryken, Leland. II. Series.
BS2361.2.N38   1984   225.6'6   84-129
ISBN 0-8044-3271-6

Selections in this volume are quoted with the approval of the copyright owners and may not be reprinted elsewhere without their consent. The exact source is at the end of each selection. For acknowledgments see page 339.

CONTENTS

Notes on Editorial Procedure

As editor I have sometimes omitted illustrative material in order to reproduce a critic's framework of generalizations. In so doing, I have been able to preserve the flow of a critic's argument and do justice to the overall line of thought. I have indicated my omissions with elliptical marks.

The only liberty I have knowingly taken with a text is to raise a lower case letter to a capital to indicate the beginning of a new sentence in my excerpted version.

For major entries, such as those on individual books or a form such as gospel, I have arranged the selections around topics (e.g., "structure," "unifying motifs"). Headings for these topics appear at the beginning of each group of selections on a common theme. I have also supplied cross references when a given topic is closely related to another entry in the book. The best guide to finding material on a given topic is the table of contents.

Leland Ryken
Wheaton College

ABBREVIATIONS OF JOURNALS

CBQ	Catholic Biblical Quarterly
C & L	Christianity and Literature
Int.	Interpretation
JBL	Journal of Biblical Literature
JETS	Journal of the Evangelical Theological Society
JR	Journal of Religion
JTS	Journal of Theological Studies
NT	Novum Testamentum
NTS	New Testament Studies
PTR	Princeton Theological Review
R & E	Review and Expositor
YR	Yale Review

INTRODUCTION

What Kind of Book Is This?

This is a book of excerpts of literary criticism on the New Testament. All of the selections have been taken from previously published material. A century ago Matthew Arnold proclaimed the virtue of knowing the best that has been thought and said on a given topic. This book contains the best that has been said on the literary aspects of the New Testament by an impressive array of writers and scholars.

I have generally selected excerpts that state overriding principles that apply to a whole topic or book of the New Testament. The selections rarely provide detailed commentary on a specific passage but instead state general principles or suggest a methodology for reading the New Testament. Ralph Waldo Emerson once said that the purpose of principles is that they give us eyes with which to see. The selections in this book provide eyes with which to see the New Testament in its literary dimension.

In keeping with what I have just said, and because of the relative brevity of the selections, this is a book that activates a reader to complete what it begins. The excerpts are a catalyst. They do not exhaustively illustrate a thesis. Instead, they invite a reader to apply the general idea or procedure to the New Testament. This is the best type commentary because it provides the impetus for a reader to embark on a process of discovery. For those who wish to see the details of a given critic's thesis, this book is a handy bibliographic guide.

The commentary in this book is practical. I agree completely with the critic who writes that what people interested in knowing more about the literature of the New Testament "need to hear most from literary critics is that old-fashioned critical concepts of plot, character, setting, point of view, and diction may be more useful than more glamorous and sophisticated theories."*

---

*Except where otherwise noted, the quotations in this introduction have all been taken from the selections included in the book, and I have accordingly not documented their source here.

Because of its practical bent, this book will have special appeal to several groups. One group is people who teach the Bible as literature, whether in literature or religion courses. Another group that will especially benefit from the book is students enrolled in such courses. The book is also tailor-made for people who have had their curiosity aroused in regard to the literary approach to the Bible but who have not known where to begin their exploration.

This book is a roadmap to both the agreements and disagreements among literary critics of the New Testament. I have sometimes included selections that state similar conclusions to suggest areas where a consensus exists. I have more often chosen comments that supplement each other. For entries on individual books of the New Testament, for example, you will find multiple perspectives on the structure of the book. I have sometimes included selections that contradict each other in order to suggest areas of disagreement among critics.

Finally, the commentary in this book represents a *literary* approach to the New Testament. I have taken the title of the series to which this book belongs seriously. It is a library of literary criticism on the New Testament. The rest of this introduction explains what constitutes a literary approach to the New Testament. What follows, therefore, is both a set of principles that can be used as ''eyes'' with which to look at the New Testament and an explanation of the rationale underlying my selection of excerpts for the book.

Is the New Testament Literature?

The New Testament has always been felt to be less literary in nature than the Old Testament, with its gallery of vivid characters and colorful stories and abundance of poetry. By comparison, the New Testament has seemed less obviously similar to familiar types of literature. *Is* the New Testament literature?

That question has been debated virtually from the beginning. The early church Fathers could not make up their minds on the question. Origen decided that the New Testament did not measure up to Greek standards of literary style, and he gave a religious explanation for that fact, namely, that if the New Testament writers had been eloquent, the power of their writing would not have been perceived as coming from God. Augustine disagreed, believing that Paul's ''wisdom is his guide, eloquence his attendant.'' Chrysostom came up with impressive statements on both sides of the question.

This ancient controversy about the literary merits of the New Testament illustrates something that pervades any discussion of the New Testament: the New Testament is distinctly religious in nature. In the Western world, it has been a sacred book and has never been viewed as only a work of literature like Shakespeare's plays or Milton's epics. The literary features of the New Testament cannot be separated from its religious meanings, a fact that has unjustifiably inhibited discussion of literary traits that are definitely present in the New Testament.

The question of how literary the New Testament is has continued in the twentieth century, though other criteria (such as the literary genres of the New Testament) have overshadowed the stylistic criterion that preoccupied the early Fathers. There has been a general shift during the twentieth century away from Adolf Deissmann's view that the New Testament is written in a predominantly unliterary style, to a more generous estimate of the literary excellence of New Testament writing.

Although few of the writers who are excerpted in this volume consciously set out to discuss the New Testament "as literature," they all implicitly confirm that the New Testament does, in fact, have much that is literary about it. Most of the comments collected here are examples of actual literary commentary, not theoretic statements about what makes the New Testament literary. Yet their critical analyses presuppose the literary principles that I delineate in the remarks that follow, and the anatomy of literary principles that I provide correspondingly explains why I chose the excerpts that I did.

The New Testament possesses traits that allow us to consider it as literature. Yet it is not all equally literary in nature. The framework that I provide should not be regarded as establishing a "great divide" in which the New Testament either is or is not literature. Instead, we should picture a continuum on which some parts of the New Testament are more literary and other parts less literary.

It is also important to note that whether or not we regard the New Testament as literary depends partly on the way in which we decide to approach it. The criticism in this book illustrates what it means to talk about the New Testament with literary terms and tools of analysis. None of the critics who have undertaken this task has denied that the New Testament can at the same time be approached as history and theology, to cite the other two commonest approaches. The excerpts in this book do not do everything that needs to be done with the New Testament. But they represent a necessary approach to the New Testament and one that has been neglected far too long.

The Experiential Concreteness of the New Testament

To begin, we can identify literature by its content. The subject of literature is human experience, concretely presented. Literature *presents* human experience instead of telling *about* it. It is incarnational in nature. It embodies its meanings in some type of concretion, whether an image or character or event. A work of literature does more than *tell* us something: it *shows* us.

We can, in other words, distinguish between the expository or documentary use of language and the literary use. The documentary impulse has as its aim to tell us, as objectively as possible, the facts and information about a subject. Literature, by contrast, appeals to the imagination (the image-making capacity) within us. Its aim is to recreate an experience in sufficient detail and concreteness to enable a reader to relive it.

Everywhere we turn in the New Testament, we find an unusual mixture of the documentary and literary impulses. Bare, factual passages exist side by side with concretely elaborated ones. It is, indeed, this bewildering mixture of types of writing that largely accounts for the fact that throughout its history the New Testament has not struck most readers as being literary in the way that Homer or Shakespeare or the Old Testment is.

Yet in the New Testament we constantly encounter the sights and sounds and quality of real life. The New Testament again and again shows evidence of the literary impulse to embody experience as concretely as possible. When asked to define "neighbor," Jesus told the story known as the parable of the Good Samaritan.

And if writers of literature thus depend on the imagination, so do good readers of literature. They read with active imaginations that visualize as much as possible. They maximize the sensory dimension of stories and poems. A literary approach to the New Testament is one that makes a reader sensitive to the sensations and vividness and experiential qualities of a passage.

This sensitivity to the concreteness of much of the New Testament characterizes numerous excerpts in this book. Several critics catalog the concrete images that appear in the sayings and parables of Jesus. Others note the abundance of concrete imagery in Paul's writing and the epistle of James. There are good comments on the kaleidoscope of actions, settings, and characters in the book of Acts and the gospels. G. Wilson Knight observes that "the Gospels are rich with tangible, physical, sensuous . . . life." And then there are Erich Auerbach's famous comments about the everyday realism of the gospels, which record events and portray characters that are "entirely real, average, identifiable as to place, time, and circumstance."

Literature as Interpretation

For all its concreteness, literature is not an objective portrayal of its subject. Documentary writing is far more objective than literature, where the writer is consciously interpretive. For one thing, a literary author always selects from the available material and distills some aspect of it for presentation. An author never records reality as a camera does. A writer selects and molds the material around one or more themes.

This interpretive impulse is not distinctive to literature. It is shared by the writer of an essay or history book, for example. But it is important to acknowledge that literature has a much stronger interpretive dimension than a news report or statistical summary. To read the New Testament as literature is to discern the interpretive perspective from which a given writer has presented the material.

In the New Testament, the gospels and book of Acts provide the best examples of the interpretive bias that pervades literature. These books are first of all stories about characters and events. But each of the five works tells its story from a discernible perspective. As various critics have noted, the interpretive slant in these New Testament stories is discernible partly from what a writer decided to include and omit, and partly from the way in which an author presents a given character or event. A prevalent theme in the excerpts of this book is, accordingly, the specific perspectives that distinguish a given New Testament book or writer from others.

For the entries on the major books of the New Testament, I have included a section of excerpts that I have labelled "unifying motifs." Many of these motifs are themes—implied or stated ideas that a New Testament writer communicates by means of his literary construct. The interpretive element in New Testament literature ranges from such a specific motive as Matthew's view that Jesus is the fulfilment of Old Testament prophecy or Lukes's championing of the outcast to the general quality of encounter in the New Testament—a quality that leads Auerbach to claim that everyone who reads the New Testament is "required to take sides for or against it." All of these instances are part of the interpretive and persuasive and therefore literary nature of the New Testament.

Artistic Beauty

Literature is an art form. One of the criteria by which we classify something as literary is the presence of beauty, form, craftsmanship, technique. These qualities can characterize a whole work or a small part, but wherever they are strongly in evidence, we rightly consider a text to have literary properties.

The elements of artistic form, in literature as well as the other arts, include these: pattern or design, theme or centrality, organic unity (also called unity in variety), balance, contrast, symmetry, repetition or recurrence, variation, unified progression. When judged by such criteria of aesthetic form or beauty, the New Testament suddenly emerges as an artistic and literary masterpiece.

Many of the selections in this book reveal exactly this aesthetic quality of the New Testament. Several critics discuss the adherence of Jesus' parables to such narrative principles as unity of impact, completeness, repetition, contrast, and end stress. Others point out the recurrence of key words as a unifying pattern in the book of James, or the intricate patterns of contrast, parallelism, and triplets in Paul's famous encomium on love (1 Corinthians 13), or the pairing of a miraculous sign and an accompanying discourse in the Gospel of John, or the artistic parallels between the stories of John the Baptist and Jesus in Luke 1–2.

What functions are served by this type of artistic beauty? And why is it important to be aware of this dimension of the New Testament? Artistic form serves the purpose of pleasure, delight, enjoyment. A literary approach to the New Testament differentiates itself from other approaches by placing a high value on the artistic quality of the writing. Literary critics relish a piece of writing as an artifact, a thing of beauty, the product of verbal and imaginative skill. A literary approach to the New Testament values the individual works as products of an author's craftsmanship.

In view of this, it becomes natural to ask whether the New Testament authors were consciously artistic when they wrote or spoke. Critics with literary intuitions overwhelmingly assume self-conscious artistry on the part of New Testament authors. Biblical scholars, by contrast, tend to assume an absence of self-conscious artistry and are not very excited by it when they find it. In this, as in other areas, readers tend to see in a text what they expect to find. Biblical scholars have often spoken of the New Testament writers as "simple and unlearned," and of "unliterary beginnings" for the New Testament. By contrast, literary critics who assume literary skill in New Testament writers have found abundant evidence of it.

As editor of this volume, I was on the lookout for commentary that was sensitive to the artistic dimension of the New Testament. Most of these excerpts come from writers who are professional biblical scholars. What I found, though, is that their comments were often peripheral "asides"— remarks that did not excite their enthusiasm or prompt them to elaborate their insight beyond a brief paragraph or two. The *proportion* of commentary on artistic form and beauty that appears in this volume reflects my literary approach but is atypical of the general tenor of most of the sources I quote.

Literary Genres

One of the standard ways of defining literature is by its genres ("types"). Through the centuries, people who deal with literary texts have agreed that certain genres belong to the canon of literature.

The New Testament is made up of three main literary genres: story or narrative, letter or epistle, and vision or apocalypse. All three are common literary genres, and this by itself goes a long way toward justifying the claim that the New Testament can be approached as literature.

In addition to the three large genres, the New Testament is made up of a host of smaller forms, which I have often labelled "subtypes." In the New Testament, a literary genre can be as small a unit as a proverb or poem or hymn, and there are sections on all of these in this volume.

There are several reasons why the study of genre is important in a literary approach to a text. Every literary genre has its "rules" of operation and its underlying principles. Being aware of them tells a reader what to expect and look for. Literary genres are also important to literary taxonomy and as such provide the basic framework for how we organize individual works and literature as a whole. And since every genre has its own set of procedures, placing a work into the right literary family can be a prerequisite to the correct interpretation of a text.

All of this explains why the topic of literary genre looms large in the selections in this book. Some genres have separate entries, including gospel, parable, proverb, epistle, hymn, and satire. Similarly, the entry for the book of Revelation has a section on the genre of the book, and much of the material on other individual books likewise helps to build a definition of the genre of the book.

One of the purposes of this book is to provide a roadmap that shows a reader what to look for in various parts of the New Testament. Where can one find the poems and hymns of the New Testament? How do parables work? What is important about the New Testament genre known as apocalypse? What critical tools are best when talking about a gospel? Questions such as these receive very practical answers throughout this book.

Are the New Testament genres unique, as is often claimed, or do they have affinities with familiar genres, ancient and modern? This has been a question of scholarly debate for a long time. I have tried to do justice to both sides of the debate in the selections that I have included. From these specimens will emerge what I think is the most accurate solution: there are no exact models for the New Testament gospels, parables, "acts," epistles, and apocalypse, but each of these has enough affinities with familiar literary forms to allow us to apply many of the usual categories of story and poetry (for example) to them. Certainly we do not need an esoteric critical vocabulary for dealing with most of the New Testament, and one of the weaknesses of much biblical scholarship in this century is the way in which it has encrusted the New Testament in unfamiliar literary jargon. Why, for example, call an episode in the gospels a "pericope," which simply means "passage"?

A final thing to note about the New Testament genres is that the examples of them that we find in the New Testament tend to be mixed or hybrid forms. The Sermon on the Mount is not a poem, but it displays many of the features of poetry. The book of Revelation is not a typical story, but the standard narrative questions of who does what, and where, and with what results, are the right ones to ask when dealing with the book.

Unity

Perhaps the most basic of all artistic principles is unity. At the turn of this century, Richard G. Moulton, that pioneer of the literary approach to the Bible, wrote, "No principle of literary study is more important than that of grasping clearly a literary work as a single whole."* If Moulton's insight had been taken seriously, the course of New Testament commentary would have been virtually the opposite from what it has been.

Instead of assuming unity, biblical scholars have tended to fragmentize the New Testament. Much of this has been done in an effort to uncover the

The Modern Reader's Bible (New York, Macmillan, 1895), p. 1719.

various strata in the development of a text from its original ("primitive") form to its final written form. The following description of the methods of biblical scholarship may be taken as an accurate account of the dominant trend in biblical scholarship: "The literary critic . . . attempts to discover the original writings, to determine exactly their date of origin. . . . This means that he approaches the text with, so to say, a dissecting knife in his hand. . . . Literary criticism is the analysis of biblical books from the standpoint of lack of continuity, duplications, inconsistencies and different linguistic usage, with the object of discovering what the individual writers and redactors contributed to the text, and also its time and place of origin."*

Nothing could possibly be more alien than this to the literary methods of scholars in the humanities. The fact that biblical scholars have called their approach "literary criticism" has only confused the picture. Literary critics (as that term is used outside of biblical scholarship) accept the New Testament text in its final form as the focus of their study. Furthermore, they assume unity in the text and proceed to demonstrate its presence.

This ability to see the overall pattern of a text or passage is one of the greatest gifts of a literary approach. Much of the commentary in this book is, accordingly, preoccupied with laying out the unity of individual works. Perhaps the most important type of unity is the structure of a work. Unity can also be thematic. Or it can consist of an image pattern, or the characterization of a person or group in a story, or the progressive development of a dialogue or speech.

All of these types of unity are noted in the selections that follow. There is the pilgrimage motif in the book of Hebrews, and trial imagery in the book of Acts, and the shapeliness of Jesus' parables, and the importance of a literal and symbolic journey in Luke's Gospel and Acts, and the way in which Luke's partiality to the poor and outcast extends to virtually every facet of his Gospel. Literary criticism, rightly so called, gives a reader the big picture—a clear pathway through a book or passage.

Literature as a Special Use of Language

Literature in general, and poetry in particular, use special resources of language in a way that people through the centuries have agreed to call literary. These resources fall into two general categories.

One is the realm of figurative language. We consider literary a discourse that makes use of metaphor, simile, hyperbole, symbol, apostrophe, personification, allusion, paradox, pun, and irony. The dominant examples in the New Testament are the sayings and discourses of Jesus (see the entry on "Jesus as Poet") and the book of Revelation. But the poetic use of language

---

*Klaus Koch, *The Growth of the Biblical Tradition* (New York, Charles Scribner's Sons, 1969), pp.69–70.

permeates virtually the entire New Testament. Paul's writing is saturated with metaphor and simile and paradox. The book of James contains striking use of analogies from nature. The Gospel of John relies on such symbols as light and bread and water to communicate its meanings, as do the New Testament hymns.

The literary use of language also includes rhetorical devices—bigger units than figures of speech. Examples of such rhetorical patterns include parallel sentences (such as the parallel lines in Hebrew poetry), any highly patterned arrangement of clauses or phrases, rhetorical questions, question and answer constructions, imaginary dialogues, and the aphoristic conciseness of a proverb. In the New Testament, Paul is a master of question and exclamation and repetition and antithesis and parallel construction. The tendency toward proverb is widespread in the New Testament, and Robert Tannehill has analyzed how the proverbs of Jesus use "tensive language" to assault our patterns of deep thought. Other critics point out how the parables of Jesus are rhetorically structured to gain the approving interest of the listener until the tables are turned on him or her, with the reversal coming so suddenly that the listener cannot escape the thrust of the parable. There are also the rhetorical strategies by which the gospel writers gain a sympathetic response to Jesus and attempt to move a reader to faith.

Through the use of such figurative and rhetorical devices, literature exploits the resources of language in extraordinary ways. When it does so, literature possesses arresting strangeness, and therein lies part of its power. Literature finds ways to overcome the cliche effect of familiar statements and the impotence of abstract concepts. T. S. Eliot's famous dictum that the poet is forced continually to dislocate language into meaning is much in evidence in the New Testament.

Any one of the devices that I have listed can appear in writing that we do not consider literary, but we nevertheless recognize the devices as a literary use of language. The greater the frequency with which a text makes use of these devices, the more literary we consider it. By this criterion, too, the New Testament emerges as a literary document.

One corollary of the fact that literature represents a special use of language is that style can become a criterion of literary classification for texts whose basic genre we would not consider literary (for example, letter, speech, sermon, historical chronicle). I would personally hesitate to call the letter a literary genre. But because some of the New Testament epistles exploit the figurative and rhetorical resources of language, style becomes an avenue for approaching them as literature. Sections in this book on the epistles of James and Hebrews, as well as commentary on Paul as a letter writer, will illustrate the point.

Stylistic analyses in this book uncover some exciting aspects of the New Testament that we tend not to notice until someone calls them to our attention.

G. Wilson Knight observes the symbolic overtones of events in the gospels. Commentary on the parables of Jesus discloses the minute realism of the stories, combined with a striking universality of character types and life situations. J. H. Gardiner contrasts the clear outlines of Greek statues of the gods and the blurred edges of the visions in the book of Revelation, concluding that the latter conveys a sense of transcendence that Greek art does not.

Archetypes

The literary imagination tends to organize reality around archetypes. An archetype is an image, character type, or plot motif that recurs throughout literature. Wherever we turn in literature, we find ourselves in touch with certain powerful archetypes that make up the groundwork of our psyche and that help to organize our experiences in life. Light, darkness, initiation, the journey, the prodigal, the outcast—these are specimens of archetypes. Literature is full of them, while a history or theology book is not.

Here, too, the New Testament adheres to literary principles. A literary approach to the New Testament is one that is sensitive to the archetypes that we find there.

There is a sampling of such commentary in the selections of this book. The book of Acts, for example, is built around such motifs as journey by water, shipwreck, and rescue; one critic puts the book into the pattern of the adventure story of narrow escape. G. Wilson Knight has good comments about such archetypes as mountains, fish, pastoral settings, and fruit in the synoptic gospels. The parables of Jesus gain much of their power from such archetypal situations as lost and found, quest, master and servant, and sibling rivalry. When a critic calls the characters in Luke's nativity story "archetypes of Jewry," he at once gives them an identity (based on Old Testament literature) in our imaginations.

Providing a Literary Context

One of the commonest things that literary critics do is compare works with other similar texts. It is a highly useful thing to do, since by providing a context a critic at once illuminates the properties of the work under consideration.

Much depends, however, on the kinds of writing to which a commentator compares a work. Given their historical and theological bent, biblical scholars have tended strongly to set New Testament texts beside nonliterary works of the first century A.D. One of the clearest symptoms that a commentator has taken a literary approach to the New Testament is the presence of links between the New Testament and familiar literature of English and American and European literature. There is not much criticism of this type in existence, but I have latched onto it whenever possible, partly because as a teacher of literature I find such criticism so helpful.

In the excerpts of this book, one will find the realism of the book of James compared to the prose style of John Bunyan, and the Gospel of John compared to the tragedies of Aeschylus and Sophocles, and the Gospel of Mark compared to *Agamemnon*. The vignettes in Acts are like those in Sterne's novel *A Sentimental Journey*, according to one critic, while another believes that Luke's method of punctuating the narrative in Acts with speeches is comparable to the strategy in classical epics like *The Odyssey* and *The Iliad*. Roland Frye has argued that the gospels employ the same techniques as do Shakespeare's history plays. The absence of rhyme in Hebrew poetry is similar to the verse form of T. S. Eliot's poetry. The book of Revelation is like underground literature, and the lifelike and universal nature of the characters in Jesus' parables makes them like such classic creations of Western literature as Mr. Micawber and Falstaff.

The context need not be literary, but can be broadly artistic. I have benefited greatly from some of the analogues drawn between New Testament works and the visual arts, and I have included such commentary in this book. The book of Hebrews, says one critic, is like a medieval stained glass window. Luke's technique of portraying a character in a dramatic setting is like Rembrandt's style of painting. One critic compares the storytelling technique of the four gospels to slow-action replays on television, while another compares them to snapshots, impressionistic paintings, and portraits in arguing that they are most like the latter. The centrality of Jesus in the gospels is comparable to Holman Hunt's painting *Finding Christ in the Temple*, where the gaze of everyone in the crowded scene is focused on Jesus.

The "World" of a Literary Work

Works of literature have a self-contained quality. They do not exist primarily to point a reader beyond the text to the world of historical facts. When we read Shakespeare's *Macbeth*, for example, we do not care about the Macbeth of history. It is the Macbeth that Shakespeare created in the play that is the focus of our attention and that embodies the meanings of the work.

This distinction between self-contained and referential texts becomes very ambiguous when we turn to the New Testament, where the writers constantly claim to be dealing with the world of historical reality. In this case, the distinction between literary (self-contained) and expository or documentary writing is not so much a property of the text itself as it is of the approach that a critic chooses to take toward the text. Biblical scholars have usually taken a historical approach to the text. A literary approach concentrates on the work as it stands, realizing that there are other valid ways of viewing the text.

This literary stance implies a whole methodology. It assumes that a New Testament work is a unified world having its own settings, characters, symbols, situations, customs, and ideas. To read such a piece is to use our imaginations to enter a whole world, a world in which the details have been carefully included by the writer for a good reason. Any commentary that enhances a reader's picture of that world becomes immensely helpful.

One critic, for example, analyzes the techniques by which the writer of the Gospel of Mark "reaches out of his narrative to lead his reader on an imaginative journey into the past, plucking him out of his time and place . . . and setting him down in another time and place." The book of James, another critic observes, has the coloring of rural Palestine. Antithesis is an essential feature of how Paul perceived reality, and it accordingly characterizes the world of his letters. We can find a symbolic use of geographical regions and cities (notably Galilee, Jerusalem, and Rome) in the gospels and book of Acts. The domestic and feminine interest of Luke makes up part of the world of his gospel. Or consider a comment like this: "Zacchaeus is a thoroughly Lucan character; well-off, shady, little, unrespectable—yet responsive to Jesus. He belongs to that suspect fringe of Judaism which plays such a telling part in the book" (John Drury). Upon reading such commentary, a reader has been given a window through which to see more fully the precise world of Luke's Gospel.

Although I have not included sections labelled "world" for the entries on individual New Testament books, many of the selections help a reader to construct the world of a given story or letter or poem in the New Testament. The more fully we can enter the world of a New Testament work with our mind and imagination, the better will be our literary experience of the New Testament.

Meaning through Form

Some readers of this book will think that I have been too preoccupied with matters of form (style, structure, pattern, technique, etc.) to the neglect of content. There are two good reasons for my emphasis.

The focus on form and technique is what literary criticism is qualified to contribute to New Testament studies. Such a literary approach is not all that needs to be done with the New Testament. But it is a necessary first step in understanding what the New Testament says, and it has the additional advantage of enhancing our enjoyment of the New Testament. Historical and theological approaches to the New Testament are also incomplete by themselves, and it is no discredit to the literary approach that it leaves much unsaid.

More importantly, in any kind of written discourse, meaning is communicated *through* form. "Form" should be construed very broadly in this context. It includes anything that touches upon *how* a writer has expressed content, as distinct from *what* a writer says. Without form (beginning, of course, with language itself), no meaning is conveyed.

While this is true for all forms of writing, it is especially crucial for literature. Literary discourse has its own forms or "language," and these tend to be more complex and subtle and indirect than ordinary discourse. The storyteller, for example, speaks *with* characters, action, and setting. As a result, before we can understand what storytellers say about a given subject we must first interact with the *form*, that is, the story. In a similar way, poetry conveys its meanings *through* figurative language. It is therefore impossible to talk about what a poetic statement means without first encountering the form (metaphor, simile, etc.).

As one test case for the claim that literary form and meaning are inseparable, we might consider the element of structure that looms large in the selections of this book. Structure may look at first like a matter of form rather than content. But upon reflection it becomes evident that to determine the structure of a work one must also deal with the content. After all, it is *content* that is thus arranged into structural patterns. To lay out a work into its structural units is at the same time to interact with its content.

The literary critic's preoccupation with the "how" of New Testament writing is not frivolous. It is evidence of an aesthetic delight in artistic form, but it is more than that. It is also evidence of a desire to understand what is said in the New Testament, in keeping with the tendency of the New Testament writers to incarnate their content in literary forms that demand careful scrutiny.

Some Characteristics of New Testament Literature

A dominant impression that a perusal of this book will produce is that the New Testament is similar to other, familiar works of literature. This is in every way a beneficial discovery to make. One reason why many modern readers lack the antennae to respond well to the New Testament is that it has traditionally been isolated from the familiar landscape of our reading experience.

It would, however, be misleading to overlook the ways in which, even from a literary perspective, the New Testament is distinctive. The New Testament, for example, is from start to finish a religious book. It represents literature in the service of a strongly didactic purpose. One of the critics in this volume comments that "the gospels are distinctly religious. They are written not to please, nor even only to instruct, but to persuade, to convert, to redeem." One corollary of this is that rhetorical analysis—the analysis of the persuasive strategies by which New Testament writers try to make their readers share their viewpoint—has a big role in literary criticism of the New Testament. It is no wonder, therefore, that readers of the New Testament have paid enormous attention to determining exactly *what* the New Testament writers wish their readers to assent to, though that question falls more into the domain of the theological approach to the New Testament than of the literary approach.

Even more distinctive, perhaps unique, is the fact that the New Testament is not a self-contained book. It requires the Old Testament to complete it. Its images, symbols, and allusions convey only a fraction of their meaning unless one places them into the context of the Old Testament. Important generalizations about the relationship between the two testaments appear in the first section of this book ("The New Testament as a Whole").

Another distinctive of the New Testament is that it is a strongly oral work of literature, even though in its present form it is written. Behind the gospels and the book of Acts lie oral versions of the individual units. The letters of Paul have marked oral tendencies, and the book of Revelation was sent to the churches for oral reading.

The oral background of the New Testament influenced what we now read at every turn. Erich Auerbach directs our attention to the prominence of face-to-face dialogue in the New Testament (something that he finds unique in the writing of the time). Critics make strong claims for the essentially dramatic nature of the gospels, Acts, and the book of Revelation. The oratorical style of Jesus and Paul will also be a dominant theme of this book.

The most interesting discovery I made while doing the research for this book is the extent to which the New Testament is "folk literature." Like Homer and Shakespeare and Dickens, it speaks to every reader, not simply to a literary or intellectual elite. In the words of Deissmann, the New Testament is "a Book of the people."

This "folk literature" quality permeates every part of the New Testament. The gospels, like "popular" history plays, are intended for the whole populace, not professional historians (R. Frye). The informal nature of the New Testament epistles—indeed, even the choice of the letter as a form—shows that they arose from real-life situations and were addressed to ordinary people. The book of Revelation, too, would become a great deal more accessible if we realized that it does "not spring from the professional scribes or the official class" but is "for the most part folk-literature" (Beckwith). As might be expected, the most impressive of all the statements along these lines come in connection with the parables of Jesus, which from start to finish adhere to the rules of popular storytelling through the centuries.

Literary Criticism and Biblical Scholarship

If I have accurately described a literary approach to the New Testament, the question naturally arises how that approach compares with the methods pursued by biblical scholars. The fact that a majority of the critics included in this book are biblical scholars rather than literary critics should not be allowed to obscure the ways in which the relationship between the methods of biblical scholarship and literary criticism are largely antithetical to each other. Some of the best biblical scholars have been people with good literary intuitions, but their literary methods have set them apart from the preoccupations of their profession.

On almost every point that I have attributed to a literary approach to the New Testament, we can contrast the approach of a biblical scholarship as it has been practised in our century. Literary critics accept the New Testament as it stands; biblical scholars have constantly tried to get behind the text in an effort to trace stages in the development of the text back to its original form. Literary critics look for unified wholes; biblical scholars are more at home with fragments. Correspondingly, literary critics are interested in the self-contained "world" of a work as the key to its meaning; biblical scholars have focused on the relations between the New Testament text and historical reality.

Even when literary critics and biblical scholars talk about the same issues, their interest in the subject differs. Literary critics are preoccupied with questions of genre for what genre contributes to the correct interpretation of a text and because it sparks their interest in human artistry; biblical scholars are more likely to use information about genre to conduct "excavations" into the stages of development from an original and (assumed) authentic core. Both groups talk about style: literary critics because they value human creativity and beauty, biblical scholars in an effort to determine authorship. Both groups place the New Testament into a literary context, but not the same one; biblical scholars compare New Testament texts to other ancient documents, while literary critics are more likely to compare features of the New Testament to works of English and American literature. Biblical scholars are inclined to trace New Testament images and motifs to historical precedents; literary critics are more likely to talk about universal archetypes.

Despite the contrasts that I have drawn, the gap between literary criticism and biblical scholarship has been drastically narrowed in recent years. The literary approach has gained a foothold among biblical scholars. The literary intuitions of some of them included in this volume are equal to those of the best literary critics. A new day is dawning in New Testament scholarship. The excerpts in this book are a codification of the best literary criticism on the New Testament to date; I hope the book will stimulate further explorations in the same vein.

L.R.

THE NEW TESTAMENT AS A WHOLE

HOW LITERARY IS THE NEW TESTAMENT?

For it was not any power of speaking, or any orderly arrangement of their message, according to the arts of Grecian dialectics or rhetoric, which was in them the effective cause of converting their hearers. Nay, I am of opinion that if Jesus had selected some individuals who were wise according to the apprehension of the multitude, and who were fitted both to think and speak so as to please them, and had used such as the ministers of His doctrine, He would most justly have been suspected of employing artifices, like those philosophers who are the leaders of certain sects, and consequently the promise respecting the divinity of His doctrine would not have manifested itself; for had the doctrine and the preaching consisted in the persuasive utterance and arrangement of words, then faith also, like that of the philosophers of the world in their opinions, would have been through the wisdom of men, and not through the power of God. Now, who is there, on seeing fishermen and tax-gatherers, who had not acquired even the merest elements of learning (as the Gospel relates of them . . .), discoursing boldly not only among the Jews of faith in Jesus, but also preaching Him with success among other nations, would not inquire whence they derived this power of persuasion, as theirs was certainly not the common method followed by the multitude?

> Origen. *Against Celsus*, Book I, Ch. LXII, in *The Ante-Nicene Fathers*, IV, ed. Alexander Roberts (Buffalo, Christian Literature Company, 1885), p. 424

Here, perhaps, some one inquires whether the authors whose divinely-inspired writings constitute the canon, which carries with it a most wholesome authority, are to be considered wise only, or eloquent as well. A question which to me, and to those who think with me, is very easily settled. For where I understand these writers, it seems to me not only that nothing can be wiser, but also that nothing can be more eloquent. And I venture to affirm that all who truly understand what these writers say, perceive at the same time that it could not have been properly said in any other way. For as there is a kind of eloquence that is more becoming in youth, and a kind that is more becoming in old age, and nothing can be called eloquence if it be not suitable to the person of the speaker, so there is a kind of eloquence that is becoming to men who justly claim the highest authority, and who are evidently inspired of God. With this eloquence they spoke; no other would have been suitable for them. . . .

I could . . . show those men who cry up their own form of language as superior to that of our authors . . . that all those powers and beauties of eloquence which they make their boast, are to be found in the sacred writings which God in His goodness has provided to mould our characters, and to guide us from this world of wickedness to the blessed world above. But it is not the qualities which these writers have in common with the heathen orators and poets that give me such unspeakable delight in their eloquence; I am more struck with admiration at the way in which, by an eloquence peculiarly their own, they so use this eloquence of ours that it is not conspicuous either by it presence or its absence. . . .

As then I do not affirm that the apostle was guided by the rules of eloquence, so I do not deny that his wisdom naturally produced, and was accompanied by, eloquence. . . .

Wisdom is his guide, eloquence his attendant; he follows the first, the second follows him, and yet he does not spurn it when it comes after him. . . .

I fear lest I too should smack of the puffery while thus decanting on matters of this kind. It was necessary, however, to reply to the ill-taught men who think our authors contemptible; not because they do not possess, but because they do not display, the eloquence which these men value so highly. . . .

If any one who is skilled in this species of harmony would take the closing sentences of these writers and arrange them according to the law of harmony . . . , he will learn that these divinely-inspired men are not defective in any of those points which he has been taught in the schools of the grammarians and rhetoricians to consider of importance; and he will find in them many kinds of speech of great beauty,—beautiful even in our language, but especially beautiful in the original,—none of which can be found in those writings of which they boast so much. But care must be taken that, while adding harmony, we take away none of the weight from these divine and authoritative utterances. . . .

Again, in writing to the Galatians, although the whole epistle is written in the subdued style, except at the end, where it rises into a temperate eloquence, yet he interposes one passage of so much feeling that, notwithstanding the absence of any ornaments such as appear in the passages just quoted, it cannot be called anything but powerful [Gal. 4:10–20]. . . . Is there anything here of contrasted words arranged antithetically, or of words rising gradually to a climax, or of sonorous clauses, and sections, and periods? Yet, notwithstanding, there is a glow of strong emotion that makes us feel the fervor of eloquence.

Augustine of Hippo. *On Christian Doctrine*, Book IV, ch. 6, 7, 20, in *Nicene and Post-Nicene Fathers*, II, ed. Philip Schaff (Buffalo, Christian Literature Company, 1887), pp. 577–579, 589–590

But prove to me that Peter and Paul were eloquent. Thou canst not: for they were "unlearned and ignorant men!" . . . When the Greeks then charge the disciples with being uneducated, let us be even more forward in the charge than they. Nor let any one say, "Paul was wise;" but while we exalt those among them who were great in wisdom and admired for their excellency of speech, let us allow that all on our side were uneducated. . . .

I have said these things, because I once heard a Christian disputing in a ridiculous manner with a Greek, and both parties in their mutual fray ruining themselves. For what things the Christian ought to have said, these the Greek asserted; and what things it was natural to expect the Greek would say, these the Christian pleaded for himself. As thus: the dispute being about Paul and Plato, the Greek endeavored to show that Paul was unlearned and ignorant; but the Christian, from simplicity, was anxious to prove that Paul was more eloquent than Plato. And so the victory was on the side of the Greek, this argument being allowed to prevail. For if Paul was a more considerable person than Plato, many probably would object that it was not by grace, but by excellency of speech that he prevailed; so that the Christian's assertion made for the Greek. And what the Greek said made for the Christian's; for if Paul was uneducated and yet overcame Plato, the victory, as I was saying, was brilliant; the disciples of the latter, in a body, having been attracted by the former, unlearned as he was, and convinced, and brought over to his side. From whence it is plain that the Gospel was a result not of human wisdom, but of the grace of God. . . .

It is not a slander on the Apostles to say so, but it is even a glory that, being such, they should have outshone the whole world. For these untrained, and rude, and illiterate men, as completely vanquished the wise, and powerful, and the tyrants, and those who flourished in wealth and glory and all outward good things, as though they had not been men at all: from whence it is manifest that great is the power of the Cross; and that these things were done by no human strength. . . . And observe; the fisherman, the tentmaker, the publican, the ignorant, the unlettered, coming from the far distant country of Palestine, and having beaten off their own ground the philosophers, the masters of oratory, the skilful debaters, alone prevailed against them in a short space of time.

Chrysostom. *Homily III on I Corinthians 1.10*, in *Nicene and Post-Nicene Fathers*, XII, ed. Philip Schaff (New York, Christian Literature Company, 1889), p. 14

St. Paul . . . had a greater power by far than power of speech, power which brought about greater results too; which was that his bare presence, even though he was silent, was terrible to the demons. . . .

Now, that he was not so unskilled, as some count him to be, I shall try to show in what follows. The unskilled person in men's estimation is not only one who is unpracticed in the tricks of profane oratory, but the man who is incapable of contending for the defence of the right faith, and they are right. But St. Paul did not say that he was unskilled in both these respects, but in one only; and in support of this he makes a careful distinction, saying that he was "rude in speech, but not in knowledge." Now were I to insist upon the polish of Isocrates, the weight of Demosthenes, the dignity of Thucydides, and the sublimity of Plato, in any one bishop, St. Paul would be a strong evidence against me. But I pass by all such matters and the elaborate ornaments of profane oratory; and I take no account of style or of delivery; yea let a man's diction be poor and his composition simple and unadorned, but let him not be unskilled in the knowledge and accurate statement of doctrine; nor in order to screen his own sloth, deprive that holy epistle of the greatest of his gifts, and the sum of his praises.

For how was it, tell me, that he confounded the Jews which dwelt at Damascus, though he had not yet begun to work miracles? How was it that he wrestled with the Grecians and threw them? and why was he sent to Tarsus? Was it not because he was so mighty and victorious in the word, and brought his adversaries to such a pass that they, unable to brook their defeat, were provoked to seek his life? At that time, as I said, he had not begun to work miracles. . . . How was it, moreover, that he contended and disputed successfully with those who tried to Judaize in Antioch? and how was it that Areopagite, an inhabitant of Athens, that most devoted of all cities to the gods, followed the apostle, he and his wife? was it not owing to the discourse which they heard? . . .

How can any one dare to pronounce him unskillful whose sermons and disputations were so exceedingly admired by all who heard them? Why did the Lycaonians imagine that he was Hermes? . . . In what else did this blessed saint excel the rest of the apostles? and how comes it that up and down the world he is so much on every one's tongue? How comes it that not merely among ourselves, but also among Jews and Greeks, he is the wonder of wonders? Is it not from the power of his epistles?

> Chrysostom. *On the Priesthood*, Book IV, chs. 6, 7, in *Nicene and Post-Nicene Fathers*, IX, ed. Philip Schaff (New York, Christian Literature Company, 1889), pp. 66–68

The language to which we are accustomed in the New Testament is on the whole just the kind of Greek that simple, unlearned folk of the Roman Imperial period were in the habit of using. The non-literary written memorials of that age at length have opened our eyes to the true linguistic position of the New Testament. . . .

It is true, certainly, that it is a Greek New Testament which presents itself to the scholar for study, but within the New Testament there are portions of which "the original language" was not Greek, but Semitic. Jesus of Nazareth, the Man whose personality was the decisive impulse, did not speak Greek when He went about His public work. He spoke the local idiom of His native Galilee, the language which, in the night of betrayal, betrayed His disciple Peter to be a Galilean. This language was Aramaic, a dialect akin to Hebrew but not identical with it. . . .

The New Testament has been proved to be, as a whole, a monument of late colloquial Greek, and in the great majority of its component parts the monument of a more or less *popular* colloquial language.

The most popular in tone are the synoptic gospels, especially when they are reporting the sayings of Jesus. Even St. Luke, with his occasional striving after greater correctness of expression, has not deprived them of their simple beauty. The Epistle of St. James again clearly re-echoes the popular language of the gospels.

The Johannine writings, including the Revelation, are also linguistically deep-rooted in the most popular colloquial language. . . .

St. Paul too can command the terse pithiness of the homely gospel speech, especially in his ethical exhortations as pastor. These take shape naturally in clear-cut *maxims* such as the people themselves use and treasure up. . . . Thickly studded with rugged, forceful words taken from the popular idiom, it is perhaps the most brilliant example of the artless though not inartistic colloquial prose of a travelled city-resident of the Roman Empire. . . .

We are thus left with the total impression that the great mass of the texts which make up the New Testament, forming at the same time the most important part of the sacred volume in point of contents, are popular in character. The traces of literary language found in some few of the other texts cannot do away with this impression. On the contrary, the contrast in which the Epistle to the Hebrews, for instance, stands linguistically to the earlier texts of Primitive Christianity, is peculiarly instructive to us. It points to the fact that the Epistle to the Hebrews, with its more definitely artistic, more literary language (corresponding to its more theological subject-matter), constituted an epoch in the history of the new religion. . . .

What is natural is also beautiful, and does not cease to be beautiful until artificiality and pretence step in. Thus in our opinion the new method of philological treatment brings out the peculiar beauty of the New Testament, by establishing the popular simplicity of the language in which it is written. . . .

Taken as a whole the New Testament is a Book of the people. . . .

The Book of the people has become, in the course of centuries the Book of all mankind. At the present day no book in the world is printed so often and in so many languages as the New Testament. . . .

We must not assume that the New Testament is literature from cover to cover.

Adolf Deissmann. *Light from the Ancient East*, trans. Lionel Strachan (New York, Harper and Brothers, 1923, 1927), pp. 62, 64, 69–72, 143–144, 147–148

A good deal of currency has been given to the notion that the Greek of the New Testament was the language of the street and that the rhetoric of the book is that of the illiterate. No basis exists for either of these ideas. It is true that fresh evidence has come to light showing how widely the Greek language was used at that time by the people of western Asia and northern Africa. But what does that prove about the sacred book? . . . No doubt the Greek of the first century differed very considerably from that of Athens in the age of Pericles. But it was still rich in vocabulary and exact in syntax and was one of the most consummate instruments of expression ever contrived by human genius. It was no careless colloquial.

As to the matter of literature, the narratives and addresses of the gospels and the book of Acts surely surpass the Anabasis and the Memorabilia. The Fourth Gospel equals any dialogue of Plato's. Paul's great climaxes in his epistles, taken simply as literature, equal any of the Attic orations. The book of Revelation . . . cannot be placed below Dante's immortal Divine Comedy. The dignified literary atmosphere of the King James version truly reproduces that of the original and should by all means be preserved in every new attempt. It is not in the least inconsistent with the directness and virility of modern speech. . . .

An acceptable translation must be shaped by these ideals: to preserve the noble literary atmosphere of the old version, to say in the simplest and best English neither more nor less than the Greek says, nowhere to obtrude the translator's interpretation between author and reader, and not to make the matters in the book seem more like modern ideas and ways than they were.

William G. Ballantine. *Understanding the Bible* (Springfield, Mass., Johnson's Bookstore, 1925), pp. 19–21

Among the Jews, education was in universal demand; and everywhere, in school and synagogue, it was based on solid literary footings, partly Hebraic, partly Greek. . . . It is time surely to discard the figment of Galilaean illiteracy. It was based upon the piecemeal criticism, which builds upon the minor pedantries and amid the little trees of erudition loses sight of the main wood. Philodemus the philosopher, Meleager the epigrammatist and anthologist, Theodorus the rhetorician, and one may almost add Josephus the historian, were all of Galilee; a little later, Justin Martyr of Samaria. All Christian literature that has survived was written in Greek; it was the chosen medium of Peter, of John, of James, of Jude—of the Gospels, including that according to St. Matthew; while the theory of Aramaic originals is little more than ingenious conjecture. It is not sufficiently recognised that the Jews were the most literary of all Mediterranean nations—far more so than the Greeks, or the Romans whose literature was exotic: they gave literary form to their history, their poetry, their religion: they were *par excellence* the people of 'the Books'; in no other nation was there a literary tradition and profession and status such as were accorded to the Scribes. No nation showed readier assimilation and acceptance of the Hellenic culture, installed by Alexander.

> Gerald H. Rendall. *The Epistle of St. James and Judaic Christianity* (Cambridge, Cambridge University Press, 1927), pp. 38–39

One reason why the New Testament language was once thought to constitute a backwater from the main stream of Greek literature, and was allotted a place of its own, was that it apparently differed so much from the literature of its period and created no formal precedents in style for later Christian or secular literature. . . . Opinion during the present century no longer sees the NT language as a backwater but stresses its affinities with the vernacular. However, one may feel concerned that the literary elements in this language should not be overlooked. With a message appealing to all humanity, the NT not surprisingly is sometimes colloquial and even uses slang in one or two words, so that it is little wonder if there is a tendency at the present time to assume that its language is much closer to the non-literary Koine than to the cultured Greek of the period.

Certainly the NT in general is free from stylistic conventions such as those mentioned by J. H. Moulton, the dual number and the final optative, and contains very few atticisms. If they occur at all, it is in four books, Luke-Acts, Hebrews, II Peter, and Jude, where in refinement of diction there is a close approach to the Atticists. . . . St. Luke's preface, however, has some literary merit, and the third Gospel does attempt improvements on St. Mark's sentence-structure; II Peter is rhythmical in style and too sophisticated to substantiate any claim that it belongs to the vernacular Koine. Moffatt gives full credit to the skilful oratory of Hebrews and its sense of rhythm. . . .

Although St. Paul lacks literary artistry, simply writing or dictating the spoken word, nevertheless there are some parallels with his style in the Greek literary world. . . . Who is to say what is 'literary'? The philologist is tempted to manufacture his own canons of taste and to use them to judge, rather than merely to record, tendencies and directions in the language; but living speech inevitably modifies the literary language, and what were canons of good taste in a former period are openly flouted as time goes on.

As well as the stylistic features instanced above, we may note some literary characteristics in the realm of accidence, vocabulary, and syntax.

1. Accidence
In this sphere most NT authors display a more cultured practice than is found
in non-literary papyrus texts. There is a higher standard in orthography,
declension of nouns and adjectives, and inflection of verbs. . . .
2. Vocabulary
Mr. E. K. Simpson pointed out in a private communication how closely much
of the NT language resembles that of the extant fragments of Philodemus, a
Greek text-book writer of the previous century who lived at Gadara of Galilee,
a centre of Greek influence. Moreover, in a protest against the old position,
that NT language is that of the common people, Mr. Simpson has indicated
the literary tendencies of NT speech and its conformity in general with higher
Koine. . . .
3. Syntax
In this sphere the 'literary' quality is less apparent, but in isolated instances
(such as the use of the article with proper names) the NT is remarkable for
its classical correctness. Hebrews, James, I and II Peter . . . together with
St. Luke, exhibit the closest approach in the NT to literary syntax.

Nigel Turner. NTS. 20, 1973–74, pp. 107–109, lll

UNITY

In the New Testament we are confronted with a religious life in which everything is determined by Christ. . . .

No one, it will be admitted, can deny that the New Testament has variety
as well as unity. It is the variety which gives interest to the unity. The reality
and power of the unity are in exact proportion to the variety; we feel how
potent the unity must be which can hold all this variety together in the energies
of common life. The question raised by every demonstration of the undeniable
differences which characterise the New Testament is, What is the vital force
which triumphs over them all? . . . There can be no doubt that that which
unites them is a common relation to Christ—a common faith in Him involving
common religious convictions about Him . . . Everywhere in the New Testament . . . we are in contact with a religious life which is determined throughout by Christ. . . . In the relations of God and man, everything turns upon
Christ and upon faith in Him. There is no Christianity known to the New
Testament except that in which He has a place all His own, a place of absolute
significance, to which there is no analogy elsewhere. . . .

In spite of the various modes of thought and feeling which the canonical
Christian writings exhibit, there is really such a thing as a self-consistent New
Testament, and a self-consistent Christian religion. There is a unity in all
these early Christian books which is powerful enough to absorb and subdue

their differences, and that unity is to be found in common religious relation to Christ, a common debt to Him, a common sense that everything in the relations of God and man must be and is determined by Him. We may even go further and say that in all the great types of Christianity represented in the New Testament the relations of God and man are regarded as profoundly affected by sin, and that the sense of a common debt to Christ is the sense of what Christians owe to Him in dealing with the situation which sin has created.

> James Denney. *Jesus and the Gospel* (New York, George
> H. Doran Company, 1908), pp. 9, ll–12, 90

The absence of any genuinely literary criticism of the Bible in modern times (until very recently) has left an enormous gap in our knowledge of literary symbolism as a whole, a gap which all the new knowledge brought to bear on it is quite incompetent to fill. I feel that historical scholarship is without exception "lower" or analytic criticism, and that "higher" criticism would be a quite different activity. The latter seems to me to be a purely literary criticism which would see the Bible, not as the scrapbook of corruptions, glosses, redactions, insertions, conflations, misplacings, and misunderstandings revealed by the analytic critic, but as the typological unity which all these things were originally intended to help construct. The tremendous cultural influence of the Bible is inexplicable by any criticism of it which stops where it begins to look like something with the literary form of a specialist's stamp collection. A genuine higher criticism of the Bible, therefore, would be a synthesizing process which would start with the assumption that the Bible is a definitive myth, a single archetypal structure extending from creation to apocalypse. Its heuristic principle would be St. Augustine's axiom that the Old Testament is revealed in the New and the New concealed in the Old; that the two testaments are not so much allegories of one another as metaphorical identifications of one another. We cannot trace the Bible back, even historically, to a time when its materials were not being shaped into a typological unity, and if the Bible is to be regarded as inspired in any sense, sacred or secular, its editorial and redacting processes must be regarded as inspired too.

This is the only way in which we can deal with the Bible as a major informing influence on literary symbolism which it actually has been. Such an approach would be a conservative criticism recovering and re-establishing the traditional typologies based on the assumption of its figurative unity.

> Northrop Frye. *Anatomy of Criticism* (Princeton, Prince-
> ton University Press, 1957), pp. 315–316

When full justice has been done to the many differences of personal expression and literary form that its pages hold, it still remains true that the most remarkable characteristic of the New Testament is the basic unity which it reveals. . . . In the first place, it is partly due to the writers' common indebtedness to the Old Testament. They were all men whose outlook and thoughts and language had been molded by their early training in the traditions of the fathers. . . .

In the second place, this unity is to be explained by the fact that all the writers began with a common framework or outline. It was not a case of beginning with a blank page and seeking to devise some completely novel form for the presentation of their message. One and all began with a story. It was the story that we have come to know as the Gospel of Jesus Christ. Behind all the teaching and the exhorting and the prophesying of the New Testament there is this story of the Christ—how the way was prepared for his coming, how he lived and died, how he rose again and sent forth his Spirit to dwell in the fellowship of his Church. Everything in this collection of writings is set within the one framework. It is not surprising therefore that beneath its varied forms of expression we can discern a remarkable uniformity of basic pattern—a uniformity which binds the book together into one impressive whole.

Westminster Introductions to the Books of the Bible (Philadelphia, Westminster Press, 1958), pp. 152–153.

The concentration of the divine/human dialogue on Jesus results in stories about him dominating New Testament narrative. The epic grandeur of the Old Testament dialogue is pared down to the activity of one savior figure, upon whom rests "the whole weight of destiny expressed in the faith of Israel and in the eschatological hope." The New Testament begins with a fourfold recital of the myth of the savior. Moreover, the narrative, as it progresses from Jesus to the disciples in the church, does not leave Jesus behind. Unlike the movement from Abraham to Jacob, Moses to Joshua, or Elijah to Elisha, the disciples in the church never move beyond Jesus. They witness to him, and they perform signs and wonders in his name. Even eschatological discourse in the Revelation to John does not leave behind the crucified one; Jesus, in the figure of a slain lamb, sits beside the enthroned deity.

Stories about Jesus link with the Old Testament in at least two ways. First, texts of the Old Testament are viewed as unfulfilled promises realized in the stories of Jesus. Second, stories about him resonate overtones from the mighty deeds from of old. Overtones to the Old Testament may be explicit through quotations or implicit through patterns of action.

Leonard L. Thompson. *Introducing Biblical Literature: A More Fantastic Country* (Englewood Cliffs, Prentice-Hall, 1978), p. 232

GENRES (see also *Epistle, Gospel, Hymn, Parable, Poetry*)

As the literature of a movement and of a community, the New Testament grew up in a series of blocks or groups of writings. . . .

We may distinguish six such groups of writings within the New Testament.

(1) The *Epistles of Paul*—the earliest group, and these, indeed, separable into three main groups written some years apart.

(2) The *Synoptic Gospels*, built about earlier documents and resting upon a steadily developed tradition reaching back to the earliest days of the church's history and to the events and the Person recorded.

With these is naturally grouped the Acts of the Apostles, as the continuation of the Third Gospel and of the record of the beginnings of the church.

(3) The *Pastoral Epistles*, perhaps based upon earlier epistolary writings, and, indeed, quite possibly upon a fourth group of Pauline Epistles; but considerably modified to meet the situation toward the close of the first century—or possibly even later.

(4) The *Apocalypse of John*, apparently isolated, but really one of a large number of Jewish and Christian apocalypses, and almost certainly containing earlier Jewish as well as Christian material.

(5) A group of *Catholic Apostolic writings*, ascribed usually to apostles. . . .

(6) The *Johannine Literature*, i.e. three Epistles and a 'Gospel'. . . .

One might go on and name the types of literature produced in the church down to the time of Constantine and Eusebius—apologetic, exegetic, polemic, historical, hortatory, disciplinary, legislative, personal and biographical, epistolary, theological—and show how some of these elaborated types were already emergent in the New Testament. . . .

There was no biography for its own sake, no fiction with which to while away idle hours . . . no ambitious objective historical writing addressed, like the work of Thucydides or Polybius, to the educated world, no poetry or drama (save the solemn lyric rhythm of many of Jesus' sayings, come down out of Jewish Christian tradition, and one or two snatches of simple early hymns), no philosophy or dialogue: none of the major literary forms of the classical age or of the contemporary Graeco-Roman world is represented in the New Testament.

Frederick C. Grant. The Growth of the Gospels (New York, Abingdon Press, 1933), pp. 29–32

Interesting general points of resemblance only may be indicated between these writings of the New Testament and some of the books of the Hebrew Bible. Mark, Matthew, Luke, Acts, and John may be looked upon as the Pentateuch of the New Testament, with John representing the Deuteronomic book in relation to the others; the Epistles are comparable in some respects with the

Prophets; Revelation is a counterpart of Daniel; and there is also a New Testament Apocrypha which partly approximates the Apocrypha of the Old Testament. The specific kinds of literature which are comprised in these writings are history, legend, narrative, biography, short story, letters, sermons, orations, parables, doctrinal treatises, and vision.

Wilbur Owen Sypherd. *The Literature of the English Bible* (New York, Oxford University Press, 1938), p. 158

The reader of the New Testament would undoubtedly be greatly helped if he could see it in some conspectus of literary arrangement. Several methods suggest themselves. One is arrangement according to date. . . . The order conventional in our New Testament is due to other considerations, being accounted for partly by the chronology of subject matter (thus lives of Jesus precede the history and writings of apostles, and the latter are followed by the book which treats of "what must come to pass hereafter"); and partly by literary forms or content—Gospels together, epistles together, etc. Likewise, general ("catholic") letters are likely to be separated from those to churches, and these from letters to individuals; while, at the same time, letters by the same writer or to the same church or person tend naturally to fall into juxtaposition.

Henry J. Cadbury. "The New Testament and Early Christian Literature," *Interpreter's Bible*, Vol. 7 (Nashville, Abingdon Press, 1951), p. 36

A scene like Peter's denial fits into no antique genre. . . . This can be judged by a symptom which at first glance may seem insignificant: the use of direct discourse. . . . I do not believe that there is a single passage in an antique historian where direct discourse is employed in this fashion in a brief, direct dialogue. Dialogues with few participants are rare in their writings; at best they appear in anecdotal biography, and there the function they serve is almost always to lead up to famous pregnant retorts. . . . But here—in the scene of Peter's denial—the dramatic tension of the moment when the actors stand face to face has been given a salience and immediacy compared with which the dialogue (stichomythy) of antique tragedy appears highly stylized. . . . In the Gospels . . . one encounters numerous face-to-face dialogues. I hope that this symptom, the use of direct discourse in living dialogue, suffices to characterize for our purposes, the relation of the writings of the New Testament to classical rhetoric.

Erich Auerbach. *Mimesis: The Representation of Reality in Western Literature*, trans. Willard R. Trask (Princeton, Princeton University Press, 1953), pp. 45–46

. . . many different literary forms were employed to express the Christian message. What we call a Gospel, for instance, is a type of writing created by early Christian authors. There is no real parallel to it in non-Christian literature. The epistles of Paul are letters, but though letters were common in the first century, there are none to equal those of the New Testament for effective spiritual ministry to the needs of men. The book of Revelation is an apocalypse. This type of writing was well known among the Jews: it made much use of visions and symbols to reveal the secrets of the heavenly world and of the coming age. But Revelation shows a deep pastoral concern in its early chapters, a tenderness in its references to the martyred host, a confidence in the final victory of God, which far surpass anything else to be found in this particular type of literature. Thus the New Testament manifests both a rich variety and a superior creative quality in its literary types.

Westminster Introductions to the Books of the Bible (Philadelphia, Westminster Press, 1958), p. 150

The first thing to be said about the New Testament is that it is both a book and a collection of books; it is a text and a collection of texts brought together by the church and declared to be the New Testament. Both descriptions are important. As a book the New Testament represents a single entity of foundational importance to Christians and Christian churches; as a collection of books it is a variety of documents of different literary forms and sometimes of different religious viewpoints. . . .

In recent years we have become increasingly aware that different literary forms function in different ways. The reader of the realistic (mimetic) narrative of the gospel of Mark is caught up in the story as participant, whereas he is an observer of the sacred drama of the gospel of John. The reader of the letters of Paul, which are real letters, is directly addressed by them, but he has to wrestle with the meaning of the letter to the Hebrews, which is not a letter at all but a theological treatise. Each of these literary forms works differently and so addresses its reader differently, and it is important for the reader to know what kind of text he is reading if he is to understand it correctly.

Paralleling the differences in form are the differences in language. Not all language is alike; there are many kinds of language, and each tends to function differently. In the New Testament itself the direct discourse of the Sermon on the Mount is in form and function unlike the exalted revelatory style of the "I am" discourses in John's gospel, as also are the down-to-earth realism of the parables and the exotic imagery of the book of Revelation.

Though the books in the New Testament differ from one another in their understanding of the nature of Christian faith in the world, they are in common wrestling with the problems of that faith and no other.

Norman Perrin. *The New Testament: An Introduction* (New York, Harcourt Brace Jovanovich, Inc., 1974), pp. 17–18

The literature of the New Testament falls into four categories as we classify it according to its literary genre: gospel, acts, epistle and apocalypse.

The literary type of "acts" . . . is known to have been applied to some biographical works in antiquity, but the author of the writing *ad Theophilum* does not use the word. He . . . calls the work of predecessors in that field by the title of "stories". . . . The canonical title of "The Acts of the Apostles" was added later to the second volume in the Lucan corpus. . . .

The term "gospel" is restricted in the New Testament to the activity and substance of the early Christian preaching. "To preach the gospel" (Mk. 1:14; 1 Cor. 1:17; Gal. 1:11) is a common expression. The New Testament invariably connects "gospel" (i.e. the announcement of good news) with verbs of speaking and responding, and never with verbs of writing and reading. . . .

One of the earliest designations of the gospel records was "memoirs" (Justin Martyr), but this term did not remain in vogue. Instead, the Christians of the second and third centuries coined the title "Gospels" for these books. . . .

The major part of the New Testament corpus as regards size falls into the category of "epistle". As early Christianity spread across the Mediterranean basin and churches were formed in different localities it became necessary for lines of communication to be extended between the various centres. . . .

The fact of apostolic instruction by letter has produced a type of writing for which there are no ancient parallels. "The letter of Christian instruction was in fact almost as distinctive a Christian contribution to literary types as the written gospel" [E. J. Goodspeed].

While this statement may be true in the strict sense of letters composed for a didactic purpose, the format and style of Paul's letters follow conventional patterns known to us from methods of letter-writing in the hellenistic world. . . .

The fourth literary genre is apocalyptic. The presence of this type of Jewish material is found in the synoptic apocalypses (Mark 13; Matthew 24; Luke 21), 2 Thessalonians 1 and the book of Revelation.

> Ralph P. Martin. "Approaches to New Testament Exegesis," in *New Testament Interpretation*, ed. I. Howard Marshall (Grand Rapids, William B. Eerdmans, 1977), pp. 230–232, 234

STYLE

All the narrative of the Bible shows a combination of two sets of qualities: on the one hand it has a simplicity and a limpid and vivid clearness which make it appeal to all sorts and conditions of men; on the other hand through its whole range it has an undercurrent of earnestness and strong feeling. Thus the style clothes and transfigures even homely events with beauty and spiritual power; and the concreteness and clearness crystallize the deep feeling expressed by the strong rhythm and the varied music of the style. These two sets of characteristics, then, the simplicity and vivid clearness on the one hand, the earnestness and rich depth of feeling on the other, we may take as the most characteristic attributes of these narratives. . . .

In the New Testament, the most common type of narrrative stands between the unbroken co-ordination and simplicity of the Old Testament and the fully developed Greek style of the latter chapters of *Acts*. It is almost certain that the first three Gospels consist of material which was originally composed in Aramaic, the Semitic dialect which gradually took the place of Hebrew in Palestine after the exile. The general character of this Aramaic language, being the same as that of Hebrew, tended to fix on the narrative portions of these gospels the same general style that we find in the Old Testament; and through the influence of the Greek in which they were finally written shows in the frequency of participles and when clauses, yet there are almost no sustained periods. . . .

A good example of the average style of the New Testament narrative may be taken from the account of the death of John the Baptist in the *Gospel According to St. Mark*. This gospel is the simplest of the four, and at the same time is especially full of little touches of vivifying and convincing detail. . . .

Here the subordination of subsidiary to principal facts helps to add swiftness to the narrative; and at the same time the absence of all subtleties keeps the story real and solid. In such passages the art of story-telling, without losing any of its substantial power, is brought to a still higher degree of perfection than in the Old Testament. This variety and modulation of the style makes possible the ethereal power of the description in *St. Luke* of the shepherds watching in the field by night, perhaps the most beautiful short piece of narrative in the whole Bible. . . .

Here St. Luke's trained sense for style reaches its highest point; in recording the tradition which had come to him, he keeps its absolute simplicity; and at the same time his knowledge of the art of writing makes it possible for him to touch it with a sheer beauty of style which expresses feelings hardly known to the Old Testament. Thus without any suggestion of the somewhat palpable art which we feel in the latter part of *Acts*, the gospels seem the work of writers who lived in our half of the world and on the higher side of antiquity.

Yet when one turns from the style to the substance one feels again that all these narratives belong to another world. For these ancient writers, whether in the Old Testament or the New, there were no subtleties: they took no interest in inferences and modifications and other complications of thought which might be built upon them.

J. H. Gardiner. *The Bible as English Literature* (New York, Charles Scribner's Sons, 1906), pp. 34–35, 76–81

The Bible is a very heterogeneous book. Throughout the Authorized Version has the high qualities of simplicity and firmness in phrasing. But there is all the difference in the world between the underlying style of Genesis and Job and Matthew. The style of Genesis is possible only to a strict and almost fanatical monotheism; its tremendous simplicity overwhelms us. . . . The style of Job, on the other hand, is that of high and universal poetry. . . . And then for the third distinct kind, we have the style of the Gospels of the New Testament. In the 27th chapter of Matthew there are two masterly effects—I hardly know whether to call them effects of style. They are contained in two quite simple statements: 'Then all the disciples left Him, and fled'; and the words about Peter, after his third denial, 'And he went out and wept bitterly'. These approach to the condition of 'And the Lord said' in Genesis, in the sense that the emotional suggestion is not in the words themselves; but they differ from those simple evocations of an awful conception of God; the reserves of emotion which Matthew's simple statements liberate in us have been accumulated during the reading of the narrative. The personality and the circumstances of Christ have been given to us: no words, no art could intensify the effect of the sudden, utterly unexpected statement; 'Then all the disciples left Him, and fled'. The situation given, the force of the words is elemental. So, too, nothing more needs to be told us of Peter than that 'he went out and wept bitterly'. We know what he felt; to attempt to describe or define it would only be to take away from that which we know. And all through the Gospel narratives there are these phrases charged with a similar emotional significance. . . . And then, again, in yet another kind you have that sentence . . . of which Walter Pater said: 'There's a mystery in it—a something supernatural [Matt. 11:28–30].'

There the language itself has a surpassing beauty. The movement and sound of the first sentence is exquisite, I have no doubt a thousand times more beautiful than the Greek. . . . In whatever language that sentence was spoken to you, your depths would be stirred. Our common humanity reaches out after the comfort of the words; all that there is of weariness and disappointment, of suffering and doubt, in all men stretches out for some small share in this love that might have changed the world. Apply your coldest test to it, and it remains great style.

J. Middleton Murry. *The Problem of Style* (London,
Oxford University Press, 1922), pp.128–129

The prose of the New Testament is often of a very high order. A good deal of it approaches the rhythm of poetry in its parallelisms of thought and structure, in its cadences, and in its accent. Strength of conviction, intensity of belief, fervour of feeling are revealed in prose of great power and beauty. Simplicity, clarity, conciseness, harmony, rhythmic flow, homely figurative expression, sincerity and earnestness, and a great fundamental theme are the characteristics which elevate much of these writings about the plane of simple narrative or doctrinal exposition to the height of perfect style of its kind and into the realm of literature of universal significance.

Wilbur Owen Sypherd. The Literature of the English
Bible (New York, Oxford University Press, 1938), pp.
158–159

It is apparent at first glance that the rule of differentiated styles cannot possibly apply in this case [the story of Peter's denial in the Gospel of Mark]. The incident, entirely realistic both in regard to locale and *dramatis personae*—note particularly their low social station—is replete with problem and tragedy. Peter is no mere accessory figure serving as *illustratio*. . . . He is the image of man in the highest and deepest and most tragic sense. Of course this mingling of styles is not dictated by an artistic purpose. On the contrary, it was rooted from the beginning in the character of Jewish-Christian literature; it was graphically and harshly dramatized through God's incarnation in a human being of the humblest social station, through his existence on earth amid humble everyday people and conditions, and through his Passion which, judged by earthly standards, was ignominious. . . .

A tragic figure from such a background, a hero of such weakness, who yet derives the highest force from his very weakness, such weakness, such a to and fro of the pendulum, is incompatible with the sublime style of classical antique literature. But the nature and the scene of the conflict also fall entirely outside the domain of classical antiquity. Viewed superficially, the thing is a police action and its consequences; it takes place entirely among everyday men and women of the common people; anything of the sort could be thought of in antique terms only as farce or comedy. Yet why is it neither of these? Why does it arouse in us the most serious and most significant sympathy? Because it portrays something which neither the poets nor the historians of antiquity ever set out to portray: the birth of a spiritual movement in the depths of the common people, from within the everyday occurrences of contemporary life, which thus assumes an importance it could never have assumed in antique literature. . . .

It goes without saying that the stylistic convention of antiquity fails here, for the reaction of the casually involved person can only be presented with the highest seriousness. The random fisherman or publican or rich youth, the random Samaritan or adulteress, come from their random everyday circumstances to be immediately confronted with the personality of Jesus; and the reaction of an individual in such a moment is necessarily a matter of profound seriousness, and very often tragic. The antique stylistic rule according to which realistic imitation, the description of random everyday life, could only be comic (or at best idyllic), is therefore incompatible with the representation of historical forces as soon as such a representation undertakes to render things concretely; for this procedure entails entering into the random everyday depths

of popular life, as well as readiness to take seriously whatever is encountered
there.

Erich Auerbach. *Mimesis: The Representation of Reality
in Western Literature*, trans. Willard R. Trask (Princeton, Princeton University Press, 1953), pp. 41–44

The New Testament compresses the very essence of life. There is surely no
other book like it in the world, for nowhere else do art and history so combine
to create beyond themselves. The nearest thing to it is the Shakespearian
play, and only by seeing it on the analogy of Shakespeare can we understand
how it comes to hold a truth and a power unparalleled elsewhere. There is
no question of belief or unbelief: the New Testament is a living reality.

I answer one final objection. It might be argued that, however we may
reason, the New Testament has not the minute poetic exactitude of the Shakespearian play, and that this lack in the work of the Divine Artist is, to say
the least, curious. But the New Testament has to integrate the world of history
and value in a sense hardly done by Shakespeare. Shakespeare's is primarily
a poetic world in that it is a poet's world. The New Testament is composed
by different authors, and for this very reason its records, though clearly the
less minutely intercorrespondent with each other, are the more evidently the
result of some organic principle working in human terms yet transcending
any single human person. . . . The New Testament is always very human as
well as divine. God is not writing a book to drop from Heaven so that man
may have all his difficulties resolved; it is as though Life itself were travailing
to create it in terms of human experience.

I have tried to show that the New Testament is neither throughout poetry
nor history but a blending of the two. Often it reads like a work of art and
yet we are simultaneously aware that actuality is so stamped on it that there
can be no fiction. We also find jagged pieces, either crude fact or heightened
symbolism, that at first appear to spoil its pattern either as art or as history. . . .

We have already drawn a distinction between poets who use vivid fire or
light imagery and those whose words have a less scintillating excitement, a
more natural bloom. Both modes serve a purpose and both are found in the
New Testament. We have the Keatsian imagery of Jesus' words in the Synoptic
Gospels, but where the writer describes some visionary fact, there may be a
blaze of light such as Jesus never himself uses in his parables. St. John, an
interpretative writer, intellectualizes the imagery of the other Gospels, heightening and translating it; and St. Paul both interprets by close reasoning and
uses images of glory. 'Glory' is not a word to be associated with Jesus' own
imagery; he is more Keatsian, more natural, more homely. But the more
interpretative books are necessary to our understanding.

G. Wilson Knight. *The Christian Renaissance* (London,
Methuen and Company, 1962), pp. 56–57, 122–123

At the time of the New Testament events, Greek was the universal language of the eastern part of the Roman Empire. It was the language of government, literature, commerce, and communications. . . .

Then as now Greek existed in two separate forms: literary Greek and popular, or illiterate, Greek. Literary Greek was a continuation of classical Greek, and although it was no longer in colloquial use, this traditional but somewhat archaic language was still looked upon as the natural medium for literary work. . . .

Gradually a considerable divergence developed between the traditional language and popular colloquial language. We may imagine a Greek author, perhaps a Greek-speaking Semite, using the Hellenistic language in everyday life, but in his literary production making a determined effort to imitate models from the classical works and frequent use of his grammar and dictionary. Thus it is natural that in time people began to use the Hellenistic common language as a written language. A realm of literature came into existence written in a so-called ''illiterate'' language. Purely literary works were written in the classical language, but technical works and writings with a wider appeal for the common people . . . were written in less ambitious literary style, even if still intended to be Attic Greek.

Thus when New Testament language is said to be ''popular'' or ''illiterate,'' one must remember that the dividing line set between the literate and the illiterate differs greatly from that posited in our modern world. Purely literary works . . . were reserved to a small group, while the popular language was the property of everyone, including the literary author when he talked with his family. But as in the development of the language on Greek soil, the two languages began to merge. The literary author . . . would be quick to insert a few classical expressions in his conversation with other educated men. Like Luke, he would speak different kinds of Greek with different kinds of people, depending on the topics and the participants in the conversation. Or, to give another example: Paul's letter to the Romans is indeed ''popular'' and ''illiterate'' but its subject matter precludes our shedding light on it from the papyrus letters of ordinary people. . . .

This common language was already spoken by non-Greek populations who were obliged to use a universal language. This was the case in Palestine: the native language, Aramaic, was itself a language known throughout the East, yet at this time Greek was dominant to such an extent that many people considered it to be the future universal language of the East—to be spoken in addition to their native tongue. . .

In such bilingual areas as the Semitic countries a merging of the universal language with the native tongue was possible. This is the reason for the controversies among scholars over ''semitisms'' in the New Testament. . . . As the New Testament books were written records of a religious message first delivered in Aramaic, all kinds of semitisms may occur, including the new use of a Greek word to cover content hitherto expressed only in Semitic.

Johannes Munck, *The Anchor Bible: The Acts of the Apostles* (Garden City, Doubleday and Company, 1967), pp. xxv–xxvii

New Testament language, like that of the Old, is markedly realistic and concrete, but in the New Testament there is a tension—Auerbach even calls it an antagonism—between that concrete language and the meaning transmitted through it. . . . The passion and crucifixion of Jesus are presented with total realism in vivid, concrete language. The teachings of Jesus also incorporate commonplace activities such as planting corn, catching fish, eating, drinking, buying, and selling.

Yet that language, closely allied to the commonplace, sensory world, is constructed so that a reader is called upon to look beyond the concrete images in order to find their meaning. . . . Planting corn becomes a figure for the kingdom of God. Language is used in such a way as to turn the reader's attention from "the sensory occurrence and towards its meaning." From that necessity of turning arise the rhetorics of indirection which permeate both the New Testament and the Christian interpretation of the Old Testament.

Leonard L. Thompson. *Introducing Biblical Literature: A More Fantastic Country* (Englewood Cliffs, Prentice-Hall, 1978), p. 223

RELATION TO THE OLD TESTAMENT

Between these two parts which make up our Bible there are, of course, wide and radical differences. The first is that of space and of time. The New Testament is only one-third as large a book as is the Old; its writings all belong to the same age and cover a period of only one hundred years, whereas the Old Testament reflects the life of at least eleven centuries. Moreover, the literature of the New Testament is confined to one subject, the life and the teachings of Jesus and of His followers, for even the apocalyptical drama of Revelation arises from and is dependent upon that material; the literature of the Old Testament, on the other hand, includes every type and every subject. Except for the few songs and hymns interspersed among the narratives of the New Testament and inherited in every case from the Old, its medium of expression throughout is prose, whereas the Old Testament contains practically every form of poetry. . . . The purpose of the New Testament is overwhelmingly religious, and its literary excellence arises almost entirely from the religious fervour of its authors; the Old Testament is a work of literature as well as one of religion, and as literature it is vastly superior to the New.

Mary Ellen Chase. *The Bible and the Common Reader* (New York, The Macmillan Company, 1944), pp. 261–262

. . . The New is neither a merely natural development from the Old, nor the substitution of something unrelated. . . .

So far as the books of the Jewish Old Testament Canon are concerned, these were accepted as sacred by the Christians from the start. The New Testament makes constant appeal to them, and takes for granted their authority in such a way that it is not intelligible without reference to the Old. . . .

This does not of itself mean that the two Testaments belong together. Milton's *Paradise Lost* is so full of allusions to classical mythology that it is unintelligible without some knowledge of that mythology. We need, therefore, to consider in what respects the New Testament allusions to the Old differ from these in fundamental character. . . . the relation of the New Testament to the Old is not that of *Paradise Lost* to the literature of Greece and Rome. There is a fundamental unity, so that with all their diversity they belong so intimately together that the New Testament cannot be understood without the Old, and *neither can the Old Testament be fully understood without the New.* . . .

The Old Testament continually looks forward to something beyond itself; the New Testament continually looks back to the Old. Neither is complete without something beyond itself. . . .

In many other ways we have similar patterns in the New Testament and the Old. Yet the new pattern is never a mere repetition of the old. It is on a new level, or in terms of new conditions, and it brings a new message and a new power.

H. H. Rowley. *The Unity of the Bible* (Philadelphia, Westminster Press, 1953), pp. 91, 93–95, 98

. . . the most remarkable characteristic of the New Testament is the basic unity which it reveals. . . . it is partly due to the writers' common indebtedness to the Old Testament. They were all men whose outlook and thoughts and language had been molded by their early training in the traditions of the fathers. They had been brought up on the ideas and imagery associated with the promises made to Abraham, the redemption of Israel from Egypt, the inauguration of the covenant at Sinai, the establishment of the kingdom under David, the development of the sacrificial system, the hope of the coming of the Messiah. They had fed their minds and imaginations upon the messages and metaphors of the prophets. They had been instructed in the familiar commands of the Law. It is no wonder, therefore, that they tended to use the

same metaphors, the same parables, even the same terms. They were steeped
in the language of the Old Testament and they naturally expressed themselves
by the aid of its basic forms. It is true that they believed that through the
work of Jesus Christ a new age had dawned and a new stage had been reached
in the fulfillment of God's purpose. Yet when it came to the expression and
the interpretation of that great fact they could use only the forms of language
ready to their hands. Because all its roots are in the Old Testament, the New
Testament, like a tree, reveals a remarkable symmetry of form.

Westminster Introductions to the Books of the Bible (Philadelphia, Westminster Press, 1958), pp. 152–153.

Typology . . . is the science of discerning types which lie behind the records
of the New Testament. Those types may be of three kinds. First there will
be Old Testament types. St. Paul says that Adam is the type of Christ in the
cosmic effect of his action; or Jesus said that Elijah was the type of John the
Baptist (Mark 9.13). Secondly there are types within the gospel story itself,
as when the raising of Lazarus prefigures the raising of Christ, or . . . the
transfiguration is the type of the ascension. Thirdly there are times when the
events of the gospel are types of things still to come. In this sense the last
supper is the type of the messianic banquet and the resurrection of Christ is
the type of the resurrection of the Church. . . . There is clearly a real connection in each case between type and antitype. The divine power which
raised Lazarus to thirty years more of earthly life is the divine power which
raised Christ to eternal life. . . .

Much criticism could be dispelled if it were realized that almost all typology
is cumulative. . . . There is in the New Testament systematic and sustained
typology. . . .

It cannot fail to strike us that the story of the massacre of the innocents
in Matt. 2 is very similar to the story of the massacre of the Jewish boys by
Pharoah in Ex. 1. . . . Fear inspires the tyrant in each case to the slaughter
of young children; but in each case the future saviour of Israel is delivered. . . . The massacre of the innocents is associated with the flight into
Egypt, which is recorded immediately before the massacre in Matt. 2.13–15.
Now before the massacre in Ex.1 comes nothing that is relevent to our
argument, but as soon as we allow our eye to wander back into the book of
Genesis it strikes us at once that the closing chapters of that book are concerned
with Joseph bringing his family down to Egypt. Here then is a second coincidence in both Testaments closely preceding the first one. . . . In each
case the man responsible is called Joseph. In each case he brings his family
from Palestine to Egypt. And St. Matthew tells us himself that these families
were the old and the new Israel, for he quotes Hosea for their return journey:
"Out of Egypt have I called *my son*." . . .

St. Matthew's quotation from Hosea shows that he has the exodus in mind for his description of the New Testament return: God called Israel his son out of Egypt then, and so it is now. And, lest we should be in any doubt, he appends a quotation from the early chapters of Exodus to underline his intention. God said to Moses (Ex. 4.19), "All men are dead which sought thy life": the angel says to Joseph (Matt. 2.20), "They are dead which sought the young child's life". . . .

Systematic typologies *do* occur in the New Testament. There is nowhere in the New Testament so extended, continuous, and transparent a passage modelled upon the Old Testament as Matt. 1–5. . . .

It is worth while asking how much accumulation of evidence will be taken to establish that a particular Old Testament or other passage was in the evangelist's mind. This will depend, naturally, upon the closeness of the words and the clearness of the motive for making the alleged typology. . . . In general it will be found that three or four points of correspondence suffice to form a convincing catena. One or two obvious points may carry some less certain ones. An indefinite number of uncertain ones establish nothing.

> M. D. Goulder. *Type and History in Acts* (London, S.P.C.K.,1964), pp. 1–3, 6–7

These themes are all present in the Old Testament, and many feel that they are sufficiently delineated there. When we come to the New Testament, however, we encounter a group of writers who are convinced that more needs to be said, and who declare that the Old Testament themes are both summarized and completed in the life and work of Jesus. It is clear that the New Testament writers regarded the work of Jesus in both particular and universal terms. Here, they believed, the particular tradition of Israel came to its climax and fruition, here the teachings of the law and the prophets were fulfilled. Beyond these particular terms, they also held that what happened in and through Jesus was of universal significance, affecting not only the Jewish race but all races of men. . . .

In these and other ways Jesus and his disciples consciously carried on the central traditions of the Old Testament. Even at the point of their most radical breaks with the Judaic community of the first century A.D., the early Christians believed themselves to be merely testifying to the fulfillment by God's action of what had been carried on through the Old Testament period. In what they regarded as the unique and incomparable person of Jesus the Christ, they found the dramatic continuation and culmination of the whole former process of God's disclosure of himself, and of his will for individuals and communities. Thus, whether or not a person regards the New Testament as a valid religious culmination to the Old Testament (and honest men differ on this question), it does unmistakably maintain a literary and dramatic continuity with it.

We can see this literary continuity in the preservation of the pervasive

Biblical emphasis on the characterization of God, of man, and of human community. The New Testament writers find these three elements brought to a final clarification in the person of Jesus Christ and the events of his life on earth. It is here, they hold, that men can find the fullest understanding of God. . . .

We have referred to the suspicion on the part of the Biblical writers of any abstract, philosophical definition of God: throughout, the Bible prefers to present the characterization of God in terms of action and in terms of vivid figurative language. What the New Testament writers maintain is that such means have been ultimately dramatized in a single person, Jesus Christ. Though God is not to be defined in statemental forms, he has defined himself dramatically in and through Jesus Christ. It is this conviction which permeates and gives form to the various literary developments of the New Testament.

> Roland M. Frye. "Introduction," *The Bible: Selections from the King James Version for Study as Literature* (Boston, Houghton Mifflin, 1965; rpt. Princeton University Press, 1977), pp. xxii–xxiii

Without the Old Testament the New Testament does not begin to make sense.

(i) Every page of the New Testament has words or phrases—Messiah, Son of Man, New Covenant, 'Christ our Passover', etc.—which send us back to the Old Testament for clues to their meaning.

(ii) Next, from Genesis to Revelation we can trace a series of biblical patterns or recurring themes which bind the two Testaments together. To say this is . . . to hold an *organic* view of the Bible's unity—to see it as the story of one long unfolding purpose of God from Genesis to Revelation.

Consider, for example, three of the threads that run through the great tapestry of the Bible:

(a) the idea of the *covenant* (or relationship between God and man, in which God Takes the initiative). We find this first in the story of Noah, in Abraham (Gen. 15), in the old covenant made at Sinai (Ex. 24), in Jeremiah's prophecy of a new covenant (Jer. 31), and in Christ's words at the Last Supper.

(b) the idea of the *Exodus*, i.e. of God as Saviour of his people, can be traced from the story told in Exodus, to the 'exodus', or deliverance, of the Cross and Resurrection (Luke 9.51), to St. Paul's comparison of Christ and Baptism (1 Cor. 5.7, 10.2). . . .

(c) the idea of '*the Day of the Lord*'. We find it first in Amos, then, in apocalyptic form, in Joel and Daniel, then in 'the day of the Son of Man' in the Gospels, and finally in Paul's concept of 'the day of Christ'.

All these subsidiary themes converge on a greater one running through both Testaments—God's gracious coming to man in mercy and judgment. So the Old Testament becomes the indispensable record of the preparation for the Incarnation, for God becoming man in Jesus Christ.

(iii) This brings us to our third and final point. If we are to understand the titles Jesus applied to himself, or the apostolic writers applied to him, we cannot do without the Old Testament. . . .

. . . the New Testament writers think of themselves as the inheritors of the promises made to Israel as the people of God. (Paul calls the Church 'the Israel of God'.) For them Abraham was no obscure and ancient patriarch but the founder of the divine commonwealth to which they belonged. The Gospel, or *kerygma*, of the apostles was that 'the scriptures had been fulfilled', that the hopes and prayer of the Old Testament saints had now come true. The mission and vocation of Old Israel had passed to the new Israel, the Chuch of Christ, now called to fulfil the world mission that God had set before the old one.

A. M. Hunter. *Bible and Gospel* (Philadelphia, West-minister Press, 1969), pp.11–13

If one stops reading the Bible with the Old Testament, there is no sense of incompleteness. . . .

If, however, one continues reading into the New Testament, the Old Testament—without its text changing—is transformed into a book of promises and scenes of waiting expectation which are fulfilled in the Christian community. The Old Testament loses its autonomy and becomes subordinated to the New Testament. . . .

The syntaxes and dynamics of the Old Testament continue to operate in the New. Song, story, and saying are the basic units from which more complex structures are built. The Christian community continues the line of the covenantal people living in dialogue with God. . . . Within those syntaxes and dynamics, however, significant modulations occur. The syntaxes join together to create new structures such as gospels and letters. God and man enter into dialogue through new forms which center upon Jesus the Christ. Changes in the divine/human dialogue create new rhetorical dimensions in the language of the New Testament. . . .

Novelty in the New Testament gains legitimation from the Old. New Testament writers sometimes strain to discover common elements between their message and the Scriptures. They establish common elements through typology, through an extension of the mighty deeds from of old to include Jesus' death and resurrection (cf. Acts 7), and through a structure of promise and fulfillment (cf. Mr. 1-2). . . . New mythic patterns join with Old Testament Scriptures to form a new whole. There is something new "apart from the old," but the new needs the old to "bear witness to it" (cf. Rom. 3:21). The new myth is seen as completing and fulfilling the old; and the old provides the categories for interpreting the new. As completion and fulfillment, the

new claims the greater reality: it is the realization of an earlier "shadow."
In providing the categories for interpretation the old claims the greater reality:
the new is a copy of it.

Leonard L. Thompson. *Introducing Biblical Literature:
A More Fantastic Country* (Englewood Cliffs, Prentice-
Hall, 1978), pp.215–216,227

The New Testament writers, then, regard the Old Testament as a source of
anticipations of the events in the life of Christ. These are often explicitly
alluded to, and the source given. Thus, in the Crucifixion, the piercing of
Jesus' hands and feet, and mockery of the passers-by, and the fact that his
legs were not broken on the cross, are related to passages in Psalm 22. . . .

There is a very large number of these references to the Old Testament in
the New: they extend over every book—not impossibly every passage—in
the New Testament; and some New Testament books, notably Revelation and
the Epistle to the Hebrews, are a dense mass of such allusions, often with
direct or oblique quotations. . . . The New Testament, in short, claims to be,
among other things, the key to the Old Testament, the explanation of what
the Old Testament really means. Jesus' disciples could not understand even
the Resurrection until Jesus had explained its relation to Old Testament Prophecy (Luke 24:44).

The general principle of interpretation is traditionally given as "In the
Old Testament the New Testament is concealed; in the New Testament the
Old Testament is revealed." Everything that happens in the Old Testament
is a "type" or adumbration of something that happens in the New Testament,
and the whole subject is therefore called typology. . . . Paul speaks in Romans
5:14 of Adam as a *typos* of Christ. . . . What happens in the New Testament
constitutes an "antitype," a realized form, of something foreshadowed in the
Old Testament. . . .

This typological way of reading the Bible is indicated too often and
explicitly in the New Testament itself for us to be in any doubt that this is
the "right" way of reading it—"right" in the only sense that criticism can
recognize, as the way that conforms to the intentionality of the book itself
and to the conventions it assumes and requires. The typological organization
of the Bible does present the difficulty, to a secular literary critic, of being
unique: no other book in the world, to my knowledge, has a structure even
remotely like that of the Christian Bible.

Northrop Frye. *The Great Code: The Bible and Literature* (New York, Harcourt Brace Jovanovich, 1982),
pp. 78–80

ACTS

STRUCTURE

Robert F. Horton has happily expressed the history contained in Acts under the figure of six successive waves of the advances of faith from Jerusalem to Rome. This is the most interesting way to study the contents of the book. The first wave (1:1–6:7) carries the faith from the first little church in Jerusalem through the whole city. The second wave (6:8–9:31) carries the gospel throughout Palestine. The third wave (9:32–12:23) advances to Antioch and covers all Syria. The fourth wave (12:25–16:5) goes over to Asia Minor. The fifth wave (16:6–19:9) goes over to Europe and occupies Macedonia and Greece. The sixth wave (19:10–28:31) reaches the capital of the world.

Herbert R. Purinton and Carl E. Purinton. *Literature of the New Testament* (New York, Charles Scribner's Sons, 1925), pp. 111–112

The Acts of the Apostles became the most literary book in the New Testament.

We can easily recognize the means by which the author solved his problem, viz. the right sequence is given to the events by grouping and connecting the materials. Among the single stories, which are frequently of marked individual character, collective records are introduced which expand the single event into a type (*vide* i, 13–14; ii, 43–7; iv, 32–5; v, 12–16; similarly also vi. 7; ix, 31; and xii, 24). . . . But in particular, speeches are composed and introduced into individual scenes to give vividness and instruction, to illuminate and upbuild. . . .

The first part . . . deals with the commencement of events in Jerusalem (chaps. i–v). . . . The second part, which describes the mission in Palestine and Syria (chaps. vi–xii), begins with the martyrdom of Stephen, amplified by a speech. . . . By means of dexterous transitions, a proof of conscious literary work, the author joins to this first martyrdom the conversion of Paul, of the Samaritans, and of the Antiochenes.

The third main section is almost entirely concerned with Paul's mission and imprisonment. . . . In this section the course of Christendom as a whole falls into the background. The journeys of a single man are told, and a kind of diary of a journey—an enumeration of halts and church foundations—constitutes, at least in chapters xiii–xxi, the skeleton with which the single stories and the speeches are connected, occasionally with rather harsh transitions. In the course of this journey-narratvie, however, the record is given in the first person plural in certain passages (xvi, 10–17; xx, 5–xxi, 18; and later, also xxvii, 1–xxviii, 16). . . . This author-like desire led to a special piece of literary composition, particularly in describing the journey to Rome (Acts xxvii and xxviii), which is not altogether independent of journey-narratives to be found in literature proper.

> Martin Dibelius. *A Fresh Approach to the New Testament and Early Christian Literature* (New York, Charles Scribner's Sons, 1936), pp. 262–264

It is made up of a blocking or grouping of . . . dramatic episodes into six sections or units, which are contained approximately within the following chapters: chapters 1 to 6, those taking place in Jerusalem; 6 to 10, in other places in Palestine; 10 to 13, from Palestine to Antioch in Syria; 13 to 16, in districts of Asia Minor; 16 to 19, in Macedonia and Greece; and 20 to 28, those incidents that precede St. Paul's arrival in Rome. It is in no sense necessary to keep clearly in mind these respective sections, but it is interesting to note them, since their arrangement proves St. Luke's careful designing of his book and since they serve to show both the wide extent of its background and the spread of Christianity in terms of geography.

It is rather the nature of the episodes themselves which is of paramount interest to the reader. They may be compared to highly coloured or brilliantly illuminated vignettes in prose, such as those which Laurence Sterne gives us in *A Sentimental Journey* and in which he highlights either the main character or the dramatic instant; or to some of the finely lined portraits of Rembrandt by means of which one's imagination is spurred on not only to reconstruct characters but actually to see those characters in fancied situations. It is easy to understand why so many of the incidents in St. Luke's Gospel and in his Acts of the Apostles formed the subjects for numberless artists in the Middle Ages and in the Renaissance.

Once the book of Acts has been read as a whole in order that the reader may become aware of the extent of its background and of its value as history, perhaps the best means of appreciation of the best of these single dramatic episodes is to lift them out of their context and to look at them as units of narrative. For unless one employs this method, many of them are likely to be lost among material of relatively little value as literature.

> Mary Ellen Chase. *The Bible and the Common Reader* (New York, the Macmillan Company, 1944), pp. 281–282

The contents fall into six distinct parts: (1) the founding of the Church in Jerusalem (1:1–6:7); (2) the dispersal of the Christains over Palestine following the martyrdom of Stephen (6:8–9:31); (3) the spread of the Church in Palestine and Syria (9:32–12:25); (4) Paul's first missionary journey to Cyprus and Asia Minor and his return to Jerusalem (13:1–16:5); (5) Paul's journeys to Macedonia and Greece (16:6–21:14); and (6) the opposition to Paul, and his journey to Rome (21:15–28:31).

Although this arrangement of material is neatly chronological, it is perhaps not the most convenient for literary analysis. Throughout Luke's thirty-year drama several major figures appear on the stage at various times. Let us single out the five most important characters, gather up the scattered passages pertaining to each, and consider one by one the five groups of passages. Our principal *dramatis personae* will be Peter, Stephen, Philip, Barnabas, and Paul.

> Buckner B. Trawick. *The Bible as Literature: The New Testament* (New York, Barnes and Noble, 1964, 1968), p. 71

The first thing that strikes a reader who stands back from the Acts enough to view it as a whole is that it is a *cyclical book*. Mighty works of God are expounded by the Church in preaching which achieves both the conversion of the open-minded and the alienation of the hard-hearted. While the converted flood into the Church, and enrich it with their charity and devotion, the alienated raise persecution against her leaders. The faithfulness of those leaders in tribulation is answered by divine intervention triumphing over the powers of darkness; and so to more mighty works, and fresh preaching to expound them, and round the cycle again. The movement of the book is like a spiral, always moving on and out into new territory, into deeper trials, into new communities, like a series of waves breaking higher and higher on the sea-shore. The overlapping points on the spiral are often marked with care by the author. . . .

Luke allows his story to develop *in cycles*: building up from three short cycles in Jerusalem to the fuller length cycles in the middle of the book, and closing with the long section on the passion and deliverance of Paul. . . . Luke found certain basic elements in the life of the Church: God's choice of new ministers for the preaching of the gospel; God's mighty works through them; the crowd that is drawn, the word that is preached, the converts that it brings, their faithfulness and charity; and on the other side the rejection of the preaching, especially by the Jews, who are led therefore to persecute, try, assault, and martyr the Christian leaders. But God always retains the last word, and from the Church's faithfulness he brings new opportunities, and new leaders, for a new cycle. . . .

We showed the structure of Acts to be built up in a series of nine cycles:

three brief cycles under the ministry of the apostles at Jerusalem, one fuller cycle in which Stephen's martydom leads on to the ministry of Philip and the conversion of Saul, one in which Peter is the instrument of God and the action is laid for the most part in Judea, and finally four in which the protagonist is Paul. The first of these cycles stops short of persecution. . . . The second and third cycles, contain mounting persecutions, bearing the marks . . . of the passion of Christ. In the Diaconal and Petrine cycles the typological echoes become plain and dominant; and the passion and resurrection of Jesus are the continuous background of the final journey of Paul, of his forebodings, his trials, his sufferings, and his final deliverance. . . .

The acts of the Apostles divides theologically, geographically, personally, and cyclically, into four.

The first section is concerned with the Church's mission to Israel proper, and extends over the first five chapters of the book. The whole scene is laid in Jerusalem. . . . The second section is concerned with the Church's mission to the periphery of Israel, that is to Hellenist Israel, to heretical and seceded Israel at Samaria, and to a eunich Israelite. . . . The section goes from 6.1 to 9.31. . . . The third or Petrine section from 9.32 to 12.24. Its preponderant incident is the preaching to Palestinian God-fearers at Caesarea, its hero is Peter, now for the first time on his own. . . . Cornelius is the thin edge of the wedge: the admission of Palestinian God-fearers into the Church leads on to the wholesale admission of Gentiles at large in Section IV, the Pauline section, 12.25 to the end of the book. Here the gospel is carried from Jerusalem to Rome.

M. D. Goulder. Type and History in Acts (London, S.P.C.K., 1964), pp. 16, 32–33, 46–47, 65–66

The . . . five-fold division of Acts is this: (1) 1.9 to 8.3; (2) 8.4 to 11.18; (3) 11.19 to 15.35; (4) 15.36 to 19.20; (5) 19.21 to 28.31.

Jerusalem is . . . important for this set of divisions. Stephen's martyrdom is the signal to take the gospel from Jerusalem to Judea and Samaria, and to Antioch and beyond, providing both the first and the second break in the story (8.4 to 11.19). At the beginning of each of these second and third sections the Jerusalem Church specifically approves and watches over the new missionary efforts, by sending Peter and John to Samaria (8.14–25) and by sending Barnabas to Antioch (11.22ff). The second section ends with Peter's reporting back to Jerusalem after he has baptized Cornelius, and receiving the blessing of the Jerusalem Church on his work (ll.18). The break between the third and fourth sections is marked by the important Jerusalem Council in which, significantly, James, the leader of the Jerusalem Church, and not Peter, the first of the Apostles, takes the principal part. The final section begins with Paul's making his fateful decision to return to Jerusalem and to go from there to Rome.

In the whole of Luke-Acts Jerusalem controls the history. It is at the same time the city which God redeems (Luke 2.38) and the city where he is rejected. It becomes the centre of the mission to the Gentiles, but it rejects the gospel for itself. Jerusalem is both the Heavenly City and the Earthly City. The story ends at Rome because Jerusalem has rejected her saviour, but Rome will be the centre of the Church, and Jerusalem will be in subjection, only "until the times of the Gentiles are fulfilled" (Luke 21.24).

J. C. O'Neill. *The Theology of Acts in Its Historical Setting* (London, S.P.C.K., 1970, pp. 72–73

Brief comment needs to be made yet regarding the missionary sermons of the journey. Myres has pointed out the importance of speeches in the classical epic for punctuating the narrative and for emphasizing turning points in the story. Duckworth has amply illustrated from the Vergilian epic of Rome that the focal point of the story is often a significant speech. Thus, in the middle section of the triadic structure of the *Aeneid*, where the national and patriotic theme comes through most strongly, the speech of Anchises with its stress on Roman heroes, the greatness of Augustus, and the Romans' task is centrally placed. Also Luke, in the concluding section of Acts, which deals with the bringing of the gospel to Rome, uses the speeches of chapter 28 in a vital way to signal the passage of the gospel from the hardened Jews to the receptive gentiles.

In respect to the missionary journeys narrative, the symmetrical and climactic placement of the three larger Pauline sermons suggests a careful Lukan design in keeping with the theme of Acts. The placement of two of Paul's three major journey sermons at the first and last itinerary points to which Luke devoted considerable space in his story and the positioning of the Athens sermon at the center of the entire structure do not appear to be literary accidents or coincidences. The architectonic patterns discovered for the other speeches in Acts add substance to the suggestion of Dibelius that "the selecting of the occasion and the elaboration of the speech is in each case the work of the author." Why, for example, should the single model Pauline sermon to the gentiles be placed in Athens? . . . Luke was purposeful in selecting Athens for the only recorded sermon of Paul on Greek soil. The piety and the philosophy of Athens were "the heart of the spiritual life of Greece." The Athens speech symbolizes Paul's penetration to the center of the Hellenistic cultural world. Luke's placement of a sermon at this spot is suggestive of the outreach of the gospel.

The three major Pauline sermons within the missionary journeys structure exhibit great variety, as well as progression. One of the speeches is in a Jewish synagogue, given to Paul's countrymen; the second address is before the gentiles; and Paul's pastoral farewell is delivered to the elders of a Christian congregation. The sermons are placed symmetrically within the missionary journeys structure. The Antioch sermon is given near the start of Paul's first of three missionary journeys; the Athens sermon is dramatically placed near the center of Paul's second missionary journey; the Miletus address fittingly comes near the end of the third missionary journey. The Antioch sermon shows that the gospel was given first to the Jews, who rejected it; then it was delivered through the Athens sermon to the gentile world; finally, it was entrusted to the church, comprised of both Jews and Greeks, through the testament offered to the elders at Militus.

> Donald R. Miesner. "The Missionary Journeys Narra-
> tive: Patterns and Implications," in *Perspectives on Luke-
> Acts*, ed. Charles H. Talbert (Danville, VA, Association
> of Baptist Professors of Religion, 1978), pp. 212–213

STORYTELLING TECHNIQUE

At first sight as a church history the Acts is very disappointing, because it is so incomplete. There are such great gaps. . . . But the feeling of disappointment is really due to want of ability to appreciate S. Luke's historical method. As he knew that the secret of history lies in personality, so he knew that the true way of writing history is not to compile bare records but to draw living pictures. Accordingly instead of writing a dictionary of historical names and ecclesiastical usages, he gives us a succession of vivid pictures which present to us a living church. Thus we have pictures—of the preaching in the Temple (ii, iii), of the apostles before the Sanhedrin (iv, v), of the internal discipline of the church (v), of the working of signs (iii, ix, xiv), of the election and ordination of church officers (vi), of a martyrdom (vii fin.), of apostolic laying on of hands, and of the work of a Christian prophet (viii). We assist at a proconsul's court (xiii), a sabbath service in the synagogue (xiii), a city riot (xix), a meeting for Christian worship (xx 7–12) and so forth. This method really gives us all we want. For these scenes are intended for typical pictures. Having once filled in the details in one picture, S. Luke does not repeat them elsewhere: we must take them for granted. Thus we have no doubt that vi 1–6 is meant for a typical ordination, viii 14–17 for a typical apostolic confirmation of the newly baptized, xv 5–29 for a typical Christian 'council,' and xx 7–12 for a typical Christian service. In the same way we have a typical sermon to the Jews (xiii), a typical address to philosophers (xvii), a typical appeal to the unenlightened heathen (xiv), and a typical defence before a Roman governor (xxiv).

> Richard B. Rackham. *The Acts of the Apostles* (London,
> Methuen and Company, 1901), pp. xlix–l

No other New Testament book equals Acts in the variety and number of the persons described. Here we meet kings and other leading men and women of the Roman Empire; distinguished Jewish rabbis, high priests, and especially Gamaliel, the president of the college in Jerusalem; and most important of all, Peter, Paul, and scores of men and women who helped carry Christianity from Jerusalem to Rome.

Peter, who denied Christ, is found in chapter 2 preaching on Christ with such effect that three thousand people are converted in one day. The first half of Acts is filled with the doings of this impulsive follower of Jesus. The last half of the book is given to a description of Paul and his missionary work in Asia and Europe. Other noteworthy characters who help make Acts the greatest biographical book in the Bible are John, Stephen, Philip, Cornelius and the Roman, Barnabas, Mark, Lydia, Dorcas, Priscilla.

> Herbert R. Purinton and Carl E. Purinton. *Literature of the New Testament* (New York, Charles Scribner's Sons, 1925), p. 114

The Acts is a book of persons, not things; of personalities, not institutions and church organization. Some critics hold that great events in history are naturally grouped round great personalities. The history of Christianity in Luke's narrative centres in Peter and Paul. Luke has made them cover the early growth of the Church, as Peter fights its home battle, and Paul the battles abroad. The selection of these two, with Stephen as a link between, has given something of a unity to the book. Luke has not made the mistake of ranging too widely.

The Acts, then, has all the liveliness of a book of personalities. The very title strikes the personal note. This is fortunate. It is the only kind of book that could have been sufficiently readable, coming just after the peerless gospel memoirs. Suppose our only record of the Church had been written by a dull chronicler with a passion for names, lists of officials and their duties, who might have given us the genealogies of the seven deacons or the times and places at which they distributed relief, with no appreciation of the outstanding personality of Stephen! The impression might have been as flat and uniform as a bad photograph. On the contrary, how quickly Luke passes from the deacons as an institution to the spiritual work of Stephen, and to the tale of Philip and that interesting eunuch. . . .

Luke has a characteristic way of introducing his big people. Space being limited, and the action pressing, the introductions are brief and rapid, and yet smoothly and quietly done. Notice how Peter is brought to the front. 'In those days Peter stood up *among the disciples* and said (their number was about 120). . . .' Yet the unanimity of the band acting with him is quietly stressed, 'But Peter standing up *with the eleven* . . .', 'they said to Peter *and to the rest of the Apostles*', 'then Peter *and the other Apostles answered* . . .'.

> P. C. Sands. *Literary Genius of the New Testament* (Oxford, Oxford University Press, 1932), pp. 105–106, 109

He proposes to sketch the beginnings of Christianity, especially of Greek Christianity, into which the Christian movement had developed. The thread of the narrative is no mere biography but the providential fashion in which the gospel had groped its way out of Judaism into widening circles—Roman and Ethiopian, proselyte and Samaritan—until at length, in Antioch, the apostles began to preach to Greeks with no Jewish preparation and then to the whole Mediterranean world. No man plans it, not even the apostles. It happens involuntarily but inevitably, in an almost casual way, by human contacts. . . .

Old chapters and verse divisions . . . have blocked and obscured the swiftly running current of the Acts with its rapid, exciting action, which ought by all means to be read, as it was intended to be read, at a single sitting. Where within eighty pages will be found such a varied series of exciting events—trials, riots, persecutions, escapes, martyrdoms, voyages, shipwrecks, rescues—set in that amazing panorama of the ancient world—Jerusalem, Antioch, Philippi, Corinth, Athens, Ephesus, Rome? And with such scenery and settings—temples, courts, prisons, deserts, ships, seas, barracks, theaters? Has any opera such variety? A bewildering range of scenes and actions passes before the eye of the historian. And in them all he sees the providential hand that has made and guided this great movement for the salvation of mankind.

The narrative which began in Jerusalem culminates in Rome, where Christianity has already been mysteriously established. The style, which is full of strange variety in the opening chapters of the Acts, settles into the writer's own manner when Paul takes the center of the stage—a strong hint that the author is here on his own ground.

Acts may appear at first little more than a storybook of the early Christian movement, but this means only that the writer has skilfully concealed his didactic and left the instrinsic interest of his materials to carry the reader on. Each story has a point of its own, but the whole has a larger meaning of its own too, which the writer has not spoiled by elaborating but has left to the intelligence of his readers. And he has told his story to the end, for with Christianity established in Rome accounts of its further extension to obscure places in Gaul or Spain would be sheer anti-climax. There is an obvious propriety in a narrative which, beginning in Jerusalem, the historic seat of the old religion, ends in Rome, the center of its field, which was to be the world.

> Edgar J. Goodspeed. *An Introduction to the New Testament* (Chicago, University of Chicago Press, 1937), pp. 186–189

We can say that his aim is to write an edifying work for Christians, which will at the same time present the case for Christianity to Gentiles. This comes to light in different ways. The author is a very skillful narrator, and possesses a great gift for dramatic presentation. We can see this not only in the composition of the narrative passages, but also in speeches particularly, those which comprise about a third of the whole work. . . . As far as content is concerned they are closely linked with the narrative framework. The hearers in fact are the readers of Acts, and the purpose of the speeches is to bring the past to life. In other words, the ultimate aim behind Luke's account of history is not so much to present the past but rather to speak to the present. The author achieves this by turning "history" into "stories." It is in this way that the Church is "edified," for it learns how the Word of God has triumphed over all opposition and can therefore be confident that it will continue to triumph. . . .

It is noticeable that the aim here is to show that Christianity is not something "done in a corner" (xxvi. 26). Its success is carefully brought out by references to the numbers of converts. . . . It is also emphasized that influential people have either become Christians themselves of have entered into serious conversation with the missionaries. . . . This is of course meant to make the Christian faith more attractive, but there is obviously a further special intention here. The author does not seem to be thinking any longer in terms of a sweeping success in the mission to Jews (xxviii. 28), but he emphasizes the fact that the Christian message is not opposed to the Jewish.

W. Marxsen, *Introduction to the New Testament*, trans. G. Buswell (Philadelphia, Fortress Press, 1968), pp. 170–171

Every history also has to be a story; the multiform experience of everyday reality has to be organized into some sort of pattern. As shown above, the organizing pattern for Luke is history of salvation, a history of the accomplishment of God's purpose. This linear narrative points to an end, a future fulfillment, but Luke has restructured it so that the real emphasis lies on the "middle of time," the story of Christ related in his Gospel. Read on this level, Luke-Acts is a key stage in the incorporation of the story of Jesus into a coherent story of God's relation to the world.

Yet there is another level of story in Acts, which works as a kind of counterpoint to the story of the working out of God's purpose. The Book of Acts, however it is analyzed in detail, falls into two main parts. In the first, the church discovers its identity: in the second, it reaches out into the world. The outreach is dramatized in the journeys of Paul. In this part of the story it is easy to recognize the narrative motif of the journey or quest. Unlike the journey of Odysseus, that of Paul does not bring him back to his home. The quest becomes an open journey, an unfinished one. The particular narrative device which highlights the quest theme and emphasizes its unfinished character is the very simple one of the narrow escape, a form of narrative which is more at home in the tale or romance than in history. Paul's story is made up of a whole series of narrow escapes. . . . Further depth is given to the narrow escape theme by the fact that Paul's career is paralleled on a smaller scale by the narrow escapes of Peter. . . .

When Acts is read with an eye to the level of human quest or journey as well as with attention to the overarching divine purpose of sacred history, the whole vision of existence communicated by the book becomes an open one and is released from the theological rigidity which it receives in some interpretations. The firmness of the divine purpose is set in counterpoint to the peril and expendability of its instruments—Stephen is martyred, Peter disappears from the story without comment, and Paul goes through his many escapes to die, presumably, before his plans have been accomplished (cf. Acts 20:25). The open structure of the ending of Acts is fully appropriate to the vision of existence which the book as a whole communicates.

> William A. Beardslee. *Literary Criticism of the New Testament* (Philadelphia, Fortress Press, 1970), pp. 50–51

DRAMATIC ELEMENT AND SPEECHES

Luke's sense for pictures and scenes and drama is most evident of all in the last nine chapters. Memoirs have an advantage over history, in that the writer is freer to select from his material, develop a part which has dramatic possibilities, in which too he may have a personal interest, and while observing proportion, not be a slave to it. The last chapters of the Acts may be disproportionately full of detail, but by allowing himself this amount of disproportion and confining his story to his hero Paul, Luke has given the Acts a dramatic close. One is always happy while the chief actor is on the stage, and in these chapters Luke has concentrated on what has been called 'the Passion of Paul'. If Luke did not know Greek drama, he at least knew the device of 'dramatic irony'. The end of the drama, Paul at Rome, is deftly prepared for by a verse in chapter xix, Paul's remark at Ephesus about his plans, 'After I have been there, I must also see Rome.' He was not thinking of going there in chains or that his seeing Rome would first entail more hairbreadth escapes than he had yet experienced. 'I must also see Rome.' How artless it seems in the narrative, but to Luke it meant drama, and he proceeds to work up this drama with unusual detail, the stages of the journey of Jerusalem, the farewells of the churches, the ominous predictions of danger on the way, everything that can intensify the feeling of an approaching crisis. . . .

The trials all excite interest. You feel Paul straining to penetrate the prejudice against him, and yearning to reach the better feeling of his countrymen. But as the word 'Gentiles' wrecks him with the mob, so 'resurrection' cuts short the patience of the council. . . . Luke adds many an interesting touch from his own observation or inside information; 'the captain *took* the boy by the *hand*'—a kindly captain; 'Felix trembled'; the promptness of Festus and his pride in it , in contrast to the dilatoriness of Felix, is quietly expressed by facts. Luke makes you feel as if you were listening yourself by giving you a gesture of the president, or a look of the speaker, as he stands on the rostrum: 'the governor *beckoned* to him to speak', Paul '*looking earnestly* at the council'; and while abridging the speeches Luke always contrives to leave a firsthand impression of the speaker and the court. . . .

The story of Paul before Agrippa is as stirring as that of Elijah on Mount Carmel. It is the old issue in a revised form: 'If the Lord be God, follow him.' 'If Jesus be the son of God , follow him.' Each plea is made before a king, with the people as witnesses. Luke has written up the tale with such care that he evidently felt it to be the climax of the history. His artistry consists in the fidelity with which, while making a précis, he preserves the salient facts of the scene and the spirit of the speeches and dialogue. The scene comes through to us as he saw it, and the actors speak for themselves.

P. C. Sands. *Literary Genius of the New Testament* (Oxford, Oxford University Press, 1932), pp. 114–116

Christian speeches reported in the Acts of the Apostles . . . fall into four main groups, which we may call evangelistic, deliberative, apologetic, and hortatory. The first group must further be subdivided according to the nature of the audience, for the methods of presenting the Good News to pagans was naturally different from the method of presenting it to those who had some acquaintance with the OT revelation. . . .

To this latter kind of evangelistic oratory belong the speeches of Peter to Jewish audiences in chapters ii, iii, iv, and v, his address in the "god-fearing" household of Cornelius in ch. x, and the sermon preached by Paul to an audience of Jews and "god-fearers" in the synagogue of Pisidian Antioch in ch. xiii. To the other class of evangelistic speeches belong the addresses at Lystra in xiv, 15ff., and at Athens in xvii, 22ff.

To the deliberative group we may assign Peter's speech to his fellow-disciples in i, 16ff., preceding the election of Matthias to fill Judas Iscariot's vacant place, and the speeches at the Council of Jerusalem in ch. xv. The apologetic speeches include Stephen's defence before the Sanhedrin in ch. vii, Peter's defence of his entering and eating in the house of Cornelius (xi,

4ff.), and Paul's successive defences before the Jerusalem populace (xxii,1ff.), the Sanhedrin (xxiii, 1ff.), Felix (xxiv, 10ff.), Festus (xxv, 8ff.), Herod Agrippa II (xxvi, 1ff.), and the Jews of Rome (xxviii, 17ff.). Paul's address to the elders of the Ephisian church in xx, 18ff. belongs mainly to the hortatory class. . . .

When a student of the classics reads Luke's twofold work, he realizes that in several ways Luke has inherited the traditon of Greek historical writing, handed down from the time of Herodotus and Thucydides in the fifth century B.C. One feature of that tradition was the composition of appropriate speeches for appropriate occasions. Thucydides himself at the outset of his *History of the Peloponnesian War*, makes it clear how he proposes to tackle this business. . . .

That was . . . the fashion of the time, and against this background we must look at the speeches in Acts. At once we are struck by a difference, for these speeches can by no means be called the summit of Luke's literary perfection. For an author who could write such idiomatic Greek as the Prologue to the Third Gospel, the Greek of some of the speeches in Acts is surprisingly awkward.

We must not consider the speeches in Acts in isolation from those in the former part of Luke's history. The speeches in the Third Gospel can be compared with their parallels in the other two Synoptists, who did not inherit the traditions of Greek historical writing. On the basis of such a comparison, the general conclusion of Synoptic students is that Luke has preserved his Sayings source or sources with great faithfulness. . . . If Luke comes off so well in reports of speeches where his fidelity to his sources can be tested, we should not without good reason suppose that he was less faithful where his sources are no longer available for comparison. . . .

We need not suppose that the speeches in Acts are *verbatim* reports in the sense that they record every word used by the speaker on the occasions in question. Paul, we know, was given to long sermons (cf. Acts xx, 2, 7, 9; xxviii, 23); but any one of the speeches attributed to him in Acts may be read through aloud in a few minutes. But I suggest that reason has been shown to conclude that the speeches reported by Luke are at least faithful epitomes, giving the gist of the arguments used. Even in summarizing the speeches, Luke would naturally introduce more or less of his own style; but in point of fact it frequently seems to be less, not more. Taken all in all, each speech suits the speaker, the audience, and the circumstances of delivery.

F. F. Bruce. *The Speeches in the Acts of the Apostles*
(London, Tyndale Press, 1942), pp. 5–8, 27

The speeches of Acts are not like the speeches of Thucydides. The latter are "a possession forever" as unexcelled reflections on the story of the Peloponnesian war, and as such detachable from it, but there is also a complete and admirably told story. The speeches of Luke are an essential part of the story itself, "the story of the proclamation of the Word of God." Without them the book of Acts would be a torso consisting chiefly of a miscellany of episodes and summaries. Some primary dependence of Luke in the composition of his speeches on Greek-hellenistic historiography in general and on Thucydides in particular cannot be ruled out. In both cases, Thucydides and Luke, formal speeches occupy about one fourth of the total composition. . . . But if Luke was influenced in some way by Thucydides, he made one radical change, in that by his speeches he no longer gives "heightened meaning to the moment," but transforms the Thucydidean tradition by making the speeches an integral part of his story itself, as the story of "the proclamation of the Word of God." In the Acts, at a conservative estimate, the speeches and their immediate settings—the latter chiefly preparatory but also subsequent to the speeches—occupy 74% of its whole text, while in Thucydides they occupy no more than about 25%. The settings, in the best Thuchdidean style of brevity, hardly occupy any space and therefore do not detract from his main narrative at all.

Paul Schubert. JBL. 87, 1968, p. 16

Luke was most anxious to impress upon his readers that the Roman authorities treated the Christian missionaries with benevolence and acknowledged them to be politically harmless. . . . Luke was therefore obliged to show in concrete stories how friendly and correct had been the behaviour of Roman officials toward Paul. . . . Consequently, like a dramatist, he produces a rapid succession of vivid and lively scenes (25.14–26.32):

Scene 1:   in the palace of the Roman governor; Festus and King Agrippa in close conversation . . .

Scene 2:   next day; the audience-chamber is filling; the Caesarean authorities and the officer-corps are already here, and the governor too. Enter King Agrippa with his sister Berenice and an imposing retinue. But the real centre of interest is Paul, who is now brought in by a legionary. . . .

Scene 3:   Paul—in close-up, as it were—speaks. It is of course the readers of the book who are his real public. They hear the story of his life for the second time form his own lips. . . . Then comes dramatic by-play between Paul and Festus (who can again make neither head nor tail of the resurrection-message), then Paul and the king, who, however non-commitally, expresses his appreciation to the Christian. The final scene is a short consultation in an adjoining room, Agrippa summing up in these words: Paul could have gone free had he not appealed to the emperor.

Thus we may clearly discern Luke's dramatic technique of scene-writing in an episode where, untrammelled by tradition, he enjoyed freedom of movement.

Ernst Haenchen. *The Acts of the Apostles: A Commentary*
(Philadelphia, Westminster Press, 1971), pp. 106–107

The book of Acts records seven episodes which have been taken as trial scenes by various interpreters: Paul's speech on the Areopagus (Acts 17:19–32); the defense before the Hebrews in the temple court (Acts 21:27–22:29); the hearings before the Sanhedrin (Acts 22:30–23:10); before Felix (Acts 24:1–23), before Felix and Drusilla (Acts 24:24,25), before Festus (Acts 25:6–12), and before Festus and Herod Agrippa II (Acts 26:1–32). Only four of these accounts include a speech: the temple scene, the apprearance before Felix, that before Festus and Agrippa, and the Areopagus meeting. . . .

The speeches of Paul are set in a framework very similar to the pattern [of defense speeches in ancient literature]. All elements found in the opening and closing frameworks of the typical form are found in the Lukan compositions.

The introductions to the Pauline speeches likewise show great affinity with the defense speech model. The opening remarks were clearly defined, identified the speech as an apology, were comparatively short, and generally used a term of address. . . .

The bodies of the Lukean speeches also appear to be in general harmony with the pattern. They open with a refutation of the charges and treat the accusations levelled at the defendant. They consist largely of first-person verb forms and use a term of address. They also stress the innocence of the accused. . . .

It would therefore appear reasonable to conclude that the defense speeches of Paul in Acts exhibit the same form, the same arrangement, and the same general elements which are characteristic of defense speeches in other narrative literature form ancient times.

Fred Veltman. "The Defense speeches of Paul in Acts,"
in *Perspectives on Luke-Acts*, ed. Charles H. Talbert
(Danville, VA, Association of Baptist Professors of
Religion, 1978), pp. 253, 256

UNIFYING MOTIFS

Luke writes his book largely by the use of biographical sketches.

But it is not a haphazard jumble. He has two heroes, Peter and Paul, but Paul is the dominating figure of Acts next to Christ, whose words and deed overshadow all (Acts 1:1). . . .

Luke has demonstrated his artistic skill by welding this complex variety of persons and places, times and seasons, characters and circumstances, into one whole—a whole so complete that we entirely forget the variety, we are unconscious of the author and his method. We are swept on with the onward march of Christianity from Jerusalem to Rome. We see the greatest of all revolutions transforming Peter and Paul from Jewish pride of privilege to world evangelization and Christian freedom in Christ.

> A. T. Robertson. *Luke the Historian in the Light of Research* (New York, Charles Scribner's Sons, 1930), p. 235

A writer will reveal his particular concern by his selection of materials. The writer of Acts had to be highly selective. When he set out to cover a period of thirty years in the scope of one papyrus roll, it is obvious that he had to omit far more than he included. . . . Within the narrow confines of his brief pamphlet he has chosen to repeat and emphasize some things at the expense of totally omitting others. His whole pattern of interspersing detailed narratives with compact summaries shows selectivity at work.

We have seen that this is true of *persons*. It is by conscious purpose that Peter and Paul successively dominate the book. The amount of space devoted to *speeches* is more than a literary convention. It reflects the basic theological concern of the book. Certain *events* are forced on our attention by repetition: the conversion of Cornelius, the conversion of Paul, the apostolic decree.

But it is the selectivity of *place* that is most striking. Jerusalem and Rome are the *foci* of the book. The expansion of the church in other directions is resolutely ignored. . . .

Jerusalem dominates the first part of the book. Thus Luke . . . centers on Jerusalem as the place where Jesus gave his final intructions (Acts 1:4,12) and the sole place where the church came into being (Acts 2). Jerusalem is the center from which the preaching of the gospel proceeds (Luke 24:47, Acts 1:8). . . . The missionary labors of Paul are presented in the pattern of "missionary journeys" which begin and end at Jerusalem (Acts 12:25, 15:2, 15:30, 18:22, 21:17). . . .

Toward the end of the book, there is a similar emphasis on Rome. As early as 19:21, Luke lets his readers in on the secret that the journey to Jerusalem is in reality a journey to Rome. This is enforced by the vision in 23:11. . . . Finally, the book moves to its climax with a detailed account of the voyage, the shipwreck, and the arrival at Rome at last. The reader cannot miss the peculiar emphasis of 28:14: "And so we came to Rome." With the statement that Paul had an unhindered ministry in Rome for two years, the book comes to an abrupt halt, leaving the reader unsatisfied, but apparently satisfying the writer that his purpose has been achieved.

If what we have said up to this point has any weight, there must be a theological motive for such selectivity, Jerusalem must have a theological significance, and Rome also. This is not hard to discover. Jerusalem is the world center of the chosen people. To her the tribes go up. To her belongs the promises of the Scriptures. And Rome is the world center of the Gentiles. . . .

For Luke the outstanding ''thing that has been fulfilled among us'' is that the gospel which began at Jerusalem, in the bosom of Judaism, is now preached at Rome, the center of the Gentile world. The theological significance of this fact leads him to omit any record of expansion in other directions, to take only those men who played a strategic role in the Gentile mission as his heroes, and to tell of their lives only those portions which contributed to this one development.

This is not a question of mere geographical transfer, of the familiar dotted lines on the maps of Paul's journeys. There has been a theological transfer. God's great deed for his People has been rejected by them and accepted by the Gentiles.

Albert C. Winn. Int. 13, 1959, pp. 148–150

The book of Acts shows tremendous interest in the idea of witness. . . .The facts of the Christian faith and their significance are being presented in an atmosphere of hostility, contention and debate. . . . Under these conditions it is not strange that Luke should make use of the language of the courtroom. Indeed, the importance attached to legal language in the Book of Acts is part of the author's theological intention.

The prominence of legal scenes in Acts is nowhere more obvious than in the five trial scenes of Paul (xxii 30–xxiii 10; xxiv 1–23; xxiv 24–25; xxv 6–12; xxvi 1–32). . . . The prominence of legal language in the trial scenes of Paul is clearly a part of Luke's purpose; both Paul and the Jerusalem apostles work in an atmosphere of hostility and contention. . . .

The frequent use of legal language in connection with real courts of law is germane to Luke's presentation and part of his theological intention. The claims of Christ are being debated, and Luke intends by the use of lawcourt scenes and legal language to draw attention to this fact. The Messiahship and Lordship of Jesus are in dispute, and this challenges Luke to demonstrate these claims 'by many convincing proofs'. . . . An important part of his task is the presentation of the courtroom evidence in such a way that it will bear witness to Christ.

Allison A. Trites. NT. 16, 1974, pp. 278–279, 284

The coincidence of sea voyages and first person plural narration in the Acts is striking. There are four we-sections in Acts; 16:10–17; 20:5–15; 21:1–18; 27:1–28:16. In each instance, a sea voyage begins as the first person plural narration emerges. While this observation can lead the interpreter in various directions, it points vividly to accounts of sea voyages in antiquity. . . . Sea voyage narratives in Greek and Roman literature become a distinct genre. One of the features of this genre is the presence of first person *plural* narration. Undoubtedly the impetus for this is sociological; on a sea voyage a person has accepted a setting with other people, and cooperation among all the members is essential for a successful voyage. Therefore, at the point where the voyage begins, the narration moves to first person plural.

The author of Luke-Acts employs the sea voyage genre with great skill. His narrative builds toward a conclusion that is reached through a dramatic sea voyage. First plural narration emerges in the sections that present "mission by sea". . . .

All of the features of this genre arise out of the dynamics of sailing on the sea, landing in unfamiliar places, and hoping to establish an amiable relationship with the people in the area where the landing occurs. During the short stay on land, before resuming the voyage, two kinds of episodes are especially frequent. First, an event often occurs in which some people of the area are friendly toward the voyagers. This event usually leads to an invitation to stay at someone's home. The voyagers seldom remain neutral visitors in a locale where they land. Thus, a second event will divide the people of the area over whether or not these voyagers are to be trusted. Usually the leader of the voyage will become involved in a major episode in which his extraordinary abilities are displayed. Often he will speak eloquently and perform some unusual feat. If the voyagers are not driven forcibly from the place where they have landed, an emotional farewell scene occurs in which the people bring provisions and other gifts to the boat.

A sea voyage account often opens with a statement regarding the purpose of the voyage, a comment about preparations for it, and a list of some of the participants in it. When the voyage is under way, there is an account of the places by which the voyagers sail, and frequently short descriptive comments are given about the places. Also, the length of time it takes to sail from one place to another usually is indicated, and frequently the span of time is linked with the direction and force of the wind. Gods are portrayed as determining the fate of the voyage. Visits of the gods, and signs and portents, frequently attend the voyage. In response, prayers are offered, altars are built, and sacred rituals are enacted. At some point, almost every good sea voyage account portrays a storm that threatens or actually ends in a shipwreck.

Virtually all of the features of ancient sea voyage literature are present in the we-passages in Acts.

Vernon K. Robbins. "By Land and By Sea; The We-Passages and Ancient Sea Voyages," in *Perspectives on Luke-Acts*, ed. Charles H. Talbert (Danville, VA, Association of Baptist Professors of Religion, 1978), pp. 216, 229–230

STYLE

The scenes he saw so vividly owe much of their vigour to his special vocabulary, such words as 'looking steadfastly at' of the speaker taking in his audience, 'shaking downwards with his hands' as he beckons for silence. His most expressive words are often post-classical, that is, of the time when words took on metaphorical meanings, and are more highly coloured, than when they were first used. For instance converts in Athens *'glued themselves'* to Paul (A.V. 'clave to'), and Paul and his company *'tear themselves away'* from the elders of Ephesus. . . . Then Apollos was *'boiling'* in spirit or 'fervent', the audience at Pentecost were *'pricked* in their heart', and Stephen's hearers were *'cut to the heart,'* (lit. sawn asunder), Paul *'makes havoc of'* (lit. 'sacks') those who believed. . . . Luke treasures up anything vigorous or expressive that he finds in his sources: 'What will this *seed-picker* say?' the Athenian slang word for the superficial trifler who picks up scraps of knowledge like a bird picking up seed. . . . 'This thing was not *done in a corner'* is Paul's expressive idiom before Agrippa. 'Paul *shook out his lap,* and said . . . ' preserves another gesture, and 'knower-of-hearts' is Peter's favourite word twice reported for us. . . .

When we come to phrase-making, Luke's simplest phrases give a fine pictorial effect, like the *'rushing mighty wind'* of Pentecost, or as when 'the crowd of believers *had one heart and soul'*, or 'the lame man *jumping up stood and walked around,* and went with them into the Temple, *walking round and jumping* and praising God', exactly what he would do, feeling the new life in his joints, first standing, then trying a walk round, then walking and jumping in turn. . . .

Consciously or unconsciously Luke collected words to give *atmosphere.* Impressed by the greatness of Ephesus, but equally impressed by Paul's progress there, a great victory over a great stronghold, Luke punctuates his account with words expressing the greatness and power of the Christian forces. Apollos *'powerful'* in the scriptures...*'keenly and thoroughly confuted'*...Paul 'spoke with *great power'* and 'exercised no *common powers'*. The man with the spirit *'mastered and prevailed over them both'*. *'So mightily* grew the word of God and *prevailed.'*

Necessity drove Luke to economize in words, and of all economies none infuses more vigour into style than 'direct speech'. 'Men and brethren, what shall we do?' 'Stand up, I myself also am a man.'. . . . Then by his skilful use of Greek syntax Luke packs important matter into relative clauses and prepositional phrases, but more striking are his short cuts, as for instance from indirect to direct speech, 'he commanded them to wait for the promise of the Father, *which ye heard from me*'. . . .

> P. C. Sands. *Literary Genius of the New Testament* (Oxford, Oxford University Press, 1932), pp. 121–123

The Acts of the Apostles ranks high as a work of literature. It has much of the same radiance, warmth, tenderness, and enthusiasm which we have found to be characteristic of Luke's Gospel. The author shows superb skill in presenting dramatic episodes: the events at the time of Pentecost (2:1–41), Philip's running to the chariot of the Ethiopian eunuch (8:26–39), Paul's conversion (9:1–9), and Paul's shipwreck (27:14–44). There are, furthermore, many striking portraits of interesting people: the bold and confident Peter, the shrewd and opportunistic Simon Magus, the deceitful Ananias, and the learned and zealous Paul. The narrative moves smoothly and logically according to a preconceived plan: the tracing of the Gospel farther and farther from Jerusalem.

Luke's dramatic, descriptive, and narrative abilities so impressed Ernest Renan that he labeled the Acts "a new Homer."

> Buckner B. Trawick. *The Bible as Literature: The New Testament* (New York, Barnes and Noble, 1964, 1968), p. 70

Cadbury has also pointed out the versatility of Lucan style. It was taken for granted by Luke that Apostles should speak with dignified biblical expressions, especially on solemn occasions. Thus came into being those speeches which to our ears have a remarkabley stilted, no to say artificial ring: those speeches of Paul (13.10f), Peter (15.7–11) and James (15.14–21) that have so troubled the exegetes. But when Luke does not feel compelled by the occasion to employ these solemn tones, he is capable of painting a scene easily and expansively, dwelling lovingly on details, in almost conversational tones, as in the visit of Paul's nephew to the tribune, 23.17ff. Luke may have found the story of the rescue of Peter (Ch. 12), with its popular bluntness, in tradition—left to himself, he would probably have had the angel treat Peter with a little more courtesy!—but he left this down-to-earth style untouched because it renders so credible the reality of this miraculous incident. . . . He varies his style according to the tone required and the situation he is depicting, and the stylistic contrast in the alternation of dry log-book and exciting 'legends' does much to heighten the effect.

Ernst Haenchen.*The Acts of the Apostles: A Commentary* (Philadelphia, Westminister Press, 1971), p.80

FIRST CORINTHIANS
(Chapter 13)

I Corinthians xiii illustrates the effect of repetition along with balance or 'antithesis'. Balance or antithesis by itself is stately but cold, repetition by itself is emphatic and warm; this passage is a blend of the two. . . .

Paul settles down, as far as he can, to a slower rhythm. For once he does not hurry. His balance of phrase is undisturbed by rhetorical question or rapture, his theme mastering him, the praise of love, but himself the master of his theme, because of his intense experience of what it deals with, 'love suffereth long'. While the sentences roll off so easily, he is thinking steadily of what he has seen in the church at Corinth. Each phrase describing love corresponds to some weakness in his converts. Tongues, prophecy, knowledge were at present their all in all: envy, conceit, censoriousness, divisions, were some of their faults. . . .

The music of the passage will be found to depend mainly on balance strengthened by repetitions. . . . There are other merits, of course. It is all about the abstract quality of love, and yet it is all concrete—what things love does, and how it wears better than any other gift, better than all those partial things, which will fade in the light of the perfection to come. The brevity, again, in the Greek is wonderful, especially in ver. 8, where twelve words only represent all the English. The whole of vv. 4–11 in Greek looks like a mass of verbs, which do more work than any other part of speech. Then there is the epigram to close, with its compactness and pleasant rhythm, ending aptly on the word 'love', the theme of the whole.

P. C. Sands. Literary Genius of the New Testament (Oxford, Oxford University Press, 1932), pp. 142–144

The beauty of the passage lies in the choice of words, in the structure of the sentences, and in the figures of speech; in the design and rhythm of the whole. . . .

In part one (vv. 1–3), there are three very different parallelisms, and yet they are bound together by an harmonious rhythm; in the second part (vv.

62

4–7), there are five parallel lines, which are nearly all again divided into two; in the third part (vv. 8–13), groups of three (vs. 8), three (vv. 9f), five (vs. 11), five (vs. 12), three again in v. 13. . . . We leave it to the reader to make a careful and detailed analysis of it, merely pointing out that here also the fundamental elements of Pauline composition are found, namely parallelism and antithesis. . . .

The chapter on Love . . . fits so loosely into its real context (viz, the explanation concerning the charismata, I Cor., chh. 12, 14) that one doubts whether it really belongs here, whether it was fashioned for this particular place, or whether it is not really an independent picture which carries its purpose in itself. We need not safeguard ourselves against a foolish misunderstanding when we say that this gem of religious art is 'created.' Yes, 'created,' like a poem of Goethe or a song of Schubert, yet likewise created through the impulse of strong inner feeling. What we mean is that he did not 'shake it out of his sleeve,' or toss it off while dictating something relative to an entirely different matter; when Paul composed it he had forgotten all about the dispute concerning the speaking with tongues. This work of art came into existence as a result of the deepest reflection and through the impetus of an almost unconscious feeling for form and literary style. . . . Here one must guard himself against any supposition of improvisation; such fruits do not fall except after long previous ripening. One will certainly form a false picture of the literary work of Paul if he imagines that such widely comprehensive works—for they really are small books—were in a few hours and without much reflection bubbled forth into a single stream. They are, for the most part, long, well thought-out, gradually-formed conceptions, and often many chapters, like, perhaps, I Cor. 7 or 15, or Rom. 1:18–3:20, or Rom. 9–11, represent the entire literary output of one or several days.

What we wish to say is this: Paul, in his letters, gives only now and then an impulsive improvisation, of the kind the ordinary letter writer gives us. He works rather like an author or artist, and often enough he embodies in his letters previously formed or prepared speeches, to the use of which he is led not only by the practical purpose of the moment, but also by the urge to give to his thought an all-embracing, complete, and rounded form. And indeed very often this has a simple though strongly marked artistic form, usually produced by the use of symmetrical parallelism, written down, as the occasion demanded, in free rhythmical cadence.

Johannes Weiss. *Earliest Christianity*, Vol. II, trans. Frederick C. Grant (New York, Harper and Brothers, 1937), pp. 407–408, 411

In 1 Corinthians 13 we find a prose encomium that praises an abstract quality. The subject of this discourse is love, which is praised by using some of the standard motifs of the encomium.

The encomium begins by praising love as being the indispensable ingredient of the Christian life (vss. 1–3). . . . The next section of the discourse (vss. 4–7) praises love by listing its qualities and acts. Love is personified in the passage, which is permeated with parallelism. . . .

The concluding section (vss. 8–13) praises love by declaring its permanence, as opposed to the transience of three spiritual gifts. It is a variation of the superiority motif so common in encomia. The first sentence of the passage asserts the main theme to be developed: "Love never ends" (vs. 8). Paul develops this idea by contrasting love to three spiritual gifts that are not permanent (vs. 8). In typical Pauline fashion, the writer goes on to analyze how it is that prophecy, tongues, and knowledge will pass away (vss. 9–12), emphasizing the process of maturation that makes earlier phenomena unnecessary.

Paul clinches his point with a concluding aphorism about the superiority of love. In contrast to the transience of prophecy, tongues, and knowledge, there are three spiritual qualities that endure: "So faith, hope, love abide" (vs. 13). Then, in the climax of the whole discourse, the writer singles out love as being the greatest of the illustrious group of three permanent qualities: "but the greatest of these is love" (vs. 13). The first sentence in the next chapter belongs with the encomium on love, since it represents the familiar conclusion found in many encomia, the command to emulate: "Make love your aim" (1 Cor. 14:1). . . .

Balance, parallelism, and contrast are the basic rhetorical forms used in the discourse, with many of the smaller units falling into threefold patterns.

The first triad comes at the very beginning. In three successive verses, Paul uses the threefold formula, "If I . . . but have not love, . . . nothing." Within this formalized structure, Paul makes use of further repetition and contrast (vss. 1–3).

The subsequent passage (vss. 4–7) is also a triplet, as the list of the acts of love consists of three successive clauses that have the word "love" as the subject of the verbs that follow (English translations tend to obscure Paul's rhetorical pattern in verses 4 to 7). The passage is replete with parallelism and contains an example of antithesis in verse 6.

Verse 8 is based on a contrast between the permanence of love and the transience of three spiritual gifts, with the latter group falling again into the pattern of a triplet. . . . The triad pattern continues in verses 9 and 10, which use the word "imperfect" three times and also contain a contrast between the concepts of "imperfect" and "perfect". . . .

Repetition and contrast pervade the next verses, where Paul uses analogy to explain the reason for the transience of the three spiritual gifts. The figure of childhood immaturity falls into another triplet of clauses (vs. 11). The next clause introduces a contrast: "when I became a man, I gave up childish ways." Verse 12 continues the antithetical mode, mentioning contrasts between "now" and "then," "dimly" and "face to face," "in part" and "fully." The threefold pattern reaches its climax in the famous aphorism that concludes the discourse.

Leland Ryken. The Literature of the Bible (Grand Rapids, Zondervan, 1974), pp. 209–210, 324–326

Paul's hymn to love is composed in three strophes: verses 1–3, 4–7, and 8–13.

a. Strophe 1. The dominant feature in the three verses is the pattern "If I but have not love, I am (or, I gain)_____." Love is the essential element without which other virtues or achievements have no value. . . .

In the second and third sentences, the virtues selected tend toward a climax. The second sentence ends with faith that can remove mountains (probably an allusion to the familiar saying of Jesus recorded in Matt. 17–20). The ending of the third climaxes both the individual sentence and the series with the supreme test of religious devotion, martyrdom. Even this most extravagant testimony to one's convictions gains nothing without selfless love (agape).

b. Strophe 2. In the second stanza the hymn personifies love and describes it in terms of what it does and does not. Contrast is basic to the structure of the strophe. Verses 4 and 5 state the first contrast, positives (line 13) followed by a series of negatives. Verse 6 is a self-contained contrast, this time beginning with the negative and ending with a positive. The two series of contrasts are carefully balanced, forming a chiasm: positive, negative—negative, positive. . . .

c. Strophe 3. The third unit picks up three virtues introduced in the first strophe and develops the contrast between them and more lasting virtues, notably love. Three virtues introduced at the beginning, at verse 8 (prophecy, tongues, and knowledge), are balanced by three virtues at the end: faith, hope, and love (verse 13). The contrasts in the strophe point up the transient, impermanent character of tongues, prophecy, and knowledge. The child metaphor (verse 11) and the mirror metaphor (verse 12) stress that the present strains toward a future, the partial toward completion. . . .

Donald Juel. An Introduction to New Testament Literature (Nashville, Abingdon Press, 1978), pp. 323–324

EPISTLE AS A LITERARY FORM
(See also *Paul as Letter Writer.*)

DEFINITIONS

What is a letter? A letter is something non-literary, a means of communication between persons who are separated from each other. Confidential and personal in its nature, it is intended only for the person or persons to whom it is addressed, and not at all for the public or any kind of publicity. A letter is non-literary, just as much as a lease or a will. There is no essential difference between a letter and an oral dialogue; it might be described as an anticipation of the modern conversation by telephone, and it has been not unfairly called a conversation halved. It concerns nobody but the person who wrote it and the person who is to open it. . . . Its contents may be as various as life itself, and hence it is that letters preserved from ancient times form a delightful collection of the liveliest instantaneous photographs of ancient life. The form of the letters also varies greatly; but in the course of centuries a number of formal peculiarities were developed, and we not infrequently find the same forms becoming stereotyped into formulae in civilisations apparently quite independent of one another. But neither contents, form, nor formulae can be decisive in determining the characteristic nature of a letter. . . .

What is an epistle? An epistle is an artistic literary form, a species of literature, just like the dialogue, the oration, or the drama. It has nothing in common with the letter except its form; apart from that one might venture the paradox that the epistle is the opposite of a real letter. The contents of an epistle are intended for publicity—they aim at interesting "the public." If the letter is a secret, the epistle is cried in the market; everyone may read it, and is expected to read it: the more readers it obtains, the better its purpose will be fulfilled. The main feature of the letter, viz. the address and the detail peculiar to the letter, becomes in the epistle mere external ornament, intended to keep up the illusion of "epistolary" form. Most letters are, partly at least, unintelligible unless we know the addressees and the situation of the sender. Most epistles are intelligible even without our knowing the supposed addressee and the author. . . . The epistle differs from a letter as the dialogue from a conversation, as the historical drama does from history. . . . The letter is a piece of life, the epistle is a product of literary art.

Of course there are things intermediate between letter and epistle. . . .

In the New Testament there are both non-literary letters *and* literary epistles.

The letters of Paul are not literary; they are real letters, not epistles; they were written by Paul not for the public or posterity, but for the persons to whom they are addressed. . . .

St. Paul was not a writer of epistles but of letters; he was not a literary man.

> Adolf Deissmann. *Light from the Ancient East*, trans. Lionel Strachan (New York, Harper and Brothers, 1923, 1927), pp. 228–230, 233–234, 240

Out of twenty-seven books in the New Testament, twenty-one are in letter form. They are all described as 'Epistles,' and as a literary art epistle writing is to be distinguished from the writing of letters. The epistle proper is the product of much more conscious art than the letter. It is meant for a wide public, and has something of the character of a written speech, designed for preservation. A letter, on the other hand, is spoilt by signs of conscious art. Its interest is, as a rule, passing, and it is essentially individual and intimate. . . .

The epistles of the New Testament have features characteristic both of the technical epistle and of the letter. They are several of them addressed to a wide public and are obviously intended to be more than merely ephemeral; but they have one particular aim, and they express much intrinsic personal feeling. This intimate, emotional quality is to be found in all St. Paul's Epistles, and in the second and third Epistles of John. These two Epistles of John, and four among St. Paul's, those to Philemon, Timothy, and Titus, are all addressed, not to groups but to individuals. These may therefore be classed as letters proper, rather than as epistles.

> Kathleen E. Innes. *The Bible as Literature* (London, Jonathan Cape, 1930), pp. 230–231

The epistles represent a homogeneous literary category which, if we disregard oral traditions, was the oldest and most important within the early church.

Partial precedents in Jewish and Greek practice contributed to the development of the New Testament epistle form. . . . Standard phrases of Jewish and Greek letters are reflected in the openings and conclusions of the New Testament epistles. . . .

On the other hand the central parts of the New Testament epistles do not reflect the influence of Jewish and Greek letter traditions in the way that the salutation and conclusion do. The heart of the epistles is generally a doctrinal section followed by a series of admonitions. These may be regarded as following the forms of Jewish, Greek, and Christian preaching. . . .

Most New Testament epistles are not literary substitutes for conversation, like private letters, but ways of speaking publicly to congregations that could not be addressed in person. . . . So the rhetorical setting, which was always of great importance in antiquity, must be kept in mind. If a church authority could not visit the believers he wanted to address, he preached to them in writing. Someone read his epistles aloud to the congregation and the people were able to listen to the voice of the writer, as though the latter were speaking personally. As inspired communications that still preserve the characteristics of preaching, the New Testament epistles are unique literary productions.

The rhetorical core is stronger in the later New Testament epistles, inasmuch as the forms of preaching continued to evolve. One example is the baptismal sermon which consisted of catechetical instructions and exhortations presented to candidates for baptism. Another form of preaching, though only practiced as a literary genre, was the "testament." . . . The form and imagery of the epistles treated here may often be explicated by a reference to such preaching traditions. In James and Jude we find hortatory preaching in general, in First Peter and First John reflections of baptismal sermons, in Second Peter the pattern of a "testament."

It is worth noticing that the authors of Hebrews and the General epistles, which are the latest epistles of the New Testament, have diluted and partly dropped the phrases traditionally belonging to a letter and concentrate on rhetorical expsition. . . .

The amount of preaching in these writings did not prevent the church from calling them "epistles." Fundamentally they were written messages like the Pauline epistles, and some of them still have a few resemblances to actual letters. It was possible to present them as epistles in spite of the predominant rhetorical element because from the very beginning the apostolic epistles were intended to be read publicly to the congregations.

> Bo Reicke, *The Anchor Bible: The Epistles of James, Peter, and Jude* (Garden City, Doubleday and Company, 1964). pp. xxx–xxxii.

A letter is a *literary* product, intended for a *private or public* reader/s, originally or only formally in letter form. *Letter form* is distinguished by 1) *being sent* or intended for sending; 2) *from a writer* or from writers; 3) *to an addressee* or to addressees; 4) with greetings, conclusion, or other *formally stylized components*; and usually 5) with reference to or clear *intent to be a letter*.

As a broadest possible framework, this definition suggests an awareness on the part of the writer/s or addressee/s that the writing occurs within *the epistolary situation*: someone wishes to communicate in writing with someone else distant from them in space (primarily) or time. That this communication is closely related to the oral mode of discourse has been emphasized throughout the history of the form ever since (if not before) Artemon spoke of the epistle as "half of a dialogue." . . . The epistolary form is intimately related to informal oral communication: in each case there is a sense of personal intimacy not at hand in more sterotyped written or oral modes. . . .

While the central concern is the delineation of the public open letter (the "epistle") from the private letter, this factor is also necessitated by the fact that we approach all the letters through collections and editions: it is often impossible to determine whether their author intended to have them brought out in public form. . . .

The criterion of *letter form* is necessary to distinguish epistolary writings from literature-in-general. Such a distinction is along purely formal lines (addressee, sender, greetings—or omission of one of these; or explicit purpose—as within an intended collection—of being a letter; or being referred to as a letter), much as an alternation of speakers characterizes a dialogue or a drama or a metric form, style, and rhyme characterize a poem. . . .

Certainly we do not have to have a grasp of the whole range of Hellenistic epistolography to comprehend the NT letters, for they are almost all located toward the "more private" end of the spectrum. I should classify the letters of Paul and his school as "more private" in type, even though several of them show characteristics of "more public" letters (as Romans, which served as a public and discursive summary of Paul's later theology). The Johannine letters are public and discursive, and remind me of Hellenistic school exercises. The letters in the Apocalypse are imaginary. Philemon is an administrative letter into which Paul intrudes theologizing. The Universal letters are least private both in terms of formal conventions and in their didacticism. Hebrews has so little relation to private correspondence as to omit epistolographic conventions. We have before us in the NT only a few of the Hellenistic epistolary types, but our interpretation of these letters is greatly enriched when we recognize characteristics, diction, and sometimes formal fragments from the whole range of Hellenistic epistolary literature.

The absolute distinction between Letter and Epistle should be dropped. Instead we should give specific letters a relative position somewhere in the spectrum of private, intimate letters and open, public letters, taking their formal conventions and their content fully into account.

William G. Doty. CBQ. 31, 1969, pp. 193–195, 197–198

In general, the New Testament epistles do not conform closely to any existing models. For one thing, they show an unusual mixture of the personal letter and the more formalized literary epistle. They contain the personal notes, salutations, and news that informal letters contain, and they are addressed, for the most part, to specific readers (in contrast to literary epistles intended for publication, which assume a generalized audience and lack specific addresses to a reader). But along with this informality, there is much that is obviously formalized in the epistles. Their tone is more public than intimate. The personality of the writers is much less important than the religious content of their letters. The writers, indeed, do not write primarily as individual persons but in their role as apostles—as the conveyors of divine truth in a manner reminiscent of the Hebrew prophets. The destination of the epistles is usually the believing community, either a local church or a group of churches. Everything considered, the New Testament epistles are an extension of the Gospels. Both were written by authoritative Christian leaders and both existed to explain the life and teachings of Jesus.

Leland Ryken. *The Literature of the Bible* (Grand Rapids, Zondervan, 1974), p. 317

Of the twenty-seven works that make up the New Testament, twenty-one are called *epistolē*, a Greek word that may be translated either as "epistle" or as "letter." The distinction is important, because in the ancient world a "letter" was a personal communication between individuals, or groups, or individuals and groups; it was a deliberate surrogate for personal conversation and was intended to be direct, personal, and geared to a specific occasion or concern. An "epistle," however, was a deliberate literary creation intended for wide dissemination. Its form as a letter was merely a literary convention; in the ancient world it served the purpose that today would be served by an essay or article, an open letter, a short treatise, or a communication to a journal or newsaper. The letters of the apostle Paul are most emphatically letters, not epistles. . . .

The letters of Greco-Roman antiquity normally followed a set pattern: a greeting, a thanksgiving and prayer for the well-being of the addressee, the central message, a conclusion, and a final greeting. Paul normally follows this pattern, with suitable Christianizations of the greetings, thanksgivings, and prayers. . . . The central message of the letters shows the characteristic New Testament mixture of proclamation and parenesis, of doctrinal argument and exhortation.

Paul wrote his letters to meet the immediate needs of the congregation he was addressing in a particular situation. This concreteness gives them their existential element of direct confrontation. But with the exception of Philemon, they were not letters to individuals, but to congregations, which meant they would be read aloud at that congregation's meeting. This fact gives them their element of engagement with the group at large and their concern for the common life of the community as a community.

Norman Perrin. *The New Testament: An Introduction* (New York, Harcourt Brace Jovanovich, Inc., 1974), pp. 96–97

The two types of correspondence described by Deissmann need to be borne in mind. He distinguished between an epistle, which is a conscious literary effort intended for publication, and a letter, which is private in character, written for a specific occasion and of ephemeral duration. If we accept this distinction, it seems that the New Testament pieces of correspondence without exception fall into the former category. Many signs in the epistles point in this direction. (a) Paul and Peter compose in a carefully thought-out style. . . . John's first epistle contains recurring patterns of thought which have bewildered the commentators but the overall impression is that John is pursuing certain lines of pastoral counsel with deliberate intention. (b) Apostolic authority runs through the major epistles of Paul showing that he was conscious of his teaching office as "apostle to the Gentiles". This is true even in those parts of Pauline correspondence which are usually regarded as his "tender" pastoral letters (Philippians: see 1:1; 2:12; 3:17) and private communications. . . . (c) Paul intends that his letters will be read out in assemblies of Christian worship (1 Thes. 5:27) and will circulate among other Christian groups as they are sent on from the addressees (Col. 4:16). (d) He has in his mind's eye a picture of the church assembled for public worship as he writes (1 Cor. 5:1ff.; Col 2:5) and in greeting one part of the church in his epistle he takes into account also the wider company of the church in every place (1 Cor. 1:2). This vision of an "ecumenical" church (as in 1 Pet. 1:1, 5:9; Jas. 1:1) enforces the belief that these epistles are all "catholic" inasmuch as their scope reaches out to embrace the Christian brotherhood in the world. Perhaps the only exceptions to this rule are 2 and 3 John, which seem to be individual.

> Ralph P. Martin. "Approaches to New Testament Exegesis," in *New Testament Interpretation*, ed. I. Howard Marshall (Grand Rapids, William B. Eerdmans, 1977), p. 232

In letter writing, there is a continuity between private and public letters. As is well-known, A. Deissmann distinguished between "true" or "real" letters, directed to a particular recipient in a certain situation, and epistles which are "literary" in the sense that they are designed for repeated use; writings standing intermediate between these he regarded as "bad letters". In reality, however, all writing participates in both particularity and generality, even though in different degrees and in divergent ways. The medium range between the two poles represents by no means an anomaly, but may furnish some of the very finest expressions. . . .

The letters of the New Testament play a complementary role in relation to the Gospels. To a large extent, Christian tradition regarded the Gospel materials (which, like the Pentateuch, include both narrative and ethical words) as fundamental; the letter writers did not seek to replace these, but—like prophecy—directed themselves more especially to particular circumstances, and—like Wisdom—included their own reflection as a subsidiary source of insight. . . . Paul treated specific issues at such a basic and theoretical level that his writings were worthy of being shared and preserved, as was true of the messages of the great Israelite prophets.

> Martin J. Buss. "Principles for Morphological Criticism: With Special Reference to Letter Form," in *Orientation by Disorientation*, ed. Richard A. Spencer (Pittsburgh, Pickwick Press, 1980), pp. 73–74

GROUPINGS

The Epistles may be placed in the literary category of the 'letter.' They are of four main classes: (1) Purely personal, such as Philemon and 3 John; (2) treatises or discussions in letter form, such as 1 and 2 Thessalonians and 1 and 2 Corinthians; (3) pastoral letters such as 1 Timothy; and (4) discourses which are letters in title only, such as 1 John, James, and Hebrews (save for the concluding verses). These epistles connect themselves naturally with similar remains of epistolary literature not only from the time of the Apostles but from preceding and succeeding ages. Specific reference may be made to the letters of Epicurus, of Seneca, of the younger Pliny, of gnatius, of Polycarp, of Clement of Rome, and to the letter of Barnabas.

> Wilbur Owen Sypherd. *The Literature of the English Bible* (New York, Oxford University Press, 1938), p. 170

Primitive Christian literature—insofar as it records have been preserved—began in letter-form. It is in this form that we find twenty-one out of the twenty-seven books of the New Testament.

There are certain distinctions we need to make here. Not all these letters are . . . real letters. Sometimes an author uses the letter just as a literary art-form, which was very popular in the ancient world, but there is very little evidence of this kind of influence in the New Testament. A much stronger influence is that of the Pauline letters. . . .

Deissmann made the suggestion that we should make a distinction in terminology between letter and epistle, 'letter' being taken to mean a real letter, and 'epistle' a literary document which uses the letter form. This distinction has been widely adopted, and it can be valuable, although it is not always possible to make an exact division. . . . Quite apart from this, however, these descriptions are not adequate. Heb. for example has the form of a homily, but its form changes into that of a letter in the closing verses. . . . I Pet. presents similar problems. . . . The question—letter or epistle?—is significant in so far as the author has particular recipients in mind or is writing quite generally for his contemporaries. One thing that is certain is that according to this distinction the 'genuine' Pauline letters are to be regarded as letters.

> W. Marxsen. *Introduction to the New Testament*, trans.
> G. Buswell (Philadelphia, Fortress Press, 1964, 1968),
> pp. 23–24

Before focusing on the Pauline collection, we need to have before us a quick overview of the range of use of letters in primitive and early Christianity. . . .

The earliest Christian letters which concern us are those written by Paul around the middle of the first century. While we may not assume that there were no other letters written before Paul's, or that we possess all the letters Paul wrote, transmitted tradition has been restricted to the canonical Pauline letters as the earliest literary products in primitive Christianity. . . .

A second group of materials in letter form appeared in sequence with and probably in dependence upon the Pauline letters, namely, those writings in the general style of Paul and in his name, which are variously called the Post-Pauline, Deutero-Pauline, Psuedo-Pauline, or more traditionally, the Pastoral Letters (1 and 2 Timothy, Titus). . . . Some of these materials begin to spring the true-letter framework, tending to become essays or treatises, a tendency especially prominent in a group of writings associated with the name of John, the Johannine Epistles (1, 2, and 3 John). A fourth set of letters can be identified in the second volume of Luke's two-volume account of primitive Christianity, in Acts 15:23–29 and 23:26–30.

A fifth group of letters is associated with the names of prominent leaders: the Universal (''Catholic'') Letters, comprised of 1 and 2 Peter, James, and Jude. And finally, within the canon of the New Testament, a group of letters is recorded in the Apocalypse to John (Rev. 2–3).

Twenty of the twenty-seven New Testament writings purport to be letters and we have seen that two of the seven remaining writings, Acts and the Apocalypse of John, contain materials purporting to be letters. Even if we exclude additional materials which are letters in only part of their formal structure—Hebrews, James—it can still be seen that the dominant literary form found within the Christian canon is the letter.

> William G. Doty. *Letters in Primitive Christianity* (Phil-
> adelphia, Fortress Press, 1973), pp. 18–19

STRUCTURE

Personal or private letters have features in common, and may run something like this:

i.	Dear. . .	Salutation.
ii.	I am glad to hear you are well. . . I congratulate you on. . .	The health and interests of the person written to.
iii.	I have been not too well myself. . . I have been very well since I saw you. . .	Ditto of the writer.
iv.	I want to explain. . . They tell me you have. . .	Information or criticism.
v.	My advice is. . .	Advice.
vi.	I shall be seeing you soon. . .	The next meeting.
vii.	Keep well. . . . Do your best to. . .	Closing injunctions.
viii.	Remember me to. . .	Greetings sent.
ix.	Yours affectionately. . .	Signature.

We may follow out the above scheme in St. Paul's letters.

P. C. Sands. *Literary Genius of the New Testament* (Oxford, Oxford University Press, 1932), p. 128

The preceding observations permit us to posit the following working hypothesis concerning the substructure of the Pauline letter form: (1) salutation (sender, addressee, greeting); (2) thanksgiving; (3) body, with its formal opening, connective and transitional formulas, concluding "eschatological climax" and travelogue; (4) paraenesis; (5) closing elements (greetings, doxology, benediction). It should be emphasized that these elements are subject to variation in both content and order, and that some items are optional, although the omission of any one calls for explanation. It is put this way around on the view that Paul is not rigidly following an established pattern, but is creating his own letter form—in relation, of course, to the letter as a literary convention.

Robert W. Funk. *Language, Hermeneutic, and Word of God* (New York, Harper and Row, 1966), p. 270

We have seen that the basic form of the Hellenistic letter contains a threefold division: an introductory section, the main body of the letter, and a concluding section. (Indeed, I would argue that any communication carries three such features, and that means that the three features must be more clearly subdivided for identification and study.) Paul's letters fit the Hellenistic pattern in most respects, although we shall see that he developed certain subunits and expanded others.

The basic form which we may identify as belonging to the Pauline way of writing letters is as follows:

Opening (sender, addressee, greeting)

Thanksgiving or Blessing (often with intercession and/or eschatological climax)

Body (introductory formulae; often having an eschatological conclusion and/or indication of future plans)

Paraenesis

Closing (formulaic benedictions and greetings; sometimes mention of the writing process).

> William G. Doty. *Letters in Primitive Christianity* (Philadelphia, Fortress Press, 1973), p. 27

A recognizable structure is fairly consistent throughout Paul's epistles:

Opening
    Sender
    Recipient
    Salutation
Thanksgiving
Body
"I appeal to you"
Closing
    Benediction
    Concluding greeting

> Donald Juel. *An Introduction to New Testament Literature* (Nashville, Abingdon Press, 1978), p. 301

The current definition of letter structure may be outlined as follows:

Hellenistic Letter Structure	*Pauline Letter Structure*
Opening (sender, addressee, greeting for good health)	Opening (sender, addressee, greeting)
	Thanksgiving (prayer for spiritual welfare, remembrance of addressee, eschatological climax)
Body (with introductory formulae)	Body (with introductory formulae, eschatological appeal, travelogue)
	Paraenesis
Closing (greetings, final wishes, occasionally dating)	Closing (final greetings, benediction)

> Ronald Russell. *JETS.* 25, 1982, p. 297

STYLE AND MOTIFS

Martin Dibelius noticed the traditional nature of Paul's ethical instructions (paraenesis). We know now that the apostle drew on pre-Pauline or even pre-Christian traditions for his moral exhortation. Characterized by a terse, gnomic style, these materials usually fall near the end of Paul's letters (e.g., Gal. 5:13–6:10; 1 Thess. 4:1–5:22; and 2 Cor. 13:11) and possess a certain uniformity in content and vocabulary. Admonitions to do good and to avoid evil, warnings against immorality, exhortations to nonviolence, and encouragement of subjection to leaders, edification of the church, and kindness to outsiders all appear in more than one of Paul's letters. . . .

It is generally agreed that Paul borrowed his ethical injunctions, but whether he deployed them appropriate to each addressee is still debated. . . .

Types of Paraenetic Tradition

a. Wisdom Sayings
   (1) Whatever a man sows, that he will also reap. (Gal. 6:7)
   (2) He who sows sparingly will also reap sparingly, and he who sows bountifully will also reap bountifully. (2 Cor. 9:6)
   (3) Bad company ruins good morals. (1 Cor. 15:33)
   (4) A little leaven leavens the whole lump. (Gal. 5:9)

b. Vice and Virtue Lists
   (1) They were filled with all manner of wickedness, evil, covetousness, malice, . . . envy, murder, strife, deceit, malignity, . . . gossips, slanderers, haters of God, insolent, haughty, boastful, inventors of evil, disobedient to parents, foolish, faithless, heartless, ruthless (Rom. 1:29–31; see also 5:19–21; 1 Cor. 5:10–11; 6:9–10; 2 Cor. 12:20)
   (2) The fruit of the Spirit is love, joy, peace, patience, kindness, goodness, faithfulness, gentleness, self-control. (Gal. 5:22–23. . . .)

c. Imperative Cluster
   Let love be genuine; hate what is evil, hold fast to what is good; love one another with brotherly affection; outdo one another in showing honor. Never flag in zeal, be aglow with the Spirit, serve the Lord. Rejoice in your hope, be patient in tribulation, be constant in prayer. Contribute to the needs of the saints, practice hospitality. (Rom. 12:9–13)

d. Developed Exhortation (or Topical Moral Essay)
   (See the sustained admonition concerning the mutual responsibility of the strong and weak in Rom. 14:1–15:13; also note 1 Thess. 5:1–11).

Calvin J. Roetzel. *The Letters of Paul: Conversations in Context* (Atlanta, John Knox Press, 1975, 1982), pp. 35–37

Authors of letters in the New Testament are highly visible in their work. At the beginning they usually announce themselves, and they remain visible as they teach, exhort, and direct the recipients of the letters. In that regard, the letter form stands in marked contrast to narrative, in which the author is generally hidden from view; he cannot reveal himself directly without destroying the story medium in which he is working. . . .

Consistently throughout letters in the New Testament the author claims some kind of higher authority than his recipients. Both author and recipients are Christians, but within Christian discipleship a clear hierarchy is present. . . .

To some extent a letter, like a Gospel, may be viewed as a structure of structures. Certain forms remain recognizable as they are subordinated and adapted to the larger letter structure. Most obvious are epistolary elements found in the opening and closing of letters. The opening designates the sender, the recipients, and the salutation. . . . In most instances the opening is followed by a thanksgiving or blessing which makes a transition to the body of the letter. . . . At the end of a letter, set forms recur. The author closes with greetings to and from various people, a benediction, and a doxology. . . .

Frequently in letters a writer witnesses to Jesus Christ through a brief creedal affirmation or hymn. One of the simplest is "Jesus is Lord" (Rom. 10:9; 1 Cor. 12:3). Paul presents a more fully developed creedal statement in 1 Corinthians 15:3–5. Even more fully developed liturgical fragments appear in Colossians 1:15–20, Philippians 2:6–11, 1 Timothy 3:16, 1 Peter 3:18–22, and Hebrews 1:2–3. All of those passages are written in a poetic, hymnic style, and like all song they represent the human voice giving praise and thanksgiving. . . . Most creeds and hymns incorporated into New Testament letters thus focus upon the death and resurrection of Jesus, the center of early Christian proclamation. Liturgical elements in the letters proclaim in brief the story of Jesus Christ.

Those forms of worship make up only a small percentage of a letter. Except for them, the letter tends to reflect upon and further explicate, rather than proclaim, the story of Jesus. In that regard the letter form stands in contrast to the four narrative works in the New Testament.

Leonard L. Thompson. Introducing Biblical Literature:
A More Fantastic Country (Englewood Cliffs, Prentice-
Hall, 1978), 280–282

PARABLE OF THE GOOD SAMARITAN

Travellers on the road between Jerusalem and Jericho, which winds between bare limestone cliffs pitted with caves, have always been exposed to the attack of Bedouin robbers. . . . The story then relates the behaviour of three separate travellers who subsequently passed along the road. The first two, each of whom, when they came upon the victim lying half dead by the roadside, went by on the other side, were a priest and a Levite respectively. Many priestly families are said to have resided at Jericho, and these men are perhaps to be thought of as returning home after completing their period of service in the Temple. At this point in the story its hearers would have anticipated the appearance of yet a third traveller, (the "rule of three"), and would probably have been prepared to identify him beforehand. Priest, Levite, *Israelite*: so ran the familiar classification of society within the Jewish Church. But, with telling effect, it is a Samaritan who is depicted as appearing finally, to save the life of the wounded man. . . .

The story demands that the third traveller should provide a contrast to the two preceding. . . . There is at once effective and unexpected contrast, and the story falls into line with a large group of parables concerned more or less closely with the mission to the outcasts. As the penitent tax-collector may rank in God's eyes before the self-righteous Pharisee, so the heretic and schismatic of more than doubtful ancestry may prove a fitter example to follow than the representatives of orthodoxy, though they may minister within the true Temple by right of birth and flawless pedigree.

B. T. D. Smith. *The Parables of the Synoptic Gospels*
(Cambridge, Cambridge University Press, 1937), 180–181

The parable begins . . . "A certain man." . . . We note the vagueness with which this character is introduced and the complete neglect of further definition. He is one of a class, and the class simply that of travelers on that road. . . . Nothing, obviously, is said of his race, color, nationality, position, or faith. He is completely anonymous, a lay figure. . . .

Details that would attract attention to the unfortunate wayfarer are omitted in order to draw attention elsewhere. The sufferer is anonymous and vaguely drawn because he is not the central actor, nor one of the principal actors, but, excepting only the innkeeper and the donkey, the least important actor. . . . More clearly drawn, this "certain man" would be a distraction. The attention is directed away from him to others. His wounds which are to be bound up, his naked state and destitution, are remarked only as occasions for the functions performed by the Samaritan.

Literary attention and dramatic interest are focused on the subsequent travelers. True, equally few words are used, but few are necessary to produce in the minds of the audience a clear and distinct impression. Priest and Levite are types well known. . . .

The "rule-of-three" . . . is invoked and dramatic skill quickly supplies the expected third figure. The hearers would probably have been prepared to identify him beforehand. Priest, Levite, *Israelite*: so ran the familiar classification of society within the Jewish Church. The substitution of a Samaritan is a master stroke. He, likewise, needs in this connection no further introduction. Since he is the surprise element, it would be difficult, as well as gratuitous, to attempt a portrait. . . . The fact that he is a Samaritan serves the purpose. The contrast as it stands is overwhelming: as against the sacred obligation of the hierarchy, the generosity of a heretic. . . .

The vagueness of the victim, contrasted . . . with the startling and vivid introduction of an alien heretic. . ., serves its purpose and must not be left out of account. The structure of the story makes the victim the *object* and the Samaritan cannot be made other than the *subject*. . . .

Attention is centered on the three who travel the road, who themselves, as far as the story is concerned, stand in no need of a neighbor to help them. . . .

From the technique employed it is clear that the focus of attention has been shifted adroitly from the question, "Who is my neighbor?" to another question, "Who proves himself neighborly?"—or, in accord with the laws of the folk tale and the suspense the rule-of-three provides—"Who is this third who will offer himself as neighbor?" Attention is directed with charm and skill, away from the man who needs a neighbor, to those to whom is presented an opportunity to show the initiative of a neighbor. . . .

The parable prepares for the question that follows it and for no other: "Which of these three, thinkest thou, proved neighbor unto him that fell among the robbers?"

Charles W. F. Smith. *The Jesus of the Parables* (Philadelphia, Westminster Press, 1948; rpt. Pilgrim Press, 1975), pp. 150–154

In comprehending the parable it is important to grasp how the hearer is drawn into the story. From what perspective is the parable told? Initially at least, the account compels the hearer to put himself in the place of that nameless fellow jogging along the wild and dangerous road. Straightway he finds himself the object of a murderous attack which leaves him stripped, beaten, and half-dead. While lying helpless in the ditch, he is aware that the priest and Levite pass by with only an apprehensive glance. It does not matter to him whether their callousness can be excused or justified, and if the hearer (as victim) is a layman, his secret anticlericalism is confirmed. The priest or Levite as hearer will, of course, be incensed. At this juncture the lay hearer will anticipate the arrival of a benign layman on the scene; the ecclesiastical listener, muttering under his breath, will expect no less. In the teeth of just such anticipations, to the utter amazement and chagrin of every listener as Jew . . . a hated enemy, a half-breed, a perverter of true religion comes into view and ministers to the helpless victim when he is powerless to prevent him. While still in inner turmoil over this unexpected turn of events, the hearer is brought up short with the question: "Which of these three, do you think, proved neighbor. . .?" It is a question on which the Jew chokes. The lawyer in the Lucan account cannot bring himself to pronounce the name of that hated "neighbor," but he can hardly avoid the answer which the parable demands.

The Samaritan is undoubtedly the primary shock, although the behavior of the priest and Levite will raise preliminary resistance in certain quarters, nodding approval in others. The first sentences of the story evoke a silent "Yes, that's how it is" from everyone. . . .

The literal, i.e., historical, significance of the Samaritan is what gives the parable its edge. . . . The Samaritan is brought into a constellation in which he cannot be anticipated. It is this surprising, odd turn which shatters the realism, the everydayness of the story. A narrative begun with all the traits of an experience about which everyone knows, or thinks he knows, is ruptured at the crucial juncture by a factor which does not square with everyday experience. The "logic" of everydayness is broken upon the "logic" of the parable. It is the juxtaposition of the two logics that turns the Samaritan, and hence the parable, into a metaphor.

> Robert W. Funk. *Language, Hermeneutic, and Word of God* (New York, Harper and Row, 1966; rpt. Polebridge Press), pp. 211–215

The tale of the Good Samaritan is so well known and speaks for itself so unmistakably that it needs little other comment than Jesus' final injunction. It occurs only in Luke and has many of his trade-marks; its length, the highly-finished Greek of the original, the theme of a journey with a turning point, the prominence of the Samaritan as a figure from the fringe of orthodox Judaism, the human sympathy which informs it all. . . . Luke knows that we need to see it happen if it is really to sink in, so doctrine becomes story. That is *the* Lucan trade-mark. The question at the outset, *who is my neighbor?* differs from the one at the end, *which of these three seems to you to have been a neighbor?* so either the tale existed in some form before it was included in the gospel, or it has turned the question round from the theoretical 'who is my neighbour?' to the practical 'who should I be neighborly to?' Notice that, like the Prodigal Son and the Crafty Steward, this is a secular story. The Samaritan's motivation is not pious in a religious sense. The kingdom of God is seen in worldly happenings.

John Drury. *Luke* (New York, Macmillan Publishing Company, 1973), pp. 120–121

We should note the importance of rhetorical highlighting effects. . . . The most obvious example in the Good Samaritan is the threefold pattern of potential rescuers. The aborted sequences with the priest and Levite provide a pattern which causes the listener to anticipate the third traveler and build up tension. Since this threefold pattern is so common in popular story telling, we also anticipate that the third traveler will be the one who will actually help. Our attention is focused on the third traveler before he arrives, and this heightens the shock when we discover that he neither fits the pattern of cultural expectation nor the pattern of expectation created by the series priest, Levite. Much of this "highlighting" may result from features of the "surface" structure, but it is not just a matter of filling in a more basic structure. Rather, it provides the focus and emphasis that makes the story the particular story that it is.

Robert C. Tannehill. *Semeia*. 2, 1974, p. 115

What is happening in the Good Samaritan is a duel between the Speaker and Hearer but at a much deeper level than that in riddles . . . or even in charms. . . . This represents an attack on the hearer at the most profound level. . . .

The Greek text gave 46 words to what preceded the Samaritan's arrival in 10:30b–32 but 60 words to what happens on his arrival in 10:33–35. This is obviously the heart of the unexpected and must be treated with great care so that the surface structure persuades the hearer and assists him from unparabled to parabled status. The hearer must see every detail of the Samaritan's "goodness" and be unable to deny its reality. Apart, then, from what we know of Jewish and Samaritan mutual relationships outside of this text, there is already sufficient evidence *within* the text for its parabolic function as an attack on the hearer's expectation at a very deep level. The deep structure that is really under attack is the security with which one knows good from evil and who or what represents each possibility within one's established world. . . .

A parable is a story whose artistic surface structure allows its deep structure to invade one's hearing in direct contradiction to the deep structure of one's expectation. It is an attack on world, a raid on the articulate.

John Dominic Crossan. Semeia. 2, 1974, pp. 96–98

The story uses several narrative techniques. There is conflict between the robbers and the victim, and contrast between the priest and Levite on the one hand and the Samaritan on the other. The motif of testing enters the story when the injured man in the middle of the road becomes a test of the humanitarian compassion of all who travel over the road. There is climax in the story, based on the folktale motif of threefold repetition. In this case, the Samaritan's actions assume greater force because of the two previous refusals of aid. Also, the appearance of the Samaritan in the third position on the list may have reversed the expectations of Christ's audience, which was accustomed to thinking in the categories of priest, Levite, and Israelite instead of (as in the parable) priest, Levite, and Samaritan. Yet another literary ingredient of the story is satire, here an attack on the ecclesiastical elite of Jesus' day.

The parable is not concerned with doctrine but with ethics—with practical Christian living as it touches upon relations with other people. We might call the story an exemplum, in the medieval definition of a story in which a character displays ideal behavior that serves as a model for others to follow. It is designed to move the listener to moral action.

Precise realism underlies the story. The violent action with which the narrative begins would not have been unexpected in Jesus' day, since lone travelers from Jerusalem to Jericho were easy victims for robbers. There is even a touch of geographic realism in the statement that the man went "down" from Jerusalem to Jericho (Luke 10:30) since the trip did involve a literal descent in altitude.

Leland Ryken. The Literature of the Bible (Grand Rapids, Zondervan, 1974), pp. 308–309

In the parable, five people are portrayed (apart from the robbers). In succession they are: the man robbed and wounded; the priest; the Levite; the Samaritan; and the innkeeper. The focus is not so much on the man who was robbed and left half dead beside the road, though he is the object of attention. . . . Also, the subject of the story is really not the priest, Levite, or innkeeper. The focus is the Samaritan. He is the doer, the agent, the main character. Hence the parable is called the parable of the good Samaritan and not the parable of the man who was robbed and wounded. The wounded man is a faceless figure whose occupation, nationality, religion, or race is not given. Perhaps the man could not be identified by priest, Levite, and Samaritan without his clothes. In short, the identity of the man does not count. He plays the part of the neighbor and that is enough—a low profile, no more.

The robbers come and go. They commit the crime and leave. . . .

The priest, and presumably the Levite, were on their way home from temple service in Jerusalem. By law, they were not allowed to touch a corpse. Should they transgress the injunction, they would inconvenience themselves socially (by being unclean), financially (by paying burial costs), and professionally (by being barred from priestly and Levitical services). . . .

Whether they were afraid of being ambushed, or were hard-hearted, or believed they might interfere in God's judgment which had struck a wayward sinner, or were too conceited as religious leaders to stoop down and help a hapless victim, we shall never know. The fact is that both priest and Levite showed no mercy.

The Samaritan as depicted finds a warm spot in everyone's heart. He is the favorite in the story. He knows what to do and he does it well. Race, religion, and class distinctions are unimportant to him. He sees a fellow human being in need and he is the man to help.

Simon J. Kistemaker. *The Parables of Jesus* (Grand Rapids, Baker, 1980), 169–170

GOSPEL AS A LITERARY FORM

DEFINITIONS

Are the Gospels *biographies* of Jesus? No or Yes, according to the connotation given the term "biography."

In the historical sense, a biography is a writing which aims to present all the important dates and facts about a person, with perspective and exactness, including his relation to other persons and to his times. This involves research, criticism, and interpretation, according to the current principles of history-writing. It is obvious that the Gospels are not biographies in this sense of the term.

In the popular sense, a biography is any writing which aims to make one acquainted with a historical person by giving some account of his deeds and words, sketchily chosen and arranged, even when the motive of the writer is practical and hortatory rather than historical. The amount, character, order, and accuracy of the historical information contained in these pragmatic writings vary greatly, according to the purposes, interests, abilities, and resources of the several authors. The Gospels may be classified with productions of this kind; in the popular sense they are biographies, and we commonly so think of them.

The Mediterranean world, in the ancient period to which the Gospels belonged, produced a host of biographies. Naturally the popular biographies exceeded the historical ones in number, attractiveness, and influence, as more suited to the common mind. . . .

Particularly is it true of the ancient biographies that they seldom had a mere chronicling purpose; they were generally written to eulogize their subjects, or to affect political opinion and action, or to teach uprightness and usefulness by example. . . .

If a writing presents a man's life with fair completeness, order, and accuracy, out of an adequate knowledge of the facts, it is a historical biography. It may at the same time have a practical purpose—eulogistic, political, social, aesthetic, or educational. On the other hand, if a writing presents only memorabilia of a man's life, disconnected incidents and sayings, without adequate chronology and connection, without showing his genetic relation to and his influence upon his times, it is a popular biography. The two classes of course shade off into each other in various ways. If the biography of a particular individual presents definite knowledge of his dates, his motives, his message, his characteristics, his personality, and his service to his period, we may classify the work as a direct contribution to history-writing. If, however, the data of the man's life are inadequately furnished by the writing, so that uncertainty exists as to the deeds, the teaching, the personality, the relationships of the man, we may classify the work as popular, because the didactic aim has operated to the neglect or the obscuration of the historical facts. Here again it is clear that the Gospels belong to the writings of the popular class, because of the extreme difficulty of recovering the historical Jesus. . . .

Biographies of the Greek and Roman intellectual leaders were written primarily to exhibit and perpetuate their teaching. The major portion of the material is quotation of their words and the main interest centers in their ideas. . . . The amount of narrative material joined with the teaching is larger or smaller, according to the picturesqueness of the philosopher or the disposition of the biographer. . . .

Among the biographical writings of the ancient Greek literature, the nearest parallels to the Gospels are the books which report the lives of Epictetus, Apollonius, and Socrates.

> Clyde Weber Votaw. *The Gospels and Contemporary Biographies in the Greco-Roman World* (1915; rpt. Philadelphia, Fortress Press, 1970), pp. 5, 7–9

One should thus realize that there is only one gospel, but that it is described by many apostles. Every single epistle of Paul and of Peter, as well as the Acts of the Apsotles by Luke, is a gospel, even though they do not record all the works and words of Christ, but one is shorter and includes less than another. There is not one of the four major gospels anyway that includes all the words and works of Christ; nor is it necessary. Gospel is and should be nothing else than a discourse or story about Christ, just as happens among men when one writes a book about a king or a prince, telling what he did, said, and suffered in his day. Such a story can be told in various ways; one spins it out, and the other is brief. Thus the gospel is and should be nothing else than a chronicle, a story, a narrative about Christ, telling who he is, what he did, said, and suffered—a subject which one describes briefly, another more fully, one this way, another that way.

For at its briefest, the gospel is a discourse about Christ, that he is the Son of God and became man for us, that he died and was raised, that he has been established as a Lord over all things. This much St. Paul takes in hand and spins out in his epistles. He bypasses all the miracles and incidents which are set forth in the four gospels, yet he includes the whole gospel adequately and abundantly. . . .

Be sure, moreover, that you do not make Christ into a Moses, as if Christ did nothing more than teach and provide examples as the other saints do, as if the gospel were simply a textbook of teachings or laws. Therefore you should grasp Christ, his words, works, and sufferings, in a twofold manner. First as an example that is presented to you, which you should follow and imitate. . . . However this is the smallest part of the gospel, on the basis of which it cannot yet even be called gospel. For on this level Christ is of no more help to you than some other saint. . . . The chief article and foundation of the gospel is that before you take Christ as an example, you accept and recognize him as a gift, as a present that God has given you that is your own. This means that when you see or hear of Christ doing or suffering something, you do not doubt that Christ himself, with his deeds and sufferings, belongs to you. . . .

So you see that the gospel is really not a book of laws and commandments which requires deeds of us, but a book of divine promises in which God promises, offers, and gives us all his possessions and benefits in Christ. . . .

When you open the book containing the gospels and read or hear how Christ comes here or there, or how someone is brought to him, you should therein perceive the sermon or the gospel through which he is coming to you, or you are being brought to him. For the preaching of the gospel is nothing else than Christ coming to us, or we being brought to him.

> Martin Luther. *A Brief Instruction of What to Look for and Expect in the Gospels*, *Luther's Works*, Vol. 35, trans. E. Theodore Bachman (Philadelphia, Muhlenberg Press, 1960), pp. 117–121

It is easier then to say what a Gospel is not than what it is, since it is a unique form. It is not a biography of Jesus as we normally understand biography. There are none of the personal reminiscences or character studies that we expect in a biography, although . . . Luke comes nearest, of all the evangelists, to giving us such a work. There is some of this human interest in Luke but it remains subordinate to the requirements of Gospel-writing. Nor is the Gospel an educational or propagandist work. A Gospel is not an educational handbook about Jesus which argues the case for belief in his divinity. A Gospel is nearer to preaching than to teaching. . . . Finally a Christian Gospel is not like a modern historical reconstruction of somebody's life which aims to get at the facts. For a Christian Gospel-writer the subject of his book, Jesus of Nazareth, is not only an historical person (although he is certainly that), but a divine being in the life of Godhead itself (the Lord Christ). And when all the facts about the historical person are agreed upon and set out, the problem of faith in the divine being is by no means settled. So the Gospel-writer believes that he must write in such a way as to enable the reader to see the double meaning of Jesus. This might seem as if a Gospel-writer is necessarily a propagandist. But if we mean by propaganda going to great lengths to work on the minds and feelings of an audience, playing on fears, prejudices and anxieties, then the New Testament Gospels are not propaganda. The remarkable thing is the way the evangelists can restrain their faith, especially their Easter faith, so as to allow the events to tell their own story. . . .

An evangelist then presents the material about Jesus in such a way as to invite primarily not interest, nor information, nor admiration, but faith.

E. J. Tinsley. *The Gospel According to Luke* (Cambridge, Cambridge University Press, 1965), pp. 4–5

In addition to such modes of dealing with the past as annals, chronicles, histories, biographies and their possible subdivisions, there is another distinctive means—the literary genre of dramatic history. This genre includes many works, most notably the history plays of William Shakespeare and G. B. Shaw, and at least one among the plays of the modern American dramatist Robert Sherwood, namely *Abe Lincoln in Illinois*. . . .

Dramatic history as a genre is directed, not to scholars whose interest in history is professional and who will read it endlessly, but to as broad a general audience as the author can attract—and this is true whether the author is writing the Gospel of Luke or the play of *Henry V*. So condensation here is even more necessary than it is elsewhere, and for a general audience brevity is more effective than prolixity. What is presented about historical characters and events should be representative of the whole, but not exhaustive. Chronology must often be telescoped, and writers in this genre also tell us that it may have to be altered, if their story is to be fairly and effectively told.

A key practice here is the use of representative persons, incidents, and actions: what is shown represents a vastly larger canvas of life which cannot be shown. *Multum in parvo* is the governing principle. . . .

All of the dramatic history which we have analyzed exhibits certain formal characteristics which are generally ascribed by scholars to the Gospels: These works are neither chronicles nor academic histories, but at the same time they are intended to provide an essentially fair representation of a tradition about persons and events which the writers regard as valid. All are written to attract and hold the attention of as large an audience as possible, and each is intended to present its own particular message convincingly to that audience. In each of these ways, then, the dramas are comparable to the Gospels. . . . Finally, these plays and the Gospels are of comparable length and all are relatively short: Luke and *Saint Joan* are probably the longest, and each can easily be read within two hours. The purpose of the literary works written in this form is to present a knowledge and interpretation of historical events and persons to an audience of all kinds and conditions of men, and to do so in a way which will move individuals to accept a new understanding. . . .

My suggestion, then, is that the gospels fit the genre of dramatic history. . . . That recognition can help us to account for a number of problems, such as differences between the Gospels themselves. Within the genre of dramatic history, such differences are to be expected. Chronology may be rearranged, incidents diversely selected, emphases shifted, and episodes presented in distinctive lights. . . .

To read such works with too precise a curiosity is to misunderstand and misinterpret them. To dissect them, put each segment under a microscope, and then reassemble the parts in some hypothetical form hopefully representing an earlier form of the tradition can be a fascinating endeavor, but again it will divert our attention and energies from a more productive kind of study.

> Roland M. Frye. "A Literary Perspective for the-
> Criticism of the Gospels." in *Jesus and Man's Hope,*
> *Vol. II,* ed. Dikran Y. Hadidian (Pittsburgh, Pittsburgh
> Theological Seminary, 1971), pp. 207, 209–212

What, then, are the essential features of the gospel as a literary kind? The gospels are collections of stories, far more packed with action than is customary in narrative. The overriding purpose of the gospel stories is to explain and praise the person and work of Jesus, who is always the moving force behind the writers' presentation. The impulse to get the facts of Jesus' life and meaning before the reader is combined with the impulse to celebrate what is recorded. The person and work of Jesus are presented through several familiar narrative devices—through His actions, through His words, and through the responses of other people to Him.

The gospels are encyclopedic forms in the sense that they are compilations of a number of individual segments that existed independently, in either written or oral form, before being brought together in a single written book. The gospels are encyclopedic also by virtue of the variety of different literary forms that they include. One form is the brief narrative, which itself can be separated into several categories. We should picture the brief narratives of the gospels as existing on a continuum that ranges from simple narrative on the one end to embellished narrative on the other. By "simple narrative" I mean a story that gives only the bare outline of an event, while "embellished narrative" refers to a story that fills out the event in relative detail. Another recurrent form in the gospels is dialogue. Also important are the utterances of Jesus, which range on a spectrum similar to the narratives. At one end of the spectrum is the brief saying of Jesus, and at the other end is the extended discourse (such as we find in the Sermon on the Mount and some of the discourses in John's gospel). Yet another form is the parable of Jesus, prominent in the synoptic gospels. The somewhat random combination of these varied ingredients probably reflects the fact that the content of the gospels existed as separate units before being brought together in a single work. The diversity of forms also sets the gospels apart from Old Testament narratives, which share the emphasis on dialogue and summarized narrative but generally lack the interspersed discourses, parables, and proclamations.

> Leland Ryken. *The Literature of the Bible* (Grand Rapids, Zondervan, 1974), pp. 275–276

This conception of tragedy as an imitation of human beings in action or subjected to stress, emphasizing the action rather than the dispositions of the characters, is not far from the Gospel as "gospel" or good news about a specific person and events related to His presence on the scene of history. Granted, the Gospel concerns essentially a person, Jesus Christ. But apart from sparse references to ephemeral shows of emotion by Jesus—such as compassion, sorrow, anger, and anguish—the Synoptics as well as the rest of the New Testament emphasize the events of Christ's ministry rather than the development of His own consciousness and character. They focus on the passion of Jesus rather than on His passions. They define the gospel as what Jesus did rather than how He felt. What they consider of first importance are deeds—how Christ died, was buried, and raised on the third day according to the Scriptures, and how He appeared to His disciples (1 Cor. 15:3–5).

> Gilbert Bilezikian. *The Liberated Gospel* (Grand Rapids, Baker, 1977), p. 53

The form of the narrative as it is recounted, event after event, constitutes its structure varies, to greater and lesser extents, as between the four gospels. The four narratives not only do not include the same material, but they do not always report common material in the same order or even in the same details.

All of this makes the gospel narratives terribly confusing if we approach them in the spirit of Aristotle—which many critics do, although perhaps inadvertently and without recognizing that their judgments of historical narrative have been more influenced by Greek philosophy than by biblical and literary standards. In Aristotle's view of narration, event should follow event in a necessary sequence, each event necessitated by what preceded it and in turn necessitating the events which follow it. Within this conception, the structural union of the parts should be such that "if any one of them is disturbed or removed, the whole will be disjointed or disturbed." On this basis, there is only one sequence of events in terms of which a story can be properly told. In the New Testament, on the other hand, we have narratives which often appear radically divergent and even in radical disagreement, from the Aristotelian point of view.

I say *appear* here, for these problems are more apparent than real, created by the presuppositions of certain readers, rather than by the accounts as we have them. The evangelists were not attempting to record a chornicle of events in accurate chronological sequence, but were intent upon recreating structures of experience into which we are invited to enter; they should be understood as narrators who construct a literary universe of experience and of value, who bring us into contact with the living personality of Jesus, and who involve us in the declaration of and response to his message.

So understood, the gospels are structured so as to introduce us to a person and to his message. They thus partake of the character of dramatic history, in which history is not ignored and is not purposefully violated, but is transmuted into a form which can attract large numbers of people who are separated from the original events by barriers of time and culture and specialized interests. We are invited to vicarious participation in happenings which are shut off from us by the irreversibility of history, but which are available to us through the imaginative involvement of literature. The narratives are recounted in orders and forms which convey the most vital and enduring impression of their significance and of the principal personality and issues involved.

Roland M. Frye. "The Jesus of the Gospels: Approaches through Narrative Structure," in *From Faith to Faith*, ed. D. Y. Hadidian (Pittsburgh, Pickwick Press, 1979), pp. 76–77

Scholars called "form critics" have argued cogently that the individual stories gathered together on the framework of each Gospel show signs of having been told and retold separately before they were written down as we now have them.

This view fits well with the fact that the stories do not appear in our Gospels in the same order. For example, the parable of the Sower occurs early in Mark's Gospel (chapter 4), a bit later in Luke's Gospel (chapter 8), and not until the middle of Matthew's account (chapter 13). . . .

One form critic has compared the separate stories of Jesus, handed down by word of mouth, to separate pearls which the Gospel writers have strung together, each in different order to present his distinctive insights into the truth. . . .

The Gospels must be understood against the background of the *kerygma*. They grew out of gospel sermons. They are not simply cold, objective biographies. They are evangelistic tracts. Their contents were selected for evangelistic purposes. . . . Every Gospel is written to give us not simply the writer's record of what Jesus said and did, but also his understanding of who Jesus really was and what he can mean to the reader. Each Gospel is a call to the decision of faith.

This is why there is so much that the Gospels do *not* bother to tell us about Jesus. What was his childhood like? We have only one story about Jesus between his infancy and age thirty (Luke 2:41–51). What did he look like? What is really the historical order of events described in such different sequence in our four Gospels? In what sense did Jesus think of himself as Messiah? Such questions are not answered for us, in part at least because they were not the theological concern of our Gospel writers.

It is true that other pious authors soon undertook to fill in the gaps in the Gospel stories. . . . These . . . incredible stories are preserved for us in apocryphal gospels. . . . Noting them points us to a second criterion of selection used by the Gospel writers. Luke tells us that, aware of other accounts of Jesus' life, he wrote his so that his reader would now know what was the truth.

Much recent scholarship has so emphasized the theological purpose of the Gospel writers that it has neglected their evident concern for reporting the facts. We have seen that they do not report all the facts. And we have seen that they do not report just facts, but also their interpretations of the meaning of those facts. But the Gospel writers were not, they tell us, producing fiction to support theology. Had they been doing so, they might well have included stories such as those just described. Each Gospel writer, like Luke, wants his reader to know the truth, the truth as he has learned it from many sources. Luke claims to have talked with "eyewitnesses.". . .

Our Gospel writers, then, have selected stories told by the early church and have strung these "pearls" together, each in his own fashion, on a thread also spun from the first sermons, to win readers to faith through confronting them with the truth.

> William M. Ramsay. *The Laymen's Guide to the New Testament* (Atlanta, John Knox Press, 1981), pp. 26, 28–29

Neither kerygma nor history is a distinctive characteristic of the genre of the gospels. . . .

The *narrative* character of the gospel genre has been realized long ago. . . . The gospels are narratives about the life and work of Jesus. A narrative such as a gospel involves a narrator's choice. Even if it reports actual events it involves the narrator's point of view. By definition it requires a story and a story-teller. This is why the narrative character of the gospel genre calls into question both kerygma and history as distinctive characteristics of the gospel genre.

The most striking characteristic of the gospel genre is 'point of view' or the way the story gets told and the perspectives ' . . . through which the reader is presented with the characters, actions, setting and events which constitute the narrative'. Mark created a story by making use of traditional material and the use of narrative techniques. In this he was followed by the other evangelists who created their own stories with the same and additional material in their own manner. Mark tells his story from an omniscient and intrusive point of view. He knows everything about his characters, what they see, hear, feel and even what they think (cf. 3. 6; 5. 28, 33; 6. 49; 8. 16; 11. 31; 15. 10). As a narrator he has *inside information*. He even knows the mind of Jesus (2. 8; 3. 5; 5. 30; 8. 12). He does not only report but comments and evaluates in order to create sympathy or dislike in his characters . . . so as to convince the receiver(s) of his story. For the consumption of the reader or hearer he makes use of narrative commentary like the translation of strange words and phrases. . . . He lets his characters act and speak in the way he prefers. In short, he creates a *narrative world* with its own set of characters, inter-textual net of references, space and time. Whether we call it a passion narrative with a long introduction. . ., a book of secret epiphanies . . . or whatever we wish, it is clear from the way it gets told that Mark presented us with *his story* of Jesus. The genre characteristics of the gospel genre are determined by the text type—they are narrative characteristics. . . .

The early Christians were story-tellers and many of the texts they produced were stories. These include the gospels. The death and resurrection of Jesus quite naturally played an important role in primitive Christianity—it had to be told and this is perhaps how the story of the life and works of Jesus started. For our present purpose, the character of the gospels as text type is more important than the *Sitz im Leben* of the gospel Gattung.

W. S. Vorster. *NTS.* 29, 1983, pp. 87, 91–92

STORYTELLING TECHNIQUE

To-day . . . nearly all technical experts agree that the contents of these three chapters [Matthew 5–7] are not one connected discourse but a selection from many. . . . But this question is of a kind, I suggest, on which academic judgment need not be taken as final. The general reader, if he be equipped with the literary sense, has a right to be heard, for literary sense perceives evidence to which merely technical learning is apt to be blind. . . . How odd is the assumption that our Lord would not repeat to different audiences the same teaching! What is the accustomed method of those who have to instruct or persuade listening crowds in many places? Certainly to reiterate the truths that seem of highest importance, and, finding in one place that some illustration or anecdote is specially effective, to use it again elsewhere. Possibly, though, they will change the wording, or add details that will appeal to the particular audience of the moment. Yet no teacher, and least of all an itinerant teacher, would shrink from repeating himself. I believe that the disciples probably heard most of the parables many times over, which explains in part why they were remembered with such exactness. And it seems mere pedantry to argue that because our Lord spoke the beatitudes in the Sermon on the Plain, recorded by Luke, He could not have spoken them also in that other Sermon on the Mount which Matthew describes.

Anthony C. Deane. *How to Enjoy the Bible* (New York, George H. Doran, 1925), pp. 84–85

They are remarkable, as are the parables, for their simplicity, their directness and their pictorial quality. Most of all, however, are they remarkable for their restraint and objectivity. There is no parallel to this in the literature of biography.

In most biography there is a strong subjective element, and most critics would feel that a certain subjectivity is an inevitable ingredient. . . . The biographer who dares to let his subject alone speak, and does not try to persuade and influence the attitude of his reader is rare indeed. In the story of the life of Jesus as told in the first three Gospels, there is neither this kind of subjectivity nor any criticism of the facts presented. The story is told simply as a record of events, without supplementary comments. Our opinions are not influenced even by the addition of an adjective praising the good or condemning the evil; there is no obvious assessing of values. Jesus is shown in many varied relations with His fellows; the things He loves and the things He enjoys are revealed in His acts and conversation. No remark of the biographer lays any stress upon particular aspects of the story. Selection of incident is the sole method used to throw His life and character into relief. And the result is the most living of personalities ever revealed through the written word. . . .

And all this is conveyed to us by direct narration of incident and speech. Not a quality is pointed out by indirect comment of the biographer. . . .

More extraordinary still is the wholly objective record of such incidents as Peter's betrayal, and the whole of Jesus' trial and crucifixion. No incident is glossed over; nothing is explained away.

Kathleen E. Innes. *The Bible as Literature* (London, Jonathan Cape, 1930), pp. 216–220

A sublime imagination interlocks with our narratives. Single events possess significance in their own right leaving pictures printed lastingly on the mind's eye. They possess the curious quality of seeming to exist poetically independently of any verbal expression; the fact itself is poetical. Such are the Journey of the Magi, led by the Star of Bethlehem; the appearance of the Angel of the Shepherds, announcing the wondrous Birth; the Baby in the manger; the Massacre of the Innocents . . . The miracles, as when Jesus walks on the waters and stills the raging winds and seas, have symbolic overtones. His life is interthreaded with sublime experience; the Voice of God claims him as a Son at his Baptism, and when he is transfigured on the mountain the Voice again pronounces an assurance and an acknowledgement. The Last Supper is a deathless memory, the prayer in Gethsemane contains all that a tragic poet need learn, all disloyalty is summed in the thirty pieces of silver received by Judas, the Crucifixion encloses and transcends the furthest agony that mortal life may endure. After the Crucifixion there is an earthquake, the sun is blackened, the Temple's veil torn asunder. Symbolism is pregnant. The number three recurs . . . Mountains are important: Jesus is tempted on a high mountain, he preaches on a mountain, he is transfigured on Mount Hermon and visits the Hill of Olives. The crucifixion is on a hill. . .

These symbolic pictures are somehow staggeringly impressive without being sensational. Most are very quietly narrated and the colourings are subdued: some are dark with a dark beauty, others light with a beauteous light. But, whether happy or unhappy in suggestion, they are all magical; they are wondrously symbolic and wondrously real at once, like Keats' poetry, the more magical for its calm . . .

Impressions of life and gentleness interthread a dark background. Nature-references are mostly pleasant . . . Gentleness is transmitted by pastoral impressions . . . Fishes blend naturally with pastoral . . . Fishes, perhaps partly from Gospel associations, are impregnated with positive beauty in many poets. The paradisal connotations of still water are present when Jesus and his disciples walk by the shores of Galilee. Fruitful nature is a dominant colouring . . . Food is mentioned often . . .

The Gospels are poetical in work and incident. The events shine as though from an inward lustre . . .

The gospels are rich with tangible, physical, sensuous and super-sensuous life pitted against disease in mind and body, evil and death.

> G. Wilson Knight. *The Christian Renaissance* (London, Methuen and Company, 1962), pp. 149–152, 171

The first observation . . . was on the great *conciseness of the story*, and this applies throughout. Apart from the Passion narrative there is no part of the story covering more than about two days' activity; only short incidents are reported, that would have occupied no more than a few minutes or hours. . . .

Throughout the law of *scenic duality* operates. Apart from Jesus and his interlocutor (or a group of interlocutors) many more people can appear on the scene—even if the number be still limited—but almost always it is only Jesus and the interlocutor who share in the significant action, though, of course, the other part can be a group. . . .

Instead of an individual person we may find *a group*, though then, conforming to primitive style, it is treated as an unity: the Pharisees, the Disciples, the Relatives, the People of Nazareth, etc. The groups speak either as a choir. . . . or by their representative; thus Peter speaks for the Disciples. . . , the High Priest for the Sanhedrin. . . .

The *motives and feelings* of Jesus and the other participants are very seldom referred to. Now and again of course motives and feelings can be clearly recognized; they are in such cases indicated indirectly by actions and words. . . .

There is the use of another means of popular speech—the *use of direct speech*. . . .

The law of repetition can be seen in such instances where either a commission is expressed in the same words, or where analogous actions are said to follow one another, very likely with the same or almost the same phraseology. . . .

Numbers play a special part in popular story telling. We have already referred . . . to the use of the *number three* in the similitudes. It can be found elsewhere: Jesus was three times tempted by the devil (Matt. 4:1–11 par.), he prayed three times in Gethsemane (Mk. 14:32–42); Peter thrice denied his master (Mk. 14:53f., 66–72 or Lk. 22:54–62). . . .

But the *number two* is of especial importance. Disciples are called twice in Mk. 1:16–20. Jesus sends the disciples out two by two in Mk. 6:7 or Lk. 10:1. Two disciples are the centre of the question asked by the sons of Zebedee Mk. 10:35ff., as in the story of the inhospitable Samaritans Lk. 9:51ff. Two disciples take the walk to Emmaus in Lk. 24:13dd.

Rudolf Bultmann. *The History of the Synoptic Tradition*, trans. John Marsh (Oxford, Basil Blackwell, 1963), pp. 307–308, 310, 312, 314

It is in the presentation of the figure of Jesus that the key to the concreteness and depth of the Gospel lies. This concreteness is not achieved by resorting to the techniques of biography or history as they were practiced in ancient times. The materials remain popular or non-literary materials, in which the person is presented through the individual incident rather than through an organized total structure. The overall outline of Jesus' work is created by putting him in the framework of a story of deliverance, a story that, as noted above, expresses both past-oriented reenactment and future-oriented hope. The materials which went into the story were quite varied. Some types were already little narratives—miracle stories or stories which climax in confrontation with a saying of Jesus (apophthegms). Another basic type is the parable, which has a narrative element but in which Jesus is the narrator, not a participant of the story. In others, . . . narrative is quite subsidiary or absent. The Sermon on the Mount will serve as an example. For the most part, the connections between these short narratives or sayings are quite loose. What counts in the Gospel form as a whole is their cumulative effect. Cumulative repetition, rather than historical development or surprise, is the way in which hese many short stories and sayings prepare for the great climax of the Gospel. . . . There is a dramatic structure to the story as a whole, and the element of surprise is often present in the way in which the individual stories overturn conventional judgments about God or about goodness, but surprise is not an element in the overall effect of the pattern. Rather, the repetition of the same sort of thing again and again emphasizes the inevitability of the outcome. . . .

What is distinctive about the Gospel form as a story of salvation is the way in which, both in the shorter units and in the passion story, which is the key to their meaning, everything centers on Jesus, who is the vehicle of the kingdom of God.

> William A. Beardslee. *Literary Criticism of the New Testament* (Philadelphia, Fortress Press, 1970), pp. 24–25

We sometimes forget that a story represents a narrator's choice. Because we are familiar with certain stories and story types, the story seems obvious and necessary. However, just as the writing of history involves interpretation, so does telling a story. This is true of both stories which have a factual foundation and those which do not. Even when it reports actual events, a story represents a narrator's choice. . . . The narrator also chooses how to tell a story. This choice will reflect the narrator's selective emphasis and values, and the story's composition helps to communicate the narrator's emphasis and evaluation to the reader. There are more ways of telling a story than we usually realize. The narrator chooses the way which fits his purpose or limits his purpose to the narrative forms at his disposal, and so his purposes are mirrored by his stories. . . .

Our imaginations are more active in reading stories than we realize. The brief scenes in the synoptic Gospels are like pen and ink sketches in which an artist, with only a few strokes, has suggested some forms, relying on the viewer to fill in the rest with his imagination. . . . We must pay special attention to the way that narrative composition indicates emphasis and suggests negative or positive evaluation of the actions of the disciples. Here we are dealing with what we might call narrative rhetoric. This narrative rhetoric reveals the standpoint of the author. . . . The rhetoric of a story also reflects, by anticipation, a dialogue between author and reader. Writing a story, although it may involve persons and events quite distinct from the world of the author and reader, is, nevertheless, communication between author and reader. At various points the author's reason for narrating this story for a group of readers may become especially apparent. Futhermore, the author has a view of his readers and anticipates how they will respond to his story. . . .

A story may arouse expectation of an event and then report the realization or nonrealization of our expectations. This not only emphasizes through repetition (our attention is drawn to the event before it happens and again as it happens) but also involves the reader through his interest in the outcome of events. . . .

A further indication of emphasis is the selective use of dialogue and dramatic scenes. The use of dialogue in a dramatic scene involves the expansion of the amount of space in a writing given to a segment of time in the story, compared to the alternative possibility of presenting an event or series of events in a brief summary. Thus dialogue in a dramatic scene emphasizes, while summary narration of events gives them a subordinate position. . . .

Emphasis and evaluation are closely related, for much of what is emphasized in a story also has negative or positive value, and the emphasis helps to communicate the evaluation. Where the evaluating voice of the implied author is especially clear, we may speak of "reliable commentary." While such commentary is often made by the narrator of a story, it need not be confined to him. . . . In the Gospel of Mark it is obvious that Jesus wears the badge of reliability and authority. . . . We are expected to judge the words and actions of others in light of the words and actions of Jesus. . . .

The implied author's evaluation of the events and persons in this narrative is very important in the communication between author and reader. . . . The author's communication with his readers is aided by the fact that, just as we constantly evaluate events and persons in everyday life, so we constantly evaluate the events and persons in stories. The author does his part by shaping and guiding our evaluation. Whatever we judge to be positive attracts us; whatever seems negative repels us. These forces of attraction and repulsion, controlled by evaluation embedded in the narrative, guide us. . . .

Robert C. Tannehill. JR. 57, 1977, pp. 387–392

In the story of the healing of the paralytic in Mark 2:1–12, the narrator begins by describing a scene in which his, and therefore the reader's perspective (point of view) is at some distance from the actors, the actions, and the setting. . . . But within four sentences the perspective shifts to a point within a house wherein the narrator and the reader, like invisible observers, imaginatively hear the words and see the actions of those within. Accompanying this auditory and visual effect, which is like that achieved with a zoom-lens on a television or movie camera, is another perspectival effect created by our narrator's knowledge of what is going on in the minds of some of the actors. . . .

The several points of view . . . produce a . . . structure of relations between: a) the narrator and his reader; b) the narrator and the characters; c) the reader and the characters; and d) between the characters themselves. Of these, the last belongs to the plotting of the actors' actions in the story. The points of view of the characters in the story illustrate the narrators' point of view in the selection, arrangement, and motivation of his actors and their actions. But the other points are more distinctly rhetorical, illustrating the ways in which the narrator reaches out of the narrative world he has created in order to lead his real-world readers into it. All four points reveal the distinctive responsiveness of narrative to the subjectivity of the narrator . . .

The narrator reaches out of his narrative to lead his reader on an imaginative journey into the past, plucking him out of his time and place, as it were, and setting him down in another time and place. . . .

It is a literary problem to grasp the narrative's world and the events that transpire in it; it is an historical problem to determine the relationship, if any. . . , between the narrative's world and the real-world events to which it may or may not refer. In either case, we must start with the narrative world, lest we lose it by assuming that it refers to real-world events we know about from other sources than the narrative we are trying to understand. . . .

Once transported into the narrator's story world the reader finds not only that his leader has marvelous mind-reading powers, but also that his leader shares this power with the central actor in the story—the one to whom all of the other actors come and to whom they all respond.

What is more, the narrator not only shares this power with the central actor, but he is privy also to the thoughts and feelings of the central actor himself. . . . Together, the distribution of points of view and the plotting of the story lead the reader to identify with, and trust, not only the narrator, but also the central actor. The reader sees and knows only what they see and know, and his judgment of the actions displayed before him is determined by their's, not, for example, by the judgment of the scribes, the paralytics, or the people who brought the paralytic to Jesus. . . .

The real-world reader is led to align himself with the central actor, to perceive this actor's world, as it were, from over his shoulder, accompanied, however, by the narrator who whispers into the reader's ear things that only he and Jesus know, i.e., the thoughts of the actors, including Jesus. From beginning to end, the reader is totally dependent on the narrator's characterization and evaluation of the actors, their actions, and their motivations.

Norman R. Peterson. *Semeia*. 12, 1978, pp. 99–102

In the Gospel of Mark there is little description of the inner states of the story characters. Instead, characterization takes place through the narration of action. We learn who Jesus is through what he says and does in the context of the action of others. Therefore, the study of character (not in the sense of inner qualities but in the sense of defining characteristics as presented in the story) can only be approached through the study of plot. We must pay special attention to the main story lines which the Gospel, for it is not only the continuing centrality of Jesus which makes Mark a single story but also the fact that certain events can be understood as the realization or fustration of goals or tasks which are suggested early in the story. These goals or tasks . . . enable us to understand key developments as meaningful within the context of the story as a developing whole. We must also study features of composition which control the "rhetorical" dimension of the story. These features show that the story has been shaped in order to influence the readers in particular ways . . . .

I prefer to speak of narrative compostition rather than narrative structure because the latter term is increasingly associated with the methods of structuralists . . . Literary composition provides clues to the nature of the act of communication which the words are to make possible. It may provide clues to the speaker's purpose, the conception of the hearers and their needs, and the anticipations of response held by the speaker. It provides clues to the type of influence which the speaker wishes to exercise with regard to the hearer. And this influence may sometimes be at a deep level, challenging the hearer to radical change, so that it is appropriate to speak of a "depth rhetoric" whose goals and methods are partly akin to poetry. This approach can also be applied to the Gospels as narratives, if we find appropriate ways of analyzing narrative composition and of understanding the results in the context of communication between writer and reader, which includes the (conscious or unconscious) intention to influence the reader in particular ways.

Robert C. Tannehill. Semeia. 16, 1979, pp. 58–59

In each of the four gospels, there is only one character with whom we cannot identify in the sense of equating ourselves with him, and this of course is Jesus; and also typical is the fact that the other characters are sketched with sure strokes, but not so fully as to preclude our identifying ourselves with them. Their faces are never so completely drawn that we cannot place our own heads on their shoulders: we could be blind man, neighbor, parent, or Pharisee, and it can be instructive for us to assume each role in turn as we read. . . .

Roland M. Frye. "The Jesus of the Gospels: Approaches
through Narrative Structure," in From Faith to Faith,
ed. D. Y. Hadidian (Pittsburgh, Pickwick Press, 1979),
p. 79

The documents . . . are theological and interpretative, designed to elicit faith within the readers. They are written from a distinctly favorable position insofar as the meaning of the events they record is concerned. Through their retrospection we are enabled to comprehend the significance of Jesus' words and deeds in a way that the actual participants could not have. . . . At the same time, however, they are recording history. . . .

In the gospels, then, we have both theology and history. The two should be seen as quite compatible, not as mutually exclusive. But how much theological "creativity" do we encounter in the evangelists' retelling of the story of Jesus? They do display considerable creativity in shaping their respective narratives and in interpreting, modifying and adapting the materials of historical tradition that they take up. . . . The fact that different evangelists can put different interpretations on the same materials should not be surprising or alarming. The deeds and words of Jesus by their nature can have several meanings and applications in the Church. Difference, therefore, is not necessarily distortion. The differences between the evangelists are thus, in the main, complementary. They are like perceptions of a multifaceted diamond, all of which trace back to and converge upon a single source, thus providing us with a richer comprehension of Jesus and his significance than any single perception could ever have done. . . .

We are the richer because our gospels are what they are. If the gospels were the written equivalents of videotapes—that is, the results of a kind of flat, disinterested reporting of "the bare facts"—we should be immeasurably impoverished. Comparatively, Jesus would be enigmatic, his words obscure, his intent confusing, his ministry bewildering. . . .

What we have in the gospels as they are is perhaps analogous in some ways to the "slow-action replay" that we encounter in television coverage of sports events. In these replays the action can be dramatically slowed down so that one is able to see much more than one was able to see in the action as it occurred. If one is given the full treatment—close-up, slow-action, forward-and-reverse, split-screen, the same scene from several perspectives, and with the verbal commentary and interpretation of an expert superimposed—one has a fair analogy of what the evangelists do. The correspondence is striking especially in that this kind of replay is in one sense what actually occurred, but in another sense is quite different from what occurred (not only in speed but also in what one individual is capable of perceiving). One might add to the force of the analogy by pointing out that the true significance of certain plays can only be known after the game is over. Now they are often seen in a new light, their true meaning dependent on what subsequently transpired. The gospels are like slow-action, analytical replays with expert commentary seen after the conclusion of the game.

The gospels are truer portraits of Jesus than they would have been had they only given us "the bare facts." The irony is that to the extent that the evangelists go beyond "the bare facts" they give us what in the last analysis is a more accurate portrait of Jesus and his significance. . . .

The interpretations are different, but compatible and complementary. We should explore, delight in and profit from the distinctives of each gospel, for in this manner we have more effective access to the meaning of the story of Jesus. It is a mistake, therefore, to attempt to make one comprehensive narrative of the four and to dull the distinctives of any of the four. We also should not feel pressured into harmonizing the gospels. . . . None of the four was meant to be read as one of four (or three).

Donald A. Hagner. *JETS*. 24, 1981, pp. 32–35

One may cautiously depict the rather broad spectrum of gospel studies in terms of three artistic expressions: (1) the snapshot, (2) the portrait, and (3) the abstract painting. Each medium gives its own expression of reality. Yet each differs from the other in the respective treatment of that reality. Consequently one expects to find a descending degree of correspondence to reality in a snapshot, a portrait and an abstract painting. Yet all three media contain specific standards of reliability that are set by the parameters of each medium, standards by which the final product may be evaluated. . . .

The Gospels as Snapshots. For many centuries—some would say from the beginning—the gospels have been viewed as verbal snapshots of Jesus' ministry. Stemming from eyewitness reports and containing a rather detailed chronicle of Jesus' life and teaching, the gospels offer a "record" of Jesus' ministry, recording the work and words of Jesus with a precision not unlike that of the *Congressional Record.* As snapshots, the gospels' primary intention was to preserve for posterity a precise verbal picture of Jesus' life and teaching . . .

The Gospels as Abstract Paintings. By contrast, since the Enlightenment in general and the work of Reimarus in particular the gosepels have been considered by proponents of a more radical criticism to be akin to abstract paintings of Jesus and his ministry. Instead of offering a "record," a "historical account," or a "biography" of Jesus and his ministry, the gospels only relate abstractly to their subject by depicting more immediately the cult, religious experience and theology of the diverse communities within the developing Church. Consequently one must read the gospels as abstractions of Jesus' impact painted with the bold brush strokes of the synthesizing community of faith. As with an abstract painting, the direction of the gospels' message aims forward to the audience or viewer rather than backward to the original subject. With so little direct correspondence, then, between the Jesus of history and the Christ of the gospels, one looks to the gospels in vain for answers to specific questions about the Jesus of the past. . . .

The Gospels as Portraits. A third perspective—the gospels as verbal portraits of Jesus and his ministry—stands . . . in a mediating position between the gospels as snapshots and the gospels as abstract paintings. Acknowledging the validity of some of the historical and literary criticism stemming from post-Enlightenment Biblical studies, this viewpoint has conceded the impossibility of maintaining the gospels to be snapshots of Jesus and his ministry. Simultaneously, by finding a basic correspondence between the Jesus of history and the Christ of the gospels, this perspective has resisted the theological reductionism of radical criticism and rejected the conclusion that the gospels offer at best abstract paintings of Jesus and his ministry.

Robert A Guelich. *JETS.* 24, 1981, pp. 117–118

STRUCTURE

Mark is not trying to write a chronicle of continuous events, or a "biography," or a travel narrative. He is giving a series of events which he deliberately strings together rather loosely. Throughout the Gospel of Mark the introductory words to each paragraph make it obvious that this is Mark's prevailing method.

Therefore it appears to be true, based on the Gospel's witness to itself, that many of these incidents were preserved orally as detached incidents. If, as tradition says, Mark embodies the reminiscences of Peter in Rome, is this not what we should expect? Authentic memory functions in this way. It can remember broad outlines; it can remember many single incidents; it can at times recall certain sequences. This is, in fact, what we find in Mark. It is very likely . . . that Peter in his preaching and teaching used many events from the life of Jesus, which he vividly and accurately remembered, to illustrate Jesus' message and mission. The important thing is not the order or sequence of events; it is rather who Jesus was and how it came about that the Son of God was crucified. . . .

The conclusion that the Gospels are in part topical arrangements of material which was preserved in distinct units appears also in the recorded teachings of Jesus. All three Gospels record a day of parables (Mark 4, Matt. 13, Luke 8), but do not agree in the parables spoken on this occasion. . . .

The conclusion is inescapable that Matthew and Luke deliberately arrange their materials not in terms of how they think the events they record happened historically, but in terms of the portrait of Jesus' person, mission, and message they wish to sketch. This may well be due to the fact that many of the sayings of Jesus were preserved as independent units and were arranged by the Evangelists to suit their purposes.

> George Eldon Ladd. *The New Testament and Criticism*
> (Grand Rapids, William B. Eerdmans, 1967), pp. 165–168

The freedom felt by the gospel writers to rearrange the order of events in the gospel tradition for programmatic or literary purposes is shown by Luke's placing Jesus' rejection at Nazareth at the outset of his public ministry (Luke 4), whereas in Mark it comes in the middle of the story of Jesus' activity (Mark 6:1). The miracle stories of Mark (Mark 1 and 2) are moved by Matthew to a point following the Sermon on the Mount (Matt. 5, 6, and 7) because that best suited Matthew's arrangement of material in alternating panels of activity and discourse. The sense of movement and sequence that the reader receives in Mark's gospel comes from Mark's own arrangement of the tradition.

> Howard Clark Kee. *Jesus in History: An Approach to
> the Study of the Gospels* (New York, Harcourt, Brace
> and World, 1970), pp. 124–125

The relationship between heroic narrative and gospel illustrates the difficulty of identifying this New Testament genre. Like heroic narrative, the gospel centers on the life and exploits of the heroic protagonist. The gospel, however, is structured differently from the Old Testament heroic narratives, which are more unified as stories. . . . The stories of Joseph, Gideon, Samson, Ruth, and Esther are structured around a single chain of related events. Equally important is the fact that in these stories approxiamtely the same cast of characters is present from the beginning of the story to the end. Even when characters appear only temporarily, they usually make some contribution to a causally related chain of events that constitutes the plot. In a word, Old Testament heroic narratives are single plots. By contrast, the gospels are collections of stories. They are, accordingly, more fragmented in structure than the heroic narratives. The synoptic gospels in particular, are very episodic. A given fragment in the gospels can usually be rearranged or omitted without affecting the overall movement of the narrative. Many of the characters who encounter Christ in the gospels appear only once and then drop out of the story. Compared to the unified Old Testament literary narratives, the gospels are kaleidoscopic in their ever-changing, episodic account of the life of Christ.

It is true there is another category of Old Testament narratives that are less unified than the stories I have just described. Many of these stories, such as the stories of Moses, David and other kings, Samuel, Elijah, and Elisha, have the episodic and fragmented structure I have claimed for the gospels. A look at these more diffuse narratives will show, however, that they are usually intertwined with other historical material. This material suggests that the writer's motive was not the biography of an individual but the history of a nation or an era. In these instances the story of the individual is not self-contained, as in heroic narrative, but is part of the larger historical survey. By contrast, the gospels keep the focus on Jesus, whose story is continuous instead of being interrupted by extraneous historical material. This sustained devotion by the gospel writers to a single person rather than a historical period makes the gospels different in narrative structure from the diffuse biographies of the Old Testament.

> Leland Ryken. *The Literature of the Bible* (Grand Rapids, Zondervan, 1974), pp. 173–274

The first experiments in structuralist analysis have been made upon texts in which narrative plotting was very clearly manifested. This is the case with folktales, which demand from the listener or the reader the perception, without ambiguity and delay, of its global meaning and of the interaction of its sequential parts. . . . The autonomy of the successive episodes and of the various textual features is reduced to aid their integration into the overall signifying organization. . . .

By contrast, in other cases the autonomy of the sequences asserts itself more distinctly and the unifying principle is kept in the backround of the linguistic manifestation. The reader then tends to treat each episode separately and more or less to forget the overall perspective of the text. This change of level in the perception of the signifying phenemenon has repercussions upon its analysis: the narrative model, applicable without too much difficulty to each micro-narrative, becomes more problematic for the description of the whole, whereas the discursive model, associated with the thematic dimension of the text, is often more effective. . . .

The Gospels belong to this second category. The structural description of each of their elements is relatively easy, but the elaboration of a descriptive model of the whole remains more problematic. It is well known that the usual reading of these texts proceeds through a consideration of each pericope or each group of pericopes on its own and according to an order which does not always respect the sequence proposed by the Gospel text. One also knows how difficult it is to establish a plan which makes explicit in a satisfactory manner an organization of the sequential parts about which various readers could agree as the one account for the progression of the text. Uncertainty concerning textual segmentation always signals the interference of several principles of organization and the absence of a dominant narrative criterion.

Jean Calloud. Semeia. 16, 1979, pp. 132–134

A continuous biography, such as would be appropriate for someone existing continuously on our own level, would be out of the question; a series of mysterious apparitions by some kind of disembodied phantom would be equally so. The gospel writers solve this problem by the device sometimes called "pericope," the short discontinuous unit normally marked by a paragraph sign in most copies of the AV. Jesus appears in a certain context or situation that leads up to a crucial act, such as a miraculous healing, or to a crucial saying, such as a parable or moral pronouncement. Hence the Gospels are, as one scholar says of Mark, a sequence of discontinuous epiphanies.

Northrop Frye. The Great Code: The Bible and Literature (New York, Harcourt Brace Jovanovich, 1982), pp. 215–216

JESUS AS PROTAGONIST

You know how books of tales are written, that put one man before the reader and shew him off handsome for the most part and brave and call him My Hero or Our Hero. . . . Christ . . . is the hero of a book or books, of the divine Gospels. His is a warrior and a conqueror; of whom it is written he went forth conquering and to conquer. He is a king, Jesus of Nazareth king of the Jews, though when he came to his own kingdom his own did not receive him. . . . He is a thinker, that taught . . . divine mysteries. He is an orator and poet, as in his eloquent words and parables appears. He is all the world's hero, the desire of nations. . . .

There met in Jesus Christ all things that can make man lovely and loveable. . . .

He was the greatest genius that ever lived. You know what genius is— beauty and perfection in the mind. . . .

A witness to his genius we have in those men who being sent to arrest him came back empty handed, spellbound by his eloquence, saying, Never man spoke like this man.

A better proof we have in his own words, his sermon on the mount, his parables, and all his sayings recorded in the Gospel. . . . No stories or parables are like Christ's, so bright, so pithy, so touching; no proverbs or sayings are such jewellery: they stand off from other man's thoughts like stars, like lilies in the sun; nowhere in literature is there anything to match the Sermon on the Mount. . . .

Far higher than the beauty of the body, higher then genius and wisdom the beauty of the mind, comes the beauty of his character, his character as man. For the most part his very enemies, those that do not believe in him, allow that a character so noble was never seen in human mould. . . . No heart as his was ever so tender, but tenderness was not all: this heart so tender was as brave, it could be stern. He found the thought of his Passion past bearing, yet he went through with it. He was feared when he chose: he took a whip and singlehanded cleared the temple. The thought of his gentleness towards children, towards the afflicted, towards sinners, is often dwelt on; that of his courage less. But for my part I like to feel that I should have feared him. We hear also of his love, as for John and Lazarus; and even love at first sight, as of the young man that had kept all the commandments from his childhood. But he warned or rebuked his best friends when need was, as Peter, Martha, and even his mother. For, as St. John says, he was full both of grace and of truth. . . .

From all that might be said of his character I single out one point and beg you to notice that. He loved to praise, he loved to reward. He knew what was in man, he best knew men's faults and yet he was the warmest in their praise.

> Gerard Manley Hopkins. Sermon for Sunday Evening, Nov. 23, 1879, in *Poems and Prose of Gerard Manley Hopkins* (Baltimore, Penguin Books, 1953), pp. 136– 141

While the Gospels agree in the great essentials, they differ in many little details. Yet these differences only accentuate the fact that all the great lines point toward the figure of Jesus Christ. A good illustration of this is Holman Hunt's painting entitled, *Finding Christ in the Temple.* It is a very complex picture. There is a large, ornate building, several groups of hostile people, besides Joseph and Mary and Jesus. As you study the picture, whether you look at Mary or at a rabbi or one of the women in the background, you will see that the lines of composition focus on the face of Jesus. So it is in our three Gospels.

> Herbert R. Purinton and Carl E. Purinton. *Literature of the New Testament* (New York, Charles Scribner's Sons, 1925), pp. 58–59

The life of Jesus is told in narratives which are both convincingly factual and artistically significant. It pursues an unswerving tragic rhythm, showing an individual's clash with his environment. Generally in drama the tragic hero, though conceived on a grander scale than his community, can be said to fall partly at least through some fault. Here the protagonist is in every way a more perfect being than his world, the usual tragic relation being to this extent reversed. Jesus' life distils the quintessence of human reality: his story presents an absolute, finished and complete life in harmony with a supreme ethic. . . .

We see Jesus silhouetted against a world of formalized religion, hypocrisy, envy, evil and suffering. It is a world of death; of spiritual death and of bodily death. To this world he would bring life. . . .

Jesus' life is complementary to his words. By picture-language and by dramatic example his work is done. . . . Jesus is human and real to us; we grow to know his naturalistic and humanistic poetry, his sympathy and endurance, his flashing wrath and prophetic ardour; but his personality, human though it be, is also symbolic, radiating a mysterious and mystic power. His life is framed by light, melting into the divine at either end; his birth is divine, he rises from the dead, and at choice moments he is vividly superhuman, as when the heavens open and God speaks at his baptism and at his transfiguration.

> G. Wilson Knight. *The Christian Renaissance* (London, Methuen and Company, 1962), pp. 149, 169, 171

The primary characteristic of all of the books in the New Testament is undoubtedly the central role played in them by the person of Jesus Christ. This is especially obvious in the four Gospels. They were written exclusively in order to present Jesus. Other people of course appear in them too: Jesus has his followers; he soon has his bitter opponents; the masses respond to his activity, first receptively, only to turn against him later. The disciples, the opponents, and the masses all play distinctive roles, and as a rule the evangelists describe them with great care. But the spotlight is always on Jesus. The purpose of the Gospels is to describe him and no one else: *his* appearance in Isreal, what *he* said, what *he* did, what happened to *him* . . .

If one thinks about it, it becomes extremely difficult to imagine that there ever was a time when Jesus' followers were not interested in preserving his teachings and in committing his deeds to memory. And if we orient ourselves historically, and remind ourselves how students in the Jewish milieu hung on the words of their teachers and attentively followed their activities in order to learn how to live properly, it then becomes difficult to believe that Jesus' disciples could have been less concerned to hear their master, to observe his way of doing things, and to store up all of this in their memories.

As the Gospels also reveal, this concentration upon Jesus in regard to content is matched by a formal concentration upon Jesus. The evangelists are conscious theologians; this is clear from the way they design their work, group their material, form connecting notices, omit formulations, add formulations, alter formulations. But they do not see it as their task to write a reasoned presentation of Jesus, setting forth his message and doctrines in their own words mixed in with theological comments, doctrinal argumentation, or hortatory speeches. They permit Jesus to speak for himself, as a rule in direct discourse. They report episodes involving Jesus tersely and to the point. They do not allow themselves to comment—except for occasional, concise, and scarcely noticeable remarks in links between pericopes.

> Birger Gerhardsson. *The Origins of the Gospel Traditions* (Philadelphia, Fortress Press, 1977), pp. 47–49

ORAL BACKGROUND AND NATURE

It goes without saying that the earliest evangelical narratives were oral. . . . The existence of oral tradition is not only a basic presupposition of the written Gospels (see once more the Preface to Luke), whose form and contents can by no means be explained otherwise; but we actually have evidence of the existence of this tradition in the period prior to the earliest of them. Not only does the earliest preaching of the Christian message, reflected in the opening chapters of the book of Acts, imply the repetition of teaching about Jesus, his words and 'mighty works'; but in a famous passage in I. Cor. xv, St. Paul reminds his readers that he 'delivered unto them first of all that which he also had received' (vs. 3)—viz. the tradition of the Passion and Resurrection of Christ. And it was the testimony of 'the eyewitnesses' referred to by Luke which doubtless became their message as 'ministers of the word.'

> Frederick C. Grant. *The Growth of the Gospels* (New York, Abingdon Press, 1933), p. 39

Jesus left nothing written. This was not exceptional in the case of prophetic persons of the Orient. . . .

An Oriental is accustomed to pass on orally the traditions of his practical philosophy and of his history. . . . Hence the Oriental teacher, prophet, or narrator employs such forms as have been customary among these peoples from time immemorial, viz. proverbs, parabolic narratives, riddles, fairy-tales, and so on. A casual glance at the gospels and especially at the three earliest . . . proves that the traditions assembled in them exhibit Oriental forms in this sense. This is equally true both of the sayings and the doings of Jesus. . . .

The time when these oral traditions came to be written down depended upon the need for writing and the memory of those who conserved the traditions. . . .

When [Jesus'] parables were handed down, they would be repeated in a form which soon came to be definite and fixed, just as was the case with other stories which belonged to popular tradition. The Talmud shows that the Jews in particular were very fond of telling "parables" and were able to keep them intact through further repetition.

The same observation holds good in regard to the proverbial sayings, the shortest form of utterance playing a part similiar to the parables. The evidence of the Gospels shows that Jesus often used the form of a proverb or "gnome" to give succinct expression to well-recognized truths or those of a paradoxical nature. By virtue of this brevity, often aided by a metaphor and sometimes by a paradox, the sayings were more easily retained in the memory. . . .

In the majority of cases, the adherents of Jesus handed them on without context, as is customary with proverbs or popular rules. This fact is proved by the way in which the sayings have been assembled into the "speeches" or "sermons" of Jesus.

Still other sayings of Jesus could be firmly held in the memory because of their connection with Old Testament passages, whether by way of agreement or criticism. . . .

Thus the very form of the words used by Jesus contained the quality which made for their preservation.

> Martin Dibelius. *A Fresh Approach to the New Testament and Early Christian Literature* (New York, Charles Scribner's Sons, 1936), pp. 27–33

Among the Jews, the teaching of a Rabbi was preserved and transmitted by his disciples by word of mouth. They were not allowed to write it down. Obviously their memories were far better trained and more accurate than ours usually are: we are so dependent on print. The disciples of Jesus adopted the same method as a matter of course. . . . If you call to mind the teaching of Jesus as we have it in the Gospels, it is remarkable how much of it is given in forms peculiarly easy to remember. There are the parables; who could fail to remember the parable of the Lost Sheep or the Good Samaritan? There are crisp epigrams that stick in the mind like burrs: . . . 'What shall it profit a man if he gain the whole world and lose his soul?' There are whole passages that run almost like verse (in the original language they may have been in regular metre); they are nearly all complete within the compass of a few verses. In all this we can catch the accents of the living voice.

How early the tradition of the sayings of Jesus began to be written down, it is hard to say. At a guess, I should suspect it was not long after the Church moved into Greek-speaking countries. The Greeks were a bookish people, like ourselves, and liked to have things in writing. So by degrees they compiled fly-sheets with a few sayings on some special topic. Then the fly-sheets were brought together into more comprehensive collections. It seems certain that there was a considerable number of collections of sayings of Jesus in circulation. Some of them were used in the composition of the Gospels. . . .

The disciples of Jesus not only handed down what he taught. They laid at least equal stress upon certain facts about him. When Gospels came to be written, these facts bulked largely. . . .

In . . . I Corinthians xi. 23–25 Paul refers . . . to the tradition he received and passed on. He says it included also an account of what Jesus said and did at his last supper. . . . We have already noticed Mark's account of the same occasion. We learn now that it was the custom of the Church, when it met for worship, to repeat the words and actions of Jesus. . . . But at this time none of the Gospels was written. They drew on living memory. Sunday by Sunday, without intermission, from a time when the events were quite recent, the Christian congregation in many different places deliberately renewed the memory of facts which they could not allow to fall into oblivion. . . . The Church not only remembered and reported the facts. It lived them. If we have understood this, we are near to the secret of the Gospels.

It is this living tradition, carefully guarded, constantly repeated, that lies behind Mark's work.

C. H. Dodd. About the Gospels (Cambridge, Cambridge
University Press, 1950), pp. 16–17, 19–22

Until the writing of the first written sources, the only medium for circulating the story of Jesus was the spoken word. The first written documents may have been nothing more than *aide-memoires* devised to preserve in a fixed form the stories that were propagated orally. If the bulk of the Gospel consists of an assemblage of written transcripts of oral tradition, it is not inconceivable that features characteristic of oral communication have been conserved in its final form. Thus, in regard to its origins, it may be permissible to describe the Gospel as the "spoken Gospel." Should this be the case, the definition could also extend to its transcripted form. If the Gospel is a transcript *of* oral discourse, it is ipso facto a transcript *for* oral discourse. It was written down as it was heard, to be heard again. The Gospel was written not to be read silently but to be heard publicly.

This point furnishes a clue to many of the peculiarities, the incongruities and stylistic paradoxes, that have been surveyed above. If these be considered faults, they are imputable to the spontaneity and freedom of the spoken word. The shocking constructions, the capricious thought sequences, the seemingly extraneous details, the euphonious words, the startling confusion of pronouns and tenses—all betray . . . intent to deliver the Gospel with the vividness, expressiveness, and persuasive power of verbal interpretation.

> Gilbert Bilezikian. *The Liberated Gospel* (Grand Rapids,
> Baker, 1977), p. 119

That Mark owes much to his oral past is evident. . . . Many of the gospel's individual forms and genres are recognizable as orally fixed and mangageable compositions. We have already adverted to the existence in the gospel of controversy stories (Mark 2), parables (Mark 4), miracles (Mark 4–6), apophthegms (Mark 10), and *logoi* (Mark 13). Their presence in cluster-like density betrays Markan indebtedness to the oral habit of hoarding like experiences. The simple linking together of sentences by *kai* parataxis, . . . the preference for direct speech, the predominance of the historical present, the lack of an artistically reflected prose, an incomplete characterization of the Jesus figure, the gospel's exposition as a series of events, and little enthusiasm for the abstract—these and many other features indicate Markan allegiance to the vitality of the spoken word.

> Werner H. Kelber. *Semeia*. 16, 1979, p. 34

SUBTYPES

The shape into which the tradition came to be cast was conditioned by the *forms of speech* which Jesus used.

Among these the best known and most clearly differentiated form is that of the *parabolic narrative*. . . .

Jesus often used the form of a proverb or "gnome" to give succinct expression to well-recognized truths or those of paradoxical nature. . . .

We can easily understand why the words of Jesus were preserved in tradition, for they had a direct bearing upon the activity of the church. On the other hand it is not so easily apparent why the story of events in the life of Jesus should have been recounted. . . . A glance shows that the narrative sections of the gospels are not at all concerned with giving a chronicle of events, with biography, or with making a connected historical record. What is set down is essentially stories in narrative form, complete in themselves. In form at least they are similar to our anecdotes, and they deal with separate incidents in the life of Jesus. They would not have come down to us rounded off and complete in themselves, at any rate in Mark's Gospel, if they had not been current separately in the first instance, passed on from mouth to mouth independently of of each other. . . .

Many of them are founded upon some saying of Jesus, and the circumstances are described because they help to explain it. . . .

Very shortly, however, a second interest was added. . . . Their objective was to depict the appearance of Jesus on the scene not as a biographer or a historian would do it, but in the way a religious inquirer ought to see it if he wanted to understand and take part in Christian missionary work. . . . Here in these short stories of healings, miracle-working utterances, authoritative judgements . . . were the needful signs, works, and miracles. . . .

That in the majority of the shorter stories about Jesus . . . we are dealing with such examples for sermons, can be clearly seen from the style of these stories. In the first place they are characterized by their terseness and by the fact that they deal only with that which is essential. Everything is concentrated on what Jesus says and does; what others say and do is only important as the occasions of His intervention. . . . And just as portraiture is lacking so also is landscape. . . . We shall best understand the process if we picture to ourselves the meaning of these narratives as examples. They were meant to serve the preaching of salvation, to prove its content and to provide references; in short to bear witness to Jesus. . . .

Alongside of the short narratives about Jesus with which we have already dealt there are, however, still others whose vivid portraiture is familiar to every Bible reader. . . . We possess here another, more detailed, and also more secular, style which enables us to call these narratives "Tales". . . . Here even the unliterary Bible reader is struck by the emphasis given to certain secondary circumstances: references to numbers, e.g. to the number of people who had been fed and the basketfuls of fragments; or again to the age of the girl who was ill and the length of the illness—such remarks assure the accuracy of the record just as small dialogues between Jesus and other persons vivify it.

Martin Dibelius. *A Fresh Approach to the New Testament and Early Christian Literature* (New York, Charles Scribner's Sons, 1936), pp. 28, 31, 35–38, 40

There is a considerable amount of agreement among the form critics regarding the description of the forms, though the nomenclature varies.

1. The first of the forms is that which Dibelius calls the *paradigm* and Bultmann the *apothegm*. The question about tribute to Caesar (Mark 12:14–17) is a good example of this form. It consists of a dialogue, often controversial, sometimes associated with a miracle, which leads up to a striking pronouncement by Jesus capable of general application. The interest of the pericope is centered in this saying, not in other details or persons. For this reason Vincent Taylor prefers the name "pronouncement stories." . . .

2. The second of the forms is the *miracle story*, which is recognized fundamentally by its content. . . . Here the interest is in the display of power, and a regular pattern appears—description of the trouble, description of the method used, and report of the effect. A true miracle story is likely to be longer and more colorful than a paradigm, since the interest is in the event itself; but there is little in the style to distinguish it from a biographical anecdote.

3. A third classification is that of the *sayings*, to which Dibelius gives the name *paraenese* ("exhortations") because he believes these sayings were preserved for the instruction of new converts. This class really includes a number of forms—parable. poetic stanza, maxim, and so forth. . . .

4. There remains a group of stories in which the practical interest is less apparent. . . . Most of these are stories about associates of Jesus, from Peter to Zacchaeus, where a frank biographical interest appears. Finding an analogy in the tales of saints, Dibelius terms these *legende*. With them he would also include the nativity legends. . . .

5. Finally, Dibelius adds a very small group of *myths*—much larger in Bultmann's view. He uses the term myth to describe pieces in which the action is clearly that of a divine, not a human, person. Such would be the story of the Transfiguration (Mark 9:2–8) and Dibelius would also include a few sayings, such as the familiar 'Come unto me, . . . and I will give you rest" (Matt. 11:28), which convey a divine reassurance.

6. Besides agreeing on the forms of the independent pericopes most form critics agree that one section of the gospel tradition had a connected sequence almost from the beginning. This is the *passion story*, which gives a connected account from the inception of the final plot against Jesus (Mark 14:1) to his death on the Cross (Mark 15:39), though not including resurrection stories or some of the minor incidents now in the narrative. Such a story of how and why Jesus died was essential to the gospel preaching from the very beginning.

Alfred M. Perry. "The Growth of the Gospels," *Interpreter's Bible*, Vol. 7 (Nashville, Abingdon Press, 1951), pp. 69–70

The extensive and sharply differentiated material can be divided very roughly into narrative and sayings material.

(a) The miracle stories make up a large part of the narrative material, but we cannot speak of them as a uniform type. Alongside the nature miracles. . . , the miracles of Feeding. . . and Peter's Draught of Fishes . . . there is a great number of different kinds of healing miracles. The account is often very general and does not aim to relate what happened in the greatest possible detail, but aims rather to underline the miracle as such and so glorify the figure of Jesus. . . .

If the purpose of these miracle-stories is to make clear—generally indirectly—who Jesus is, then the same purpose is achieved—but more directly—

in another group of stories in which the person of Jesus is at the centre: the Baptism, the Temptation, Peter's Confession and the Transfiguration. According to their style these stories are legends (but this term is not meant to express any historical evaluation). In some of the other legends the connection with the person of Jesus is only indirect (e.g. Peter's Denial). The various Easter stories (with the Empty Tomb and the detailed accounts of the appearances) belong to this category, as well as the account of the so-called "Institution" of the Lord's Supper.

(b) An intermediate stage between narrative material and sayings material is formed by the large number of shorter stories which contain a saying by Jesus in the framework of a brief scene. In some cases the saying interprets the scene, in others the scene illustrates the saying ("ideal scenes"). Among examples are the eating with publicans (Mk. ii. 15p17), the question of fasting (Mk. ii. 18-22), the blessing of the children (Mk. x. 13-16) and the story of the Tribute Money (Mk. xii. 13-17). The form here is often that of the dialogue or disputation. . . .

(c) A large part of the sayings material is taken up by the parables. Here again we cannot speak of a uniform type, but have to draw distinctions. However, a number of mixed forms make it difficult to differentiate very sharply. The metaphor is the simplest form, in which one concept stands for another and the image and the object are identical (king-God; father-God; wedding feast-feast of consummation).

In the simile and the parable proper . . . the image stands alongside the object. . . .

The remaining sayings material, which in general is much briefer, is very varied both in form and content, and it is very difficult to divide it into categories. We can mention some of the groups. In the prophetic-apocalyptic sayings, very often with borrowings from traditional concepts and material, the irruption of the reign of God is announced, and this can take the form of the beatitude. . . .

In the so-called "Christ-sayings" the meaning of the hour is expressed in "personal" terms. They include the group of "I am come" saying (Mk. ii. 17; Lk. vii. 49), and also the Son of Man sayings, which speak of the present and active Son of Man . . . and the suffering, dying, and rising Son of Man.

W. Marxsen, *Introduction to the New Testament*, trans. G. Buswell (Philadelphia, Fortress Press, 1968), pp. 121–124

What Mark received came to him in isolated pericopes of two main types: sayings tradition and narrative tradition.

SAYINGS TRADITION

1. Aphorisms. Example: He who has ears to hear, let him hear" (Mark 4:9). . . .

2. Parables. Example: the Parable of the Productive Seed (= the Parable of the Sower) (Mark 4:3–8). . . .
3. Sayings clusters. These are of two types:
   a. Topical groupings. Example: the salt words (Matt. 5:13–16).
   b. Formal groupings. Example: the Beatitudes and woes (Luke 6:20–26).

NARRATIVE TRADITION

1. Anecdotes. Example: the story of the demoniac in the synagogue at Capernaum (Mark 1:23–26). These are brief biographical narratives.
2. Aphoristic narratives. Example: the plucking of grain on the Sabbath (Mark 2:23–28). A mixture of narrative and sayings material, these are narratives that culminate in pithy sayings.
3. Wonder stories. Example: Mark 5:1–20. In these stories the main point is the wonder itself, the miraculous as such.
4. Legends. These are narratives in which the divine is directly or publicly manifest. They are of two types:
   a. Biographical legends. Example: the temptation story. . . . The main interest is in the divine as disclosed in Jesus' life or activity.
   b. Cult legends. Example: the Feeding of the Five Thousand (Mark 6:30–44). The main interest is in authorization of or grounding for the church's cult.
5. Passion story. This is the only connected account preserved in the gospel tradition, although the sequence was not rigidly followed by all the gospel writers.

> Howard Clark Kee. *Jesus in History: An Approach to the Study of the Gospels* (New York, Harcourt, Brace and World, 1970), pp. 125–126

One . . . form or type of tradition is "the pronouncement story." These are brief episodes about Jesus that give a particular setting, generally refer to some action in Jesus' encounter with other people, and are climaxed by a significant saying or pronouncement of Jesus. One of the best examples of this type of form is Mark 12:13–17 (Matt. 22:15–22; Luke 20:20–26). . . . The setting for many of these stories must be viewed as a typical or ideal setting rather than as an actual historical setting in the life of Jesus. Many of the references in the Gospels, such as "on the sabbath," "in the synagogue," "early in the morning," and so on, illustrate this typical quality.

A second form is "the miracle story," which consists of a description of the circumstances, the cure or miraculous act worked by Jesus, and a recreation by those involved in or witness to the miracle. . . .

A third form of tradition is "the parable." The term "parable" and its Hebrew counterpart *mashal* were applied to a wide variety of picturesque forms of expression, such as illustrative story, metaphor, simile, riddle, and so on. It is one of the most frequent forms of tradition in the Gospels. . . . Parables were used in a number of contexts and for a number of reasons in the early church—to proclaim a call to Christian commitment, to illustrate the nature of Christian behavior, and to interpret the content of Christian faith.

Another form in the teaching traditions is what might be broadly called "sayings" or "aphorisms." These tend to be very similar to parabolic teaching except that the elements of illustration and narrative are omitted. An example of a saying tradition is found in Mark 4:21–25 (Luke 8:16–18), where several sayings have been brought together. . . . The sayings of Jesus are very similar to the wisdom proverbs of the Old Testament but oftentimes with obvious Christian perspectives. . . .

The sayings of Jesus were used by the early church in its teaching and preaching and perhaps were circulated in independent form. . . . Evidence of collections of such sayings appear in the Gospels. For example, Luke 6:27–38 contains a number of sayings in which love is a central consideration and possibly a theme providing an organizational principle.

Other forms of Gospel tradition are more difficult to categorize. Several units or pericopes are stories about Jesus, such as the account of the baptism, the temptation, the entry into Jerusalem, the resurrection, and so on. These may have been used in various contexts in the early church and served as vehicles for the church's declaration of its faith in Jesus. The longest of this type of material is the passion narrative concerning Jesus' betrayal, trial, crucifixion, and burial. This seems to have existed as an extended and connected narrative from the earliest days of the church. . . .

Form criticism has contributed greatly to an understanding of the Gospel traditions in their preliterary form. It has shown that the majority of these traditions circulated as independent units before being brought together to form small collections.

John H. Hayes. Introduction to the Bible (Philadelphia,
Westminster Press, 1971), pp. 331–333

It is well known that the Old Testament supplies us with a virtually stereotyped pattern for the annunciations of the forthcoming births of famous figures in salvation history, narratives obviously written in retrospect after the figure had become famous. Regularly there are five features in the pattern:

—Appearance of an angel or of God, sometimes greeting by title the subject of the vision.

—Fear or prostration on the part of the subject confronted with this supernatural presence.

—The annunciation message, sometimes prefaced by the injunction not to fear and the mention of the visionary's name. The basic message contains the following items:

(a) the woman is or is about to be with child;

(b) she will give birth to the child;

(c) the name by which the child is to be called;

(d) an etymology interpreting the name;

(e) the future accomplishments of the child.

—An objection on the part of the visionary as to how this is to come about.

—The giving of a sign to reassure the visionary.

In comparing Matthew and Luke's accounts of the annunciation of the birth of Jesus (to Joseph and Mary, respectively), we find that Matthew preserves three of the features while Luke preserves all five.

> Raymond E. Brown. "Luke's Method in the Annunciation Narrative of Chapter One," in *Perspectives on Luke-Acts*, ed. Charles H. Talbert (Danville, Virginia, Association of Baptist Professors of Religion, 1978), p. 131

[In pronouncement stories], setting and saying are related as stimulus and response. Careful study of this relationship reveals six types of pronouncement stories in the synoptic Gospels: 1. *Correction stories*, in which the climactic response corrects the views or conduct of the person or group provoking the response. 2. *Objection stories*, in which the behavior of the responder (the one who utters the climactic pronouncement) or the responder's followers is the cause of an objection and the climactic response is an answer to that objection. 3. *Commendation stories*, in which the responder commends or praises something said, done, or represented by another person. 4. *Quest stories*, which begin when someone approaches the responder in quest of something very important to the well-being of the quester. The suspense generated by the uncertainty of success in the quest is central to the story, and the story comes to an end with an indication of the quest's success or failure. The responder's pronouncement (sometimes accompanied by action) plays a crucial role in this success or failure. 5. *Test stories*, in which someone approaches the responder with a question, request, or proposal designed to test the responder. Like the objection story, the suspense in this type of story focuses on the responder, who must extricate himself or herself from a difficult situation. Unlike the objection story, this suspense does not arise from an objection against something already said or done by the responder. 6. *Inquiry stories*, in which the basic features of the other five types are absent and the responder simply responds to a question or request for information by supplying the information.

The two parts of a pronouncement story are correlative, i.e., the function of the stimulus part must correlate with the function of the response part or the story will be malformed and confusing. It is only by considering both parts in relation to each other that the type can be defined. The fact that Jesus is asked a question does not immediately tell us that the story is an inquiry, for Jesus may respond by correcting an assumption behind the question (a correction story), or the question may actually be a demand for justification of previous behavior (an objection story), or the question may announce a quest or pose a test. . . .

"Hybrid" pronouncement stories, combining several of the types in a single story, are fairly common in the synoptic Gospels. . . .

The movement from the provoking occasion to the response may also represent a movement from one attitude to another on important issues of religion and life. . . .

Most pronouncement stories are brief, containing one or sometimes two exchanges of dialogue. . . . The imaginative force of the language is important, for it must awaken new thought about an unconsidered or poorly considered possibility. A brief pronouncement need not put an end to thought. It can awaken imaginative thought by pointing to possibilities beyond the prison of old assumptions in which most of our thinking is trapped. For this purpose the impact of the words, their rhetorical power, is important. The climactic pronouncement is often carefully shaped to increase its impact, and in correction stories the setting of the pronouncement also increases its impact through contrast.

Robert C. Tannehill. "Attitudinal Shift in Synoptic Pronouncement Stories," in *Orientation by Disorientation*, ed. Richard A. Spencer (Pittsburgh, Pickwick Press, 1980), pp. 184–86

Form critics have attempted to analyze these stories on the basis of the forms or patterns in which they seem repeatedly to occur. Such critics have not always agreed in their analyses, but three such patterns or forms will be noted here.

The most obvious form is that of the *parable*. . . . One can readily see how these little stories could be remembered easily and handed down orally.

A second form has been called the *pronouncement story*. It consists of a saying of Jesus embedded in an account of some incident of his life, so that the two would be remembered together. For example, Mark 2:23–28 tells how Jesus' disciples, walking through a grain field on the Sabbath, plucked and ate bits of wheat. When the Pharisees accused them of desecrating the Sabbath by threshing grain on the holy day, Jesus replied, "The sabbath was made for man, not man for the sabbath." Story and saying would be remembered together. . . . Incidentally, it should be noted that many, many of Jesus' saying are in this style of witty couplets or balanced phrases which would be easy to remember and pass on orally.

The third form is the *miracle story*. In a typical miracle story, (1) a need is noted; (2)Jesus' help is sought; (3) there is an expression of faith; (4) a memorable miracle is performed, and (5) the story ends with a notation about the response of those who saw the miracle. The response may be one of faith, astonishment, or even anger. Matthew 9:1–8 contains all five of these elements in its account of the healing of a paralytic.

> William M. Ramsay. *The Layman's Guide to the New Testament* (Atlanta, John Knox Press, 1981), pp. 26–27

TRAGEDY OR COMEDY?

My task is to isolate the unique "act" of the Christian faith, and the unique "act" of the comic, and to compare and contrast these two archetypal acts. For it is in the notion of "act" that we have perhaps the best conceptual instrument for relating the religious imagination to the dramatic imagination. . . .

The Christian tradition has not seen fit to reduce the meaning of the act of Jesus Christ to a single formula, but it has attempted to explicate the work of Christ in various figures and metaphors. Following the Judaic conception of sacrifice and offering, one strand of interpretation has spoken of Christ as the Victim. . . . Another strand, rooted in apocalyptic imagery of demonic forces, has interpreted Christ as Victor. . . . And a third strand of the Christian tradition has attempted to conjoin these two images from the metaphorical worlds of altar and battlefield by speaking of Christ as the *Victim-Victor*, or, in the words of Saint Augustine, Christ was for us "both a Victor and a Victim—a Victor because a Victim."

Each of these three metaphorical expressions is used in the Gospel account of the action and the passion of Jesus Christ. These patterns of meaning, these various literary structures, are built into both dramatic comedy and the biblical drama. . . .

In the Gospels, the stress upon the victory that follows humiliation and surrender is repeated over and over: "He who humbles himself will be exalted"; "Some are last who will be first"; "He who loses his life for my sake will find it"; and finally in parabolic form: "Unless a grain of wheat falls into the earth and dies, it remains alone: but if it dies, it bears much fruit" (Luke 14:11; 13:30; Matt. 10:39; John 12:24). . . .

The Gospels are replete with . . . "comic assurances," although the disciples, like many spectators of a drama, did not always realize the implications of the clues until after the drama was completed. . . .

It is precisely in what Jesus Christ did—in his patient suffering, in his sacrificial death, in his triumphant resurrection, and, most of all, in what the Christian tradition has called his reconciliation—that we find a clue as to what it is that constitutes the archetypal comic action. For some of the phrases used in the discussion of comedy . . . are echoes of what the Christian faith understands by the Incarnation, the Atonement, the Resurrection, and especially, the reconciliation of Christ. . . .

The three dramatic structures of comedy (those of the Victim, the Victor, and the Victim-Victor) provide a bridge between the archetypal acts of the comic and of the Christian faith. The three structures are descriptions of the action and passion of Jesus Christ as well as of the protagonist of comedy. . . .

Dante in the movement of his work not only employs the journey as a pattern of Christian life, but he also clearly indicates that the movement in *The Divine Comedy* is an analogue of the divine action of Jesus Christ: the movement from misery to happiness. For the structure of the *Comedy* indicates that Dante is in some sense retelling the story of the Christ, and, in so doing, is viewing it as a comedy. . . .

On all three levels of Dante's story, the work of Christ is understood as a comedy: literally, in his earthly body a comedy begins in a manger and ends in the triumph of the Ascension; allegorically, in his mystical body a comedy begins outside Eden and concludes in Paradise regained; and, analogically, in his sacramental body a comedy begins in the breaking of bread and ends in the festive union with the redeemed. . . .

The ultimate manifestation of Christ's identity with men and his power is expressed by his enemies: "This man receives sinners and eats with them" (Luke 15:2). Here identification, and therefore reconciliation, is complete, and comic dimensions of the Christian story are again eveident.

Nelvin Vos. The Drama of Comedy: Victim and Victor
(Richmond, John Knox Press, 1966), pp. 14–15, 18–
19, 28–29, 106–107, 110

What, then, . . . is the form of the Gospels? To debate the question of whether or not the Gospel form should be called a definite literary genre would not be as fruitful as to consider concretely its kinship with and differences from the Western literary tradition. In the Gospels we see Jesus seeking and intending to bring to men the gracious presence and rule of God, but his efforts resulted in conflict and finally in his death. On the cross he suffered the tragic recognition that his good purpose had produced forsakenness by God. The resurrection, however, shows that he was not really abandoned, although he believed that he was, and proves his death to have been in truth a victory. From the standpoint of plot, then, the Gospel form might be called the tragedy of an innocent sufferer which is followed by a post-tragic redemptive episode or, similarly, a tragedy which paradoxically includes victory. In view of the emphasis which the Gospels clearly put on the resurrection, however, it seems more appropriate to speak of the Gospel form as a comedy in which the tragic is included and overcome. The ease and appropriateness with which the categories of tragedy and comedy can be used of the Gospels manifest their affinity with the literary tradition. . . .

We might say that the Gospel form is the tragicomedy of the God-man which proclaims and offers to other men the comic overcoming of their tragic loss of existence.

> Dan Otto Via, Jr. *The Parables: Their Literary and Existential Dimension* (Philadelphia, Fortress Press, 1967), pp. 179–181

A persistent doubt about the assertion that no literary work can be both Christian and tragic leads to the more basic question, are not the gospel narratives themselves fundamentally tragic stories? They certainly seem so to the disinterested observer—the main character, who possesses both courage and integrity, conducts his life as he believes he must, even in the face of overwhelming opposition; and as a direct result of this behavior, he is put to death. . . .

When those who deny the possibility of Christian tragedy attempt to describe the main features of tragic drama, their generalizations apply at least as well to the gospel narratives as they do to any literary tragedy. . . .

A "tragedy" is a literary work, predominantly somber in tone, in which the main character encounters some significant misfortune for which he himself is partly, though not wholly, responsible. . . .

The suffering which tragedy represents is neither accidental nor inevitable; the hero's action is, to be sure, one cause of that suffering, but the effect goes far beyond what we can explain by means of that one cause. Nevertheless, the hero accepts the suffering voluntarily though reluctantly. . . .

The central event recorded in the gospels is the crucifixion, and it is here that the obvious similarity to the tragic pattern lies. . . . Whatever else it may also have been, the crucifixion was for Christ a "significant misfortune," which he accepted "voluntarily though reluctantly." This fact is clearly revealed in his Gethsemane prayer: "My Father, if it be possible, let this cup pass from me; nevertheless, not as I will, but as thou wilt" (Matt. 26:39). . . .

The gospel narrators were striving to present Christ as the agent of destiny and yet to preserve his freedom in that destiny. They sought to convince their readers that his self-sacrifice was of cosmic significance and that it was at the same time freely offered. In order to do this, they had to show that the disciples arrived at such an understanding of Christ's role only retrospectively, whereas Christ himself was fully conscious of this destiny at a much earlier point.

This attitude of the gospel writers has very interesting implications. It means, for instance, that from their point of view Christ conducted his life with full consciousness of his destiny, and that when he took decisive action, knowing what the consequences would be, he acted in a way to *fulfill* that destiny, not to avoid it. . . .

Because Jesus was at least partly responsible for what happened, his suffering cannot be described as accidental. The emphasis which the gospel writers place upon Christ's being an agent of destiny precludes this possibility. They make it perfectly clear that Christ knew his course of action would lead directly to a collision with the authorities—hence the prediction of his suffering and death. But on the other hand, the collision was not inevitable, because Jesus was at all times free to abandon his mission—that is, to deny his identity as the son of God. This indeed is the meaning of his being tempted in the wilderness (Matt. 4; Luke 4). . . .

Christianity has at its center a suffering God. That is, both tragedy and Christianity perceive a meaning in unmerited but necessary suffering. . . .

The relationship between Christianity and tragedy must be stated as a paradox. . . . Christ submits himself so totally to tragic experience that in the end he totally liberates himself from it. . . .

We can say, then, with Neibuhr that Christianity stands beyond tragedy— but not because Christianity is untragic. On the contrary, it does so only because Christianity is so profoundly and uncompromisingly tragic that it ends by seeming to lose its tragic character, by coming out on the other side.

Roger L. Cox. *YR.* 57, 1968, pp. 546, 550, 558, 560, 562–563, 569

If Mark is both comic and serious, as I shall argue, then what we need is the genre-category tragicomedy. . . .

Tragedy and comedy both arose from essentially the same kind of death and resurrection ritual, and the two genres separated by virtue of whether the emphasis was placed on conflict and death, or on resurrection and marriage. We have observed that comedy and tragedy can deal with the same situations, but from different perspectives and with different emphases. The central element in both is conflict.

Prior to the eighteenth century tragicomedy meant a work which mixed various tragic and comic elements in succession. But since that date it has meant a work which fused the two so that both kept their identity and were strengthened while each was made identical with the other. A given situation is seen *simultaneously* as both tragic and comic. Mark might be thought of as tragicomedy in the old sense: death is *followed by* resurrection. But in a number of ways Mark is a "modern" tragicomedy. There is simultaneity of the tragic and comic because the new which finally issues in resurrection is there from the beginning: the time is fulfilled. And the old world, the opposition which penultimately kills Jesus, is also there from the outset.

Mark is primarily tragicomedy because of the global and detailed presence of the death and *resurrection* or *life*-through-death motif. . . .

> Dan Otto Via, Jr. *Kerygma and Comedy in the New Testament* (Philadelphia, Fortress Press, 1975), pp. 99–101

Like the fairy-tale world, the world of the Gospel is a world of darkness, and many of the great scenes take place at night. The child is born at night. He had his first meal in the dark at his mother's breast, and he had his last meal in the dark too, the blinds drawn and everybody straining to catch the first sound of heavy footsteps on the stair, the first glint of steel in the shadowy doorway. In the garden he could hardly see the face that leaned forward to kiss him, and from the sixth hour to the ninth hour the sun went out like a match so he died in the same darkness that he was born in and rose in it, too, or almost dark. . . .

In the world of the fairy tale, the wicked sisters are dressed as if for a Palm Beach wedding, and in the world of the Gospel it is the killjoys, the phonies, the nitpickers, the holier-than-thous, the loveless and cheerless and irrelevant who more often than not wear the fancy clothes and go riding around in sleek little European jobs marked Pharisee, Corps Diplomatique, Legislature, Clergy. It is the ravening wolves who wear sheep's clothing. And the good ones, the potentially good anyway, the ones who stand a chance of being saved by God because they know they don't stand a chance of being saved by anybody else? They go around looking like the town whore, the village drunk, the crook from the IRS, because that is who they are. . . .

And as for the king of the kingdom himself, whoever would recognize him? He has no form or comeliness. His clothes are what he picked up at a rummage sale. He hasn't shaved for weeks. He smells of mortality. We have romanticized his raggedness so long that we can catch echoes only of the way it must have scandalized his time in the horrified question of the Baptist's disciples, "Are *you* he who is to come?" (Matt. 11:13); in Pilate's "Are you the king of the Jews?" (Matt. 27:11) you with pants that don't fit and a split lip; in the black comedy of the sign they nailed over his head where the joke was written out in three languages so nobody would miss the laugh.

But the whole point of the fairy tale of the Gospel is, of course, that he is the king in spite of everything. . . . There is no less danger and darkness in the Gospel than there is in the Brothers Grimm, but beyond and above all there is the joy of it, this tale of a light breaking into the world that not even the darkness can overcome.

That is the Gospel, this meeting of darkness and light and the final victory of light. That is the fairy tale of the Gospel with, of course, the one crucial difference from all other fairy tales, which is that the claim made for it is that it is true, that it not only happened once upon a time but has kept on happening ever since and is happening still.

> Frederick Buechner. *Telling the Truth: The Gospel as Tragedy, Comedy, and Fairy Tale* (New York, Harper and Row, 1977), pp. 89–90

MIRACLE STORIES

Within the Gospels, the stories of the miracles and exorcisms functioned in several ways. (1) They bore testimony to the belief that Jesus was no ordinary person. The power of God was present and active in his work. (2) They sought to offer to the reader, and, in their oral form, the hearer, a way of faith in him whose whole life had been a miracle. The exalted Lord was none other than the wonder-worker Jesus of Nazareth. (3) The miracles of Jesus were seen as the fulfillment and transcendence of Old Testament prophecy. Just as Moses and the Hebrews in the wilderness and Elijah and Elisha in their service had witnessed the miraculous and had been granted the power to perform the unusual, so also Jesus. (4) The miracles were declared to be evidence of the coming of the Kingdom, the dawning of the new age, the arrival of the eschatological time. . . . In other words, the miracles were signs that the Messiah had come, the new day had dawned. . . . (5) The Gospel writers sought to depict the time of origin, the beginning of the Christian movement, as a unique period, as a "type-time." The events from which the subsequent Christian movement flowed were events whose origin was transcendental not terrestrial.

> John H. Hayes. *Introduction to the Bible* (Philadelphia, Westminster Press, 1971), pp. 354–355

It is now well established that the Synoptic miracles, by and large, are to be understood eschatologically. The exorcisms, healings, and other miracles themselves bring the blessings of the kingdom. The miracles are presented in the Synoptic Gospels at least partly as the fulfillment of OT prophecies and Jewish expectations regarding the new age. It is also generally agreed that the miracles sometimes function as "signs" even in the Synoptics, that is, that they point to realities beyond themselves. That means, essentially, that what a miracle effects in the physical order has its analogy in spiritual: the healing of the paralytic (Mk 2:1–12), for instance, signifies the forgiveness of sin; as noted, the miracle performed for the Syrophoenician woman (Mk 7:24–30) signifies salvation to the Gentiles; and the healing of the blind man (Mk 8:22–26), the spiritual seeing, or faith, enjoined throughout Mark's Gospel. . . .

It is not necessary to strain this observation to the point of calling the miracles acted parables. A parable is always a literary composition, a verbal artifact; a miracle is an action or event. Parables and miracles are quite different phenomena and nothing is gained by confounding them. It is important, however, to know that the miracles, as they are treated in Mark, are similar to the parables in having more than one level of meaning and are thus subject to the same misunderstanding as the parables.

> Madeleine Boucher. *The Mysterious Parable: A Literary Study* (Washington, D. C., Catholic Biblical Association of America, 1977), pp. 79–80

Jesus' ministry, as recorded in the Synoptic Gospels, emphasizes the working of miracles. He performs over twenty of them—not counting slightly differing versions of some stories and the numerous summaries of the multitudes whom he healed.

Although most of his miracles are healings or exorcisms, the stories appear in a variety of forms and serve many functions. Some contain little detail, the miraculous act serving only as an occasion for raising important, often controversial, questions. For example, in the story of his healing the man with the withered hand (Mark 3:1–6 and parallels), the miracle is subsidiary to the main issue: work on the sabbath. Other miracles serve primarily a didactic function, exemplifying the power of faith. Such stories are particularly common in Matthew—for example healing the Canaanite woman's daughter (Matt. 15:21–28) and the two blind men (9:27–31). Sometimes the miracle story is a symbol or allegory within the narrative, as in cursing the fig tree (Mark 11:12–14, 20–21) and healing blind Bartimaeus (10:46–52). Finally, an extended miracle story is told with an apparent relish for detail and serves almost exclusively as testimony to Jesus' power. Instances of this last type are raising Jairus' daughter (Mark 5:21–43) and healing the Garasene demoniac (verses 1–20).

> Donald Juel. *An Introduction to New Testament Literature* (Nashville, Abingdon Press, 1978), p. 114

To understand what the Gospels want to report with this kind of story we have to know something of the way such stories were treated and told and regarded in the world within which the New Testament arose. People who could do such extraordinary things populated the imagination of the Graeco-Roman world of the first century of our era. There were figures, Greek and Jew alike, to whom such powers were attributed and about whom such stories were told. . . .

A regular pattern developed best suited to this kind of material. The pattern had basically three elements, each one of course capable of expansion and complexity. First of all, the problem was stated. A person was sick or possessed by a demon or blind or dumb or deaf or endangered or the like. Accompanying the statement of the problem, there was frequently an appeal for help, either by the subject or by someone else on the subject's behalf. Secondly, the miraculous solution was recounted. Through a gesture, or a phrase from some exotic language, or some manipulation, or the use of some dried plant or herb, or any combination of the those, the problem was resolved. The third element was some demonstration that the problem had indeed really been resolved and that it was not just an illusion or trick of some kind. . . .

Problem, solution, and proof are thus the three elements, in that order, which characterize the normal Hellenistic miracle story. Not surprisingly, the Gospel miracle accounts fall into that pattern. Long or short, that is the skeletal framework upon which they are constructed. . . .

What is important is what is included in such a story that is not necessary just to tell a miracle. Obviously, if there are elements in the story that go beyond the basic parts of the miracle story, then some other point is being made than just the recitation of an act of power. For what it is worth, there are very few miracle stories recounted of Jesus without some material being included that was extraneous to just the telling of a miracle. . . .

If a miracle story therefore is to convey anything more than the impression that the person performing the miracles is something out of the ordinary, that impression must be built into the story itself. In other words, to reduce or eliminate the ambiguity, the correct interpretation must somehow be built into the story. It should perhaps come as no surprise to learn that that is the case with most of the Gospel accounts of Jesus' mighty acts.

Paul J. Achtemeier. Int. 35, 1981, pp. 164–166

PASSION STORY

Jesus himself was the climax. The Passion and the Resurrection are the climax of the Gospel history. Poetry and painting have tried to adorn them. The searchlight of criticism has played upon them. Year after year musical versions of them move great audiences. No story has ever been the cause of so much emotion. The word 'pathos' might be reserved exclusively to apply to it. It is the greatest of dramas, and the greatest of miracles. The people who recorded it were affected by the facts they relate in their whole life and conduct. Yet the narrative itself is plain and matter of fact. Never were witnesses more restrained in tone and style. There is no need, and apparently no desire, to embellish. The only comments are small explanations or parallels noted to prophecies in the Old Testament.

The four Gospel records of these events could hardly be expected to cover the same ground. It was not a case of all having to give everything, but of selecting. The exhaustive and exhausting compilations of modern historians are made from a different standpoint. The account had to be kept short, if the writer wished to keep his matter within the limits of a 'roll', rolls being of a certain standard length, and also dear.

> P. C. Sands. *Literary Genius of the New Testament* (Oxford, Oxford University Press, 1932), p. 93

From the Synoptic Gospels we may gather that this journey [of Christ to Jerusalem] had early acquired in Christian thought the character of a solemn procession to the place of sacrifice (Mark x. 32–4, Luke ix. 51, xiii. 31–5). The way from Galilee to Jerusalem is a *via dolorosa*, in all gospels, and apparently in the *kerygma* which lies behind them. This symbolic value of the journey to Jerusalem is deeply embedded in the scheme of the Fourth Gospel.

> C. H. Dodd. *The Interpretation of the Fourth Gospel* (Cambridge, Cambridge University Press, 1953), p. 384

The Marcan traditions concerning Jesus' ministry in Jerusalem and the events associated therewith may be broken down in the following daily sequence:

Sunday:	"Triumphal Entry" (Mark 11:1–11)
Monday:	"Cleansing of the Temple" (Mark 11:12–19)
Tuesday:	(a) Teaching in the Temple (Mark 11:20 to 12:44)
	(b) Private Instruction of Peter, James, John, and Andrew (Mark, ch. 13)
Wednesday:	At Bethany (Mark 14: 1–11)
Thursday:	The Last Supper, Betrayal, and Hearing before the High Priest and Sanhedrin (Mark 14:12–72)
Friday:	Trial before Pilate, Crucifixion, and Burial (Mark, ch. 15)
Saturday:	Sabbath
Sunday:	Visit to the Tomb by the Women (Mark 16:1–8).

> John H. Hayes. *Introduction to the Bible* (Philadelphia, Westminster Press, 1971), p. 360

The passion story of Jesus is the climax not only of the individual gospels but of the whole story of the Bible. It is the center toward which the rest of biblical literature points either forward or backward. It is the fulfillment of the Old Testament ceremonial laws and prophecies, of Old Testament types (foreshadowings), and of the biblical archetype of the suffering servant. The substitutionary atonement represented by Jesus' death on the cross is also the basis for the "good news" that pervades the New Testament and is the foundation for the whole edifice of New Testament theology.

The resurrection of Jesus from the grave is the climax of the gospels. It is the ultimate triumph of the protagonist, proof of His uniqueness and divinity.

It is also the ultimate fulfillment of the literary archetype of movement through death to renewed life. In terms of plot stucture, the resurrection is the final phase of the U-shaped comic plot of the gospel. The gradual isolation of the protagonist which prevailed in the tragic phase of the story is now followed by the gradual reintegration of the hero into His society. It is evident that the inherent form of the New Testament gospels is comedy, not tragedy, as is somtimes claimed. If the plot did not end in triumph, the term ''gospel'' would be a misnomer.

> Leland Ryken. *The Literature of the Bible* (Grand Rapids, Zondervan, 1974), p. 290

The Gospel also contains the third element deemed essential to tragedy by Aristotle, the pathos, variously called the *suffering*, the deed of violence or horror, the tragic incident. He defined it as ''an action of a destructive or painful nature, such as murders on the stage, tortures, woundings, and the like.'' . . .

As a further refinement in poignance, Aristotle advised that such deeds be committed within the circle of personae bound by natural ties. . . . In tragedy the most shameful and therefore the most pathetic acts of shame appear to be acts of betrayal or rejection.

These categories are applicable to the passion story, which stands in the Gospel as the counterpart of the deed of violence in tragedy. The account of Jesus' suffering and death is revolting not only because of the physical violence unjustly perpetrated upon a righteous person, but especially because of the unthinkable horror of the situation. It is clear to the reader that Jesus is the Messiah. But the leaders of His own people fail to recognize their deliverer and put Him to death because of His very claim to messiahship. . . .

The tragic incident of the Gospel occurs among those who in reality are bound by natural ties. It is a story of rejection, betrayal, and regicide. But as Aristotle allowed, the murderer may accomplish his deed ''in ignorance of his relationship, and discover that afterwards.'' The resurrection assures the eventual vindication of Jesus as Messiah, but not until the full fury of human pride has wasted itself against the outpouring of divine mercy.

> Gilbert Bilezikian. *The Liberated Gospel* (Grand Rapids, Baker, 1977), pp. 102–103

Even if the story of Jesus' Passion were the only narrative in the New Testament, Amos Wilder would be justified in saying that ''the narrative mode is uniquely important in Christianity.'' The reader is persuaded to recognize the crucified one as the Christ, not by means of a carefully argued essay or homily, but through story. The apogee of the Christian Bible is created through narrative. I shall follow the Markan text, for it is the simplest, briefest, and probably most effective of the four Passion narratives.

Apart from Jesus, characters in the story fall into two opposing groups: (1) Jesus' followers and disciples, and (2) the chief priest and scribes who seek to destroy Jesus. The story opens with Jesus in the company of his followers; it ends with him in the power of the priests who engineer his death. The narrative turns on the scene in which Jesus is transferred from the company of his followers to the company of priests (Mk. 14:43–52). Jesus says about that moment of transferral, "the hour has come" (Mk. 14:41). The two halves of the story parallel each other, with the exception of the anointing scenes, which form a kind of inclusion around the Passion narrative as a whole.

Throughout the action Jesus is misunderstood and ill-treated. Priests plot against him and finally convict him after an unfair trial. Pilate finds him guilty of no crime, but he betrays Jesus to the crowd. Even his disciples fail to understand the time in which they live. . . . The actions of disciples and enemies alike evoke from the reader a sympathetic attitude toward Jesus.

More, however, is required than gaining the reader's sympathy. For the crucifixion to be theophanic and saving, Jesus must be more than the victim of evil forces. A Christian narration of the Passion must present Jesus' suffering and death fully and realistically, but so that the irony of the deed is visible. . . .

Two forces operate in the narrative to initiate and to move the action along. Action proceeds initially from the priests' plotting (Mk. 14:1–2). The unfolding story at no time breaks the relism of that intrigue. But another force, "the great and mysterious imperative of God," runs counterpoint to the priests' intrigue. . . .

Gethsemane portrays dialogue between Jesus and God. The issue is whether God will remove his fateful hand from Jesus. . . . After Jesus' speech in Gethsemane, the priests' plot is carried out in a realistic fashion; yet, because of Gethsemane, the reader is fully convinced that the action is initiated by more than conspiracy. Jesus submits to his divinely appointed destiny: "It is enough; the hour has come" (14:41). The reader recognizes that the silence and passivity of Jesus in the second half of the narrative witness to his submissiveness to God's will. . . .

Jesus' humiliation and death do not bring the final word. The Passion is penultimate; Jesus will return in power and glory. The crucifixion is reconciled here with Jesus' messiahship through a temporalizing of humiliation/exaltation: now humiliation, weakness, and death; later, exaltation, power, and life.

Leonard L. Thompson. *Introducing Biblical Literature: A More Fantastic Country* (Englewood Cliffs, Prentice-Hall, 1978), pp. 242–244

In all four Gospels, Jesus' death dominates the story. Mark devotes more than one-third of his Gospel to the last week of Jesus' life, almost half of that to his trial and death. In each of the Synoptics, Jesus predicts his own death on three separate occasions. Although successful as a teacher and miracle worker and immensely popular with the common people, Jesus encounters opposition by religious Jews, the guardians of tradition, from the outset. Plots form against him almost at once. The hostility grows more and more intense until, during the festival of Passover in Jerusalem, it climaxes in Jesus' arrest, trial, and execution.

Increasing specificity in each of the four narratives also testifies to the centrality of Jesus' death. Earlier episodes in Jesus' life are usually vague in details; from the moment Jesus arrives in Jerusalem, however, people, places, and times become important and specific. . . .

The martyrdom of a hero was not a motif unique to the New Testament. There were stories about Jewish martyrs who had died at the hands of foreigners rather than forsake their faith, and perhaps the most famous martyrdom in antiquity was that of Socrates. The story of Jesus' trial and death, however, is distinctive in many respects. Paradoxically, his death is a triumph—not only for the truth, but for himself as well. . . . In his death that is more than a death, Christian storytellers understandably might have found it necessary to modify traditional literary models.

The passion story is also distinctive in its imagery. Here the Gospels portray Jesus as a king, the Messiah-King. His entry into Jerusalem has details from the book of Zechariah that describe the coming of the king. . . .

In these last chapters of Jesus' life the narrators' hostility to Jews intensifies.

Donald Juel. An Introduction to New Testament Literature (Nashville, Abingdon Press, 1978), pp. 137–139

HEBREWS

Curiously enough this author, although he addresses an epistle to "Hebrews," is the least Hebraic writer in the New Testament. Except, of course, in quotations from the Old Testament—which are invariably from the Septuagint and never from the Hebrew—there is scarcely a trace of Semitic influence in his work. The author has a rich vocabulary at his command and uses it with great skill.

The style is even more characteristic of a practiced scholar than the vocabulary. In the first place the Greek text of the epistle is distinguished among the prose works of the primitive church by its rhythmical cadences, so much cultivated by "good" Greek authors. Again, the author likes to choose his words to produce alliteration. . . .

Besides being acquainted with these tricks of the ancient rhetorician . . . this unknown author displays a most remarkable capacity for an architectonic style of composition. Unlike Paul, whose emotions occasionally run away with him, making havoc of syntax, this author knows at each moment precisely what his next sentence will be, and he follows meticulously an elaborate outline. In fact his treatise involves the longest sustained argument of any book of the New Testament. With delicate finesse he suggests an idea before he develops it at some subsequent point. For example, in 2:17 he mentions "high priest" and takes it up again at great length at 4:14ff.; in 5:6 he mentions Melchizedek, but defers the full development of this typology to 6:20ff. He deftly employs parenthesis and asides, sometimes of considerable length (e.g., 3:7–11; 5:13–14; 8:5; 11:13–16). These and many similar features betray the hand of a careful and skillful author, whose work is easily recognized as coming closer to the definite literary style of a master of the Greek language than anything else in the New Testament.

Bruce M. Metzger. "The Language of the New Testament," *Interpreter's Bible*, Vol. 7 (Nashville, Abingdon Press, 1951), pp. 46–47

At first reading, the Letter to Hebrews will probably both attract and perplex us. It is like a work of art from another time and place—a mediaeval stained-glass window, for example, whose general meaning and beauty are clear enough, but whose style and details are strange and puzzling. . . .

Hebrews is a work of art. It may well attract us with its magnificent language, its vivid images, and the sweep and subtlety of its argument: but its world of ideas and its methods of reasoning are so different from those of today that we shall probably feel that we are missing a great deal of its meaning. . . .

The real contrast in Hebrews is a threefold one: (i) between the Old Covenant and the New (a chronological contrast); (ii) between the Jewish sacrifices and that of Jesus (a contrast of outward and inward); and (iii) between the earthly tent and heaven. This last is expressed in Platonistic language, but its real basis is the Hebrew contrast of the creator God and the created world. . . .

An adequate analysis into large sections is possible, because there are certain main turning-points in the argument of Hebrews. The turning-points, however, occur within paragraphs, so that commentators do not agree on the precise limits of the main sections. In Hebrews the main turning-points occur in the paragraphs 4:14–16 and 10:19–39, and the N.E.B. accordingly puts its three headings before chapters 1, 5, and 11. These headings are *Christ Divine and Human*, *The Shadow and the Real*, and *A Call to Faith*. . . .

Throughout the letter the writer alternates between two types of discourse—doctrinal exposition and practical exhortation. The latter arises from the former, but the former is there for the sake of the latter. Paul in his letters usually puts all the doctrine first (e.g. Romans 1–11) and all the exhortation second (Romans 12–16). Our writer alternates throughout: and the alternation is for the most part so clearly marked that if the doctrinal passages are read continuously, and the exhortations omitted, the main argument displays its underlying continuity and coherence. The following table analyses the letter in this way.

Doctrine	Exhortation
1:1–14	2:1–4
2:5–3:6	3:7–4:13
4:14–5:10	5:11–6:20
7:1–10:22	10:23–39
11:1–12:2	12:3–17
12:18–29	13:1–25

Analysis by main themes . . . does most justice to the overlapping of the writer's three main ideas: (i) *Christ's supremecy as God's word to man*. This is announced at the beginning, and developed by two contrasts, with the angels (1:5–14) and with Moses (3:1–6). (ii) *Christ's supremacy as man's way to God*. This proves to be more important than (i). It begins in 2:5–18, develops in 4:14–5:10, and is fully expounded in chapters 7–10. (iii) *The need for faithfulness*. This is urged as a consequence of (i) and (ii). It appears, chiefly in its negative form of warning, in the first four sections of exhortation . . . and, more positively, in chapters 11 and 12.

J. H. Davies. *A Letter to Hebrews* (Cambridge, Cambridge University Press, 1967), pp. 1, 13–16

The title "to the Hebrews" is undoubtedly secondary. It serves, however . . . to characterize the document as a letter and to assimilate it formally to Pauline letters by referring to recipients in a particular area, which is a feature otherwise peculiar to the Pauline letters. But can we really call it a "letter"? The conclusion, where we are told that the author has written briefly to his readers (xiii. 22–25), suggests that we can reasonably do so. Besides, quite apart from the greeting, there are a number of observations which clearly suggest a letter. On the other hand, it is surprising that it begins without preface. It has sometimes been supposed that this is connected with the near-eastern letter form, which was a development from the oral message in which the messenger expressed the greeting and then delivered the substance of the message. If this message was given to the messenger in writing, he would read it aloud after he had delivered the greeting, but if the message was sent without a special messenger the address was written on the cover. In the letter itself, therefore, the preface was sometimes omitted. . . .

The description that most readily springs to mind for i. 1–xiii. 21 is that of a "treatise." But as the style, train of thought and method of argument show many parallels with the form of the Jewish-Hellenistic homily, an even better description for i. 1–xiii. 21 would be that of a "sermon." In any case the author was obviously familiar with the rhetorical rules of synagogue preaching. If what we have here is really the form of the homily . . . then the lack of a preface is no longer suprising and the ending in xiii. 21 also become intelligibile. . . .

It is possible to imagine circumstances in which the author might have composed his work in the literary form of the synagogue sermon, although he thought of it from the start as a "letter," but if this were the case it would be difficult to understand why his "homily" says much less about the readers and their situation than one would expect in a document addressed to particular circle of readers. Finally, we must allow for the possiblity that xiii. 22–25 is purely fictitious in character. . . . In this case we should not think in terms of any particular "recipients" of the letter who can be geographically located, but of "readers" whose particular situations vary greatly but have general features in common. In other words, the author is addressing his own times in his homily. . . .

It is obvious that the author makes use of a familiar baptismal confession (cf. iii. 1; iv. 14; x. 19 ff.), which he applies by way of interpretation to the situation of the church. He begins with the declaration of the glory of the

Son of God who is now exalted over all, expressed in hymn-like language (ch. 1). . . .

The standpoint of Heb. has a great structural similarity to that of Rev. . . . The important thing is not to think of the unique events merely as something that happened in the past, but to take one's stand upon them now. The readers' gaze is directed to the consummation . . . in order that they will be able to endure in the midst of all that threatens them and continue on their journey with confidence.

W. Marxsen, Introduction to the New Testament, trans.
G. Buswell (Philadelphia, Fortress Press, 1968), pp.
217–218, 220–221

Faith is the subject of an encomium found in Hebrews 11–12:2. The encomium begins with a brief definition of exactly what quality will be praised (vs. 1). The second verse adds the idea that such faith has divine sanction: "For by it the men of old received divine approval." The motif of ancient and distinguished ancestry is latent in the idea that it is men "of old" who possessed this kind of faith.

The main part of the encomium, beginning with verse 3, is a catalog of the mighty acts of faith. Part of the artistry of the list comes from the repeated formula used to introduce the illustrations: "By faith. . . ." The repetition of sentences beginning with this phrase has a tremendous cumulative effect as the catalog progresses. The structural principle underlying the list is historical chronology. We begin with an allusion to the creation of the world (vs. 3) and then march straight through Old Testament history: Abel (vs. 4), Enoch (vs. 5), Noah (vs. 7), Abraham (vss. 8–19), Isaac (vs. 20), Jacob (vs. 21), Joseph (vs. 22), Moses (vss. 23–28), the Isrealites who lived through the exodus and conquest (vss. 29–31), the judges and kings (vs. 32). This means that the chief literary device used in the encomium is allusion, with the writer managing to evoke all kinds of positive reponses to his subject (faith) by linking it to the high points of the national history of his Hebrew audience. . . .

The catalog ends with a rhetorical flourish that carries the reader along by means of its sheer eloquence. The passage begins with the inexpressibility motif. The acts of faith are so numerous that the writer declines even to try to recount them all: "And what more shall I say? For time would fail me to tell of Gideon, Barak, Samson, Jephthah, of David and Samuel and the prophets" (vs. 32). Then, in a passage replete with parallelism, we get a whole barrage of mighty acts of faith (vss. 33–38). . . .

The first two verses of Hebrews 12 complete the enomium with a conventional motif, the command to emulate. . . . The writer, in a brilliant stroke, allows the reader to place himself in a long and distinguished line of heroes. To call the heroes of faith "witnesses" is to use a metaphor from the courtroom, conveying the idea that they testify to the reality and worthwhileness of faith in God. Calling these Old Testament characters a "cloud" of witnesses is a veiled allusion to the pillar of cloud used by God to guide the Israelites through the wilderness. The implication is significant: the heroes of faith listed in Hebrews 11 are intended to serve as a guide and model for believers of later ages. Appropriately, Jesus is held up as the crowning example of faith to whom the reader is urged to look for guidance and the very perfection of his own faith.

> Leland Ryken. *The Literature of the Bible* (Grand Rapids, Zondervan, 1974), pp. 210–212

Christian literature, whether devotional or scholarly, frequently makes reference to a pilgrimage motif in the book of Hebrews. The idea of pilgrimage itself, however, is increasingly remote in western man's thought: the modern concept is a vague amalgam of Pilgrim Fathers, Canterbury Tales and *Pilgrim's Progress*. Consequently, allusions to pilgrimage in Hebrews lack precision. . . .

H.B. Partin . . . has set out the religious "structure" of pilgrimage. He finds four essential elements:

(1) Pilgrimage entails a separation, a leaving home. . . .

(2) Pilgrimage involves a journey to a sacred *place*. The mere act of religious wandering in itself does not constitute pilgrimage.

(3) Pilgrimage is made for a fixed *purpose*, such as purification or forgiveness of sins. The attainment of this purpose is linked to arrival at a sacred place.

(4) Pilgrimage involves *hardship*. Physical difficulties and religious trials make the threat of failure a grim possiblity. . . .

The phenomenological model of Partin is satisfied at each point by the data of Hebrews. . . .

(1) The idea of having left home (separation) is strong in Hebrews. . . .

(2) Their journeyings are not aimless wanderings: they have their eyes fixed on "the city which has foundations, whose builder and maker is God" (11:10). This is the "real" city, for it is invisible. . . .

(3) Likewise with purpose: the Christians' journeying signifies a dissatisfaction with what is "home" to others, pointing to a translation of values in which the "real"—the supreme value—is to be found only beyond the world. . . .

(4) But the way is difficult. There are perils, both physical and spiritual. Sin beckons with its pleasures as of deceitful power to erode faith and faithfulness. . . .

It seems incontestable that the pilgrimage motif as found in Hebrews displays parallels with the phenomenological model of pilgrimage. Partin's work is even more enlightening, however. In his concluding discussion of pilgrimage as a religious phenomenon, he argues that the practice *in toto* is to be viewed as a *rite de passage*, i.e., a religious transition from the profane to the sacred. The three stages in such rites—separation, transition, and incorporation—apply to pilgrimage: separation indicates those rites of leave-taking; transition those rites along the way, obligatory for the pilgrim community; and incorporation those rites at the sacred place itself. Likewise with Hebrews: the three states parallel the eschatological pattern of the book:

Then (past)	separation (baptism, persecution)
Now (present)	transition (journeying, proleptic participation)
Not Yet (future)	incorporation (attainment of the city, see God)

This understanding of Hebrews in terms of the religious "structure" of pilgrimage enables us to appreciate better what is possibly the most arresting passage of Hebrews: 12:18–29. . . .

It is apparent that the pilgrimage motif in Hebrews displays features other than those developed in Partin's model. In at least three significant points—the figure of Jesus, the nature of the goal, and the concern with an event in the past—Hebrews cuts its own path. . . .

We now discern the manner in which the pilgrimage motif is integrated into the overall structure of Hebrews. Divorcing ourselves from common (loose) definitions of pilgrimage and seeing it as its own deeply religious form, we see that the Christians of Hebrews are viewed as a *cultic community on the move*.

William G. Johnsson. *JBL*. 97, 1978, pp. 239, 244–249

HUMOR

Certain conventions of Christianity have made its founder the gloomiest visage in history. . . . Such a nature, so responsive, so subtle, so rich in emotions, in imagination, in understanding of his fellow-men, would have been an anomaly had it marked and felt only the tragedy, never the comedy, of the incongruous. But we need not altogether theorize: a few of his jests are on record.

According to the first chapter of the earliest gospel, Jesus founded his little order with a jest. . . .Jesus was passing one day along by the sea of Galilee; and he saw Simon and Andrew, the brother of Simon, casting a net into the sea, for they were fishers. And Jesus said unto them, "Come ye after me, and I will make you to become fishers of men". . . .

His fancy indulged at times in grotesque exaggerations, which need but to be pictured by us as they were by his original auditors to be recognized at once. The picture of a busybody with a stick of timber in his eye, solicitous for the sight of a neighbor with a fleck of dust in his, is itself ludicrous, and doubly as a type of the fault-finding hypocrite; thus, also, punctiliously to strain out the gnat before drinking a cup of wine, only thereafter to swallow a camel, is ludicrous, and doubly as a type of the punctiliousness and inconsistency of religious formalists. . . .

It was Jesus, too, who conceived the desperate anxiety of self-interest in terms of the short man trying by worrying about it to add a cubit to his stature. . . ; and we remember the comparison of the difficulty of the rich man, worming his way into heaven, with the easier feat of the camel, squeezing, legs, hump, and all, through the eye of a needle.

Thus the Jester could riot in wild and grotesque whimsies; but perhaps oftener to his mood was the delicate humor of a gentle realism: . . . the disgruntled householder roused in the night by an important neighbor come after bread for his guest, and constrained to open the door at last because the man kept up such a merciless knocking; the judge who yielded to the widow, not because he feared God or regarded man, but simply to get rid of her continual coming; the recipients of an unwelcome invitation who straightway began to make conventional excuses, especially the much-married man who could not remain away from his wife. . . .

And may not the Knower of men have smiled . . . at the simple shepherd and the women who, finding their lost possessions, gleefully called in their neighbors to gossip about it all?—or at the unseemly haste of the guests when he marked how they chose out the chief seats? . . . May not a sense of humor have reinforced his appreciation of the zeal of the little Zacchaeus with whom he decided to take lodgings? Was there not grim humor as well as bitter rebuke in his comment on those who think they shall be heard for their much speaking, and on those who disfigure their faces to be seen of men to fast? No man could look through human nature, as Jesus looked through it, without smiling sometimes in very truth.

Humor is as old as speech. Laughter rings round the world. And even Galilee had its mirth; and even we can hear it.

William Ellery Leonard. The Poet of Galilee (New York,
B. W. Huebsch, 1909), pp. 87–93

We are not left to mere conjecture regarding the humor of Jesus. His recorded utterances are before us bearing incontrovertible evidence that his genial spirit found expression in kindly pleasantries and humorous suggestions. His colloquy with the Syrophoenician woman (Mark 7) is a good-natured challenge of a heathen's right to ask anything of him until he has attended to all the applications of his own people. The mother's rejoinder is unmistakably witty, and is apparently very much relished by Jesus. . . .

Observe his quaint characterization of those who carefully cleanse the outside of the cup and platter, forgetting that they drink and feed from the inside of these vessels; of men who carefully strain out a gnat but incontinently swallow a camel. Notice how he hits off the absurdity of trying to serve two masters, of feeding pearls to swine, of putting a light under a bushel, of proffering a stone for bread. . . . What a grotesque thing it is for a camel to try to squeeze through the eye of a needle, or for a blind man to attempt to lead another sightless mortal, with the result that both pitch into the gutter. How preposterous it is for a man with a beam in his eye to offer to remove a mote from his brother's eye. Consider the ludicrous plight of the architect who places a house on the shifting sands, of the general who goes to war without thinking it worthwhile to estimate the possible resources of his enemy, of the man who makes himself the laughing-stock of his town by commencing to build a tower which he has no means to finish. These are delicious bits of our Lord's humor with a high moral purpose.

. . . Remember the pathetic humor of his response when the Pharisees warned him that Herod was on his track: "Go ye, and tell that fox, Behold, I cast out devils, and I do cures to-day and to-morrow, and the third day I shall be perfected . . . for it cannot be that a prophet perish out of Jerusalem." . . . Run through his parables, and observe how rich a vein of humor pervades all of the more important ones.

George P. Eckman. *The Literary Primacy of the Bible* (New York, Methodist Book Concern, 1915), pp. 119–121

We read again and again of the interest men and women found in [Jesus'] preaching and teaching—how they hung on him to hear him, how they came in crowds, how on one occasion they drove him into a boat for a pulpit. It is only familiarity that has blinded us to the "charm" they found in his speech—"they marveled at his words of charm" (Luke iv. 22)—to the gaiety and playfulness that light up his lessons. . . .

[One example] is that of the Pharisee's drinking operations. We are shown the man polishing his cup, elaborately and carefully; for he lays great importance on the cleanness of his cup; but he forgets to clean the inside. Most people drink from the inside, but the Pharisee forgot it, dirty as it was, and left it untouched. Then he sets about straining what he is going to drink—another elaborate process; he holds a piece of muslin over the cup and pours with care; he pauses—he sees a mosquito; he has caught it in time and flicks it away; he is safe and he will not swallow it. And then, adds Jesus, he has swallowed a camel. How many of us have ever pictured the process, and the series of sensations, as the long hairy neck slid down the throat of the Pharisee—all that amplitude of loose-hung anatomy—the hump—two humps—both of them slid down—and he never noticed—and the legs—all of them—with whole outfit of knees and big padded feet. The Pharisee swallowed a camel—and never noticed it (Matt. xxiii. 24, 25). It is the mixture of sheer realism with absurdity that makes the irony and gives it its force. Did no one smile as the story was told? Did no one see the scene pictured with his own mind's eye—no one grasp the humor and the irony with delight? Could any one, on the other hand, forget it?

T. R. Glover. *The Jesus of History* (New York, Association Press, 1926), pp. 47–48

Any attempt to discover why Jesus used humor and how he employed it is limited not only by our tendency to view first-century situations through 20th-century eyes, but also by the traditional gravity with which the New Testament is read. We have not been moved to laughter because we have regarded the gospel message as essentially solemn—as though it were written on pages bordered in black, like Victorian funeral notices.

It is not particularly difficult, though, to recognize several cases in which Jesus, the master public speaker, seems to have employed humor for its catalytic effect upon listeners.

Modern readers tend to see nothing but the text of a sermon in the saying recorded in Matthew 11:7 (cf. Luke 7:24–25). But Jesus was speaking to herdsmen and farmers—men accustomed to outdoor life who had gone to considerable trouble to hear that strange zealot whom they called John the Baptist.

" 'What did you go out into the wilderness to behold?' " Jesus demanded. " 'A reed shaken by the wind?' "

One can almost hear him pausing for laughter before adding the jibe: " 'Why then did you go out? To see a man clothed in soft raiment?' " Obviously, a dandy was the last person one would seek in the Palestinian desert. . . .

Other statements appear incongruous and laugh-provoking when seen from the viewpoint of Jesus' actual hearers. More than once he referred to such brilliant exploits as lighting a lamp and placing it "under a bushel, or under a bed." (Mark 4:21; Luke 11:33; Luke 8:16) He asked his followers to imagine one blind man asking another blind man to guide him. (Luke 6:39)

And he told a delightfully refreshing story about the stupidity of a group of young women who went to an all-night party without sufficient oil for their lamps. That was like the modern lass who starts on a long trip without checking the gas tank of her car. . . .

Analyzing the problem of self-criticism in religious leadership, he used language perfectly familiar to men who worked with their hands. " 'Why do you see the speck that is in your brother's eye, but do not notice the log that is in your own eye?' "

In this passage, humor grows out of exaggeration—a special form of incongruity. Notice, however, that this is not laughter for its own sake. This is a polemic, directed against religious legalists and designed to discredit them. . . .

In addition to these relatively lengthy instances in which humor was a more or less prominent factor, there are dozens of cases where Jesus seems to have engaged in word play. He took delight in epigrams and near puns, used words with such invigorating freshness that nearly everything he said can be read in more than one sense. . . .

In terms of sheer bulk, the humor of Jesus is of more than passing importance. He employed laughter both as a device for gaining listener interest and as a weapon in his attack upon established ideas.

Gary Webster. Laughter in the Bible (St. Louis, Bethany Press, 1960), pp. 109–112, 115–116

The germ of the idea which has finally led to the writing of this book was planted many years ago when our eldest son was four years old. We were reading to him from the seventh chapter of Matthew's Gospel, feeling very serious, when suddenly the little boy began to laugh. He laughed because he saw how preposterous it would be for a man to be so deeply concerned about a speck in another person's eye, that he was unconscious of the fact his own eye had a beam in it. Because the child understood perfectly that the human eye is not large enough to have a beam in it, the very idea struck him as ludicrous. . . .

One reason for our failure to laugh is our extreme familiarity with the received text. The words seem to us like old coins, in which the edges have been worn smooth and the engravings have become almost indistinguishable. . . .

A second reason for our widespread failure to recognize the humor of the Gospels is their great stress upon the tragedy of the crucifixion and the events immediately preceding it. . . . The events of Good Friday and Easter, because of their dramatic appeal and profound significance, began, very early in Christian history, to occupy the center of interest. Because the tragic aspect is intrinsically unhumorous, men came to see the sad picture as the whole picture. . . .

We have many reasons for being grateful for the production of the Synoptic Gospels, but one of the greatest reasons is that they provide a powerful antidote to the subsequent distortion. The Person they present has many contrasting features. He is a Man of Sorrows, but He is also a Man of Joys; He uses terribly rough and blunt language; He expresses blazing anger; He teases. . . .

Perhaps our greatest failure in creating a false picture of Christ has been a failure of logic. We assume that an assertion of sadness entails a denial of humor, but there is no good reason to suppose that such is the case. There is abundant evidence to show that contrasting elements of character, far from being mutually incompatable, are often complementary. The fact that Christ laughed does not, and need not, mean that He did not also weep. . . .

We make a mistake if, in studying the Gospels, and watching for evidence of humor, we look only for that which brings full laughter. Frequently there is only a slight touch of humor. . . . Often the smile comes because Jesus reveals to us some of the absurdity of our own lives, where we need help to recognize it. A good illustration of this is . . . the story of the judge who would not help the mistreated widow because her cause was just, yet finally helped her because he got tired of being bothered. He found it easier to do the right thing than to be pestered forever (Luke 18: 1–5)! . . .

It is very important to understand that the evident purpose of Christ's humor is to clarify and increase understanding, rather than to hurt. Perhaps some hurt is inevitable, especially when . . . human pride is rendered ridiculous, but the clear aim is something other than harm. . . . Most of Christ's humor belongs to what Meredith calls "the laughter of comedy." . . . The satirist may work on a "storage of bile," but this seems utterly absent in the humor preserved in the Gospels. The attack may be strong, when the object is the Pharisaic spirit, but it is not an attack upon an individual Pharisee.

Elton Trueblood. *The Humor of Christ* (New York, Harper and Row, 1964), pp. 9, 19–21, 50–51

Let us turn first to the commonly ignored element of the book which I should like to underscore here simply because it is so little noted: this is its humor of which there is a surprising amount. . . . In the teachings of Jesus, especially in his response to questions and objections, we find the humor of the well-turned phrase and the apt repartee which is close to the heart of true wit. Even Peter can be made the butt of a significant thrust of humor which throws light on the imperceptive response of even the most faithful men to Jesus' entire ministry when, at the Last Supper, Jesus comes to wash Peter's feet, and Peter impetuously asks him to wash "not my feet only, but also my hands and head" (John 13:6–10). Indeed, a remarkable element in Peter's greatness as the leader of the apostles is shown by the fact that his fellow Christians not only preserved accounts of his betrayal of Jesus but also treasured the story of his ridiculous reaction to the transfiguration of Jesus in the presence of Moses and Elijah. (See Luke 22:55–62 and 9:33.) If the one instance was tragic and utterly unfunny, the other preserved an attractively humorous insight into Peter's complex character. It was possible not only to admire and even revere Peter, but to see his weakness and to smile at his follies.

Roland M. Frye. "Introduction," *The Bible: Selections from the King James Version for Study as Literature* (Boston, Houghton Mifflin, 1965; rpt. Princeton University Press, 1977), pp. xii–xiii

HYMN
(See also: *Luke, Gospel of, Nativity Hymns.*)

In I Cor. xiv, 26 Paul speaks of each having a psalm. . . . He presupposes the regular use of such hymns (Col. iii, 16) in public worship and employs a number of expressions for them. Thus we may infer that there was a certain wealth of materials of this character in the early Christian period. This is quite comprehensible if a fund of hymns of Jewish origin were brought by converted Jews into the public worship of the Christians, and if these hymns were given a Christian transformation. We find an interesting example of such transformation in the two hymns introduced according to an ancient narrative custom into the record of Luke I, viz. the Magnificat of Mary (i, 46–55) and the Benedictus of Zechariah (i, 68–79)—the Latin names to which we are accustomed are the first words in the hymns. If we read the texts, but omit the verses which refer to the story (i, 48 and i, 76–9), we shall find that they contain nothing Christian, but are only a Jewish laudation of the Messiah.

We must pass a similar judgment upon the numerous short hymns which occur in the Revelation of John. . . .

Apart from the hymns which have a special relationship to the events seen by the seer, there remains a considerable number which gives us a conception of the nature of early Christian hymns. Some may have come from Judaism just as they stand (Rev. vii, 12; xv, 3,4; xix, 5). In other cases the Christian element can be separated out (v,13; vii, 10; xii, 10–12). Others, such as the hymns to the Lamb (v,12; xix, 6–8), are entirely Christian. . . . Certain other citations in the New Testament may come from hymns, e.g. Eph. v,14, and especially I Tim. iii, 16, which is a fragment in three couplets arranged not historically but purely rhetorically, and on this very account possessing poetic character. Probably also Matt. xi, 5 and I Cor. ii, 9 come from hymns.

> Martin Dibelius. *A Fresh Approach to the New Testament and Early Christian Literature* (New York, Charles Scribners's Sons, 1936), pp. 246–247

Ephesians v, 14 is usually regarded as the most cogent example of early Christian hymnology. . . .

As a whole the verse contains an invocational appeal addressed to the Christian and summoning him to action. At the same time it offers him the promise of Divine favour and aid. The first two lines are a rousing summons to moral activity; and the third line is the accompanying promise of God.

In view of these contents, couched in the language of exhortation and using a combination of metaphors (sleep, death, light) applied to the spiritual life of the Christian at his conversion and entry into the Church's fellowship, the most natural event with which the verse is to be associated is Christian baptism. . . .

Those features which make Ephesian v, 14 stand out from its context are to be found in other places also. Scholars have looked for passages which have a lyrical quality and rhythmical style, an unusual vocabulary which is different from the surrounding context of the letter in which the passage appears, some distinctive piece of Christian doctrine (usually associated with the Person and work of our Lord Jesus Christ) and hints that the passage in question finds its natural setting in a baptismal or Communion service. From these features it is possible to identify and classify with a reasonable degree of accuracy and certainty the following New Testament hymns.

(i) 1 Timothy iii, 16
After an introductory sentence: 'Great indeed, we confess, is the mystery of our religion,' the verse falls into six lines of rich truth concerning the Person and action of Jesus Christ. By a series of antithetical couplets in which a second line complements the thought of the first line, the Gospel message of the Church's Lord is set forth. It treats of two world orders, the divine and the human; and shows how Christ has brought together the two spheres by His coming from the glory of the Father's presence into this world . . . and by His lifting up of humanity back again into the divine realm. Thus heaven and earth are joined, and God and man reconciled. . . .

(ii) Philippians ii, 6–11
. . . This is one of the finest Christological portions in the New Testament, and powerfully portrays the drama of Christ's pre-temporal glory with the Father, His abasement and obedience upon earth, even to the death of the Cross, and His exaltation to God's presence and cosmic triumph and lordship which all the spiritual powers confess. There are various suggestions as to how the verses should be arranged. An analysis into a six-stanza hymn or a three-verse hymn are some widely accepted proposals. . . .

(iii) Colossians i, 15–20
. . . The two stanzas cover two subjects: Christ and the creation (verses 15–18a) and Christ and the Church (verses 18b–20). Moreover, the two parts are

comparable in a number of ways and certain stylistic peculiarities are present which cannot be there by chance. For example, we may note the repetition of words and phrases in the two halves, and in some cases the words are repeated in exactly the same position in each stanza. . . .

(iv) Hebrews i, 3

. . . By the threefold test of theological content, stylistic construction and unusual vocabulary we may confidently assess this verse to be a Christ-hymn. . . .

To the passages above may be added: John i, 1–14; 1 Peter i, 18–21; ii, 21–25; ii, 18–22; and parts of the Revelation which contain distinctively Christian adoration (e.g., v, 9f.; 12; xii, 10–12; xix, 1 ff.).

> Ralph P. Martin. *Worship in the Early Church* (1964; rpt. Grand Rapids: William B. Eerdmans, 1974), pp. 47–52

A tentative list of passages treated as hymnic by various scholars can be made, with the reservation that identification of precise hymnic boundaries or definite hymnic structure for any particular passage is often hotly disputed by critics. The categories often overlap. . . .

Sacramental—Baptismal and Eucharistic: Eph. 2:19–22 (14–18?), 5:14 ("Awake, O sleeper, and arise from the dead, and Christ shall give you light"); Titus 3:4–7; Rom. 6:1–11(?); Col. 2:9–15.

Initiation Hymns: Eph. 2:4–10; Rom. 3:23–25; Titus 2:11–14, 3:3–7; 2 Tim. 1:9–10 (Eph. 1:3–12, Col. 1:12–20).

Confessional: 1 Tim. 6:11–16; 2 Tim. 2:11–13; Col. 3:16; Eph. 5:19; Heb. 13:15.

Christ Hymns: Heb. 1:2–4, 5:5, 7:1–3; Col. 1:15–20; Phil. 2:6–11; 1 Pet. 1:18–20, 2:21–24, 3:18–22; 1 Tim. 3:16.

Hymnlike meditations: Eph. 1:3–14; Rom. 8:31–39; 1 Cor. 13 (12:31–14:1?).

Scriptural Centos: Rom. 9:33, 1 Pet. 2:6–7.

Means of identifying hymnic and liturgical materials are similar to those used for identifying confessional materials; in addition . . . , hymnlike passages are frequently opened by a relative clause and continued by participles; rhythmical quality is pronounced; conscious parallelism or other grammatical features may be present; rare terms or terms unique to an author in this particular passage may produce an elevated style; introductory formulae may be used (Eph. 5:14, "Therefore it is said, . . ."); concluding statements may summarize the point of the quotation; and part of the contents of the passage may be extraneous to the reasons why the material has been inserted.

> William G. Doty. *Letters in Primitive Christianity* (Philadelphia, Fortress Press, 1973), pp. 61–62

One distinct advantage of reading the Old Testament in a modern version is that one is able to see at a glance which parts of the text are cast in poetic and hymnic style. . . .

The reader of the New Testament needs the same guidance to show him at a moment's glance what are the poetic portions of the literature. The more apparent examples come in Luke 1, 2 which preserve some early canticles doubtless treasured in the Jewish Christian community, and possibly forming part of their liturgical worship. These are the *Magnificat* (Lk. 1:45–55), the *Benedictus* (Lk. 1:68–79), and the *Nunc Dimittis* (Lk. 2:29–32). All the Latin titles are drawn from the opening words of the poetic pieces. . . .

Snatches of hymnody based on the Old Testament model are seen in the Apocalypse of John. Scattered through the series of visions are songs of the heavenly world (Rev. 4:11; 11:17, 18; 14:7; 15:3, 4). . . .

Poetic and hymnic forms were more consciously adopted and made the vehicle of theological expression in the era when the church moved out into the hellenistic world. Three prime examples of this style of writing are seen in the Pauline corpus. . . .

1 Timothy 3:16. The chief literary feature here is the use of antithesis to express two stages of Christ's existence. These are denoted . . . by the terms: flesh/spirit (cf. 2 Cor. 5:16 for the formula).

Since the pioneering work of E. Norden, other literary forms have been detected in this short, creed-like statement. The authority for these forms is the rhetorician Quintilian in his *Institutio Oratoria*. The repetition of the verb at the beginning of each line and in the same grammatical form produces a species of rhythm known as *parison* and *homoioptoton*. . . .

Ephesians 5:14. This single verse provides another good example of Greek poetic structure. The text of this baptismal chant divides into three lines. . . .

Philippians 2:6–11. Since Lohmeyer's study this passage has been recognized as hymnic in form and capable of division into strophes. Lohmeyer postulated six such stanzas. Later attempts to improve on this arrangement produced a three strophe hymn in which the device of *parallelismus membrorum* was utilized and a tacit acceptance was given to Aristotle's judgment that a perfect literary composition requires ''a beginning, a middle and an end'' (*Poetics* 145b 26). This is held to correspond to the three states of Christ: pre-existent, incarnate, enthroned. . . .

It may be thought that the classification of parts of the New Testament according to the basic patterns of poetic and hymnic form is an interesting exercise but nothing more. This is not so. . . .

We see that much of the hymnic language is poetic and suggestive of deep spiritual reality rather than prosaic and pedestrian. The early Christians . . . were seeking to interpret their understanding of God's salvation in a way which defied rational and coherent statement. Hence they had recourse to the language of symbol and "myth". Examples of the symbolism used in the hymns will come readily to mind, e.g. the imagery of light and darkness; Christ is likened to the sun which banished gloom and the shadows; the totality of the universe is summed up in phrases such as "every knee should bow, in heaven and on earth and under the earth" (Phil. 2:10), or "thrones or dominions or principalities or authorities" (Col. 1:16).

Ralph P. Martin. "Approaches to New Testament Exegesis," in *New Testament Interpretation*, ed. I. Howard Marshall (Grand Rapids, William B. Eerdmans, 1977), pp. 235, 237–240

JAMES

All the more striking is the abundant illustration which the Epistle of James receives from both the manner and the substance of Hellenistic popular moral addresses, or Diatribes. . . .

It is not strange that the diatribe had a profound and far-reaching effect on the forms of Christian literature for centuries, that its influence is clearly traceable in the epistles of Paul, and that it serves to explain much, both of the form and the content, of the Epistle of James.

To the most characteristic traits of the style of the diatribe belong the truncated dialogue with an imaginery interlocutor . . . and the brief question and answer. . . . Good instances of both are found in Jas. 2:18f. and Jas. 5:13f. These traits serve well to illustrate the aim of immediate impression, appropriate to popular hortatory address, which has largely controlled the formation of this literary type. . . .

The transitions are often made in the same way as with the Greek sermonisers—by raising an objection (2:8), by a question (2:14, 4:1, 5:13). . . . The imperatives are not only numerous (nearly sixty times in the 108 verses), but, as in the diatribes, are sometimes ironical (5:1, perhaps 4:9). Rhetorical questions (e.g., 2:4, 5, 14–16; 3:11f; 4:4f.) are numerous, and 4:1f. shows the characteristic form of statement by "catechism-like" question and answer. The apostrophe to the traders and the rich (4:12–5:6) is quite in the style of the diatribe, and does not in the least imply that the persons addressed were expected to be among the readers of the tract. Even personifications are not lacking (1:15; 2:13; 4:1; 5:8f.). . . . Figures are abundant in all kinds of popular address, but in those of James there is direct resemblence to the diatribes. Some comparisons are conventional, traceable for centuries previous in Greek writers (especially, with others, the rudder, the bridle, the forest fire, in 3:3–6); as in the diatribes, many are drawn from the works of nature, others from the common life of man (1:25; 2:15; 5:7), and they are sometimes double or with repetition (3:3–6, 10–12). Examples from famous individuals are found here, too (Abraham, Rahab, Job, Elijah), and they are, as with the Greek preachers, stock instances, well-known representatives of the qualities mentioned.

In general the Greek preachers were well aware that in their diatribes they were awakening sinners and inculcating familiar but neglected principles, not engaged in investigating truth or in carrying thought further to the conquest of the unknown. Not originality but impressiveness was what they aimed at. The argument is from what the readers already know and ought to feel. They appeal to analogy (cf. Jas. *passim*). Harsh address to the reader is not absent in James. . . .

Other traits of style show resemblance. As in the diatribes, there is a general controlling motive in the discussion, but no firm and logically disposed structure giving a strict unity to the whole, and no trace of the conventional arrangement recommended by the elegant rhetoricians. The method of framing the sections in by a general statement at opening and close is to be seen in James at 1:2–12, 19–26; 2:17–26; 3:11–12, 13–18. The characteristic methods of concluding a section are found: by a sharp antithesis, 1:26; 2:13, 26; 3:15–18; 4:12; by a question, 4:12, 5:6; by a quotation, 5:20. . . . A key-word often runs through a passage, or is repeated so as to give a sense of reference back. . . .

Like a diatribe, the epistle begins with a paradox (1:2) and contains others (1:10, 2:5). The general principle that popular estimates of values are false and must be reversed underlies James. . . .

Of course, any one of these traits of language, style, and mode of thought could be paralleled from other types of literature. What is significant and conclusive is the combination in these few pages of James of so many of the most striking features of a specific literary type familiar in the contemporary Hellenistic world. The inference from details is confirmed by the general tone and character of the whole epistle—direct, plain, earnest, sensible—lively, even on occasion descriptive and dramatic (cf. 2:1ff.), full of illustration and concrete application—not aiming at profundity of speculation, popular and hortatory throughout.

James Hardy Ropes. *A Critical and Exegetical Commentary on the Epistle of St. James* (New York, Charles Scribner's Sons, 1916), pp. 10, 12–15

The style is short and energetic, with a certain ruggedness resulting from the high moral tension at which the author writes. . . . The phrasing has a force and pungency, which convey the impression of character and conviction, accompanied by gifts of illustration and of racy observation, such as lend charm and physiognomy to Bunyan's prose. In its colloquial turns and interrogations, its dramatic forms of address and second-person appeal, the work is clearly that of the preacher rather than the pamphleteer, and of the preacher of the aphoristic and prophetic not the homiletic type, the preacher of few words intensely felt, having the accent 'of authority and not as the scribes.' The adages and maxims introduced, such as '*Slow to speak, slow to wrath'* (i. 19), *'Mercy glorieth against judgment'* (ii. 13), *'Faith without works is dead'* (ii. 26), are not impromptus, but summaries of reflection and experience, familiar probably upon his lips. . . .

Metaphor is a feature of his style—more frequent and vivid than in any other of the Epistles. Its general character is aphoristic—reminding us of the Synoptic teaching of our Lord—enforcing moral truths by similitudes from nature. These are drawn in part from the language of the prophets and of the Wisdom literature (i. 11, iii. 18, iv. 6, v. 2, 5), in part from personal experience. In all the latter, the colouring is genuinely Palestinian, from scenery familiar to St. James. Some are from peasant life (iii. 18), like that of the husbandman, long-suffering in expectation of *'the early and the latter rain'* (v. 7). The culture is of the fig, the olive and the vine (iii. 12). Even more local is that of *'the sun rising with the scorching wind'* (i. 11). . . *'and withering the grass,'* worked out in terms adapted from Isaiah, Job and Jonah. Others are maritime, drawn from the Sea of Galilee, and vividly impressionist: *'The light spray whisked . . . from the curling wave'* (i. 6) is his picture of instability; and yet more vivid is the presentment in iii. 4—*'Look again at the boats, big as they are and driven by gusty squalls, yet veered by a tiny blade, as the stroke of the steerer listeth.'*

> Gerald H. Rendall. *The Epistle of St. James and Judaic Christianity* (Cambridge, Cambridge University Press, 1927), pp. 34–35, 37–38

The Epistle of James is today usually regarded as either a general epistle or as a sermon. Both descriptions are accurate but fall short of characterizing the letter. It is actually a Wisdom teaching which was dictated and distributed as a general letter. Its conglomerate impersonal nature would be disconcerting in a personal letter, but it is typical of Wisdom products. Like the Wisdom teachings of Jesus, it is not an overt attempt at literature but the transcription of verbal instruction. It does not personify Wisdom, nor does it use the parallelism of Jewish poetry. The factors which merit its classification as Wisdom literature are: its use of proverbs and parables, its teaching of universally applicable moral truths, and its use of traditional Wisdom themes.

The proverbs employed or coined in James include those on the dangers of injudicious speech, a Wisdom theme. The epistle says, "The tongue can no man tame; it is an unruly evil, full of deadly poison" (3:8). . . . Proverbs had handled the same theme thus—"In many words sin will not be absent; but he who holds his tongue is wise" (Prov. 10:19). . . . Other Wisdom themes among these proverbs are humility (4: 6b; 4:10), the folly of trusting riches (1:10,11), and the final authority of God (4:14, b + c).

The parables in the epistle treat similar themes. The parable of the self-sufficient (4: 13–16) contains the proverb "Life is a vapor which appears for a little while and vanishes away." The parable itself is an elaboration of the theme expressed by Proverbs 27:1, "Boast not of tomorrow, for you know not what a day may produce. . . ."

Terence Y. Mullins. *JBL*. 68, 1949, pp. 338–339

The brief Epistle of James shares many of the literary characteristics of the Epistle to the Hebrews. It too is written in excellent Greek and in a strikingly elevated and picturesque style resembling that of the Hebrew prophets. Though the tone is distinctly Jewish, there are very few Hebraisms in the epistle. . . . As to his vocabulary, he freely employs rare words and compounds, all of them correctly formed and some of them possibly formed by himself. He shows great rhetorical skill, making use of not a few figures of speech which were affected by the best koine authors. He exhibits a marked tendency to link together clauses and sentences by the repetition of the leading word or some of its cognates, a device known as paronomasia or assonance. . . .

On the whole his sentence structure is terse, vivid, and rhythmical, being marked by a certin epigrammatic conciseness.

Bruce M. Metzger. "The Language of the New Testament," *Interpreter's Bible*, Vol. 7 (Nashville, Abingdon Press, 1951), p. 47

The Epistle may be considered to best advantage as a series of eight homiletic-didactic discourses. Each discourse has a principal theme but is developed either by way of a series of subsidiary topics or by a list of appropriate *exempla*. Skilful use of word-links and thematic recapitulations knit together the several sections into a single whole, which the author presents in the form of a literary epistle. The varied sources of the author, whether oral or written, are freely adapted to suit his own style and interest. The main discourses or sections may be briefly outlined as follows:

	Greeting	1:1
1.	Endurance of Trials	1:2–18
2.	Hearing and Doing	1:19–27
3.	Respect of Persons	2:1–13
4.	Faith and Works	2:14–26
5.	Evil-speaking	3:1–12
6.	Factiousness	3:13–4:10
	Recapitulation	4:11–12
7.	Two Woes: On the Rich	4:13–5:6
8.	Patience	5:7–18
	Summary	5:19–20

Most of these discourses are built around, or contain, a central *macarism* or gnomic saying, adapted by the author to his particular theme. Thus sections 1 and 8 are based upon a macarism (cf. 1:12 and 5:11) whose original core was something similar to this:

Blessed are those who endure (evil):
For (they) shall receive (good things).
The macarism of sec. 2 is clearly 1:25. The gnomic basis of sec. 3 is more problematic, but it may be embedded either in 2:5 (with an ending similar to the macarism of 1:12) or in 2:10. In sec. 4, the key saying is clearly comparable to 2:20 and 2:26. Sec. 5 has a macarism, 3:2 in which "perfect" has been substituted by the author for "blessed." The gnomic saying of sec. 6 is 4:4. . . . The two Woes of sec. 7 are distinct in form from the other discourses, being in the nature of prophetic denunciations. But they contain a saying in 5:17 that is loosely connected with the context. It may be noted also that secs. 4 and 8 are similar, and distinctive, in structure by their use of *exempla* taken from the OT coupled with illustrations drawn from contemporary church life.

Massey H. Shepherd, Jr. JBL. 75, 1956, pp. 41–42

The principal purpose of the letter is to convince its readers that "faith without works is dead" (2:26). It is clear that the author interprets "faith" to be mere intellectual assent to Jesus' Messiahship and to the truth of his teachings. . . .

The Epistle of James is similar in spirit, style, and content to several other Biblical books. It is similar in spirit and content to some of the Old Testament prophets, notably Amos, Isaiah, and Micah, in their stern condemnation of those who give lip service to God but who fail to perform righteous deeds. . . .

In form and style the epistle sounds like a combination of the Epistle to the Hebrews and the Book of Proverbs, for it is a sermon filled with practical precepts for daily living (notice especially Chapter 3, on "taming the tongue"). It is memorable for its fifty-four imperatives (in 108 verses), its irony, its humor, and its vigor.

Buckner B. Trawick. The Bible as Literature: The New Testament (New York, Barnes and Noble, 1964, 1968), pp. 139–140

JESUS AS POET
(See also entries on *Poetry* **and** *Proverb as a Literary Form*.)

POETIC STYLE

All His words together which have been preserved to us would not occupy more space in print than half-a-dozen ordinary sermons; yet it is not too much to say, that they are the most precious literary heritage of the human race. . . .

The form of preaching of Jesus was essentially Jewish. The Oriental mind does not work in the same way as the mind of the West. Our thinking and speaking, when at their best, are fluent, expansive, closely reasoned. . . . The Oriental mind, on the contrary, loves to brood long on a single point, to turn it round and round, to gather up all the truth about it in a focus, and pour it forth in a few pointed and memorable words. It is concise, epigrammatic, oracular. A Western speaker's discourse is a systematic structure, or like a chain in which link is firmly knit to link; and Oriental's is like the sky at night, full in innumerable burning points shining forth from a dark background.

Such was the form of the teaching of Jesus. It consisted of numerous sayings, every one of which contained the greatest possible amount of truth in the smallest possible compass, and was expressed in language so concise and pointed as to stick in the memory like an arrow. . . . They have found their way into the memory of Christendom as no other words have done. Even before the meaning has been apprehended, the perfect, proverb-like expression lodges itself fast in the mind.

But there was another characteristic of the form of Jesus' teaching. It was full of figures of speech. He thought in images. . . . There were no abstract statements in it; they were all changed into pictures. Thus, in His sayings, we can still see the aspects of the country and the life of the time as in a panorama—the lilies, whose gorgeous beauty His eyes feasted on, waving in the fields; the sheep following the shepherd; the broad and narrow city gates; the virgins with their lamps awaiting in the darkness the bridal possession; . . . and a hundred other pictures that lay bare the inner and minute life of the time.

James Stalker. *The Life of Jesus Christ* (New York,
Fleming H. Revell, 1891), pp. 68–69

Jesus did so much for religion and practical life that his great contribution to literature and artistic beauty has not often been brought to mind. Yet he was "earth's supreme literary artist." Newell Dwight Hillis . . . said: " . . . Charles Dickens was the great master of the pathetic style. When the novelist was asked what is the most touching story in literature, he answered, 'The story of the Produgal Son.' Coleridge took all knowledge to his province, and his conversation sparkled with jewels of thought, yet, when asked for the richest passage in literature, he answered, 'The Beatitudes.' Edmund Kean was a great actor and artist, but there was one passage so full of tears that he thought no man could properly render it—the one beginning, 'Come unto me all ye that labor and are heavy-laden, and I will give you rest.' "

> Herbert R. Purinton and Carl E. Purinton. *Literature of the New Testament* (New York, Charles Scribner's Sons, 1925), p. 89

One of Jesus' great lessons is to get men to look for God in the commonplace things of which God makes so many, as if Abraham Lincoln were right and God did make so many common people, because he likes them best. . . . When Jesus speaks of the very highest and holiest things, he is as simple and natural as when he is making a table in the carpenter-shop. . . .

The sense of fact and the gift for sympathy are the foundations, so to speak, of the imagination which gives their quality to the stories and pictures of Jesus. He thinks in pictures, as it were; they fill his speech, and every one of them is alive and real. Think, for example, of the Light of the world (Matt. v. 14), the strait gate and the narrow way (Matt. vii. 14), the pictures of the bridegroom (Mark ii. 19), sower (Matt. xiii. 3), pearl merchant (Matt. xiii. 45), and the men with the net (Matt. xiii. 47), the sheep among the wolves (Matt. x. 16) . . . , the fall of the house (Matt. vii. 27)—or the ironical pictures of the blind leading the blind straight for the ditch (Matt. xv. 14), the vintagers taking their baskets to the bramble bushes (Matt. vii. 16), the candle burning away brightly under the bushel (Matt. v. 15; Luke xi. 33), the offering of pearls to the pigs (Matt. vii. 6)—or his descriptions of what lay before himself as a cup and a baptism (Mark x. 38), and of his task as the setting fire to the world (Luke xii. 49). There is a truthfulness and a living energy about all these pictures—not least about those touched with irony. . . .

The great "Son of Fact," he went to fact, drove his disciples to fact, and (in the striking phrase of Cromwell) "spoke *things*." And we can see in the record again and again the traces of the mental habits and the natural language of one who habitually based himself on experience and on fact.

> T. R. Glover. *The Jesus of History* (New York, Association Press, 1926), pp. 54–56, 59

Jesus . . . followed Jewish native traditions in many ways.

He adopts all their resources, such as, their use of *metaphor*:

'Ye are the salt of the earth,' 'I am the Bread of life',
of *simile*:
'As a hen gathereth her chickens . . .'
of *allegory*, as in the talk of the Good Shepherd;
of *hyperbole*:
'if thy hand offend thee, cut if off . . .'
of *paradox*:
'he that findeth his life, shall lose it.'
of *rhetorical question* and *irony*:
'if he ask for bread, will he give him a stone?'
of *repetition*:
'If thy hand offend thee, cut if off: it is better for thee . . . (where their worm dieth not . . .), and if they foot offend thee, cut if off: it is better for thee . . . (where their worm dieth not . . .), and if thine eye offend thee, pluck it out: it is better for thee . . . (where their worm dieth not).'
of *parallelism*:
'Heaven and earth shall pass away,
but my words shall not pass away.'
of *apostrophe*:
'O Jerusalem, Jerusalem, that killest the prophets . . .'
of *epigram*:
'the foxes have holes, and the birds of the air have nests,
but the Son of man hath not where to lay his head.'
The cast of this epigram reminds us of Isaiah's
'the ox knoweth his owner, and the ass his master's crib,
but Israel doth not know, my people do not consider.'
The *analogy*, the *balance*, and the *compactness* are similar in both.

P. C. Sands. *Literary Genius of the New Testament* (Oxford, Oxford University Press, 1932), pp. 75–76

The eye that rested on the children at play in the market-place, on the unemployed waiting for work, on the funeral or the wedding procession with its cries of woe or joy, on the eagle or vulture, the raven, the sparrow, the dove, and the field-birds watching the sower and stealing his seed, on the wild flowers and the creatures of the wild, on the sheep and the goats and their patient vigilant herdsmen, on the housewife at her work, and the husbandman on his land, and the fisherman at his nets, and the traveller on his ass or camel, and the Pharisee and publican at worship, was the eye of a poet of nature as well as a prophet of righteousness. . . . His words pulse with poetic emotion. . . .

It is startling to realize how simple and limited is the range of words at His disposal. The vocabulary which He employs is not more ample than a child or a peasant might command. . . . Maxims, counsels, exhortations and ideals that are inexhaustible in their truth and wisdom are turned, even in our childhood, into familiar commonplaces. . . .

At his very homeliest, as when He uses the simile of the hen and her chickens, or the physical analogy of the uncleanness from within the human body that defiles a man, He stands in the Old Testament tradition. It is profoundly significant that in the literatures of the world, modern not less than ancient, the vehicle of literary expression to which the highest value and prestige are accorded has always had the same character, for by common consent it is required of lyric poetry, both by the artist in words and by the reader or the singer, that it shall find utterance only through elemental terms for ideas and emotions which all may share. . . . We demand that the poet shall employ essentially simple and even childlike speech, as if convinced that like the Kingdom of Heaven the realm of poesy is open only to the spiritually humble and lowly, the poor in spirit, the babe at heart.

If as Jesus said, the Seed is the Word, the Sower Himself is seen to be one who on His business travelled light across the field. His equipment is austerely bare, ascetically simple. Although, for example, His message is religious, ethical and spiritual all the way, the words religion and religious, spiritual and ethical, have no place in His store. Unlike us, He does not speak of truth and beauty in the abstract, of feelings, motives, influences, reasons, instincts. He has no word for conscience. For tendency He has no other word than leaven. Even when the innermost things are His theme, He speaks with a lyrical concreteness and directness. He penetrates the depths without sacrifice of clarity and light. . . .

The teaching is Oriental. . . . In its unlaboured simplicity, its swift intuition, and its pervading symbolism, it comes to the more prosaic West with all the piquancy of foreign things, and with the refreshing sound of living water, fresh from eternal springs in the heights above.

William A. Curtis. *Jesus Christ the Teacher* (London, Oxford University Press, 1943), pp. 104–106

He speaks through a kind of poetry, poetry being the authentic language of the space-time vision, using images of the birds, the lily, the vineyard and fig-tree, harvests and the marriage-banquet. . . . His parables are more than stories; they are works of art where the spatial quality of the whole is as important as the time-sequence of events. Jesus speaks through imagery and example. He is less a teacher than a poet and an exemplar, creating the one pattern equally in his mind-pictures and the picture-drama of his life.

Jesus' language is poetry: the poetry comes first, and this he elaborates, but the application he leaves vague, couched often in the most usual terms such as 'Heaven', 'God' and so on. He is a poet before being a theologian. Often he leaves his story uninterpreted. . . . Poetry is not parasitic on the teaching; rather there is a teaching that flowers from the poetry. Jesus thinks naturally through pictorial and emotional associations. The Christian flock is to be compared with sheep or lambs; the disciples are to go out as 'lambs among wolves' (*Luke*, X. 3); Jesus pities the people, 'harassed and dejected', seeing them as 'sheep without a shepherd' (*Matthew*, IX. 36). . . .

We have seen that Jesus' poetry is richly imaginative yet rarely flashes or scintillates. It has an assured mastery and quiet grace. It is homely, realistic and magical.

G. Wilson Knight. *The Christian Renaissance* (London, Methuen and Company, 1962), pp. 16–17, 154, 168

If one examines the words of Jesus in the synoptic Gospels—sayings and parables—one is struck by their artistic form. . . . The sayings of Jesus in the synoptic Gospels do not have the character of everyday words or of casual repartee. Nor can they be arbitrarily selected portions of sermons or of doctrinal discourses. Rather they consist of brief, laconic, well-rounded texts, of pointed statements with a clear profile, rich in content and poetic in form. The artistic devices show through clearly even in the tradition's Greek form: picturesque content, strophic construction, *parallelismus membrorum*, verbatim repetition, and so on. . . .

The intent here is not simply to instruct or to clarify in general terms, but to provide the listeners with certain ''words'' to ponder and discuss. The speaker in this context does not engage his hearers in conversation, nor does he lecture them, but rather presents them with a parable; he delivers a proverb to them. They receive it somewhat in the way one receives a curious object which one must examine in order to find out how it can be used. They are given a text upon which they can ruminate and discuss with one another in an effort to clarify its meaning. What is more important here is, of course, not that people learn the text, but they that understand its meaning—but much of the meaning is dependent on the wording.

If one looks at the *form* which these sayings take, one notes that they are brief, pointed, and pregnant. The sayings have been formulated so that they can be easily remembered. . . . In the light of the ancient Jewish methods of teaching, it seems entirely clear to me that Jesus presented such a saying two or more times in an effort to impress it upon the minds (''hearts'') of his hearers.

Birger Gerhardsson. *The Origins of the Gospel Tradition* (Philadelphia, Fortress Press, 1977), pp. 68–69, 71–72

METAPHOR

Above all, it is essential that the profoundly metaphorical and symbolic character of the language of Jesus should be clearly appreciated and continually kept in mind. If Peter, James, and John, and Nicodemus were many times at fault, unpardonably obtuse as we are apt to think, because they took literally and for prose what He had said in poetry, we are only too prone to repeat their error with increase. The language of Jesus belongs in the deepest sense to the Old Testament and prophetic order. It is charged, it is saturated, with metaphor. In the opening episodes of the ministry—His baptism, His temptation, His first address in the synagogue at Nazareth—figurative terms and ideas abound. . . .

Throughout the whole range of bodily function Jesus, like Isaiah and Jeremiah, found metaphorical material for the description of conditions and experiences of spiritual life. Men had come into the world, born of women: they must enter the Kingdom, born of God. They had life: they must have life eternal and abounding. They knew bodily hunger and thirst and weariness; but there was hunger and thirst and weariness of soul to be recognized and allayed. Worse than blindness, deafness, dumbness, paralysis, and leprosy of the body, were blindness, deafness, dumbness, paralysis, and leprosy of the spirit. Death of the body they dreaded and evaded with all their power, but death of the soul they suffered without alarm or even consciousness. Bondage to Rome galled them, but captivity to self and sin gave them no concern. . . .

After the same fashion He turns to figurative account a wealth of everyday and homely details drawn from human and even animal life. . . . He can picture a human character by means of a single telling symbol. Herod is 'that fox'. Simon is 'a rock'. James and John, who urged Him to let them call down fire from heaven upon His rejectors, are veritable 'sons of thunder'. . . . The Apostles are lambs among wolves, a little flock, babes and sucklings in respect of legal knowledge, and they are to be 'wise as serpents' while 'innocent as doves', the 'light of the world', the 'salt of the earth'. As in proverbial wisdom so in His speech the camel and the gnat, the beam and the mote, the mountain and the mustard-seed, stand for contrasted things great and small. The unlighted street, 'the outer darkness', cheerless and forbidding after night falls, the refuse-fires of a vineyard or a farm or of Gehenna's valley below the City's walls, tares in the corn, and the dunghill, fishes unfit for the catch, are symbols of the destiny of wasted and worthless lives. . . . External piety He names 'play-acting', hypocrisy, a thing no better than the grave of a religion, a glistening whitewashed structure without, darkness, foulness, mustiness, a charnel of dead men's bones within.

William A. Curtis. Jesus Christ the Teacher (London,
Oxford University Press, 1943), pp. 99, 101–104

A prosy literalism not only misses the wry humor, when humor is present, but, what is worse, misses the point of the teaching. Christ taught in figures nearly all of the time, and everyone knows that no figure is to be accepted in its entirety. No one could suppose that when Jesus said He was the door, He meant that He was made of wood. . . .

Christ seems to have noted . . . connections everywhere, starting with the most common experiences of ordinary life. His metaphors concern the plow, the seed, the yoke, the salt, the light, the leaven, the door, the coin, the jewel, the fire, and many more. Each one is placed in an association which we can never forget but which we did not discover with our own unaided powers. Some of these are humorous and some are not, but it is reasonable to suppose that they represent only a few of Christ's flashing insights.

> Elton Trueblood. *The Humor of Christ* (New York, Harper and Row, 1964), pp. 41–42

Jesus is one of the world's most famous poets. If we are unaccustomed to regarding Him as such, it is because His poetry is so natural and apparently artless that it enters our consciousness without striking us as being poetic. Upon analysis, His speech shows total mastery of poetic forms.

Jesus' speech is saturated with metaphors and symbols. Using the resources of the poetic imagination, He repeatedly drew upon one area of human experience to shed light on another. According to Jesus, calling people to belief in God was like gathering a harvest (Matt. 9:37–38). Sending the disciples to minister in a hostile world was similar to sending "sheep in the midst of wolves" (Matt. 10:16). Living a life of self-sacrifice for the sake of Christ called to Jesus' mind the picture of picking up a cross and bearing it (Matt. 10:38), while the ordeal of His own death was a cup whose contents had to be drunk (Matt. 26:39). Jesus compared the hypocritical Pharisees to "whitewashed tombs, which outwardly appear beautiful, but within they are full of dead men's bones and all uncleanness" (Matt. 23:27), and to "graves which are not seen, and men walk over them without knowing it" (Luke 11:44). . . . Many of Jesus' comparisons drew upon archetypal images, as when He spoke about living water (John 4:10), the bread of life (John 6:35), the light of the world (John 8:12), and the good shepherd (John 10:11). Jesus' reliance on analogy as the most effective way of explaining His saving ministry reaches its climax in the parables, where the kingdom of God is compared to a field, a mustard seed, a treasure, a pearl, a vineyard, a banquet, and a wedding.

> Leland Ryken. *The Literature of the Bible* (Grand Rapids, Zondervan, 1974), pp. 291–292

HYPERBOLE

Christ had even a literary style of his own, not to be found, I think, elsewhere; it consists of an almost furious use of the *a fortiori*. His "how much more" is piled one upon another like castle upon castle in the clouds. The diction used *about* Christ has been, and perhaps wisely, sweet and submissive. But the diction used by Christ is quite curiously gigantesque; it is full of camels leaping through needles and mountains hurled into the sea. Morally it is equally terrific; he called himself a sword of slaughter, and told men to buy swords if they sold their coats for them. That he used other even wilder words on the side of non-resistance greatly increases the mystery; but it also, if anything, rather increases the violence.

G. K. Chesterton. *Orthodoxy* (London, Bodley Head, 1909), pp. 269–270

Jesus used an extraordinary rhetoric. For he had a unique purpose. . . . .In his discourses he suggested great truths by parables, by questions, by metaphors, by paradoxes, by hyperboles, by every device which could elude the semblance of fixed legislature or judicial formulas. . . .

Even the hastiest reader of the gospels must see that Jesus, in his teaching, constantly used the rhetorical figure which is called Hyperbole, a figure the most unsuitable conceivable for the statement of laws. The word "hyperbole" is derived from two Greek words meaning *to throw beyond*. . . . Jesus apparently aimed to startle into thought the most indolent and to fix his suggestions in the memories of the most forgetful. His remarks often lack absolutely the characteristics of precise definition, and seem rather, as Matthew Arnold so well expressed it, "words flung out" toward great ideas.

Whatever may have been his reason for using this surprising rhetorical figure, it undeniably abounds in the discourses of Jesus. It makes all attempts at consistent literalism hopeless, and it leaves the reader in many cases at a loss for any explanation. . . .

Jesus said, "If any man comes to me and does not *hate* his father and his mother and his wife and his children and his brothers and his sisters, yes, and his own life also, he cannot be a disciple of mine" (Luke, xiv, 26). This is most extraordinary language in regard to entrance on a life of love. . . .

Jesus said: "If your right eye is a snare to you, pluck it out and cast it from you . . ." (Matt. v.29, 30). But no one of us would encourage a young man who, finding temptation through the eye dangerous to purity, should propose to destroy his own sight, or who should, under any circumstances, amputate his right hand.

The most perplexing hyperboles of Jesus are those in which he spoke of power of faith and prayer. He said . . . , "I tell you truly, if you have faith like a mustard seed you will say to this mountain, 'Remove from here to there,' and it will remove, and nothing will be impossible for you" (Matt. xvii, 20). . . . Any attempt to consider these promises literally will seem to savor of irreverent levity. Everybody knows that these are figurative.

One is astonished at the language in which Jesus sometimes spoke of his own purpose and mission on earth. He said: "I came to cast fire on the earth, and what will I, if it is already kindled?" "Do you think that I came to give peace on earth? No, I tell you, but dissension" (Luke xii, 49, 51). . . .

Jesus is the poorest possible authority for a literalist. He says the most unqualified things and then never seems bound by them.

> William G. Ballantine. *Understanding the Bible* (Springfield, Mass., Johnson's Bookstore, 1925), pp. 64–66, 68, 70, 81, 83–84, 88

Certain of the sayings of Jesus are marked by what can only be called obvious absurdities. When Jesus bade the critic consider the beam in his own eye before he offered to take the mote from his brother's eye: when he accused the Pharisees of straining out the gnat and swallowing the camel: when he said that it was easier for a camel to go through a needle's eye than for a rich man to enter into the kingdom of God . . . ; in all these cases his figures are undeniably absurd. So much has this been felt that attempts have been made to mitigate them, but in vain. Despite the best endeavours of exegetes the beam remains a beam, the camel refuses to be reduced to a cable and the needle's eye to be enlarged to a wicket-gate. . . .

When Jesus said, "It is easier for a camel to go through a needle's eye, than for a rich man to enter into the kingdom of God," his mind was envisaging something rather absurd than impossible. . . .

After the lustful stare is condemned as adultery, Matthew adds, "And if thy right eye causeth thee to stumble, pluck it out, and cast it from thee: for it is profitable for thee that one of thy members should perish, and not thy whole body be cast into hell. And if thy right hand causeth thee to stumble, cut it off, and cast it from thee: for it is profitable for the . . . etc." (Matt. v. 29f). . . . How in such a matter could the right eye be guilty and not the left? And how would the excision of one eye lessen the evil so long as the other eye remained? It is, of course, agreed that it would be the greatest folly to take the words literally and act upon them. . . . And the absurdity is increased by reiteration, till we have a procession of one-eyed, one-armed, one-legged men entering into "*life*." To be unconscious of these absurdities would argue a slow mind in the speaker, and we have therefore to assume that they were intentional.

> A. T. Cadoux. *The Parables of Jesus: Their Art and Use* (London, James Clarke and Company, 1930), pp. 243, 245–246, 249–251

In close relationship to Jesus' use of parable and proverb and paradox is His deliberate recourse to *hyperbole*, picturesque exaggeration. Some of the proverbial expressions He quotes or applies contain this element with its tinge of humor. If paradox daringly affirms what is apparently self-contradictory, hyperbole in the same spirit ventures to state what is apparently impossible or incredible or unnatural. It does not so much distort truth as overstate it,

heightening its form in order to impress dull vision with its existence. . . .
A beam of timber in the censorious eye, a mountain that a grain of faith can
remove, a 'camel' or boat's cable that can pass through a sewing-needle's
eye, a camel, largest of familiar beasts in Palestine slipping down the throat
that would stickle over a gnat, the whole world stuffed into the pocket of a
grasping profiteer, the left hand unaware of the right hand's doing, the eye
gouged out and the right hand cut off by wise self-surgery to save a man's
true life, the trivial jot and tittle in the alphabet of the Law that are yet
imperishable, the hairs of a man's head numbered by His Maker, the hating
of parents and brethren and children and of life itself, the burying of the dead
to be left to the dead, rise up from His teaching as clear examples of His
hyperbolic method. A stone instead of bread for a hungry child, a serpent for
a fish, a scorpion for an egg, may serve as lesser examples of it. The duty
of forgiving, on repentance shown, is in like manner phrased as extending
to seventy-fold seven times. . . . What do we not owe to these stimulants of
our flagging attention, these irritants of our prosaic imagination? The world
uses the like devices continually in the service of wholesome satire, comedy,
and laughter. Jesus enlists them, not without a smile, in the service of truth
and seriousness.

William A. Curtis. Jesus Christ the Teacher (London,
Oxford University Press, 1943), pp. 94–95

Of all the mistakes which we make in regard to the humor of Christ, perhaps
the worst mistake is our failure, or our unwillingness, to recognize that Christ
used deliberately preposterous statements to get His point across. When we
take a deliberately preposterous statement and, from a false sense of piety,
try to force some literal truth out of it, the result is often grotesque. The
playful, when interpreted with humorless seriousness, becomes merely ridiculous. An excellent illustration of this is a frequent handling of the gigantic
dictum about the rich man and the needle's eye, an elaborate figure which
appears in identical form in all three of the Synoptics. "It is easier," said
Jesus, "for the camel to go through the eye of a needle than for a rich man
to enter the kingdom of God" (Mark 10:25). This categorical statement, given
with no qualification whatever, follows, in all three accounts, the story of a
wealthy man who came to Jesus to ask seriously how he might have eternal
life. He claimed to have kept the standard commandments, but he went away
sorrowfully when told that, at least in his case, it would be necessary to divest
himself of all of his possessions.

We are informed that Christ's hearers were greatly astonished, and well
they might have been, if they took the dictum literally, as they apparently
did. . . . For humorous purposes this is evidently the same camel swallowed
by the Pharisee when he carefully rejected the gnat. . . .

By making the statement in such an exaggerated form, termed by Chesterton the *giantesque*, Christ made sure that it was memorable, whereas a

prosy, qualified statement would certainly have been forgotten. Te device is mirrored in our conventional Texas story, which no one believes literally, but which everyone remembers. . . .

We spoil the figure, and lose all the robustness, when we tone it down. Christ had a revolutionary message to give and He knew that He could not make Himself understood by speaking mildly. . . .

Christ seems to employ exactly that amount of shock which is necessary to make people break through their deeply ingrained obtuseness. In some cases only the extreme form will suffice. An illustration of this is the figure of the dead undertaker. A would-be follower seeks to excuse himself for what seems to us a justifiable reason: he has to bury his father. Jesus, apparently tired of excuses, blurts out, "Leave the dead to bury their own dead; but as for you, go and proclaim the kingdom of God" (Luke 9:60). . . . A manifest impossibility is advised, as a clear means of making a point, where a milder figure would not have been as successful. When Christ said not to cast pearls before swine (Matt. 7:6), He was employing the patently absurd to make His point.

> Elton Trublood. *The Humor of Christ* (New York, Harper and Row, 1964), pp. 46–49

Jesus was equally adept at using hyperbole. There is obvious exaggeration in the statement that "it is easier for a camel to go through the eye of a needle than for a rich man to enter the kingdom of God" (Matt. 19:24), and in the satiric comment that the Pharisees are guilty of "straining out a gnat and swallowing a camel" (Matt. 23:24). Another of Jesus' humorous exaggerations occurs in His satire against self-righteous judgment: "How can you say to your brother, 'Brother, let me take out the speck that is in your eye,' when you yourself do not see the log that is in your own eye?" (Luke 6:24). Some of Jesus' hyperbolic statements will be misinterpreted if they are taken literally. For example, Jesus was not stating a reasoned ethical position when He said that "if any one comes to me and does not hate his own father and mother and wife and children and brothers and sisters, yea, and even his own life, he cannot be my disciple" (Luke 14:26). Rather, He was using hyperbole to assert the priority that a person must give to God over other relationships.

> Leland Ryken. *The Literature of the Bible* (Grand Rapids, Zondervan, 1974), p. 293

PARADOX

What Christ said was true, but it was never a truism. The escape from truism came by the consistent employment of paradox in which there is always a hint of the laughable. For example, the paradox of the blind leading the blind is absurdity carried as far as it can go (Luke 6:39). It is clear that, though

Christ's use of paradox was appreciated by the perceptive, it was missed by the unhumorous and the literal-minded. An illustration of the latter response is the literalistic question of Nicodemus when faced with the radical metaphor of new birth. Such use of paradox became a means of selection among hearers, with the consequence that many did not really hear, though there was nothing wrong with their physical ears. . . . Unjust as it sounds, it is a fact, at least in the realm of understanding, that the rich get richer and the poor get poorer (Mark 4:25).

Christ's use of paradox is dazzling. The entire process of finding similarity in apparent difference, which makes parable possible, is deeply paradoxical. At first sight the different metaphors which Christ uses to explain the character of the new redemptive fellowship which He is establishing, particularly *salt*, *light*, and *leaven*, seem radically different, but, on closer examination, all mean the same thing. Each is a figure of *penetration*, and each fulfills its function only by spending or by losing itself. Thus the theme of the cross, i.e., of saving by losing, is far more pervasive of the Gospel than it at first appears to be. . . . It is the ultimate of paradox. So moving was it to the restless mind of Dostoyevsky that he used the paradox as an epigraph for his final and greatest work of fiction, *The Brothers Karamazov*. At the beginning of the book are the words, "Verily, verily, I say unto you, except a corn of wheat fall into the ground and die, it abideth alone: but if it die it bringeth forth much fruit." (John 12:24, A.V.).

> Elton Trueblood. *The Humor of Christ* (New York, Harper and Row, 1964), pp. 42–43

Jesus also used paradox. He asserted, for example, "My yoke is easy, and my burden is light" (Matt. 11:30). The effect of paradox depends, of course, on the listener's resolution of the apparent contradiction. In this case, Jesus is making the claim that submission to Him, symbolized by the yoke and burden, brings freedom and salvation to a person. In stressing the need for his followers to deny themselves as a condition for gaining eternal life, Jesus made the paradoxical statement, "For whoever would save his life will lose it, and whoever loses his life for my sake will find it" (Matt. 16:25). The ideal of service to others is captured in Christ's statement that "whoever would be great among you must be your servant, and whoever would be first among you must be your slave" (Matt. 20:26–27), while the biblical commonplace that God's standards of judgment run counter to the world's evaluation of success was made memorable in Jesus' remark that "many that are first will be last, and the last first" (Mark 10:31). On another occasion Jesus told His disciples, "If any one would be first, he must be last of all" (Mark 9:35). It becomes evident that paradox was rooted in the nature of Christ's message, which challenged conventional attitudes at so many points.

> Leland Ryken. *The Literature of the Bible* (Grand Rapids, Zondervan, 1974), p. 292

JOHN

STRUCTURE

John did not set himself to write a complete history, but only to enforce a given view of the Christian revelation in the light of selected facts. He is thus left free to shape his narrative on a deliberate artistic plan, and it unfolds itself with something of the ordered majesty and simplicity of a Greek tragedy. First, in a solemn prologue, our minds are prepared for the action which is to follow; and then the divine life passes before us in its cardinal episodes. In the first four chapters the Light is seen rising on the world, and all men appear to welcome it and respond to it. Then follows a period of uncertainty, when friends and enemies begin to take their sides (v. and vi.). In the next section (vii.–xii.) the world settles down into definite antagonism, while the few whom Jesus has chosen are drawn to Him ever more closely. At last He is left alone with this small company of His true disciples, and reveals His inmost heart to them in the quiet of the supper-room (xiii.–xvii.). Meanwhile the hatred of His enemies, like the love of His chosen friends, has reached its height, and in the remaining chapters we see Him overwhelmed by the powers of darkness, yet in the end rising victorious.

The story thus groups itself around one central motive, that of the judgment, the sifting out of men, effected by the coming of Christ. After the first wonder has spent itself, the two classes of children of light and children of darkness begin to emerge definitely. Those who are repelled from Jesus become more intensely hostile, while those who accept Him are won to an always deeper and more intimate faith. This separation of men by their attitude to the Light is the governing motive of the book, and as such it serves an artistic as well as a theological purpose. By his conception of Jesus as the Logos, the writer was compelled to regard Him as a stationary figure. There could be no inward development of His character or consciousness, no reaction of circumstances upon His life. As the story of the Incarnate Logos the Gospel could be nothing more than a series of repetitions, without any real sequence or unifying interest. The difficulty is overcome by the aid of that other motive, which enables the narrative to march forward with a natural dramatic purpose.

Jesus Himself remains sovereign and impassive, awaiting His ''hour''; but the effect of His presence on the world becomes more and more decisive. A judgment is in process, and we follow it stage by stage to the great climax.

> E. F. Scott. *The Fourth Gospel: Its Purpose and Theology* (Edinburgh, T. and T. Clark, 1906, 1908), pp. 16–18

The ominous note of tragedy is struck in the Prologue (i, 1–18) itself,—''He came unto his own, and his own received him not''; not only the note of tragedy but we have also sharply contrasted modes of thought, Light and Darkness, Life and Death, Faith and Unbelief. These contrasts indicate that a clear line of division has been introduced into the world by the coming of Jesus Christ. . . .

If we examine the incidents, and the discourses that follow them, we shall find that in them also these contrasts reappear. The scheme of the work appears as a series of movements or cycles. All of them illustrate this conflict of Light with Darkness, Life with Death, Faith with Unbelief. The climax is reached in Chapters xiii–xx, which tell the story of the final conflict between the Lord of Light and the Prince of Darkness; the Lord of Life and the lords of Death. Therein is seen the final triumph of Faith and the defeat of Unbelief.

> R. H. Strachan. *The Fourth Evangelist: Dramatist or Historian?* (London, Hodder and Stoughton, 1925), pp. 16–17

What he gives us is no ordinary narrative, where one thing follows another in a simple succession. The links that connect one episode with another are extremely subtle. It is rather like a musical fugue. A theme is announced, and developed up to a point; then a second theme is introduced and interwoven with the first, then perhaps a third, with fresh interweaving, until an intricate pattern is evolved, which yet has the unity of a consummate work of art. The Fourth Gospel is more than any of the others an artistic and imaginative whole. . . .

In one sense, each several incident contains the whole truth of the Gospel, as John unfolds it; and yet, as we read, we are aware of movement and progression. We are being led step by step towards a climax. The climax comes in the latter part of the book, where the author tells once again the story of the sufferings, death and resurrection of Jesus Christ, and sets forth after his own manner the meaning of these momentous events.

> C. H. Dodd. *About the Gospels* (Cambridge, Cambridge University Press, 1950), pp. 41, 43–44

The book naturally divides itself at the end of ch. xii. The division corresponds to that which is made in all the gospels before the beginning of the Passion-narrative. But here it is made more formal. The gospel is divided at this point virtually into two books. What follows in chs. xiii–xx or xxi, if we include the appendix, may properly be called The Book of the Passion. The earlier chapters correspond to the account of the Ministry in the other gospels. . . . We may fitly call it The Book of Signs. This book begins with ch. ii. Ch. i forms a proem. I shall therefore examine the gospel under these three heads: A. The Proem; B. The Book of Signs; C. The Book of the Passion. . . .

The Book of Signs, chs. ii–xii . . . seems naturally to divide itself into seven episodes, each consisting of one or more narratives of significant acts of Jesus, accompanied by one or more discourses designed to bring out the significance of the narratives. . . .

The Book of the Passion is constructed on a pattern broadly similar to that of each individual episode of the Book of Signs. There is a single continuous narrative, that of the arrest, trial, crucifixion and resurrection of Jesus Christ, in chs. xvii–xx; and a long series of discourses, partly dialogue and partly monologue, in chs. xiii–xvii, commonly called the Farewell Discourses. If in this case the narrative follows the discourses, instead of the discourses following the narrative, as is the general rule in the Book of Signs, that difference is necessitated by the difference in situation. The narrative includes a certain amount of dialogue, chiefly in the account of the trial of Jesus, as well as in the post-resurrection narratives. The discourses similarly include a narrative element, in the account of incidents at the Last Supper. But the character of chs. xiii–xvii as discourse, and of chs. xviii–xx as narrative, is unmistakable.

Having in view the parallelism in structure with the episodes of the Book of Signs, we should be disposed to expect that the discourse would serve to elucidate the significance of the narrative. Such appears to be the intention of the evangelist. . . .

Chs. ii–xii . . . form an organic whole. A continuous argument runs through them. It does not move along the direct line of a logical process. Its movement is more like that of a musical fugue. A theme is introduced and developed up to a point; then a second theme is introduced and the two are interwoven; then a third, and so on. A theme may be dropped, and later resumed and differently combined, in all manner of harmonious variations. The themes are those of life, light and judgment, the passion and the glory of Christ, and the like. Each is enunciated and exemplified in various ways, and by the end of Ch. xii they have all been brought into a unified presentation of the whole truth about Christ and His work; the whole truth, for although the story of His death and resurrection remains to be told, and there is much to be said about its far-reaching significance, yet in principle the Christ of the Book of Signs is the Christ who dies and rises again. . . .

The Book of the Passion corresponds in structure with the several episodes of the Book of Signs, in that it consists of a narrative accompanied by an interpretative discourse. In this case the discourse precedes, in the form of the dialogues of Jesus with His disciples on the eve of His Passion. The narrative is that of the arrest, trial and crucifixion of Jesus, His burial, the discovery of the empty tomb, and His appearance to the disciples.

C. H. Dodd. *The Interpretation of the Fourth Gospel* (Cambridge, Cambridge University Press, 1953), pp. 289–291, 383, 423

The structure of the gospel is simple in outline, complicated in detail. The book falls into four clear parts, with an appendix, as follows:

(a) 1.1–18, Prologue;

(b) 1.19–12.50, Narratives, Conversations, and Discourses;

(c) 13.1–17.26, Jesus alone with his Disciples;

(d) 18.1–20.31, the Passion and Resurrection;

(e) 21.1–25, and Appendix. . . .

The bulk of the gospel falls into sections (b) and (c). (b) contains a great variety of material. There are simple narratives containing little or no teaching (e.g., 4.46–54; 6.16–21); conversations, simple (e.g., 1.45–51), or, more commonly, controversial (e.g. 8.21–59); and, often merging into the conversations, prolonged discourses pronounced by Jesus (e.g. 5.19–47). This disparate material is not left in juxtaposed fragments, but narrative, discourse, and debate are woven together into units, which in turn stand in recognizable relationship to each other. To take the clearest of examples: the discourse on the bread of life (6.26–59) clearly arises out of the miracle in which Jesus supplies a multitude with bread (6.5–13). In the "sign" . . . the truth of the discourse is implicit; the two are complementary. Again, it will be remarked at once that the "bread of life" chapter forms a complement to the "water of life" discourse (4.10–26). The discourse does not always follow the sign it explains; for example, it is at 8.12 that Jesus announces that he is the light of the world; the corresponding miracle (the gift of sight to a man born blind) is found in ch. 9. There are moreover abundant cross-references; for example, "light" appears also at 3.19–21; 12.35f., 46 (cf. 11.9f.), as well as in the Prologue. The total number of distinct themes is small: Life (including water of life and bread of life), Light, the relation of Jesus to the Father, the Shepherd, Sabbath controversy: these cover nearly all the material in chs. 1–12. . . .

The last night of the life of Jesus, contained in chs. 13–17, . . . is on a larger scale, but follows a pattern similar to that of the earlier units. It opens with a symbolic action, the washing of the disciples' feet, and then proceeds through dialogue to what is, in chs. 15f., almost pure discourse, uninterrupted by question and answer. The conversation and discourse serve to bring out the meaning of the relationship established by the feet-washing and of the approaching passion of Jesus, which is itself prefigured in the humble love embodied in the act of service he performs for his friends. After this exposition the crucifixion is recounted . . . in plain terms with little theological comment. . . .

If this analysis of the gospel be received, two consequences must also be accepted. (a) Since the material is disposed in accordance with a theological and literary scheme, it is idle to seek in John a chronology of the ministry of Jesus. . . . (b) Theories of dislocation . . . are not proved when it is shown that, by manipulation, the components of the gospel can be reshuffled into a neater narrative. The question is whether these components, as they stand, take their proper place in the theological structure of the book.

> C. K. Barrett. *The Gospel According to St. John* (London, S.P.C.K., 1955), pp. 11–14

A literary approach to the gospel will concern itself . . . with the narrative unity and design of the work. The impact of any long narrative depends in part on the overriding structure that the writer is able to impose on his details. The gospel of John is built on several unifying principles that span the work as a whole.

The general outline of the book follows the chronology of the protagonist's career. The gospel thus begins with an account of Jesus' divine origin. It then proceeds through the preparatory ministry of John the Baptist, the early events of Jesus' public ministry, some main incidents of His career as an itinerant religious teacher, and finally, His trial, death, and resurrection. This is clearly a story with a beginning, middle, and end. . . .

Another element of narrative structure is the progressive intensification of plot conflict and a corresponding movement toward the climax of the story. The writer begins his story with events that evoked no conflict . . . , and then moves to acts of Jesus that elicited extreme conflict. . . . Finally there is the overt conspiracy to kill Jesus and at last the crucifixion itself. . . .

Yet another aspect of the structural unity of the gospel of John is the overriding conflict between belief and unbelief. Keeping Jesus always in the center of the focus, the writer presents a series of responses by people who come into contact with the protagonist. At root, these responses show either belief or unbelief in the saving work of Christ. . . .

The writer's narrative skill is seen not only in his management of large narrative patterns but also in his construction of smaller units. One of these elements of design consists of the combining of an event involving Jesus with a discourse that interprets the meaning of the event. Typical examples include Jesus' request for a drink from the Samaritan woman followed by His statements about the water of life (ch. 4), the healing on the sabbath linked to Christ's words about His divine authority (ch. 5), the feeding of the five thousand related to the discourse on the bread of life (ch. 6), and the raising of Lazarus accompanied by Jesus' remarks about His being the resurrection and the life (ch. 11). . . .

The organization of the gospel of John is based on narrative principles. One of these is variety of episode. With a storyteller's instinct, the writer mingles long and short episodes, as well as mighty acts and spoken discourses. Events that carry their own meaning are interspersed with acts that are accompanied by interpretive discourses. Jesus' encounters with individuals are balanced by appearances to large crowds. Stories that end in belief are juxtaposed to episodes that lead to conflict and unbelief.

In addition to the narrative principle of variety, the gospel of John is structured as a series of progressions. These patterns include the progressive intensification of plot conflict, the movement toward the climax of Christ's execution, . . . and the continuing plot conflict between belief and unbelief.

> Leland Ryken. *The Literature of the Bible* (Grand Rapids, Zondervan, 1974), pp. 276–278, 291

STORYTELLING TECHNIQUE

Every reader has been struck with the contrast between the prevailing tone of mystical thought and the vivid realism of many of the separate pictures. The book abounds in clearly drawn portraits of character. Disciples who in the Synoptics are little more than names stand out in John with definitely marked features. The more prominent actors in the history (e.g. Peter, Judas, Pilate) are carefully individualized. Even those persons who have no real part in the action, and are only introduced for the purposes of doctrinal discussion (Nicodemus, the woman of Samaria, the blind man), are endowed with some distinctiveness of character. In like manner the writer delights in little pictorial touches which serve to give a concrete reality to his narrative. He records dates, hours, names of places. He works out special episodes with a wealth of lively detail. He adds an individual reference to vague statements in the Synoptics. (Peter was the man who struck, and Malchus the man wounded; Judas objected to the waste of ointment; Thomas is the representative of the "some who doubted".) He introduces, often with wonderful effect, dramatic contrasts and circumstances. ("And it was night." "Jesus wept." "Behold the man!" "What is truth?") These are but a few examples of that study of the vivid and concrete which forms one of the best marked characteristics of the Fourth Gospel, abstract and theological as it is in its main teaching. . . . It can be shown that many of the apparently lifelike details have a symbolic value. . . .

A manner of writing is adopted which admits of singularly little variation, so that it is difficult at times to distinguish between the words of Jesus Himself and the commentary which follows them. This monotony of the Johannine style, due to a certain uniform, semi-rhythmical construction of sentence, . . . is evidently intentional, and imparts to the whole book an air of majesty and religious awe, in keeping with its high argument.

> E. F. Scott. *The Fourth Gospel: Its Purpose and Theology* (Edinburgh, T. and T. Clark, 1906, 1908), pp. 18–20

The most striking literary features of the Fourth Gospel are to be found in its conception of Christ, its style of composition, blending incident and discourse, its precise and circumstantial narrative, and its dialogues. Its conception of Christ as Christ the Lord, a dominant conception from the first page to the last, is one of the sources of its unity. . . . This impression of Christ is subtly conveyed in the talks of Jesus, and his prayer to his Father (xvii). In Mark men are making up their minds about the Son of Man. In John men are judged for unbelief in the Son of God. . . .

The style of composition increases the impression of the book's unity, its appearance of being 'woven without seam', as Strauss said, in spite of certain dislocations of sections in our present text and in spite of the comments interspersed by the evangelist. . . . It is part of the subtlety of John's style that incident and talk, narrative and editorial comment show the same features and are blended into a unity. The style is one throughout, and what appear to be the evangelist's own comments are so merged with the other matter that it is not always easy to say where they begin and end. . . .

When we turn to the narrative of the Gospel, the outstanding feature from a literary point of view is its particularity of detail. It reminds us in this respect of Mark, but with a difference. Mark's account is distinguished by graphic details of action and gesture, especially of Jesus himself. This Gospel gives details rather of time, place, numbers, names of speakers, even where not specially important, and explanatory circumstances.

It carefully notes the historic sequence of events, especially of the incidents which impressed themselves on the memory when Jesus first came upon the scene. . . . Whether notes were made at the time, is not known, but they are set down later with the confidence of a diarist. . . .

Places are inserted with equal deliberation, and even added at the end of an incident, when not previously specified. . . . These and other instances show anxiety to make the topography clear to readers Jewish and Gentile. Especially interesting is the fixing of the place as well as the time of the long talks of Jesus, most of which revolve upon some striking saying, as the discourse in v.17 arises out of the curing of the infirm man on the Sabbath, and leads up to the saying 'the dead shall hear the voice of the Son of God and live'. . . .

His habit of recording quantities and measures is part of the same exactness, and not to be explained by symbolism or an effort of fiction.

To all this particularity of detail add the constant references to the attitude of the audience, as if this witness were keeping his finger, so to speak, on the pulse of the audience of Jesus, and drawing a chart of their belief.

After every striking discourse or miracle he takes stock of its effect on the crowd or the disciples. . . .

> P. C. Sands. *Literary Genius of the New Testament* (Oxford, Oxford University Press, 1932), pp. 48–49, 55–57, 59

The great differences between John and the synoptics strike one immediately. In the latter we find pieces of tradition, stories, and sayings, in a more or less significant context, whereas in John both events and isolated sayings (e.g. in chaps. vii and viii) are often only opportunities for introducing speeches or conversations of Jesus with His opponents and disciples. . . . Again, in the dialogues, the parties do not endeavour to work out certain conceptions by means of question and answer. Rather, by foolish questions and very erroneous misunderstandings, the hearers repeatedly give Jesus occasion to state again what He has said, in what might be called a monologue. Of course, the reader grasps the meaning from the very antitheses to the misunderstandings.

The theme of the speeches and conversations is the revelation of God in Jesus.

> Martin Dibelius. *A Fresh Approach to the New Testament and Early Christian Literature* (New York, Charles Scribner's Sons, 1936), pp. 96–97

You will recall the scene in Mark where Jesus fed a multitude of people with bread in the wilderness. Mark observes, with some emphasis, that there was something about it which no one understood at the time. John re-tells the story in his own way (vi. 1–14); but instead of leaving it with a cryptic hint of a secret not divulged, he appends a long discourse on the theme of 'bread of life'; by which he means the invisible, divine powers that nourish the spiritual life of men. . . . The reader is thus encouraged not to think so much about what happened by the Sea of Galilee one evening in March about A.D. 30, but to consider what it is to be spiritually starved, and to learn how Christ satisfies the hunger of the soul. In a word, the incident has become what John calls a 'sign', or symbol, of something which is true always and everywhere, and which the reader, whoever he is, can prove in his own experience.

In this way, all the actions of Jesus that John records—and he gives only a small selection compared with the wealth of incident in the other Gospels—are treated as 'signs', or symbols, of some deeper truth. When Christ cleanses the temple, it is a sign that the old way of religion, with its sacrifices and ceremonies, gives place to the worship of God 'in spirit and in truth'. When he gives sight to a blind man, it means that he enlightens the spiritually blind with the light of truth. When he raises dead Lazarus to life, it stands for the awakening of the spiritually dead to life worthy of the name.

To say that these events are symbolic does not, of course, mean that they are imaginary, or that they never happened as events in history. . . . Gradually, as he meditated, over a period of years, one incident and another became transparent, and he saw the underlying pattern behind the mere occurrences as tradition reported them. And so, in composing his Gospel, he has re-told these incidents in such a way as to bring out the inner meaning of each of them separately and of the story as a whole. He has done this by a combination of three methods; partly by re-shaping the stories themselves in detail, partly by arranging them in a special order, which is not necessarily the order or time in which they happened, and partly by placing alongside a story a discourse which expounds its deeper meaning. Mark was always hinting at a secret—'the mystery of the Kingdom of God'. John has told the secret, perhaps as fully as it can be told. . . .

Now we understand why John insists that we shall pause over every single incident as we go through the story, until we have got below the surface and seen what it means. Each incident is a place where we may hear the eternal Word spoken, which interprets to us our own lives and the whole universe of our experience.

C. H. Dodd. About the Gospels (Cambridge, Cambridge
University Press, 1950), pp. 38–41, 43

The unit of structure is the single episode composed of narrative and discourse, both related to a single dominant theme. The incidents narrated receive an interpretation of their evangelical significance in the discourses; or, to put it otherwise, the truths enunciated in the discourses are given dramatic expression in the actions described. Act and word are one; and this unity of act and word is fundamental to the Johannine philosophy, and distinguishes it from the abstract intellectualism or mysticism of much of the thought of the time.

The episodes are constructed upon a common pattern, subject to endless variations. Each of them tends to move from narrative, through dialogue, to monologue, or at least to a form of dialogue in which comparatively long speeches are allotted to the chief Speaker. Most of them have an epilogue or appendix, which in part recapitulates leading ideas of the episode, and in part alludes to ideas contained in other episodes, earlier or later, in such a way as to form a series of links. . . .

Each several episode . . . contains in itself, implicitly, the whole of the Gospel. The apostolic *kerygma* was centered upon the saving facts of Christ's coming, His death, resurrection, and exaltation. . . .

The Book of Signs is so constructed that each several episode contains in itself the *whole* theme of the Gospel: Christ manifested, crucified, risen, exalted, communicating eternal life to me.

> C. H. Dodd. *The Interpretation of the Fourth Gospel* (Cambridge, Cambridge University Press, 1953), pp. 384, 386

Though John's narrative contains important incidents not found elsewhere, its most striking emphases are theological and interpretative. It has a peculiar way of making its hero self-explanatory: Jesus is always interpreting himself. This is a legitimate artistic process: Shakespeare's heroes may likewise be regarded as 'interpreting' themselves and John's Gospel is a necessary link in our understanding.

Jesus interprets his own imagery: 'I am the real Vine' he says, 'and my father is the vine-dresser' (*John*, XV, I). . . . The interpretative method is maintained. Jesus compares himself to food, telling his followers that they must 'eat the flesh of the Son of Man and drink his blood' (*John*, VI. 53) if they are to have life. The author appears to be dramatizing his own reaction to Jesus' allusive speech and the tone is theological and abstract far beyond Jesus' words in the Synoptics. Life-symbols of the 'vine', 'harvest', 'water' and 'bread' are explicitly related to 'eternal life'.

It is the same with 'sight' and 'light'. . . . Physical sight symbolizes another 'sight' for which there is no exact name. There is much light-imagery, similarly interpreted. . . .

Paul presents a passionate experience of the mystic Christ; John a meditative and theological interpretation of Jesus as Son of God. Each sees a different facet of the central reality. . . . John is especially receptive to the symbolic qualities of Jesus' talk and actions; to these he calls our attention. . . .

> G. Wilson Knight. *The Christian Renaissance* (London, Methuen and Company, 1962), pp. 146–148

The conflict between Jesus and his opponents climaxes in the legal trial before Pilate (18:28–19:16), but forensic imagery is introduced much earlier in the Fourth Gospel. The first of many witnesses to offer testimony is John the Baptist: "There was a man sent from God, whose name was John. He came for testimony, to bear witness to the light" (1:6–7).

The list of witnesses is impressive:

a. Jesus has come to bear witness: [3:32; 7:7; 8:14; 18:37]. . . .
b. God is a witness [8:18]. . . .
c. Miracles are signs that provide testimony [5:36; 10:25]. . . .
d. The Spirit, called the counselor, will give testimony [15:26]. . . .
e. Followers of Jesus are appointed to be witnesses [15:27]. . . .
f. The narrator is a witness [19:35]. . . .

The consistent use of courtroom language indicates that John has fundamentally cast the story in the form of a trial. Jesus is being judged. . . .

On one level, Jesus is on trial throughout the Fourth Gospel. The characters in the story, notably the leaders of the Jewish people, must judge him. They have to weigh the testimony and decide what to do with him. For the reader, however, the trial has a deeper level. The reader sees no ambiguity about Jesus: the Father has sent Jesus, the Christ and Son of God, as the only revelation of his will. Jesus is to bear witness to the truth, to give enlightenment and life. . . .

Those who see Jesus' signs and hear his words face a crisis; they must decide who he is and whether to believe him. Everything depends on that decision; it is a matter of life and death. This personal crisis represents, John implies, an anticipation of the final judgment. How people judge Jesus determines how they themselves will be judged.

In this sense, it is not really Jesus who is on trial, but those who presume to be his judges, those to whom he has been sent. Jesus' signs and teachings have a different meaning at this deeper level: they unmask the characters in the story and provide testimony for God's verdict. . . . The climax of this level of the story comes when the religious leaders of the people, like the Pharisees in the story of the healing of the man born blind, must commit themselves. They condemn Jesus to temporal death—and in so doing sign their own eternal death warrants.

Donald Juel. *An Introduction to New Testament Literature* (Nashville, Abingdon Press, 1978), pp. 280–283

The units from which John builds his "structure of structures" are not as short and discrete as those in the other gospels. That is especially noticeable in the discourses. The Sermon on the Mount (Mt. 5–7) is a lengthy discourse, but it is made up of a series of brief legal, proverbial, and prophetic sayings, quite different from the lengthy units in John 14–17. As the Johannine narrator weaves together his stories and sayings, he freely inserts description into his narration, and in the terminology of Wayne Booth he does more "telling" in relation to "showing" than most biblical storytellers. He loves to gloss a statement, explaining a term (1:38; 4:25), a custom (4:9b), or a point in a speech (7:39).

In contrast to that of the other gospels, the language in John is simpler, more direct, and more poetic. Nouns and verbs are repeated for directness and emphasis. Time, place, quantity, measure, and personal references tend to be definite. Reactions to a statement or act are specific and enumerated. . . . Dialogues—a prominent form of discourse in John—use direct, not indirect, speech; and they are freqently structured as questions and answers. Thought rhythm, repetition, and parallel lines occur freqently in John to make his language poetic. . . .

Johannine style created a different kind of metaphoric speech from that in the Synoptics. In place of parables, John presents lengthy discourses in connection with miracles or signs. After a miracle story is narrated, Jesus enters into conversation with one of the characters. In that conversation he selects certain objects in the sign—water, bread, sight, life—and draws out their symbolic and metaphoric meanings. For the most part the objects become symbols, requiring the reader to recognize what they stand for. Occasionally the symbol-weaving discourse is punctuated by a metaphor such as "I am the bread of life" or "I am the good shepherd," which indicates what is being symbolized.

> Leonard L. Thompson. *Introducing Biblical Literature: A More Fantastic Country* (Englewood Cliffs, Prentice-Hall, 1978), p. 268

DRAMATIC ELEMENT

To what type of literary composition does it belong? Because in our Bibles it is labelled "gospel" and follows three other documents similarly labelled, it has almost universally been taken for granted that it is a document of essentially the same type as these three predecessors, i.e., a setting forth of the work and message of Jesus in narrative form. . . .

Closer comparison with the synoptic narrative shows, of course, that apart from this general likeness in large outline, likeness in detail is almost entirely lacking. There is an opening section on John the Baptist, and a considerable closing section on the Passion with its preliminaries and its sequel; between these termini there are two, possibly three, wonder-stories with synoptic parallels. Aside from these four (or five) points, the material presented by the fourth evangelist is wholly new; and, what is even more striking, within precisely these four (or five) coincidental sections the variations in detail are far more striking than even the large discrepancy in the bulk of the material. . . .

In no sense is the Fourth Gospel in form a narrative at all. . . .

It is not a narrative any more than Hamlet or the Song of Solomon or Faust is a narrative. What it tells it does not tell as items in a story; its succession has no relation to the sequences of a life-experience or the development of a plot. . . . There is throughout no progress of event or conception, no change of attitude, no perspective. . . .

Another form of art, then, from the synoptic gospels. . . . They are narrative, this is—what? My answer is: drama. . . . I mean only, a miscellany of material conceived dramatically, passages, dialogue, monologue, sketches of setting, of characters, of exits and entrances, of time and place and such like. . . .

My point . . . is that this material was conceived not as narrative, not as parallel in any way to the synoptic writings, but as a series of dramatic scenes. It is not to be read, but to be seen and heard. Its men and women are not characters in a story, but persons of a play. . . .

The thesis presented might be argued in great detail from the way the persons are sketched, from the way they appear and disappear, from the *way* they speak and the actual *lines* they speak. . . . From many other points of view the same thing might be argued: from the time and place references, from the abruptness of transitions from scene to scene, from the even more abrupt closing of scenes, as by the swift descent of a curtain, in mid-speech and mid-action, from the part played by action as itself the symbol of profound meanings, and that played by dialogue and monologue from the fact, indeed, that the gospel is here a spoken gospel, a gospel of the public utterance . . . marked by a quite extraordinary use of words designating *speech*. . . .

To begin with, there is that remarkable initial passage of eighteen verses, to which scholarshiip has inevitably, without a dissenting voice, given the title *Prologue*. Prologue: the word suggests the preface to a play; just as clearly the verses themselves suggest a striking of the great major chords whose harmony is to vibrate until the last curtain falls. . . .

We find . . . stage-directions, i.e., notes of time and place and circumstances, set down apparently whenever they happened to occur to the dramatist, often, . . . at the end, often at the beginning or intruding awkwardly into the midst of the action or dialogue. . . .

It was to be a dramatic sequence, in many particulars not unlike what we today call a pageant.

Clayton R. Bowen. *JBL*. 49, 1930, pp. 292–299

Throughout the Fourth Gospel there are abundant evidences of the use of those techniques employed frequently by dramatists. Several of these techniques deserve consideration.

Artistic Form. In the Fourth Gospel, as in the ancient classical tragedies, the catastrophe is announced in the beginning: "He came to his own home, and his own people received him not." The whole action of the narrative tends irresistibly toward the tragic close. As in Homer's *Iliad* and the tragedies of Aeschylus and Sophocles, the terrible outcome is constantly kept before the reader. . . .

Contrast. Throughout the Fourth Gospel light and darkness, faith and unbelief, life and death are frequent antitheses. Likewise in striking contrast are the critical Pharisees and the obedient disciples of John, the blind leaders of the people and the seeing blind man with his bold witness to the Messiahship of Jesus, Peter's confession and Judas' betrayal, the raising of Lazarus to life and the resultant dooming of Jesus to death.

Symmetry. Symmetry in the Fourth Gospel is apparent in the recurrence of certain characters and the skillful balancing of the parts. Nathanael appears in the first and final chapters, and nowhere else. Jesus' mother is seen only in the beginning and the end of the Gospel. At the opening of his public ministry Jesus attends a wedding feast with his disciples. Here he demonstrates his power. At the close of his ministry he is again at supper with his disciples. Here he demonstrates his love.

Variety. Variety is the spice of drama as well as life. The author of the Fourth Gospel apparently realized this. He carefully recorded the changes of the season. Incident and interlude, story and sermon, action and discourse he skillfully alternated. The marriage feast at Cana, the cleansing of the Temple, a conversation with Nicodemus in the darkness of the night, and a conversation with the woman of Samaria in the glare of the full noonday were made to follow one another in order. . . .

Irony. Dramatic irony abounds in the Fourth Gospel. . . .

Time and place indications. Whereas the writers of the Synoptic Gospels strung their material together by external links, the author of the Fourth Gospel made later events constantly refer to earlier ones. He never lost sight of chronology. From Jesus' first to his last appearance, indication of time and place were constantly recorded.

Dialogue pattern. Although the discourses in the Fourth Gospel appear to flow on spontaneously in conversational form, in reality they tend to follow a specific pattern: (1) someone makes an introductory statement or asks a question; (2) Jesus replies by uttering a profound saying; (3) this saying, often capable of a double interpretation, is misunderstood and its spiritual significance is not discerned; (4) Jesus then corrects the mistake; if a second question shows that he has done so effectively, (5) he then gives further, more detailed instruction on the subject. . . .

C. Milo Connick. *JBL.* 67, 1948, pp. 164–167

UNIFYING MOTIFS

A . . . uniformity is traceable in the conduct of almost all the dialogue in which Jesus takes part. The method invariably adopted is this; —a dark saying is thrown out by Jesus which is misapprehended by His hearers, and He then repeats the original saying, and proceeds to amplify and explain it. Whole chapters (e.g. v. vi. viii.) consist of a series of such dark utterances, misunderstood and then interpreted. A regular method is likewise followed in regard to the miracles. They are performed by Jesus on His own initiative, and embody great spiritual truths which are not apparent to the onlookers. Thus they serve as introductions to the several discourses, in which they are expounded in their inward significance.

The allegorical nature of many of the incidents and allusions contained in the Gospel has already been indicated. In the case of the miracles, John himself invites us to consider the outward event as the vehicle of a hidden meaning; and his narrative, down to its minutest details, appears to be saturated with symbolism. Even where his chief interest is to record facts as they actually happened, he is careful to place them in such a light as to bring out a deeper spiritual import which was concealed in them. . . .

A particular interest attaches itself in this connection to John's use of numbers. . . . A numerical scheme appears to be constantly before his mind. Jesus makes His journey thrice to Galilee and thrice to Jerusalem; there are three Passovers and three other feasts; the Baptist makes three appearances as witness; Jesus is thrice condemned, speaks thrice from the Cross, appears three times after His Resurrection. Seven, the other sacred number, is likewise prominent. There are seven miracles, seven references to the "hour"; the formula "I am," introducing some type under which Jesus describes Himself, occurs seven times, as also the solemn asseveration, "These things I have spoken to you," in the final discourse. It even seems probable that the structure of the Gospel as a whole is determined by these two numbers, three and seven. The book can be articulated into seven main sections, each of which falls naturally into three main parts. . . . Such a plan might seem at first sight to place a fatal restraint on the free activity of genius, but we have instances of great creative work—for example, the poem of Dante—produced under still stricter limitations. To minds of a certain type the observance of a rigid system is no burden, but rather a necessary condition to elevated and harmonious thought.

> E. F. Scott. *The Fourth Gospel: Its Purpose and Theology* (Edinburgh, T. and T. Clark, 1906, 1908), pp. 20–22

That J's purpose is not primarily biographical but religious and ideal, he really tells us himself in xx, 30 ff, where he says that he made a selection, for this particular purpose, out of a large amount of other material that was available. His words in xx, 30, that he had "many other signs" at his disposal, seem to be not only an apology for reserve, but also a frank statement that his purpose is not biographical. His positive aim has been by means of the use of a particular series of events in Jesus' life, and of His utterances, to produce a living faith in Him in the hearts of his readers. . . .

We shall, therefore, be prepared to find that "faith" or "belief" is a dominant idea in the Fourth Gospel. One point, however, is deserving of notice. The noun "faith" . . . is never used in the Gospel. The verb "to believe" alone is found. That can only indicate that the Evangelist conceives of faith as dynamic, and not as static. . . . Not faith in the abstract, but "faith," belief in action, examples of believing faith, varieties of faith illustrated in actual persons and incidents—these together with their opposites, unbelieving hostility and rejection, are the themes of the Fourth Gospel. There is a more or less formal arrangement of incidents and discourses in the Gospel, illustrating different phases, stages, and kinds of faith. The scheme of the Gospel is so conceived that every incident is an historical sermon on the growth or failure of faith, and every discourse has hardly any other theme.

R. H. Strachan. *The Fourth Evangelist: Dramatist or Historian?* (London, Hodder and Stoughton, 1925), pp. 92–94

The main truths with which this Gospel deals are transmitted by less than two dozen terms, each of which has some definite symbolic meaning. Among the most important of these are "light," "darkness," "bread," "water," "birth," "sleep," "flesh," "eating," "drinking," "shepherd," "sleep," "vine," "Father," (God), "Son of God," and "Son of man." Others like "bride and bridegroom," "thieves and robbers," "dwelling-places" (A.V. "mansions"), "grain of wheat," and "road" (way) are used only once. . . .

Certain characteristics of this imagery are immediately apparent. Whether judged by present standards or by those of the day in which the Gospel was written, these metaphors are familiar to all peoples and places. Some of them, like "sheep," "shepherd," and "vine," belong essentially to a pastoral civilization; a few, like "bridegroom," "thief," or "bond-servant," concern social position; "birth," "sleep," "eating," and "drinking" are common human actions; "water" and "bread" are staples of sustenance in any culture; "light" and "darkness" are concepts with universal connotations of good and evil; and the titles "Father," "Son of God," and "Son of man" are fairly obvious in meaning though they may have theological overtones. . . .

The figures of light and darkness define the plot of the Gospel, for they represent the opposing powers of righteousness and evil, and the contrasting results of belief and unbelief. In the introductory words of the Prologue the light is the life that was manifested in Christ. . . .

The parallel figure of darkness (1:5) represents uncertainty, ignorance, and separation from God (12:35, 46). . . .

Two common staples of life, water and bread, are illustrative of the indispensability of Christ to the believer. According to the words of Jesus, both were emblematic of eternal life (4:14; 6:51. 54). . . .

The Gospel of John contains no parables such as are found in the Synoptics. There are only two extended metaphors that resemble the teachings found in Matthew 13 and kindred passages, the figures of the good shepherd and the true vine, both of which deal with functions of Jesus' person rather than with stories of others. . . .

The physiological metaphors of birth, eating, and sleep cover the progression of Christian experience. The new birth marks its beginning: "Except one be born anew, he cannot see the kingdom of God" (3:3). . . .

The new life must be sustained by "eating" Christ, which involves a constant feeding upon Him as the bread of life (6:33). . . .

"Sleep" was Jesus' figure for the end of physical life, for He announced the death of Lazarus by saying, "Our friend Lazarus is fallen asleep; but I go, that I may awake him out of sleep" (11:11). . . . "Sleep" describes death in terms of appearance, not of reality, and as sleep presupposes an awakening, so the death of a believer must be followed by a return to life (John 11:25).

The last three important images in the Gospel are related to the personal revelation of God. They are properly titles rather than metaphors, yet the metaphorical sense underlying them demands definition. "Father" was Jesus' favorite name for God. . . .

The relationship of Christ to the Father is expressed by the phrase, "Son of God. . . ."

"Son of Man" is applied to Christ as the expression of perfect humanity.
Merrill C. Tenney. Bib Sac. 121, 1964, pp. 13–20

A . . . narrative pattern that underlies a number of individual episodes is the motif of the misunderstood statement. These dramas in miniature unfold in three stages: Jesus makes a pronouncement, a bystander expresses a misunderstanding of the utterance, and Jesus proceeds to explain the meaning of His original statement. This narrative pattern occurs no fewer than nine times in the book (3:3–8; 4:10–15; 4:31–38; 6:47–58; 7:33–36; 8:21–30; 8:31–47; 8:56–58; 11:11–15; the pattern appears with slight modification in 2:17–22). . . .

The writer of the fourth gospel makes much use of number pattern, in a manner similar to that which pervades the book of Revelation. There is repeated use of sets of three. The narrator, for example, records three Passovers and three other feasts that Jesus attended. Early in the book John the Baptist three times states his witness to Christ's messiahship. Late in the narrative Jesus is three times condemned. He also speaks three times from the cross and makes three appearances after His resurrection. There are three denials by Peter and three stages in Christ's restoration of Peter.

There is a similar use of the number seven. The writer structures the central part of his narrative around seven great miracles or "signs" that Jesus performed. The list includes the turning of the water into wine (2:1–11), the healing of the official's son (4:46–51), the cure of the paralytic (5:1–18), the feeding of the five thousand (6:5–13), walking on the water (6:16–21), the healing of the blind man (9:1–7), and the raising of Lazarus (11:1–44). Equally important is the pattern of seven statements by Jesus beginning with the formula "I am" and followed by a metaphoric description of Jesus' person and work: the bread of life (6:35), the light of the world (8:12), the door of the sheep (10:7), the good shepherd (10:11), the resurrection and the life (11:25), the way, and the truth, and the life (14:6), and the true vine (15:1). There is also a sevenfold witness to Christ: the witness of the Father (5:37; 8:18); the witness of the Son (8:14; 18:37); the witness of Christ's works

(10:25; 5:36); the witness of Scripture (5:39–46); the witness of the forerunner, John the Baptist (1:7; 5:35); the witness of the disciples (15:27; 19:35); and the witness of the Spirit (15:26; 16:14).

> Leland Ryken. *The Literature of the Bible* (Grand Rapids, Zondervan, 1974), pp. 279–280

The Fourth Gospel, like Isaiah 40–55, . . . presents a sustained use of juridical metaphor. Here we must ask what is the issue being debated, who are the participants in the debate and what is the outcome.

The issue under debate is plainly the Messiahship and divine Sonship of Jesus. It is mainly to convince his readers of this proposition that the Evangelist has written his Gospel (Jn. 20:31). . . .

The sayings of Jesus in the Fourth Gospel are often described as 'discourse', but are rather more commonly juridical debate. The discussions of Jesus with 'the Jews' sound like a lawsuit. . . . 'This whole section', Professor Johnston has pointed out, 'has the form of a great contest or assize.' The 'argumentativeness' which Burkitt found 'so positively repellent' is an integral element in the Fourth Gospel, and provides just the context of contention and debate in which one would expect to see witnesses called and evidence presented to substantiate the claims of Christ. . . .

'Witness' is one of John's favourite words. . . . The idea of witness in John's Gospel is both very prominent and thoroughly juridical, and is to be understood in terms of Old Testament legal language.

Other juridical words are notably frequent in the Fourth Gospel in the context of hostility and debate; e.g., judge, cause, judgment, accuse, convince. . . . The work of Christ is set against a background of opposition in which it would be natural to try to prove Christ's case when it was being questioned and challenged. . . .

Another feature . . . is the use of juridical questions in John. The interrogative frequently appears in the Fourth Gospel (e.g., 1:48; 4:27, 33; 9:36; 11:34; 14:5; 18:29; 20:15), but in many places, particularly in John 1–12, it is an example of lawcourt speech. The parties in the controversy interrogate one another, questioning each other's explanations. The obvious aim of these pointed questions is to shift the *onus probandi* to one's opponent. . . . Taken with other evidence, this is another indication of the importance of the controversy theme in the Fourth Gospel. . . .

The resurrection accounts of chapters 20 and 21 have an evidential ring about them. Against all would-be objectors John is concerned to maintain the identity of Christ's risen body with the one which was crucified and laid in the tomb. . . .

The 'signs' of Christ can have evidential value. A good example of this is furnished by Nicodemus, who admits that Jesus is 'a teacher come from God, for no man can do these signs that you do, unless God is with him'

(3:2). Similarly, the evidential value of signs is recognized in 6:2, where the multitude follows Christ 'because they saw the signs which he did on those who were diseased' (cf. 12:17–18). John believed that signs were important in presenting his case (20:30–1). . . .

Viewed from a juridical perspective, the Fourth Gospel has a case to present. . . . Unlike Justin Martyr, John does not seek to support his case by a large string of Old Testament quotations, for he realizes that unbelievers can give completely different explanations of the same texts. Instead he introduces a number of independent witnesses who testify on behalf of Jesus of Nazareth, whose claims have been called into question by the Jews. Thus John presents witnesses and offers evidence to substantiate the Messiahship and divine Sonship of Jesus (20:31).

> Allison A. Trites. *The New Testament Concept of Witness* (Cambridge, Cambridge University Press, 1977), pp. 78–82, 86–88

PROLOGUE

It deserves perhaps more than any part of the Gospel the three epithets sometimes applied to John's style . . . : simple, subtle, sublime. . . .

Simple as it is in diction and phrasing, it digs deep into the mysteries of the Gospel. It is an expansion of 'Jesus was with God, and became flesh to reveal God', but it touches on

(i) the ideas of *Fatherhood and Sonship* being always in God from the beginning,
(ii) Christ as the source of *light*,
(iii) God as the source of *life*,
(iv) the mysterious connexion between life and light,
(v) the incarnation of Jesus and his rejection,
(vi) the doctrine of *grace* or 'regeneration', that is, the power, from a belief in Jesus, to become new men and women,
(vii) the doctrine of 'revelation' (as opposed to the modern idea of unaided evolution).

These are the very subjects illustrated in the Gospel itself. . . .

Its simplicity is astonishing. . . .Syntax and grammar, as well as diction, contribute to this simplicity. Simple sentences are used, complex ones are rare, and as in the dialogues, simple forms of verbs are used, rarely verbs compounded with prepositions, which are much commoner in Greek authors. Particles are conspicuously absent. Instead of these and of relative pronouns, repetition of a noun or the mere order of the words makes the connexion clear. This simplicity of language, not a syllable wasted, has a wonderful effect, as in the dialogues.

A study of the verbs and nouns is interesting. How limited is their range and number! The writer plays upon ten nouns, 'word' and 'world' four times each, 'God' six times, 'light' five times, 'darkness', 'life', 'flesh', 'glory', 'man', and 'will' (all repeated), and upon five verbs, 'was', 'became', 'witness', 'receive', 'believe', of which 'was' comes nine times, and 'became' eight times. On this small range of words he builds up this stately paragraph.

This repetition of a noun or phrase is the source of the impressiveness, directness, and vigour of John's style. . . .

A second characteristic of the Evangelist [is] this habit of picking up again what seemed a lost thread, and weaving it in again. Noun echoes noun, and verb echoes verb. This must be intentional, in order to drive home certain main ideas. It is done with a quiet persistence that leaves certain outstanding truths firmly fixed in the reader's mind. . . .

P. C. Sands. Literary Genius of the New Testament (Oxford, Oxford University Press, 1932), pp. 50–53

Each of the evangelists begins his work by tracing back the activity of Jesus to its origin . . . : Mark to the work of the Baptist and the baptism of Jesus, with the descent of the Spirit and the divine pronouncement, Thou art my Son; Matthew and Luke to the birth of Jesus from a virgin; John to the creation, and beyond it. Each intends to prepare his readers for understanding the ensuing narrative; Jesus can be understood only as Messiah, as Son of God, and as Logos. John alone, however, gives the narrative about Jesus an absolute theological framework, and, though he alludes to the starting-points used by Mark (vv. 6–8) and by Matthew and Luke (v. 13), he must have regarded them as inadequate. . . .

The Prologue falls naturally into the following divisions:

1. vv. 1–5, *Cosmological.* The eternal divine Word, God's agent in creation, is the source of light and life for men. The light is surrounded by darkness, from which it is absolutely and eternally distinguished, and by which it can never be quenched.

2. vv. 6–8, *The Witness of John.* The eternal truth about the Word having been stated, the evangelist begins to move towards his account of its manifestation in time. In accordance with the Christian tradition, he first introduces the Baptist, carefully distinguishing him from the true Light, but bringing out his importance as bearing witness to it.

3. vv. 9–13, *The Coming of the Light.* The coming of the Messiah, or Light, is now reached; a coming which was an almost unmitigated failure. Even those who were most privileged did not believe when they saw the light;

though John is careful to note and allow for the few who heard, believed, and received, and so constituted the Church, whose spokesman he was.

4. vv. 14–18, *The Economy of Salvation*. The coming of Jesus the Word is dealt with in more detail, and for clarity accompanied by further reference to the Baptist. The earthly life of Jesus, though humble, was the scene in which the glory and mercy of God were displayed.

These divisions are of roughly equal length, but it does not seem possible to split them up further into poetic structure, either in Greek or in a conjectured original Aramaic. If this is true, it is impossible to strike out certain passages as prose insertions into an original "logos-ode". This is confirmed by the fact that the whole passage shows, on careful exegesis, a marked internal unity, and also a distinct unity of theme and subject-matter with the remainder of the gospel; and by the variety of the attempts which have been made to restore the original form of the Prologue.

> C. K. Barrett. *The Gospel According to St. John* (London, S.P.C.K., 1955), pp. 125–126

A preliminary glance tells us that 1.1-18 forms a whole, and has been placed at the beginning of the Gospel as a kind of introduction. . . . the section forms a whole, and is complete in itself; it is not necessary for anything to follow. . . .

And yet the Prologue is an introduction—in the sense of being an *overture*, leading the reader out of the commonnplace into a new and strange world of sounds and figures, and singling out particular motifs from the action that is now to be unfolded. He cannot yet fully understand them, but because they are half comprehensible, half mysterious, they arouse the tension, and awaken the *question* which is essential if he is to understand what is going to be said. . . .

In its form the Prologue is a piece of *cultic-liturgical poetry*, oscillating between the language of revelation and confession. . . .

The *form* of the Prologue is not loose or haphazard, but rigid and even minor details are governed by strict rules. . . . each couplet is made up of two short sentences. Sometimes both parts of the couplet express one thought (vv. 9, 12, 14b); sometimes the second completes and develops the first (vv. 1, 4, 14a, 16); sometimes the two parts stand together in parallelism (V.3), or in antithesis (vv. 5, 10, 11). This form is not foreign to semitic poetry, and recurs often in the discourses of the Gospel; but in the Prologue it is developed further by means of a special artistic device. In each sentence two words normally carry the emphasis, and the second of these stressed words often recurs as the first word emphasised in the next sentence.

> Rudolph Bultmann, *The Gospel of John: A Commentary*, trans. G. R. Beasley-Murray (Philadelphia, Westminster Press, 1971), pp. 13-15

There are several encomia embedded in New Testament writings. An example is the beginning of John's gospel (1:1–18), a poem in praise of the incarnate Christ . . . The poem conveys the impression of having been written in a moment of intense emotion. Images, ideas, and feelings tumble out abruptly and in rapid succession. There is no attempt at a sustained and logically organized pattern of development. Like a true lyric poet, the writer does not argue but asserts, and he asserts as a way of praising. . . .

The prologue is the reader's introduction to the protagonist of the Gospel story. In terms of character, He is declared to be the incarnate God—both divine and human, both heavenly and earthly. In terms of His meaning, Christ is said to be the revelation of God to man and the bringer of spiritual life.

The prologue also introduces some leading literary techniques that will be characteristic of the style of the gospel. Already we see the reliance on symbol and metaphor as the form through which the nature of God's unprecedented disclosure in Christ is conveyed. Thus Christ is presented as "the Word" and as "the light" that "shines in the darkness" and "enlightens every man." Also evident is the inclination toward antithesis and plot conflict, seen in the contrasting pairs of light and darkness, being in the world and yet rejected by the world, coming to His own home and not being received there.

Leland Ryken. *The Literature of the Bible* (Grand Rapids, Zondervan, 1974), pp. 204–205, 280

John begins his story with the creation of the cosmos. By drawing upon language from the beginning of Genesis—"in the beginning," "God," "light," and "darkness"—he presents a Christian modulation of Old Testament cosmogony. John's universe is bifurcated. Through a concentrated dose of contrasting images in the first verses of John, the realm of the creator is set over against the created world: Father/world, light/darkness, life/death, knowledge/ignorance, faith/unbelief, and spirit/flesh. Jesus mediated between the two poles. He descends from the Father into the world, becomes flesh, and thereby brings light into a world of darkness. Wherever he is present, the bifurcation is overcome; he transforms the world so that it is not in polar opposition to God. Through him, and only through him, the things of this world become signs opening to the heavenly sphere of the Father. In later scenes the words and deeds of Jesus unite the heaven/earth axis through Johannine symbols and metaphors.

Leonard L. Thompson. *Introducing Biblical Literature: A More Fantastic Country* (Englewood Cliffs, Prentice-Hall, 1978), p. 272

It is a peculiar prologue, difficult even to classify formally. It seems to be a hymn, similar to others in the New Testament (e.g. Phil. 2:5–11), to so-called wisdom hymns (e.g. Wisdom of Sirach 24:1–22), or to the non-Christian hymn to Zeus by Cleanthes. The hymn has no obvious match, but it does exhibit certain stylistic features found in Semitic poetry, like staircase parallelism:

In the beginning was the Word,
and the Word was with God,
and God was the Word.
In him was life,
and the life was the light of men.
The light shines in the darkness,
and the darkness has not overcome it. . . .

The prologue is a most appropriate introduction to the Gospel. Most of the major motifs in John appear in it: light/darkness, son/father, enlighten, life. John mentions the light/darkness opposition of 1:5 in 3:19–21 and develops it in chapters 8 and 9. The "only son" (1:14) occurs in one of the most familiar verses in the New Testament, John 3:16, and father/son language pervades the Gospel. Jesus frequently speaks of himself as the revealer (verse 18), notably in 5:19–22 and 6:46. The term "life" appears nearly forty times. . . . The prologue also introduces one of the most basic themes of the story, Jesus' coming into the world and his rejection by "his own people" (verse 11). Thus, the prologue contains most of the important clues for interpreting the work. . . .

> Donald Juel. *An Introduction to New Testament Literature* (Nashville, Abingdon Press, 1978), pp. 273–274

O God most glorious . . .
Nature's great King, through endless years the same;

. . . .
Vehicle of the universal Word, that flows
Through all, and the light celestial glows

. . . .
One Word through all things everlastingly.
One Word—whose voice alas! the wicked spurn . . .

By the time the Gospel According to John was written, men and women for three centuries had been singing Cleanthes' "Hymn to Zeus." In it they had sung of God's "Word," the *Logos*.

Bridging the gap between Pagan and Chrisian thought, John begins with another hymn about the *Logos*, the Word of God. Stoics and Christians knew that there was really only one God and that in the beginning it was through that "Word," that manifestation of the Divine Mind, that the world was created. "In the beginning was the Explanation," one could translate John's first words. . . .

Three centuries after John, the great Augustine was to write that before he became a Christian he had learned from Greek philosophy everything in the prologue of John until he came to verse 14. "And the Word became flesh and dwelt among us." That was the good news unknown to any pagan! In Jesus the *Logos* had become flesh, had become completely human. . . .

The concept of the divine wisdom in Proverbs 8 is surely part of the background of John's hymn. John begins by expressing the meaning of Christ in terms derived from the Jewish scriptures, as do the first sermons, but also in terms familiar to former pagans.

These were Gnostic terms, too. But the strong word used about the incarnation, that in Jesus the Word had become *flesh*, clearly separated John from the heretics.

> William M. Ramsay. *The Layman's Guide to the New Testament* (Atlanta, John Knox Press, 1981), pp. 243–244

PASSION STORY

Dramatic irony is particularly apparent in the account of the behaviors of the various characters involved in the closing events of Christ's life. Peter says, "I will lay down my life for thy sake," a promise that, as tradition asserts, proved true in the end. After Peter's denial, "immediately the cock crew," a symbol of the dawn of a new day in his life: but Judas goes out into Stygian darkness;—"Judas went out and it was night." . . .

The Pharisees are made to say, "Behold the whole world is gone after him," wherein they unconsciously corroborate the title given to Jesus in this Gospel, and illustrated in every chapter—"The Saviour of the World." The title on the Cross, "King of the Jews," is said to have been written in Hebrew, Greek, Latin, the languages of the three great nations of the world. It is a foreshadowing of the lofty imperial title of the world's Saviour, ironically proclaimed by the contemptuous decree of a Roman viceroy. . . . The ironical reference in xviii, 28, to the fear of ceremonial defilement on the part of Jesus' captors, and their consequent refusal to enter the Praetorium, is obvious. It is equally ironical that Pilate, representing the highest imperial authority, should be compelled to yield to their scruples.

The whole account of the dialogue with Pilate is permeated through and through with dramatic irony. Pilate makes much of his imperial "authority." . . . Our Lord replies that whatever authority Pilate is clothed with, is given him of God: the rest of the narrative shows him a mere slave to superstitious fears, to his own past, and to the malignant clamour of the populace. The cry "Thou art not Caesar's friend" is followed by the significant, "When Pilate *therefore* heard that saying, he brought Jesus forth" and with a pitiful appeal to the popular sense of humour, caused Jesus to sit,

arrayed as He was, on the imperial tribunal;—"Behold your King!" . . .
"We have no king but Caesar," shouts back the hypocritical patriotism of
the crowd. As he records that cry, the Evangelist knows that his readers will
also remember that "caesar" sacked Jerusalem. Pilate is rudely reminded of
the imperial will of which he is the slave, against his own better instincts. . . .
The final tragedy was brought about in response to a heartless demand by
Christ's own people; "He came unto his own, and his own received him
not." It is indeed true to say that the dramatic power of this Evangelist rises
to its greatest height in the story of the closing days.

> R. H. Strachan. *The Fourth Evangelist: Dramatist or
> Historian?* (London, Hodder and Stoughton, 1925), pp.
> 18–21

It is to John that we Westerners turn for the most intimate account of the
Passion and Resurrection, first for its convincing detail, the evidence of one
who, as an acquaintance of the High Priest, obtained entry to the Palace and
saw more even than Peter, and could glean his information more safely;
secondly, because the Roman trial appeals to us more than the Jewish, and
it is more fully given in John; thirdly, because of its dramatic incidents and
situations. . . .

The parts of the drama which John fills out in so masterly a way are (i)
the prelude to the arrest, (ii) the trial before Pilate, and (iii) the Resurrection.
As usual, this writer turns his searchlight upon the *motives* of the actors, and
on the thought of the Master, which engross him before everything else.

He has also preserved the dramatic order of the events; for instance, after
tracing the growing hostility of the enemy, he narrates the raising of Lazarus
not only as a climax of the "words" of Jesus, but as the work that caused
the enthusiasm of the Triumphal Entry and decided the Jewish council to take
prompt action. He now turns to Jesus and shows him to us consciously
preparing for the trial to come. In drama the audience is allowed to see
something of the mind of the hero before the final act, and Hamlet ponders
the question 'To be or not to be'. So John, while omitting the institution of
the Last Supper as known already, has given us a full account of the thoughts
of Jesus and his preparation of the disciples for the struggle.

> P. C. Sands. *Literary Genius of the New Testament* (Ox-
> ford, Oxford University Press, 1932), p. 98

The narrative itself, in chapter xviii and the following chapters, is plain,
realistic, full of dramatic detail. . . . Here and there the attentive reader will
notice unobtrusive pointers to a deeper meaning, but they are never allowed
to interrupt the flow of the narrative. But John expects us to read the story
with understanding; and he has the right to expect it, because he has already
given us, in the five chapters which immediately precede, what amounts to

a penetrating commentary on the events. His method of accompanying the record of an incident with a discourse explaining its meaning is here employed on the grand scale.

In chapter xiii John, like the other evangelists, is recording the last supper of Jesus with his followers, and the table-talk on that sorrowful occasion. Gradually the familiar table-talk takes a different tone, as Jesus begins to speak to his disciples of what lies before him, and of what it means for them and the world. Slowly, meditatively, the discourse moves from point to point, exploring one aspect after another of its great theme—the benefits of Christ's passion. Conversation gives place to prophetic utterance. Finally in chapter xvii it rises into prayer; for it is only in the language of prayer that the last truths of religion find fitting expression.

C. H. Dodd. *About the Gospels* (Cambridge, Cambridge
University Press, 1950), pp. 44–45

LUKE

STRUCTURE

There is a wide measure of agreement concerning the organization of the subject matter of Luke. The following sections would seem to represent the author's arrangement of his narrative:

(1) Preface, 1:1–4
(2) The Nativity, Infancy, and Childhood of John the Baptist and of Jesus, 1:5–2:52
(3) Preparation for the Ministry, 3:1–4:13
(4) The Galilean Ministry, 4:14–9:50
(5) Journey of Jesus and His Disciples to Jerusalem, 9:51–19:27
(6) Days in Jerusalem: The Crucifixion and Resurrection Narratives, 19:28–24:53

James L. Price, Jr. *Int.* 7, 1953, p. 200

The organization of material in this Gospel is similar to that in Mark: introduction (birth of John the Baptist and birth and childhood of Jesus), Chs. 1–2; baptism and temptation of Jesus, 3:1–4:13; ministry in Galilee, 4:14–9:50; ministry in Perea, 9:51–19:28; ministry in Judea, 19:28–22:38; arrest, trials, Crucifixion, Resurrection, and Ascension, 22:39–24:53.

Buckner B. Trawick. *The Bible as Literature: The New Testament* (New York, Barnes and Noble, 1964, 1968), p. 53

When Luke is placed beside Matthew and Mark, it is immediately apparent that the third Gospel departs completely from the order and much of the content of the other two in a lengthy central section (9:51–18:14). . . .

Once this "Central Section" is seen in proper perspective, then the basic form of the entire Gospel may be readily grasped. Whereas Matthew exhibits a five-fold pattern, and Mark and John—in different ways—develop a two-fold scheme, Luke has utilized a three-fold arrangement of his material. As with the other Synoptics, he describes first the ministry of Jesus in Galilee and concludes finally with his passion in Jerusalem. But between these two foci of the gospel ellipse he has inserted his "Great Interpolation" depicting the journey which lay between these two basic spheres of activity. Whereas the other Synoptics make only passing mention of this transition from the north to the south (Mt. 19:1; Mk. 10:1), Luke has expanded the last journey "on the way to the Cross" into his most conspicuous section.

Once the internal structure of his work was determined, Luke further supplemented Mark primarily by adding special material to the outer edges of his Gospel, thereby giving it one of the most effective introductions and conclusions of any book in the New Testament. The Infancy Narrative (1:5–2:52) artfully relates John and Jesus in parallel cycles which show how both: (1) had devout parents, (2) to whom the angel Gabriel appeared, (3) to promise supernatural conception, (4) for which both mothers gave God the glory. In each case (5) the miraculous births did occur, (6) the babies were given divinely chosen names, (7) outbursts of prophecy interpreted the events as acts of God, and (8) the children grew to spiritual maturity. The Resurrection Narrative (24:1–53) is not as elaborate as the complex Infancy Narrative but it does cluster several theological motifs crucial to Luke around the breath-taking drama of the journey to Emmaus. Both at its beginning and its ending, the third Gospel provides uniquely valuable Jerusalem-Judea source materials not found in the other Synoptics or in John.

William E. Hull. *R & E.* 64, 1967, pp. 423–242

There is good reason for believing that Luke has grouped the teaching contained in the travel narrative into two sections. The division occurs at 14.1. Just before this new section, Jesus defines again his purpose to go to Jerusalem, under pressure of the warning conveyed by the Pharisees that Herod is trying to kill him. Luke has marked the beginning of the journey by stating Jesus' firm intention to go to Jerusalem, but his purpose is not yet fully defined (9.51); at the end of chapter 13 the intention is repeated, and this time it is made clear by the lament over Jerusalem that the city will kill him as it killed the prophets before him. . . .

It is possible, then, to justify a five-fold division of the Gospel: (1) 1.5 to 3.38, Jesus comes to fulfil all the O.T. expectations; (2) 4.1 to 9.50, he preaches in the whole of Judea and Galilee and gathers his disciples; (3) 9.51 to 13.35, he begins his journey to Jerusalem and teaches the nature of discipleship; (4) 14.1 to 19.27, he concludes his journey to Jerusalem and prepares his disciples for the Passion; (5) 19.28 to 24.53, he reigns in Jerusalem by dying and rising again.

Each of the parts is governed by some sort of geographical factor, and always the geographical movement has significance for the history of salvation. The city which appears at every turn of the story is the holy city of Jerusalem, and it is important to note that at each of the breaks between

Luke's sections there stands a definitive reference to Jerusalem. At the first Jesus, after his baptism in the Jordan, is led into the desert by the Spirit to be tempted and his last temptation takes place in Jerusalem; his mission is defined near Jerusalem before he returns to Galilee to begin his ministry (4.14). At the second break he steadfastly sets his face to go to Jerusalem (9.51); at the third he renews his purpose to die in Jerusalem and laments over the rebellious city (13.31–5); at the fourth he enters it to die, having warned his disciples that Jerusalem cannot be the scene of the Kingdom's coming until it has been the scene of his death (19.11ff).

J. C. O'Neill. *The Theology of Acts in Its Historical Setting* (London, S.P.C.K., 1970), pp. 70–72

UNIFYING MOTIFS

It is easy to show that S. Luke had a special sympathy with the poor man. But that was because of the special circumstances of the poor man, because nobody else had so far shewn him any sympathy at all. His real sympathy was with every man. . . .

He did seriously believe that wealth was a terribly dangerous thing. He suspected it. And he a little bit suspects position. . . .

Consider again from this point of view his account of Our Lord's life. Born in a stable, because the public-house was occupied, in after years a manual labourer, and then a vagrant, with not where to lay His head, suspected by His brethren on the ground that He was an upstart, and by the clergy because He had no University degree, accused of all the offences of which the poor man always is accused—conceit, unworthy motives, lack of authority, trespassing on rights of property, and general impossibility—He is arrested, tried by summary process, bandied from Pilate to Herod, and back again to Pilate, finding the kind of justice that the poor man so often finds, and in the end He dies by Crucifixion on the gallows.

The greater part of Our Lord's life was lived among the poor, and therefore . . . much of His teaching is drawn from their example. His parables are about the patching of old clothes and the baking or the borrowing of a loaf of bread. . . . The Magnificat is the most revolutionary of hymns. The poor widow, the publican, and the prostitute are among the most typical of Lukan characters. The Prodigal Son, the Good Samaritan, and many others are parables of mercy.

This comes, as I say, from his belief in the Incarnation.

S. C. Carpenter. *Christianity According to St. Luke* (London, S.P.C.K., 1919), pp. 209–210

In his Gospel it is possible to see how the detached observer was carried away by admiration. The leading characteristic of his Gospel is the devotion of the author to his Hero. He has other minor but not unconnected admirations for aspects of Our Lord's message, which he shows by his description of certain types, but his main object is to draw a picture of the Son of Man. His biography is inspired, as were the biographies of Plutarch and other ancient writers, by the motive called in Latin *pietas*.

> S. C. Carpenter. *Christianity According to St. Luke*
> (London, S.P.C.K., 1919), p. 179

One of the chief characteristics of Luke is its note of *universalism*. 'Goodwill to men', is the message of the angelic host (ii. 14), and in the Infant Jesus Simeon sees 'a light for revelation to the Gentiles' (ii. 32). . . .

A strong interest in *social relationships*, especially as they concern wealth and poverty, is a further characteristic of Luke. The Beatitudes appear in the form 'Blessed are ye poor', 'Blessed are ye that hunger now' (vi. 20 f.), and are accompanied by corresponding Woes on the rich, the full, and the happy. . . . In many of His parables the illustrations are taken from finance, as in the Two Debtors, the Rich Fool, the Tower Builder, the Lost Coin, the Unjust Steward, the Rich Man and Lazarus, the Pounds. . . .

Closely connected with the foregoing is the gracious attitude of the Lukan Jesus to the *outcast*, the *sinner*, and the *Samaritan*. . . .

Luke's references to *women* are also universally noted as one of his characteristic features. It is in this Gospel alone that we read of the widow of Nain (vii. 11ff.), the woman in the city (vii. 36ff.), Joanna and Susanna (viii. 3), of Martha, who was 'distracted about much serving' (x. 38ff.), of the women who lamented Jesus on His way to the Cross (xxiii. 27ff.), and of the parables of the Woman and the Lost Coin (xv. 8ff.) and the Widow and the Unjust Judge (xviii. 1ff.). Besides these stories, . . . there are in the Birth Stories the narratives of Mary, Elisabeth, and Anna. . . .

Equally with Mark, Luke is characterized by its interest in *the Passion*. . . . Early in the story Jesus steadfastly sets His face to go to Jerusalem (ix. 51). . . .

Among other Lukan features may be mentioned the references to *joy*, *prayer*, and the *Holy Spirit*. Almost at the beginning of the Gospel stands the message, 'I bring you good tidings of great joy' (ii. 10), and at the end we see the disciples blessing God in the Temple (xxiv. 53). The references to the prayers of Jesus are especially noteworthy.

> Vincent Taylor. *The Gospels: A Short Introduction* (London, The Epworth Press, 1930, 1945), pp. 68–71

We judge the sympathies of Luke by his choice of material. The Christ of Luke is the friend of sinners. . . . In a pre-eminent sense Luke pictures Christ as the friend and saviour of sinners. The matchless parables in Luke 15 (the Lost Sheep, the Lost Coin, the Lost Son) are told by Christ, as Luke explains

(15:1f.), because, when "all the publicans and sinners were drawing near unto him to hear him," "both the Pharisees and the scribes murmured, saying, This man receiveth sinners, and eateth with them." The charge was true, gloriously true as we see, as Luke saw, but as the ecclesiastics of the time did not see. . . .

So pronounced is the sympathy of Luke with the poor that his Gospel has actually been charged . . . with class prejudice, with the modern "Soviet" conception of class domination, the poor ruling the rich. That is not true at all. Luke is interested in the rich (19:2;23:50), but he champions the poor because they needed a friend. . . . Luke records Jesus as saying at Nazareth that the spirit of the Lord had "anointed me to preach good tidings to the poor" (4:18). Luke has simply "Blessed are ye poor" in 6:20. In the story of Lazarus and the wicked Rich Man the beggar comes out ahead in the end (16:19–31). No fiercer indictment of a rich fool was ever drawn than in the parable of Jesus recorded by Luke in 12:16–21. Luke represents Christ as inviting "the poor and maimed and blind and lame" to the supper in the parable (14:21). One of the amazing things about Jesus was his interest in the poor. . . .

Certainly, then, Luke believed in the dignity of man. . . . Luke does not teach that it is a virtue to be poor, but a poor man is, after all, a man, a man worth saving, a man who may be rich toward God, and who may enrich man by the noblest qualities of manhood and service. . . .

Christ made an appeal to women, who early formed a band to help support him and his disciples (Luke 8:1–3). The rabbis in their liturgy thanked God that they were not born women. But Jesus is the emancipator of women. Luke sees this truth and emphasizes it. . . .

Luke knew how both Gentile and Jew looked down on women. He saw the difference in Jesus. So we have sketches of Elizabeth and Mary the mother of Jesus, the prophetess Anna and the widow of Nain, the sinful woman in the house of Simon and the woman with an issue of blood, Mary Magdalene and the others of her band, Mary and Martha of Bethany, the widow with the two mites and the daughters of Jerusalem, the women at the tomb. . . . Luke wrote the gospel of womanhood, full of sympathy and tenderness, full of understanding of their tasks and their service. Dante describes Luke as "the writer of the story of the gentleness of Christ." . . . Christ has enfranchised women in the true sense of spiritual privilege and prowess and service. . . . The women were last at the cross and first at the tomb. . . .

Luke tells us most about the birth and childhood of Jesus, and gives us the only glimpse that we have of the boy Jesus, with a boy's hunger for knowledge and yearning for future service, this boy who already had the consciousness of peculiar relationship to God his Father, and yet who went back to Nazareth in obedience to Joseph and Mary to toil at the carpenter's bench for eighteen more years. . . . No one who did not love and understand children could have so graphically pictured the boyhood of Jesus in this one short paragraph.

A. T. Robertson. *Luke the Historian in the Light of Research* (New York, Charles Scribner's Sons, 1930), pp. 235–239

Mark and Matthew were members of the suffering nation, and to them Jesus is the Man of Sorrows, and the persecution of the Scribes repeats the traditional persecution of the old prophets. Luke belongs to the world outside, and is absorbed in other aspects of Jesus and his message. He is interested, too, in other classes of people, for whom the message was a more joyous thing—shepherds, soldiers, taxgatherers, women, and widows and outcasts, and, what were to the Jew real 'outsiders', the Samaritans. His world is of course the non-Jewish world, whose battle the Apostle Paul, his friend, fought so hard to win in the Acts. He sees the Scribes and Pharisees with more sense of proportion, as he views them from the other end of Europe. He can even afford to be more tolerant of them. . . .

Much matter that would appeal to Jews and not to Gentiles is omitted, for instance, the teaching about the old law in the Sermon on the Mount, while the appeals to the Old Testament are few. . . .

His attitude to *women* is non-Jewish. He gives them unusual prominence; he has listened to them, used their accounts of incidents, and not forgotten the domestic side of the story. Such a domestic incident of feminine interest as Martha's complaint about Mary, and the mention of women supplying the household wants of Jesus and his band on their preaching tour, are peculiar to Luke. What feminine points of view colour the first two chapters! Their comments on the strange events, events belonging to their own sphere, their private thoughts. . . .

Mark does not mention *Samaritans*, Matthew mentions them once, John shows the prevalent contempt for them in the bitter taunt of the Jews, 'Say we not well, Thou are a Samaritan, and hast a devil?' But Luke has made them famous by the parable of the Good Samaritan, shows the tenderness of Jesus towards their intolerance, and in a miracle peculiar to his Gospel records the only grateful leper in ten as a Samaritan. So in the Acts he records the evangelising of their villages.

So it is with the outcast *Publican*. One of the most delightful episodes is the honour paid to Zacchaeus. . . . In things Roman he is always interested, and in fact the whole Gentile world, its governors and officials, is constantly before his mind. While therefore of the three hymns which he introduces in his first two chapters, the first, Mary's, is full of *personal* feeling, and the second, that of Zacharias, is full of *national* aspirations, the third, Simeon's, is full of *cosmopolitan* hope: 'all people' are to share, and 'the Gentiles' to see the light. The first teaching of Jesus, which Luke records, is on the subject of the outside peoples, and the last utterance embraces 'all nations'.

> P. C. Sands. *Literary Genius of the New Testament* (Oxford, Oxford University Press, 1932), pp. 32–34

Luke, like other writers in the New Testament (John, and the authors of Hebrews and 1 Peter), has been powerfully influenced by the part played by the idea of journeying in Old Testament religion, and seems to have constructed his two books with this picture in mind. The mission of Jesus is in the form of a journey up to Jerusalem. . . .

Luke's characteristic expression for the Christian religion is 'The Way'. . . . 'The Way' as a title for Christianity is not found only in Luke's writings; it occurs in John's Gospel where Jesus himself says 'I am the way, I am the truth and I am life' (John 14:6) and in the Letter to Hebrews where the author speaks of Jesus as 'the new, living way' (Heb. 10:20). Nevertheless, it is a theme which Luke has specially emphasized in his two volumes. The Gospel of Luke and Acts are, in fact, two books on 'the way': the 'way of Christ' in the Gospel and the 'way of the Christian' in Acts. In the manner of John, Luke announces this theme in the prologue to his Gospel and then develops it in the main body of the work. John the Baptist is to prepare 'the way' (Luke 1:76) of him who is to 'guide our feet into the way of peace' (Luke 1:79).

Jesus is in Luke's Gospel essentially a journeying figure. It appears that Luke, again like John, wants the readers of his Gospel to see in the actual travelling of Jesus, especially the journey up to Jerusalem, which is heralded as a decisive event in Luke 9:51, a symbol of the other event which is going on at the same time: the going up to God. The way up to Jerusalem (in obedience) is the way up to heaven (in ascension—Luke 9:51 and 19:28). It is therefore a way of salvation (Luke 1:77), a new exodus of Israel from sin and death . . . , a Passover celebrating Israel's freedom by enacting the journey from Egypt to the promised land. Luke uses the journeys of the apostles in Acts to make the point that Christians are those who follow in Christ's 'way', or rather that in Christians Christ, through the Spirit, is making another return journey to the Father. In the 'way of Christ' as it is presented in the Gospel Luke intends his Christian readers to see *their* way from baptism into Christ to ascension to Christ.

> E. J. Tinsley. *The Gospel According to Luke* (Cambridge, Cambridge University Press, 1965), pp. 107, 209–210

A feature of the gospel material peculiar to Luke is its numerous well-to-do characters. The Good Samaritan had money to spare, the father of the Prodigal

Son was a man of substance, Zacchaeus is more rich than honest, the rich man who ignored Lazarus is ostentatiously affluent, the women of 8.2,3 look after Jesus from their own resources. This indicates a literate and comfortable bourgeoisie as Luke's readership. . . .

Zacchaeus is a thoroughly Lucan character, well-off, shady, little, unrespectable—yet responsive to Jesus. He belongs to that suspect fringe of Judaism which plays such a telling part in the book. There, for Luke, are the people whom Jesus not only likes but chooses to stay with and eat with because they are not too encumbered with their piety and virtue to heed the gospel.

> John Drury. *Luke* (New York, Macmillan Publishing
> Company, 1975), pp. 135, 176

STORYTELLING TECHNIQUE

Luke's gospel is a regular composition, founded on anterior documents. It is the work of a man who selects, prunes, combines. . . .

We are able to say certain things in regard to his tastes and his peculiar tendencies: he is a very precise devotee; he makes it important that Jesus performed all the Jewish rites; he is an exalted democrat and Ebionite, that is, thoroughly opposed to property, and persuaded that the day of the poor is at hand; he is especially fond of all the anecdotes which place in relief the conversion of sinners, the exaltation of the humble. . . . Finally, there are in the account of the last days of Jesus some circumstances full of tender feeling and certain words of Jesus of a delicious beauty. . . .

He is less an evangelist than a biographer of Jesus. . . . But he is a biographer of the first century, a divine artist who, independently of the materials which he derived from more ancient sources, pictures to us the character of the founder, with a happiness in feature, and an inspiration in the whole, a relief which the other two synoptics have not. His gospel has the greatest charm for the modern reader, for to the incomparable beauty of the common ground, he adds a portion of art and composition which singularly increases the effect of the portrait.

> Ernest Renan, *The Life of Jesus*, trans. Charles Edwin
> Wilbour (New York, Carleton, 1864), pp. 18–19, 36–
> 37

He is fond of teaching by contrast or cumulative effect. He has in chapter xv. three "Lost" parables in succession, the Lost Sheep, the Lost Coin, the Lost Son. . . . He alone points the contrast between the two robbers on the cross, and he alone of the Synoptists between Martha and Mary. His parables include the contrasts between Dives and Lazarus, the Pharisee and the Publican, the two debtors, the priest and the Levite and the Samaritan, the Judge and the Widow, the one and the nine lepers, and the Prodigal and his brother. . . .

He is master of Tragic Irony, the making of a character in a drama say something which really tells, and is recognized by those who know the whole story as telling, in the opposite direction from that in which the speaker supposes. . . . The supreme case of the kiss of Judas, the "ninety and nine just persons," the fact that it was the Sadduccees who brought up the problem of the resurrection and a maidservant who put one of the crucial questions in the courtyard, the gibe that He saved others and if He is indeed the Christ of God, the elect, He may now save Himself—all these are part of the general tradition of the Gospels. But other examples are his own. The "is not this the son of Joseph?" (iv. 22) and the "two swords" of xxii. 38 are cases in point. . . . The parable of the Rich Fool (xii. 16f.) is another case of Tragic Irony. So is the reconciliation of Pilate and Herod over Our Lord's condemnation. . . . And the story of Emmaus, where faith is born of the very ashes of despair, is full of irony, though of a tender and more healing kind.

As a painter of portraits S. Luke excels. His short pen-pictures of Zacharias, the Virgin Mother, Martha and Mary, Zacchaeus, and the repentant robber are masterly. . . .

Once more, our Evangelist can depict a situation. He tells us how the kingdoms of the world were brought before the imagination of Our Lord by the tempter "in a moment of time." . . . One of the most dramatic situations in this Gospel is the Trial before Herod, which occurs only in S. Luke. . . . The situation of the expectant monarch and the silent Christ is one which demands, and has obtained, a great artist to depict it.

But the supremely dramatic passage in the Gospel is the picture in the last chapter of the two enthusiasts who, chilled and disappointed by a signal failure, were taking a country walk together on Sunday afternoon. They were talking of the apparent impotence of good. . . .

And, as they talked, Jesus Himself drew near. The supernatural is there, the possibility of victory, even the victory itself, but it is not recognized at first.

S. C. Carpenter. *Christianity According to St. Luke*
(London, S.P.C.K., 1919), pp. 193–195, 199–200

He was called a painter by the ancients. . . . Luke has exerted a profound influence upon Christian art by his lifelike portrayals of character in the Gospel and the Acts. He painted with his pen, if not with his brush. His pictures are drawn to the life and glow with life. . . .

He is the first great Christian hymnologist. He has preserved the psalms of praise from Elizabeth, Mary, Zacharias, the angels and Simeon. . . . He alone has preserved them because he had a soul for music and for poetry. . . .

There are abundant proofs of Luke's artistic skill. He has touches that would please cultured Gentiles like "the good and honest heart" in 8:15. . . .

Luke's fondness for "table-talk" (Luke 7:36 f.; 11:37 f.; 14:1 f.) may be due to his knowledge of the *symposia* of Greek literature. Luke knows how to make a cumulative effect by contrast as in parables in rapid succession in chapters 14–18. . . . Luke is a master of tragic irony. He knows how to make the climax tell by saying just enough and no more. The intellectual surprise is complete and abiding. The story of the two disciples going to Emmaus in Luke 24 is the most beautiful story in all the world. It is told with consummate skill. Luke can depict a situation with supreme art.

As a painter of short portraits Luke also excels. He has drawn the pictures of Jesus, Peter and Paul on large canvas with the master's hand. Luke has made his story vivid both in the Gospel and the Acts by the use of the power of personality. He understood the true principle of dealing with so vast a subject. He found the secret in personality. . . . It is not only fine workmanship that Luke gives us. He exhibits insight into human nature. . . .

He is certainly a lover of mankind who fell in love with Jesus. . . . He had the devotion to Jesus that Plutarch call *pietas*, when a biographer loves his subject. Luke was not a formal theologian, but he had the sense of mystery in the presence of Christ's overwhelming personality. . . .

Luke understood the loneliness of Jesus. . . . The humanity of Jesus in Luke is not the deity of humanity so much as the humanity of deity.

A. T. Robertson. *Luke the Historian in the Light of Research* (New York, Charles Scribner's Sons, 1930), pp. 56–60

At the outset we become aware that he is no theologian in spite of his companionship with St. Paul. He is, instead, a storyteller and a biographer. His purpose is to present the character of Jesus so that readers and hearers may become aware not only of His divine nature and message, but also of its meaning and necessity for all men throughout the world. He does not mention the founding of the Church, nor is he so much interested in Jesus, the Messiah of prophecy, as in Jesus, the man among men; in fact, it is *people* who interest St. Luke above all else, and it is through them that he reveals the personality and nature of Jesus.

He is like Boswell in his avidity for experience, and he finds it in all manner of persons: the rich and the poor, the sinful and the good, fishermen, centurions, and the rulers of synagogues; the sick in body and the troubled in soul; women and children, Pharisees, publicans, and hated Samaritans. They fill his pages with their problems and personalities: Zaccheus, who, because he was small of stature, climbed a sycamore tree in order to see Jesus; Jarius, whose little daughter was ill; Jesus at twelve in the Temple; the old man Simeon and the old woman Anna.

He is particularly interested in women, whom he pictures with a consideration and an interest not so evident in the other gospels. . . .

The genius of St. Luke had unquestionably a deep emotional quality which in less skillful hands might well have fallen into sentimentalism. This emotional quality is shown again in his presentation of Jesus as a friend of the poor and of those ostracized from society by sin or by disease. In all his scenes are evident his warm and generous sympathy, his pity and compassion, his sense of human worth: in his story of the blind man begging by the wayside, of the wretched servants beaten by the husbandmen, of Lazarus, the beggar, whose sores the dogs licked, of the poor widow casting her two mites into the treasury, and of the thief on the cross, to whom Jesus promises companionship in Paradise. In his pages more than anywhere else in the New Testament "the blind see, the lame walk, the lepers are cleansed, the deaf hear, the dead are raised, to the poor the gospel is preached." . . .

He loved also to set scenes for his stories: the house of Elisabeth and Zacharias in the hill country; the field at night with the stars above the watching shepherds; the long road to Emmaus with the two sad men walking and talking together; the house of the Pharisee on the Sabbath with all the company there watching Jesus in suspicion; the corn field through which the disciples walk and rub the ripe ears with their hands. . . .

The greatest single dramatic achievement of St. Luke is without doubt his account of the last days of Jesus, of the crucifixion, and of those miraculous happenings on the road to Emmaus and in Jerusalem. This narrative begins with chapter 22 and continues to the end of the book. More than any other gospel account of the story this one is told largely in dialogue, or perhaps more accurately, in the succinct statements of bystanders and participants. Not a word here is unnecessary. The story is carried almost entirely by verbs of sight and sound and by the most concrete of nouns. Read aloud it is seen to be, by all standards, at once the most moving and the most dramatic narrative of the four gospels.

Mary Ellen Chase. *The Bible and the Common Reader*
(New York, The Macmillan Company, 1944), pp. 272–276

[The Emmaus story in Luke 24:13–35] is one of Luke's best and most characteristic achievements, a short story whose spell-binding power comes about by a controlled line, a sober realism and a muted sense of wonder. It is his last great set piece, bringing together most of the themes he has handled throughout the work, yet with such skill that nothing strains or spoils the tale. Everything happens within it. That is typical of Luke, and so is the conjunction of ordinariness and marvel at the climax of the narrative, which so appealed to Rembrandt, the most Lucan of painters. The only things like it in the New Testament are the Prodigal Son, the Good Samaritan and the Christmas stories— all Luke's.

A number of other features are trade-marks: the length, the careful notes of time and of place in relation to Jerusalem as centre, the emphasis on interior experience. The action takes place on the road and at the supper-table—both Lucan settings. Jesus is the fulfilment of old prophecy, himself a powerful prophet, whose life is a progress through suffering to glory—a very Lucan view. . . .

A story is a story is a story. It cannot be boiled down to a meaning. Here the power is in suggestion rather than outright doctrine: the risen Jesus unrecognized because of his ordinariness, the moment of perception in the evening and the habitual ceremonies of the table. 'He comes to us as one unknown.' There is more here than a moral.

> John Drury. *Luke* (New York, Macmillan Publishing Company, 1973), p. 217

With Luke the premium is on the telling of the tale—but not as Mark told it. The mind-blowing mystery and tremendous revelation which impresses and disorientates readers of the earlier gospel must be cooled down and passed through everyday conductors to make them acceptable and appetizing to a prosperous (cf. Luke's many well-to-do characters) and peaceful world. Luke's version of Mark's story thus has a leisurely unfolding and methodical attention to temporal sequence which are lacking in the original. It is much more like history, much more realistic, much easier to read. . . .

These two dominant tendencies which govern Luke's use of the work of his predecessors, the love of both the strong story-line moving clearly through time and of salty and realistic teaching, come right into the open in all the sections which are his alone. No Christian stories are as well done or successful as his first chapters (Christmas as we know it is virtually a Lucan affair) or the walk to Emmaus in the last chapter. The care for the least and the lost (vestigially present in Mark, a distinct feature of church life in Matthew) emerges in Luke as the whole gospel, the specifically Christian thing. The stories of the Good Samaritan and the Prodigal Son combine the good story and the universal moral with unforgettable force. . . .

Luke's achievement was to write a secular gospel: the eternal God revealed in a developing story tied into human time and character, bound into the history and fate of the Jews and the church, declaring himself in an ethical demand for compassion, reconciliation and decision-for-the good which nobody could mistake or evade. Other people have been at work already, so the reader knows something of the Christian gospel [cf. the opening sentence of the book]. Luke's aim is to fill this out and order it, and he sets about it in a particular way. He is not going to do it by propositions and arguments like Paul, nor in great visions of the future like the writer of Revelation. He is going to tell a story. He is doing so because it was in a story that it happened. . . . But Luke is not neutral or dispassionate. He also tells the story because he wants his audience to enter into it and take it into their systems and their living. He wants his readers to become disciples or at least admirers of Jesus by reading his book. . . . He has recast it all in the form of an orderly and connected narrative which keeps things moving along and takes with it anyone who likes to listen to a story and lose himself in it.

John Drury. *Luke* (New York, Macmillan Publishing Company, 1973), pp. 12–13, 18

That Luke composed his gospel with care, precision and design is evident already from the introduction (1:1–4). . . . Luke carefully investigates everything from the beginning and thus writes an orderly account, though not necessarily from a chronological point of view. . . .

The gospel of Luke is characterized by a balance and precision that reveals the hand of a literary artist. Frequently men and women are mentioned in juxtaposition in order to achieve balance. In the first chapter Zechariah is introduced, followed by Elizabeth his wife; Mary has a song, and so does Zechariah. In the next chapter Joseph and Mary are mentioned, as are Simeon and Anna. The only son of the widow of Nain is raised from the dead (7:11–17), and so is the only daughter of Jairus (8:40–56). The parable of the mustard seed, which features a man planting his garden, is followed by the parable of the yeast, which portrays a woman baking bread (13:18–21). The parable of the lost sheep, which focuses attention on the shepherd (15:3–7), is succeeded by the parable of the woman who lost a coin in her home (15:8–10). And the parable of the friend who knocks at his neighbor's door in the middle of the night to ask for bread (11:5–8) is balanced by the parable of the widow who keeps coming to a judge with her request for justice (18:1–8). More examples of balance could be mentioned, but these will suffice to show that Luke's composition is beautifully structured and arranged. . . .

Luke displays artistry in listing four beatitudes followed by four woes. By contrast Matthew lists nine beatitudes and makes no mention of woes at all. . . .

The four Lucan beatitudes are skillfully balanced by the four woes that follow. That Luke adapted his material from a sermon preached by Jesus and thus reconstructed the design to create the symmetry of four beatitudes followed by four woes is most probable. . . .

Out of the material available, Luke had to select certain words and deeds of Jesus and arrange them "in an orderly account." The sequence in which Luke records these words and deeds of Jesus many times is not that of the other two synoptic writers. Luke's sequence seems to be dictated not by strict chronology but by emphases, themes, literary balance and design.

Simon J. Kistemaker. *JETS.* 25, 1982, pp. 34, 36, 38–39

STYLE

How does it happen that the Christian religion, springing, as it does, out of the Jewish, should turn so wholeheartedly to the realm of art? Who was the first artist?

It was Luke—Luke, the cultured Greek, trained in the Greek classics, a devotee of the Greek love for beauty in nature and in human nature, in the products of the hand and mind. Almost from the first he was recognized as the founder of Christian art. Indeed, there is an early church tradition that Luke was himself a painter. Rossetti has put this ancient idea into verse:

> Give honor unto Luke, evangelist,
> For he it was, the ancient legends say,
> Who first taught Art to fold her hands and pray.

. . . We do not think to-day of Luke as a painter on canvas, but he painted pen-pictures that have been the inspiration of artists of all kinds, including painters, musicians, and poets. . . . One of the earliest of church pictures, *The Shepherd with the Lost Sheep on His Shoulders*, comes directly from Luke 15. Ancient and modern painters alike have delighted in representing the scenes portrayed by Luke in the Gospel narrative. Among them may be mentioned Fra Angelico's *The Annunciation*, Lerolle's *Arrival of the Shepherds*, Hoffmann's *Christ and the Doctors*, Hunt's *Finding of Christ in the Temple*.

The music of the world owes much to Luke. From this Gospel the great oratorios and anthems have borrowed many of their most popular sentiments. But the greatest contribution is found in the current hymns of the church. The oldest of these were taken bodily from Luke. . . . Among the more recent songs that show the influence of Luke we may mention "O Little Town of Bethlehem," "Holy Night," and "The Sweet Story of Old." When we consider that these joyous hymns and many hundreds more which are sung by millions of people almost daily would never have been composed if Luke had not written his Gospel, we may consider as reasonable the statement that Luke is the most beautiful and inspiring book in the world.

> Herbert R. Purinton and Carl E. Purinton. *Literature of the New Testament* (New York, Charles Scribner's Sons, 1925), pp. 105–107

That other feature of Luke's genius, his historical and literary faculty, will best be shown by a comparison of three passages from the first chapters, two of which passages are entirely his own composition as editor (i. 1-4, ii. 1.), while the third he compiled from information that was almost certainly oral

(ii. 8–20). They present three aspects of Luke as an author, and at least two distinct styles.

The first is purely literary, a preface to his book . . . . Notice first the structure and balance of this sentence, a proper 'classical period', or complex sentence stating facts in logical, that is chronological, order, cause before effect, 'Since many . . . , just as . . . , therefore it seemed good . . .'— ending with a sentence expressing purpose, 'that you may.' . . .

Only an author with a knowledge of classical style could frame a sentence like that; a sentence that keeps the interest of the hearer to the very end, because it is not complete till the last word rounds off the sentence and the sense—a sentence in which contributory ideas are subordinated by the syntax to the chief conclusion, in this case the author's resolve.

The diction is also classical, that is to say (i) exact, and (ii) carefully arranged. . . .

Take next the prelude of the ministry of John the Baptist in chapter iii. 1. . . . Only a historian would have written like this, a man with an orderly mind, giving in a series of clauses duly subordinated to the main verb that is to follow, the names of all the officials of the country round in a particular year, and in order. . . . This orderly historical mind is evidenced by a hundred other touches in the Gospel and in the Acts.

The number of officials, named with an accuracy only possible to one writing in the period that he describes, shows Luke's carefulness to prove that his narrative may be tested by reference to contemporary official records. . . .

In these sentences then, ii. 2 and iii. 1, Luke at the outset claims to be judged as an historian, not a novelist. This is what constitutes the wonder of Luke's Gospel, when those passages are considered along with the following passage:

> There were in the same country shepherds, abiding in the field, keeping watch over their flocks by night. And lo, the angel of the Lord came upon them, and the glory of the Lord shone round about them, and they were sore afraid. And the angel said unto them, "Fear not; for behold, I bring you good tidings of great joy, which shall be to all people. For unto you is born this day in the city of David a Saviour, which is Christ the Lord . . ."

The language in which Luke has clothed it, is Greek of great simplicity and beauty of rhythm. Luke, in spite of the culture which enabled him to write fine periods, at once falls into the simple Aramaic style suited to the reports of shepherds and Hebrew witnesses. The sentences are simple constructed and the style recalls the Old Testament narrative at its best. In the monosyllabic English the language is still more simple, and for this reason perhaps even more effective, and whether it is this surprising skill of the translators, or the glamour of the anthem strains to which the words have been set, and the associations of Christmas, this passage has come to be considered one of the most melodious in the New Testament.

P. C. Sands. *Literary Genius of the New Testament* (Oxford, Oxford University Press, 1932), pp. 36–41

We are dealing with a work which in form, content, and manner of publication is essentially of more literary character than the other two synoptic Gospels. It is introduced by a genuine prologue in the form of a dedication to a certain Theophilus. Both the existence of this prologue and its wording correspond with the literary usage of the time. . . .

He makes an attempt at genuine style, firstly in the framework into which he places the tradition. He ventures to bind together matters which are distinct from each other, e.g. he points out at the end of the Temptation that the devil leaves Jesus only until an opportune moment, and that he takes possession of Judas at the beginning of the Passion. He prepares for the appearance of the women beneath the cross by introducing them as fellow-travellers of Jesus even in Galilee (Luke viii, 1–3). By interpolations he can set up historical connections, e.g. he concludes the story of the Baptist with a notice of his arrest (iii, 19, 20), introduces the public ministry of Jesus with detailed chronological data (iii, 1–2), and begins his account of Pilate by giving the points of accusation which had been brought against Jesus (xxiii, 2).

He endeavours to employ the material offered him by his sources in the manner of a biography. Thus in the case of speeches which probably were often lacking in context, he strives to explain the historical occasion; in the case of narratives he strives to give a clear report, and to remove loose threads.

Marin Dibelius. *A Fresh Approach to the New Testament and Early Christian Literature*, translated from the German (New York, Charles Scribner's Sons, 1936), pp. 62–63

Luke was a skillful writer. His language is fluent, graceful, polished, non-literary Greek (*Koiné*); his vocabulary is large, and his choice of words is exact. He replaces Mark's stringy coordinate clauses with balanced and periodic constructions. He is careful to observe the rules of Greek grammar and syntax. He excels in descriptions of scenes (the Nativity, 2:6–14), in vivid portraiture (Simeon, 2:25; Anna, 2:37; Peter, James, and John, with sleep-heavy eyes, 9:32), and in narrative power (the parables of the Good Samaritan, 10:30–37, and the Prodigal Son, 15:11–32). He has a strong dramatic sense and makes much use of psychological contrast (the Phrarisee vs. the sinful woman, 7:36–48; the Samaritan vs. the priest and the Levite, 10:30–37; Mary vs. Martha, 10:38–42). Possessing a keen appreciation of poetry, he preserves for us the earliest Christian hymns (the Magnificat, 1:46–55; the Benedictus, 1:68–79; the Gloria in Excelsis, 2:14; and the Nunc Dimittis, 2:29–32). A graceful poetic charm pervades the whole Gospel. These merits distinguish Luke as the greatest literary artist of the New Testament.

> Buckner B. Trawick. *The Bible as Literature: The New Testament* (New York, Barnes and Noble, 1964, 1968), p. 53

The relation of the ordinary world of men to another world and another reality . . . is the subject-matter of religion. There are many ways of exploring it, from cosmic myths to homely proverbs; but for the Jews it happened and was hoped for in terms of history. For them it was, above all, an unfolding story. Christianity, the child of Judaism, sees the focus of it in the story of Jesus. This, for Christians, is the place where earth and Heaven meet, and their relation to one another is clearest. *Glory to God in the highest Heaven! Peace upon earth among men of goodwill!* (Luke 2:14), and the two come together in the *baby lying in the manger* and all that follows. Luke's overriding aim is precisely this: to 'earth' the gospel of the kingdom by weaving it into the mundane, everyday world of men and time. He connects the poetry and the prose. This is what so strongly attracted Rembrandt to him when he moved religious painting away from the Italian grand manner and into the realities of street-life and home-life in Amsterdam. And this can still capture and move the modern reader.

> John Drury. *Luke* (New York, Macmillan Publishing Company, 1975), p. 11

NATIVITY HYMNS

The style and language [of the Magnificat] are those which would be natural to the speaker, as drawn from the storehouse of faith and piety, the sacred writings of her people, familiar to all by constant recitation, and dear to pious souls by use in their own devotions. In the ten verses there are as many repetitions or reminiscences of the words of Scripture. . . . Do we not all know how sentences from the Bible or the Liturgy glide into our prayers, and offer their unsought aid to express kindred feelings of our own? So here the words as well as the thoughts are those of a high-souled Hebrew maiden of devout and meditative habit, whose mind has taken the tone of the Scriptures in which she has been nurtured. We feel the breath of the Prophets; we catch the echoes of the Psalms; we recognise most distinctly the vivid reminiscences of the song of Hannah. . . .

In respect of arrangement the song is divided into two parts, presenting in natural succession two stages of thought. The first is one of personal experience in consciousness of the present fact; the second is one of prophetic foresight of its consequences to the world, and each ends with the affirmation of a great principle; the first that of mercy to all generations, the second that of faithfulness to the promises of old. . . .

Where in so few words shall we find blended together such assured faith, exalted joy, reverential adoration, and modest reserve? These are feelings not easily to be combined in due proportions; but here they breathe together in entire unison, and express a mind attuned to the perfect harmony of truth. . . .

This is a mind which looks into the distance, and sees all that is happening in its relation to the future of mankind. Thus there is a natural transition to the second part of the song, which foresees the consequences of the coming event in the history of the world, and in the fulfilment of the covenanted promises. . . .

The outlook supposes a clear view of the world as in evil state, the insolence of man exalted and the cause of God depressed. . . .

It is a great revolution which rises before her imagination. . . .

The closing words give a vast expansion to the whole meaning of the Song. If spoken within the circle of Jewish ideas, it yet looks far beyond their horizon. . . .

The *Benedictus* . . . has two parts, the first starting from the advent of Messias, the second from the mission of his Prophet; the first celebrating the work of redemption, the second the word of salvation. . . .

In passing from the *Magnificat* to the *Benedictus* we exchange the personal emotion and lively imagination of a youthful mind for the mature thoughtfulness of an old man and the spiritual insight of a priest. . . .

Promise is becoming fact. In the supernatural conception the first act has occurred, and the march of events has begun. All will be as predestined and predicted. . . .

The retrospect of prophecy and the prospect of fulfilment are commingled in the speaker's mind. . . .

The language discloses a sense of unity with the fathers and of common interest with them in what is taking place. . . .

The apostrophe to the child, so natural in the father's mouth, has the happy effect of placing the whole song in connection with the actual scene, and with the facts and feelings of the moment. . . . It will be the exceptional glory of his ministry to announce the coming of the Lord as a present fact, and to prepare his way. . . .

Certainly, by inevitable association, the whole prophecy of Isaiah ix. is present to the mind of Zacharias, as it is all reflected in his song. The great light to those in darkness, the annihilation of hostile powers, the happy deliverance of the people, the establishment of the throne of David, all these topics of the prophecy are also topics of the Song, evoked, as it is by the knowledge that the great event, which its first words announce, was then in actual occurrence.

Thomas Dehany Bernard. *The Songs of the Holy Nativity* (London, Macmillan and Company, 1895), pp. 57–63, 79–80, 83–85, 88, 91

The Magnificat is made up altogether of Old Testament phrases. These phrases are derived from no one passage, but from the most various parts of the Jewish Scriptures. The Magnificat is no mere imitation, for example, of the song of Hannah in I Sam ii. 1–10. Yet the various elements are welded together into a song of perfect unity and great beauty which preserves the parallelism of Hebrew poetry in its noblest form. . . . The author of such a hymn must have lived in the atmosphere of the Old Testament, and must have been familiar from earliest childhood with its language. . . .

The Benedictus . . . is somewhat different in form. . . . The parallelism is not quite so simple, there are more subordinate clauses and appositions and epexegetical phrases. The basic Old Testament passages are perhaps not quite so easily designated. But the Hebrew parallelism and the genuine Old Testament spirit are really almost as clear as in the case of the other hymn. . . .

But an even stronger argument for a primitive Palestinian origin is to be derived from the content of the hymns. There is nothing which can by any possibility be stretched into an allusion to Christian dogma, or even to the later history of Jesus. In the Magnificat there is no clear allusion even to the person of the Messiah. In the Benedictus the allusion is merely to salvation in the house of David. The Messianic king has come at last; but nothing more is known about Him than what was contained in Old Testament prophecy. The child John is thought of as a forerunner, not particularly of the Messiah, but of Jehovah. The coming salvation is conceived as applying not to the world, but primarily at least, to Israel. . . . That the salvation is to be not merely political, but also moral and religious (Lk. i. 75ff.) certainly does not transcend the bounds of Old Testament prophecy. . . .

The hymns are not simply Jewish hymns, composed in some unknown situation. If they were, they could not have found a place in Lk. i–ii. They must, therefore, really have been produced by the persons to whom they are attributed in the narrative—and produced at a time when Old Testament prophecy had not yet been explained by its fulfilment. The fulfilment is at the door—it is no longer a thing of the dim future—but the fashion of it is still unknown. The promised King has arrived at last; but the manner of His reign must still be conjectured from the dim indications of prophecy. The Messiah is there; but He is still unknown. The hymns belong just where the Evangelist has placed them.

J. Gresham Machen. *PTR*. 10, 1912, pp. 22–25, 36

This was a device which the historians of the time and the writers of the Old Testament particularly liked—a break in the action which enables one of the chief characters to utter a monologue explaining what has been going on. If there were any sources, they could be used. If not, it was perfectly in order for the writer to use his own resources in an appropriate way. Matthew and John in their gospels used this convention at length. Luke is more sparing because he does not like to leave his narrative out in the cold too long, but he uses it just as effectively. . . .

The models for Hebrew poetry are the Psalms. Like some modern verse (e.g. T.S. Eliot's) they are not shaped by rhymes but by a loose sustaining rhythm. Particularly Jewish is the way one half of a verse balances the other: *My heart is overflowing with praise of my Lord/ my soul is full of joy in God my Saviour.* There one half repeats the other in different words, but they can contrast: *He has satisfied the hungry with good things/ and sent the rich away with empty hands.* . . . Further instances in St. Paul's letters and Revelation show that the Christians took up the form and used it as Luke has done, particularly happily, in his three famous canticles. . . .

[The Magnificat] is rich with the Old Testament references and reminiscences of which Luke is so fond, for they show the continuity of the old order with the new. It is the same God who governs both. Hannah's song in 1 Samuel 2.1–10 and Psalm 113 are major sources which should not be missed. A well annotated Bible will provide the rest—so many of them that the Magnificat is in fact a smoothly articulated collage of old texts and reminiscences.

The determining element in the theology . . . is the God who comforts and strikes, lifting up the least and the lost, beating down the great and the secure. It is a revolutionary song for a revolutionary religion, founded in the being and doing of a God who up-ends human contrivances. Yet it is confident and happy, for God is tender as well as strong. Verses 44 and 45 clinch the matter. All this is *now.* All the generations from old father Abraham gather towards this point in time, this ordinary woman and her unborn child in the hillside town; and from this point they stream away into eternity. History is illuminated at this little point in the present. . . .

Zacharias' . . . song is about God in history. It celebrates the end of three centuries of waiting and anxiety, the return of God to his people whom he had seemed to have forgotten. As in Mary's song, a long historical perspective from Abraham through David comes to resolution in the present. The hopes for deliverance and comfort in the Psalms, for truth, light and a road to God in the prophets, all these flood back into the light of their realization.

John Drury. *Luke* (New York, Macmillan Publishing Company, 1973), pp. 29–31, 34

NATIVITY STORY

To pass from verse 4 to verse 5 of the first chapter is like passing from Gibbon to the *Pilgrim's Progress*. The Preface is in the style of the professional historian; the remainder of the first two chapters is in the style of Genesis. The reason for this sudden change . . . is because he is about to describe a scene of old-fashioned rural piety.

The contents of the section are nearly all peculiar to S. Luke. The announcement to Zacharias and Elizabeth of the birth of the forerunner is followed "in the sixth month" by the Annunciation to Mary. The Visitation, the Magnificat, the birth and naming of John, and the Benedictus complete the first chapter. The Nativity, the story of the angels and the shepherds, the Circumcision and Presentation of the Holy Child, the episode of Simeon and Anna, the return to Nazareth and the story of the Child Jesus in the Temple are the materials of the second. . . .

The first point of interest is the style in which the narrative is written. . . . The Preface is written in literary Greek, and is like the Preface to the History of Polybius or some other Greek historian. The rest is in the archaic Hebraistic style of Genesis. . . .

He may have written i.5–ii.52 in Hebraic style, because it was a Palestinian story, with close affinities to certain Old Testament narratives, e.g., the birth of Samson, the story of Elijah, and the story of Hannah. The same phenomena recur in Acts. The first part of Acts, as long as the scene is Jerusalem, is in Hebraic . . . style. The second part of Acts, where the stage is the Hellenic world, is written in ordinary, polished Greek.

> S. C. Carpenter. *Christianity According to St. Luke*
> (London, S.P.C.K., 1919), pp. 64–66, 149, 151

These stories include the following: the Promise of a Son to Zacharias and Elisabeth (i. 5–25), the Annunciation (i. 26–38), the Visit of Mary to Elisabeth (i. 39–56), the Birth of John (i. 57–80), the Birth of Jesus (ii. 1–7), the Visit of the Shepherds (ii. 8–20), the Circumcision and Presentation in the Temple (ii. 21–40), the Visit of the Boy Jesus to the Temple (ii. 41–52). The unity of these stories in respect of atmosphere and treatment, and the marked change from the style of the Preface (i. 1–4) and even from that of iii. 1ff., stamp i. 5–ii. 52 as a section derived from a special source.

> Vincent Taylor. *The Gospels: A Short Introduction* (London, The Epworth Press, 1930, 1945), p. 62

The literary structure of Luke 1–2 is generally acknowledged to consist of seven episodes in which a deliberate parallelism exists between the accounts of John the Baptist and Jesus. The annunciation to Zacharias (1:5–25) is parallel to the annunciation to Mary (1:26–38). The parallelism is interrupted by the story of the visit of Mary to Elizabeth (1:39–56), but resumes in the accounts of the births: John the Baptist (1:57–80) and Jesus (2:1–20). The two accounts of Jesus in the Temple—the first as an infant (2:21–40), and the second as a child of twelve (2:41–52)—conclude the Lukan account which, in spite of the rapid change of characters and locations, is woven into a literary unity and unfolds on the basis of the sequence of the events. . . .

In the Lukan presentation the story of the origins of Jesus begins in the Temple in Jerusalem. The scene of the earliest episode—the annunciation to Zacharias—is framed by the customs of the Temple worship which proceed with traditional regularity. God himself ruptures this regularity, and this motif of the divinely initiated interruptions of the normal events is continued and developed in the subsequent scenes in Luke 1–2. Whether this divine initiative expresses itself by angelic visitations or the action of the Spirit, the emphasis remains constant: the origins of Jesus and the movement associated with him are based on the deliberate acts of God. . . .

Luke's presentation of the origins of Jesus introduces themes and foreshadows developments that will unfold in the entire complex of Luke-Acts. Luke 1–2 is thus quite similar to the Prologue to the Gospel of John and should be considered as a carefully constructed introduction to the Gospel of Luke in particular and his entire work in general.

Harold S. Songer. R & E. 64, 1967, pp. 454, 463

The story begins in Jerusalem and in the Temple: in other words at the centre (for Luke) of religious history. The characters are archetypes of Jewry, devout old people like Zacharias and Elizabeth, Simon and Anna, the humble of heart like Joseph, Mary and the shepherds. For people like these it was a time of patient waiting, and the excitement of Luke's narrative mounts as it becomes clearer that what they have waited for is starting to happen. God is remembering his people and returning to Jerusalem (Mount Zion), his home. An outbreak of angels in unlikely places heralds his coming. The darkness of generations clears away, happy voices break into the silence, and the aching void starts to fill with the presence of God.

Like this gospel's first sentence, its first chapters are beautifully constructed. The Old Testament, Luke's Bible, is the primary surviving source of both style and content. Luke begins by stating two themes or starting two stories: John will be born, Jesus will be born. Then he brings the two together: Mary and Elizabeth meet. They separate again: John is born, Jesus is born. After this he drops his two-fold pattern because Jesus is, after all, the centre of his gospel and not John. He adds three stories about Jesus at different stages of his life: the shepherds at his birth, his religious initiation, his adolescence. The last two are set in Jerusalem, like the opening story of Zacharias. Inside these schemes Luke works out a number of themes and motifs. He is concerned with relations: of John to Jesus, of the neglected corners of human existence to its centre, and above all with the relation of the new gospel and the old Jewish religion. Except for the songs, where the underlying theology bursts out in prayer and praise, all this is done in narrative form.

John Drury. *Luke* (New York, Macmillan Publishing Company, 1973), pp. 19–20

PASSION STORY

Luke has stripped the Passion narrative of Mark of its tragic character. The anointing by the woman at Bethany, who by her action consecrates Jesus for His sacrificial death, is omitted. . . . The pathetic failure of the rest of the Apostles when the hour of crisis came is not dwelt upon. The words "they all forsook Him and fled" are omitted. . . . All the way through the Passion narrative of Luke, Jesus is presented more as a prototype of Christian martyrs such as Stephen, who continues His ministry to the end; praying for His oppressors; bidding the women of Jerusalem weep not for Him, but for themselves; providing for the future welfare of His disciples . . . ; ministering on the Cross to the penitent thief; commending His spirit into the hands of His Heavenly Father. . . . As Dibelius says: "In Luke's Passion story the martyred Hero radiates the nobility of His character even upon His adversaries, and the reader's compassion is aroused by numerous traits in the story. The oldest story of the Passion, on the contrary, seeks neither to be interesting nor to arouse emotion. It seeks to show that the events were foreordained by God, and that just in the most outrageous and ignominious incidents in the story there was accomplished the salvation of the world." . . . The whole presentation of the Passion in Luke is conditioned by the thought "that the strife was o'er, the battle won."

R. V. G. Tasker. *The Nature and Purpose of the Gospels* (London, SCM Press, 1944), pp. 54–55

It is only in Luke that we have the explicit identification of Jesus with the *suffering* servant (Isa. 53). For Luke, suffering is a vital part of the redemptive act.

Nevertheless the note of the Lucan passion narrative is not one of pathos. . . .

Luke's narrative is characterized by references to the behaviour of Jesus during the passion. This is another characteristic which Luke shares with John. Throughout the Lucan passion Jesus acts with grandeur and serenity. There is no cry of desertion from the cross. In fact on the cross Jesus continues the ministry of forgiveness (23:39–43) and finally makes an act of committal to the Father (23:46).

Christ is, in Luke's Gospel and especially in the narrative of the passion, the model martyr; the martyr-disciple is the one whose life most nearly conforms to that of his Lord. . . . Certainly the whole mission, speech and death of Stephen is presented in Acts in such a way as to recall the master, and the ministries of Peter and Paul are keyed to that of the master in the same kind of way. . . .

This does not mean that Luke is not interested in the death of Jesus as a means of delivering mankind from sin. It is true that he does not, like Mark and Matthew, refer to Jesus as the Son of Man who comes to give his life as 'a ransom for many'. On the other hand Luke does make striking use of the words 'salvation' and 'save', and in suggesting that the redeeming work of Jesus was not a piece of information put in so many words, but something to be *inferred* from what he did and said, the evangelist was near to the facts.

E. J. Tinsley. *The Gospel According to Luke* (Cambridge, Cambridge University Press, 1965), pp. 12–13

Jesus' crucifixion is linked with the punishment of two other unfortunates. . . . Jesus' prayer for his tormentors is only in Luke and is very like Stephen's words at Acts 7.60. It surely embraces the Jews as well as the Roman soldiers since he has made them the virtual executioners. There is a difference between the ordinary folk and the leaders: at verse 35 *the people* (for Luke = the Jewish people) *stood and stared* as if transfixed, while their rulers jeer. . . .

Verses 39–43 are very much Luke, the penitent criminal taking his place with other similar characters of this gospel such as the prodigal son, the unjust steward, the repenting publican, Zacchaeus and the prostitute. The reclaiming of the lost continues without interruption. The bitter words of his companion link this incident smoothly with the preceding mockeries. . . .

Luke has thoroughly rewritten the death of Jesus, using Mark's work as little more than an outline. He omits the cry of desolation (Mark 15.34) and the passage about Elijah which follows it. . . .

Luke's account of Jesus' death is quieter and less distressing than Mark's, without the theological depth of John's. But his main interests are woven into it: the compassion of Christ, the saving of the least and lost, the placing in the continuum of history. Because he is an historian in the sense of making worldly sense of things, his version has won the definitive place in most minds.

John Drury. *Luke* (New York, Macmillan Publishing Company, 1973), pp. 210–212

MARK

STRUCTURE

A . . . characteristic of the Gospel is the orderly *arrangement* of its matter. After a brief reference to John's preaching and witness, and the Baptism and Temptation of Jesus, the story plunges into the account of the Galilean Mission. A day of twenty-four hours is narrated (i. 21–38), and a selection is given of five typical narratives which culminate in the hostility of the Pharisees and the Herodians (iii. 6). After an account of the Appointment of the Twelve, and the Beelzebub Controversy, a description of the lakeside preaching follows (iv. 1–34), and then a section descriptive of some of Jesus's mighty works (iv. 35–v. 43). From vi. 30 to viii. 26 Jesus for the most part is in retirement outside Galilee proper, and from viii. 27 onwards He is mainly concerned with the instruction of His disciples. The great day near Caesarea Philippi is followed by the first prediction of the Passion (viii. 31; cf. ix. 31, x. 33f.), and the story of the Transfiguration 'after six days' (ix. 2–8). With x. 1 begins the account of the last journey to Jerusalem, the activity of Jesus in and about the city, and in xiv. 1–xvi. 8 the crowning events of the Passion and Resurrection are described.

> Vincent Taylor. *The Gospels: A Short Introduction* (London, The Epworth Press, 1930, 1945), pp. 53–54

Practically all interpreters recognize two great main divisions in the Gospel: the first representing the early proclamation of the good news by Jesus, and leading up to the climax of Peter's Confession and the Transfiguration in chapters eight and nine . . . ; the second the long Way of the Cross, that led from Caesarea Philippi and the Mount of Transfiguration to Golgotha and the Empty Tomb. . . . This division into two parts, the beginning of Jesus' ministry and the end, is so simple that nothing less could be expected of any writer of a narrative of Jesus' public activity. Embedded in the second half is the Passion Narrative, surely the nucleus of any narrative of Jesus' life from the viewpoint of the early church. . . .

When we turn from the Passion Narrative to survey the earlier contents of the Gospel, we find a singularly clear arrangement of its materials—partly chronological, but only partly so; much more definitely 'subjective,' i.e. the arrangement is by subject. . . . In brief, the incidents and sayings recorded by Mark are grouped about a dozen or thirteen great controversies in which Jesus had engaged and in which the church, a generation later, was still engaged. They are, apparently, the following:

1. The controversy over healing, i.16–ii.12.
2. The controversy over eating with sinners, ii. 13–17.
3. The controversy over fasting, ii. 18–22.
4. The controversy over keeping the Sabbath, ii.23–iii.5.
5. The controversy over the source of Jesus' 'power', iii.22–30.
6. The controversy over the external requirements of the Law, vii. 1–23.
7. The controversy over 'signs,' viii. 11–21.
8. The controversy over Elijah, ix. 11–13.
9. The controversy over the question of divorce, x. 2–12.
10. The controversy over Jesus' authority, xi. 27–33.
11. The controversy over civil obedience, xii. 13–17.
12. The controversy over the resurrection, xii. 18–25.
13. The controversy over the interpretation of the Law, xii. 28–34. . . .

The main structure of Mark was accordingly determined by the arrangement thus far observed, viz. the Passion Narrative prefaced by the controversies which led up to it. Incidentally, this provided the first answer to the perennial question, *Why* did Jesus die? . . . Mark undertakes to provide an answer: He died (1) because the Jewish leaders rejected him, and for envy (xv. 10) delivered him up to Pilate. . . . He died (2) because he willed to die, to lay down his life a ransom for many (x. 45; siv. 24). He died (3) because it was the will of God, and so it had been written of him. . . . The basic and fundamental structure of the gospel thus had a very clear and decisive motive. We may call it apologetic.

> Frederick C. Grant. *The Growth of the Gospels* (New York, Abingdon Press, 1933), pp. 103–105, 107–108

Mark gives a connected story of the general course of the life of Jesus, according to the following plan: (1) Introduction, (2) early ministry in Galilee, (3) later Galilean ministry, (4) events indefinitely placed, (5) journey to Jericho and Jerusalem, (6) teachings in Jerusalem, (7) apocalyptic address, and (8) the arrest, trial, crucifixion, and resurrection—the concluding verses 9–20 constituting an addition to the original book.

> Wilbur Owen Sypherd. *The Literature of the English Bible* (New York, Oxford University Press, 1938), p. 163

St Mark set out to write what had a beginning, middle and end, and moved steadily to an overwhelming climax. . . .

In St Mark's Gospel the paragraphs are mostly self-contained. They are strung together like beads on a string. But perhaps they are strung with art. . . .

St Mark's book is neither a treatise nor a poem, but it is more like a poem than a treatise. Now a poem of any extent has a rhythm, not in the sound only, but also in the sense. Themes and symbols recur, not monotonously but not chaotically either. The reader's imagination responds to their pattern, without being necessarily aware of it; the critic shows his discernment in discovering and analysing it. . . .

The type of pattern which I propose to explore is something in its essence more simple and elementary than a lectionary pattern. It is a quite short recurrent cycle of topics. Christ's action, according to our evangelist, constantly expresses the essentials of the Gospel, and the essentials of the Gospel are always the same. Having expressed them once within quite a narrow compass of events, Christ re-expresses them with different emphases and in different ways, and so on again until he reaches his passion and resurrection, in which he expresses these things perfectly once and for all. . . .

The cyclic order is the natural order for setting forth theological truth for anyone who is proceeding artlessly and not striving for effect. The artless speaker does not save up the main point for the end, and gradually work towards it. He gives us the whole matter 'in a nutshell' at the very start, and then goes over it again and again, developing, varying and explaining his theme as many times as he thinks fit and necessary. St Mark, indeed, is not giving a theoretical exposition of saving truth, he is showing how Christ's life was a visible enactment of it. But the cyclic form can still apply; the pattern of saving act can be gone through again and again in the action of Christ.

Everyone, in fact, who has paid the most casual attention to the sequence of topics in St Mark's Gospel has been struck by traces of cyclic recurrence. Christ calls Simon and his companions from the midst of their trade beside the sea, eats in Simon's house, and heals a man with paralysed legs, causing indignation in the Pharisees (I, 16–II, 12). Christ calls Levi from the midst of his trade beside the sea, eats in Levi's house and heals a man with an atrophied arm, to the indignation of the Pharisees (II, 13–III, 6). Christ feeds five thousand men, and then voyages over the lake; his disciples show themselves uncomprehending about the mystery of the loaves which they have just witnessed on shore (VI, 30–52). A couple of chapters later we read of a similar feeding of four thousand, another voyage, and similar uncomprehension about the loaves (VIII, 1–21). The Lord's prophecy of his own passion rings like a refrain at spaced intervals from VIII, 31 to X, 33. These are just a few of the most familiar examples of cyclic recurrence.

Austin Farrer. *A Study in St Mark* (London, Dacre Press, 1951), pp. 26, 30, 34–35

The Gospel of Mark has a very definite literary structure, through which his religious message is expressed. Five main sections may be distinguished, which are like the acts of a religious drama, each having its own particular function and mood:

I.	The Prologue and Opening Scenes	(1:1–15)
II.	The Mystery of the Messiah	(1:16–8:26)
III.	The Way of the Messiah: Suffer-ing,Service, and Victory	(8:27–10:45)
IV.	Jerusalem: Conflict and Death	(10:46–15:39)
V.	The Denouement: The Easter Story	(15:40–16:8)

1. *The Prologue and Opening Scenes* (1:1–15). The Gospel begins with a prologue, which is similar to that of a Greek drama. Classical Greek tragedies often commence with a statement by one of the actors or the chorus, which sets the mood, introduces the audience to the situation at hand, and explains the significance of the central character before he sets foot upon the stage. Through the prologue, the audience would know in advance what the central theme of the play was to be and could anticipate, to some extent, the development which would follow.

In the Gospel of Mark the prologue (1:2–8) describes the significance and role of Jesus, even before he personally appears. . . .

All of this section, the prologue and opening scenes (1:1–15), is really a unit, from a literary and structural point of view. It establishes Jesus in his messianic role. It tells what that role is to be. Jesus is to be God's Agent, to destroy the hosts of evil and usher in God's Kingdom. Mark has set the stage, not in human history alone but in eternity. This is the high moment, the commencement of the great plan conceived long ago in the mind of God.

II. *The Mystery of the Messiah* (the ministry in Galilee) (1:16–8:26). The second act of Mark's drama is a "rising action." As it opens, no one knows of Jesus' messiahship but God, Satan, and Jesus. As he goes about Galilee, his messianic power begins to be revealed. . . .

In this section of the Gospel, the emphasis is on Jesus' supernatural power, his growing fame, the mystery concerning his nature, and his desire to keep his messiahship a secret. . . .

III. *The Way of the Messiah: Suffering, Service, and Victory* (8:27–10:45). This section is quite distinct from the previous one, both in purpose and in mood. It consists of a sequence of closely knit sayings and episodes, in which Jesus interprets his role to his disciples as one of suffering, death, resurrection, and return in glory—a role which involves humility and human service, in complete obedience to God, but one which will end in victory. . . .

IV. *Jerusalem: Conflict and Death* (10:46–15:39). Again we have a distinct literary and dramatic unit. Beginning with the false splendor of Jesus' acclamation by the crowds in the "triumphal entry," it shows the inevitable conflict between Jesus and the priests and ends in the story of his martyrdom. . . .

V. *The Denouement: The Easter Story* (15:40–16:8). The final episode in

Mark's drama is completely different in mood from anything which has preceded it. It is like the gentle hush after the storm. It is full of poetic imagery, placid beauty, and prophetic anticipation. . . .

Thus we see that Mark's Gospel has a very definite literary structure. It consists of five clearly defined sections, each quite distinct in purpose and mood. The divisions are literary units—stages in mood and drama. Episodes and sayings are placed in each section because they fit the purpose of that section, not necessarily because they happened in that place or time in Jesus' life.

> Curtis Beach. *The Gospel of Mark: Its Making and Meaning* (New York, Harper and Brothers, 1959), pp. 37, 39–40, 42–45

Mark placed the traditional material on the following structural framework:
  1. Preparation for Ministry (1:1–20)
  2. The Kingdom Announced in Word and Act (1:21–8:26)
  3. What Messiahship and Discipleship Mean (8:27–10:45)
  4. Preparation for the Events of the End (11:1–14:25)
  5. The Passion and the Parousia (14:26–16:8)

The sense of urgency and tension in Mark's account is heightened not only in mechanical ways, such as his twelve-times-repeated "immediately," but also in the recurrent juxtaposition of challenge and rejection, of confession and denial, which highlights both the feeling of eschatological imminence and the importance of a faith decision.

> Howard Clark Kee. *Jesus in History: An Approach to the Study of the Gospels* (New York, Harcourt, Brace and World, 1970), p. 127

The outline of The Gospel According to Mark is rather simple: a prelude, or introduction (Mark 1:1–13); a ministry in and around Galilee (Mark 1:14 to 9:50); the journey to Jerusalem (Mark, ch. 10); Jesus in Jerusalem (Mark 11:1 to 16:8). The writer obviously wished to produce a geographical polarity between Galilee, where Jesus' ministry met with some success, and Jerusalem, where Jesus' ministry encountered hostility and ended in crucifixion. Such a geographical division must reflect the theological interest of the writer. . . .

> John H. Hayes. *Introduction to the Bible* (Philadelphia, Westminster Press, 1971), p. 338

I believe that it is possible to detect in Mark three successive and progressively worsening stages in the relation between Jesus and the disciples. The first such stage occurs in the first half of the Gospel (1:16–8:26) and is characterized by the disciples' inability to perceive who Jesus is. Despite the continuous manifestation of Jesus' messiahship before the disciples in countless healings, exorcisms, and nature miracles, they remain amazingly obtuse and obdurate in the face of their involvement in the messianic drama. . . .

The second stage of the disciples' relation to Jesus is inaugurated in Mark 8:27 ff. With the episode at Caesarea Philippi (8:27–33) a sudden change takes place in Mark's rendering of the disciples' capacity for discernment. Peter experiences a startling revelation: Jesus is the Christ (8:29). This sudden burst of insight is as inexplicable as the previous unperceptiveness. In 8:21 the disciples appear just as dense and totally unenlightened as they were in the earlier portions of the Gospel. Up to 8:29 there is no indication that they had understood or discovered any of the capabilities of Jesus which even others had discerned. Yet in 8:29 Peter, the spokesman for the disciples, suddenly makes a confession which suggests that the disciples are now as keenly perceptive as they were thoroughly lacking in perception before. . . .

Any assumption, however, that by this confession the disciples have received a complete understanding of Jesus is soon proved false by the presentation of the disciples in the subsequent chapters. What was before a period of unperceptiveness has now shifted to a period of misconception. For with the interchange between Peter and Jesus after the confession (8:30–33) it now becomes evident that, while identifying Jesus as the Christ, the disciples do not have the same understanding of the nature of messiahship as Jesus claims for himself. Whatever Peter's concept of messiahship is, it is not Jesus' concept. For Jesus, messiahship can be defined only in terms of suffering and death. . . .

With Judas' decision to betray Jesus to the religious hierarchy (14:10 ff.), Mark introduces the final phase in the relationship between Jesus and his disciples. From 8:27 to 14:10 the conflict and tension between them were primarily over a misconception of what constituted authentic messiahship. With Judas' plans to betray Jesus the conflict erupts into an outright rejection of Jesus and his messiahship. That this is true of all of the disciples and not just the traditional villain, Judas, is substantiated by the episode in Gethsemane and the incident in the courtyard of the high priest.

Theodore J. Weeden. *Mark—Traditions in Conflict*
(Philadelphia, Fortress Press, 1971), pp. 26–38

Geography structures Mark's Gospel quite simply. Jesus' preaching and healing ministry takes place in Galilee (chaps. 1–10); his final confrontation with the Jewish and Roman leaders occurs in Jerusalem (chaps. 11–15). The story ends with a promise to return to Galilee after his resurrection (16:7). This geographical division is most general, however; one cannot trace Jesus' movements in detail on a map because too much is left out. Yet the movement from Galilee to Jerusalem seems to be a significant pattern in Mark's Gospel. . . .

Jerusalem symbolizes the climactic events toward which the Gospel's story relentlessly moves. It is the religious capital of Israel, the place where the Temple is located. It is also the seat of the religious and political authorities, who will, in the name of tradition and political stability, have Jesus arrested and executed. Jerusalem is important not simply as a location but as the place where Jesus will die.

The Jerusalem phase of Jesus' career dominates Mark's Gospel. Although it comprises only one week out of Jesus' total ministry, Mark devotes more than one-third of his Gospel to that week, almost one-sixth to the last day. . . . Tying the story together, at least in a general way, is the inexorable movement toward Jerusalem, the place of death.

> Donald Juel. *An Introduction to New Testament Literature* (Nashville, Abingdon Press, 1978), pp. 180–181

UNIFYING MOTIFS

The main purpose of S. Mark was to emphasise the Humanity of Jesus Christ, and that on its purely personal side. . . . The absence of any genealogy of our Lord at the opening of this Gospel points very clearly to the distinction; there is no tracing of His Regal claims through a line of kings to David, the king. . . . S. Mark wished to paint Him in an unofficial capacity, as "a Man among men," never, however, leaving his Divinity without witness. . . .

We are quite justified in regarding the enforcement of Christ's manhood as the distinctive mark of the second Gospel. S. Mark invites attention to His look, His expressions of anger and indignation, His love and tenderness, His sympathy and sighs, His grief and sorrow, His wonder and amazement, His wants and weakness, everything, in short, which betokens His humanity. . . .

Notice His expressions of grief: even in the exercise of Divine power, he lets it be seen: before healing the deaf and dumb man, looking up to heaven He sighed (vii. 34); and when the Pharisees tempted Him, "He sighed deeply in His spirit (viii. 12). So with the manifestations of His human love: it was drawn out by something which He discerned in the rich young ruler's character; "and Jesus beholding him loved him" (x. 21). . . .

When the people "brought young children to Him that He should touch them," and His disciples tried to keep them back, He was so displeased that He put them to open shame by doing as He had done before: "He took them up in His arms," giving even more than was asked, and "put His hands upon them and blessed them." His heart overflowed with tenderness, and He made no attempt to check the impulse of His human instincts. . . .

He showed Himself sensible of the common infirmities of humanity, hunger, weariness, fatigue, and faintness. . . . Twice we are told how He was obliged to restrain His hunger, because of the exacting demands of the multitude upon His time. . . .

What a picture it gives us of tired humanity, when we are told that on the Way of the Cross, as they led Him out to be crucified, even after having pressed Simon the Cyrenian into the service, they were compelled almost to carry Him; "and they bring Him unto the place Golgotha"! The original word suggests that He was so worn out with all that He had gone through, that at last they actually put their arms beneath and assisted Him to the place of execution.

> Herbert M. Luckock. *The Special Characteristics of the Four Gospels* (London, Longmans, Green, and Company, 1900), pp. 105–110

Perhaps most notably of all, the thought of *suffering* and the doctrine of *the Cross* are stressed again and again. The story of the Passion occupies nearly a third of the record, and its shadows lie on some of the earliest pages of the Gospel (cf. ii. 20, iii. 6). The way of discipleship is the way of cross-bearing (viii. 34ff.), and implies a baptism of suffering and the drinking of a cup (x. 38f.). No saying is more characteristic of the Markan representation than the words of Jesus: 'The Son of man came not to be served, but to serve, and to give his life a ransom for many' (x. 45).

> Vincent Taylor. *The Gospels: A Short Introduction* (London, The Epworth Press, 1930, 1945), p. 56

Galilee and Jerusalem therefore stand in opposition to each other, as the story of the gospel runs in St. Mark. The despised and more or less outlawed Galilee is shewn to have been chosen by God as the seat of the gospel and of the revelation of the Son of man, while the sacred city of Jerusalem, the home of jewish piety and patriotism, has become the centre of relentless hostility and sin. Galilee is the sphere of revelation, Jerusalem the scene only of rejection. Galilee is the scene of the beginning and middle of the Lord's ministry; Jerusalem only of its end. Why he must thus pass from the one to the other, is not made clear; it can only be explained by the counsel of God; it "must" so be, 8:31; although there are suggestions that the destruction of the Son of man at Jerusalem is connected with the destruction of the jewish nation itself. But the dark passage through which he is led has an end, and this is given in the words "After I am raised up I will go before you into Galilee," the land where the divine fulfilment began and the land where it will receive its consummation.

> Robert H. Lightfoot. *Locality and Doctrine in the Gospels* (London, Hodder and Stoughton, 1938), pp. 124–125

Surprising views have been held by modern scholars about the silences imposed by Jesus on the witnesses to his works, and the hearers of his claims.

St Mark, it has been supposed, knew that Christ's contemporaries in the days of his flesh observed him neither to make messianic claims nor to do messianic works; but the hardy evangelist was not deterred by such awkward facts from painting a highly coloured messianic picture. . . . A special visitation of spiritual blindness prevented even Christ's friends (let alone his enemies) from seeing what he was and what he meant.

Unhappily for such a view, St Mark only remembers to apply the silencer about once in three times; he brings about many situations in which a conspiracy of silence is out of the question; and, most disconcerting of all, when he does report the injunction to silence, as often as not he adds that it had no effect, or served to stimulate publicity. . . .

One of the advantages which we may modestly claim for the analysis of the gospel which this book contains is that it makes good sense of the topic of secrecy, and shows the evangelist to have been both subtle and consistent in his management of it. The general lines of the solution are supplied by what we have already written on the subject of prefiguration. What is prefigured is never open, for if it were it would not need to be fulfilled or actualized. The fulfilment of the prefigured is the revelation of the hidden. A prefiguration hides seed in the ground, which will shoot up and manifest itself in the fulfilment.

It follows that the rhythm of veiling and unveiling will go with the rhythm of prefiguration and fulfilment. Now in St Mark's Gospel that rhythm is subtle and manifold. . . . Some prefigurations in the ministry await the Resurrection for their fulfilment, for example, the raising of Jairus's child. But others find their fulfilment in the next cycle of the ministry itself, and with their fulfilment comes their unveiling.

> Austin Farrer. *A Study in St Mark* (London, Dacre Press, 1951), pp. 221–222

The blindness of the disciples is usually regarded as a device of Mark and as part of his messianic secret motif. William Wrede, in 1901, said that the motif of the messianic secret in Mark was the evangelist's explanation of the fact that Jesus was not accepted as Messiah during his lifetime but was proclaimed as Messiah after the death and resurrection. . . .

Mark seems to work out this theory on three levels:

(1) The demons recognize Jesus, but they are commanded to be silent.
(2) The disciples partially recognize Jesus, but they are commanded to be silent.
(3) The Jewish authorities fail to recognize Jesus because they have been blinded.

It is the second level that engages our attention at this point. The disciples are commanded to be silent, but their recognition of Jesus is only partial, due to their blindness and their hardness of heart. Moreover, their incomplete understanding is actually a misunderstanding of the nature of Jesus. When we look closely at the incidents related by Mark in which the disciples fail to understand, then it will appear that this element is not properly a part of the messianic secret motif. It is not as if the disciples had discerned the nature of Jesus but are prohibited from broadcasting it, but it is that the disciples have a wrong conception about his nature.

There are many instances of the disciples' blindness—they do not understand the stilling of the sea (4:41), the feeding of the five thousand (6:52), Jesus' attitude toward children (10:13ff.), the saying about the rich entering the kingdom (10:23); they are characteristically unable to understand parables (4:1–20, 23 f.).

Above all, however, the misunderstanding of the disciples is connected with Jesus' threefold prediction of suffering [8: 31–33; 9:30–32; 10:32–34]. . . .

In these three predictions of suffering, not only does Mark indicate that the disciples misunderstood the nature of Jesus, but he also sees this misunderstanding as of two specific kinds: (1) No understanding of the necessity of Jesus' sufferings; and (2) no understanding of their own position in the community. The point is this: Mark is not here saying that the disciples understood that Jesus was Messiah and were commanded not to broadcast it; rather he is saying that they completely misunderstood the nature of Jesus' Messiahship, not understanding it as a suffering Messiahship but as a royal Messiahship which would issue in benefits for themselves.

Joseph B. Tyson. *JBL*. 80, 1961, pp. 261–262

The major Markan characters or groups of characters are the religious "Establishment," the ubiquitous crowds, the disciples, and Jesus. These figures enter and exit with recurring regularity from the beginning to the end of the Markan drama. Other personae such as John the Baptist, Pilate, and the Galilean women play significant roles. Their exposure on stage, however, is minimal compared to that of the major figures. If the key to Mark's intent lies in his characterization, then these major characters offer the most likely place to find that key.

It certainly requires no burst of insight to recognize that the members of the religious Establishment in Mark function as the enemies of Jesus and are responsible for the untimely and unnatural end of his life. . . . Mark's own insertion of references to the "Establishment" throughout his narrative and his positioning of the material he received on the Jewish hierarchy's antipathy toward Jesus produces such dramatic tension and movement that the hostility existing between Jesus and the authorities reflected in the Gospel must be laid to more than Mark's dispassionate passing on of tradition.

Our evangelist's staging of the conflict between Jesus and the religious leaders begins at the outset of Jesus' ministry (1:22). With rhythmic regularity and accelerated intensity the conflict is flashed before the eyes of the reader, reaching crescendos of dramatic moment at 3:6; 8:31; 9:31; 10:33; 11:18; 12:12, and culminating in the final climactic event: the death of Jesus by the insidious design of the Jewish authorities. . . .

The second ubiquitous group of characters to concern us are the nondescript masses. The fact that this amorphous gathering of humanity emerges time and time again throughout the Gospel drama and the fact that the terms used to identify it are often found in redactional passages suggest that the ubiquitous crowd has a special role in the drama. That role is to dramatize, by contrast with the religious leaders, the positive response to Jesus. The crowds flock to him with eagerness (1:32 ff., 37; 3:7–12; 4:1; 6:53–56; 9:15; 11:8 ff.), listen to this teaching enthusiastically (1:22, 27; 12:37b), and respond to his healing powers with anticipation (1:32 ff.; 3:7 ff.; 6:53ff.). . . .

Aside from Jesus, the character-group which monopolizes Mark's attention most is the disciples, specifically the Twelve. . . . At first glance one might be prompted to suggest that just as the Establishment-group is portrayed as the enemies of Jesus and the mass-group as his acclaimants, so quite naturally the disciples-group serves to dramatize the nature of proper discipleship. But such a conclusion would be drawn too hastily. For while the Establishment-group and mass-group are drawn rather simply in a one-dimensional fashion—their position is quite clear—the role of the disciples in Mark is far more intricately developed and far more difficult to interpret. . . .

This ambivalent behavior of the disciples has puzzled and intrigued scholars for some time. Though the disciples are the carefully picked confidants of Jesus, heroes of the early church, authorities for authentic christology and discipleship, ironically they emerge in the Markan drama with extremely poor performances both in terms of their perspicacity about Jesus' teaching and ministry and in terms of their loyalty to him.

> Theodore J. Weeden. *Mark—Traditions in Conflict* (Philadelphia, Fortress Press, 1971), pp. 20–24

The opening four chapters identify many of the major themes of the Gospel of Mark. . . . Certain conflicts have been suggested, our interest in the character and mission of Jesus has been aroused, the expanding nature of Jesus' authority and reputation has been established. . . . We as readers have been told he is the Son of God; but we do not know what that means. We know he will be betrayed, but not how or where or why. . . .

A first theme is the mystery of Jesus. . . . The mystery of Jesus is opened up for us in two ways. First, we gradually find out more about who he is. . . .

The mystery of Jesus is opened up in a second way by the gradual explanation of the phrase he uses when he first speaks: "the kingdom of God," he says, "is at hand." The revealing of the nature of this kingdom clarifies who or what Jesus is as Christ or Messiah. . . .

A second theme begun in these first four chapters and developed in the narrative involves the healing powers of Jesus, already demonstrated in his various miracles. Jesus, we have seen, cures physical diseases and forgives sins. The pattern of the theme is marked by a gradual deemphasis of Jesus' curing of the physically afflicted and a corresponding increase in emphasis on his cleansing or absolving the spiritually afflicted. . . .

A third theme established in the opening chapters of Mark is the concept of the secrecy of Jesus. In only one instance (5:19) does Jesus tell a man he has cured: "Go home to your friends, and tell them how much the Lord has done for you." Part of Jesus' reason for secrecy is given in the parable about the lamp (4:21–22). What is hidden, he had said, is hidden to be disclosed. Gradually during the narrative, however, Jesus becomes less concerned about secrecy. . . .

The fourth theme established in the opening chapters and then expanded in the narrative is of Jesus as a breaker of rules, an overturner of traditions, a revolutionary as far as the authorities are concerned. The emphasis indicates why those who follow Jesus and who hear his words seem to shift back and forth between believing him and not believing him. . . .

A fifth theme touched upon in the opening chapters is of Jesus as bride-groom. . . .

A sixth theme . . . is the lack of understanding of the people who hear Jesus speak. . . . Their lack of understanding leads to numerous misconceptions and ultimately to almost total denial. . . .

A seventh theme . . . is of the development of the disciples. We see, on one level, an expansion in the narrative of the disciples' various duties and powers—they are called by Jesus, formed into a band, given names, various assignments, and missions. But more interesting from a literary point of view is the disciples' increasing lack of understanding, which leads them, as it does most other people in the narrative, to misconceive and then to deny Jesus.

> Kenneth R. R. Gros Louis. "The Gospel of Mark,"
> *Literary Interpretations of Biblical Narratives* (Nash-
> ville, Abingdon Press, 1974), pp. 309–316

It is often said, accurately, that the gospel of Mark is "a passion narrative with an extended introduction," and W. Marxsen claimed that Mark composed his gospel "backwards" from the passion narrative. Certainly the passion of Jesus looms large in Mark, and our structural analysis bears this out. Every major section of the gospel ends on a note looking toward the passion, and the central section, 8:27–10:45, is concerned with interpreting it:

> 3:6 the plot to destroy Jesus
> 6:6 the unbelief of the people of "his own country"

8:21 the misunderstanding of the disciples
10:45 the cross as a "ransom for many"
12:44 the widow's sacrifice, which anticipates Jesus'.

Norman Perrin. *The New Testament: An Introduction* (New York, Harcourt Brace Jovanovich, Inc., 1974), p. 148

The author of Mark narrates a single, unified story. While the story's unity results primarily from the persistence of a single central figure, Jesus, a group of companions, or "disciples," appears early in the Gospel and plays a continuing role. . . . Because there is continuity of persons and characteristics, we can also observe developments. When, in reading a story, we encounter the same person or group more than once, it is right to ask if the relationship between the scenes enriches our understanding of the characters. Certain scenes reinforce what we already know about a character or group, other scenes reveal new characteristics, still others indicate significant shifts and developments. The meaning of each scene is enriched if we can understand it in relationship to all the other scenes. In the story each scene then becomes part of a significant development that moves toward an end. . . .

Immediately after Jesus begins his preaching, the author of Mark tells of the call of four disciples who will later take their place among the twelve (1:16–10). Jesus' command to follow him establishes a norm by which the reader can judge the behavior of the disciples. At this point the response fits the command. Later in the story Jesus will again call for followers (8:34), but the subsequent narrative (especially chap. 14) will demonstrate the disciples' failure. . . .

The first part of Mark's Gospel encourages the reader to have high expectations for the disciples and to associate himself with them. If we think in terms of consistent but static doctrine, there may seem to be a conflict between this positive view of the disciples and other material in Mark. If we think in terms of narrative development, however, we have the common story technique of encouraging the reader to contemplate one possibility so that he will feel more sharply the opposite development when it arrives. Jesus' authoritative statement about the disciples in 4:11–12 will serve as a norm by which the author will measure the disciples' failure (see 8:17–18). . . .

As the author begins to present the disciples in strongly negative terms, some of the miracle stories become contrasting scenes. It is no accident that the final sequence of feeding and discussion in the boat, with Jesus' reproachful question concerning the disciples' inability to see and hear (8:18), is framed by stories of healing a deaf man and a blind man (7:31–37, 8:22–26). . . .

In 8:31–10:45 . . . three passion announcements (8:31, 9:31, 10:33–34) become the basis of a major threefold pattern building up to a climax. Each

of these passion announcements is followed by resistance (8:32–33) or behavior contrary to that of Jesus (9:33–34, 10:35–41) on the part of the disciples, followed in turn by Jesus' corrective teaching. . . .

As the story continues we learn that the disciples desert and deny Jesus
rather than face death and that they fail to watch in Gethsemane. . . .

The importance attached to Judas' betrayal, the flight of the other disciples,
and Peter's denial appears in the fact that Jesus predicts all three of these
events. In the narrative these predictions serve both to emphasize and evaluate
these events. . . .

The disciples' story has come to a disastrous conclusion, and the author
has spared nothing in emphasizing the disaster. This ending sends reverber-
ations back through the whole preceding story. The reader who was at first
content to view the disciples as reflections of his own faith and who may
have continued to hope for a happy ending to their story must now try to
disentangle himself from them, which will mean choosing a path contrary to
their path. The possibility of this other path is recognized within the story. . . .

Robert C. Tannehill. *JR*. 57, 1977, pp. 388–389, 396,
398–403

The main unifying theme of Mark's Gospel might be called the unveiling of
the hidden Messiah. Ever since Wilhelm Wrede's work at the turn of the
century, scholars have referred to "the messianic secret motif" in Mark.
Jesus' identity is a mystery to the participants in the story, and although the
opening says that Jesus is the "Christ, the Son of God," even for the reader
there is still an enigma. What does it mean to be Messiah and Son of God?
This, too, is a messianic secret. The narrator gives no definitions, tells no
birth stories, presents no genealogy. As the story unfolds, the reader can
readily see that Jesus is not Messiah in any traditional sense. Without background information, Jesus' Messiahship is puzzling. The reader must assume
that the story will explain in just what sense Jesus is Messiah and Son of
God, and why the book should be viewed as "gospel"—that is, as "good
news.". . .

Even Jesus' disciples never achieve full enlightenment. The characters
react to each new bit of revelation with either misunderstanding or heightened
hostility. Study of the trial and passion narratives showed that the most
important revelations about Jesus come at moments when misunderstanding
is at its peak, when the participants in the drama are utterly incapable of
enlightenment. Even the empty tomb only terrifies the group of women into
withholding the good news of the resurrection. The reader's interest here,
however, lies not in the obstacles of Jesus' unveiling of his identity to the
characters in the story but in Mark's exposing of the meaning of Jesus'
Messiahship to the reader.

The progressive revelation of what sort of Messiah Jesus is seems intended only for the reader. For those in the story, the mystery surrounding Jesus becomes more and more impenetrable. Those who witness Jesus' miracles and listen to his teachings "see, but do not perceive, hear but do not understand." Their increasing confusion is a basic motif in the Gospel and acts as a counterpoint to the revelation that occurs for the reader.

Mark clearly assumed that by the time he wrote his Gospel the secret had been revealed both to the reader as well as to the disciples. From the outset, his readers know that Jesus is the Messiah, Son of God. . . .

Although the gospel account ends without the resolution of this final mystery, the whole narrative presupposes that Jesus' followers did eventually see the risen Lord and understand the meaning of his life and death.

> Donald Juel. *An Introduction to New Testament Literature* (Nashville, Abingdon Press, 1978), pp. 182–183, 190, 194–195

STORYTELLING TECHNIQUE

As some special incident is given of each journey, so some vivid detail is given of each incident, some look or gesture of Jesus, some action of the crowd, the notable words Jesus used, or the feelings aroused in him. He 'looked round on all things' in the Temple the day before he cleansed it. 'He looked round about him with anger, grieved at their hardness of heart', when the Scribes objected to the cure of the Sabbath. . . .

What little touches are added to that scene at the treasury, where Luke has merely 'Jesus looking up saw' the people casting gifts into the treasury, while Mark says so graphically "Jesus *having sat down opposite the treasury was watching how*. . . ' And the coins, he points out, were copper or brass, and the rich would need to 'cast in many' to make a decent gift. They were the current coin used by the Jews without the idolatrous symbol of the Romans engraved on them. Luke has simply 'gifts'. . . .

Nor does Jesus monopolize the observer's attention. His eye seems to pass to the patients and to the crowd. He remembers Jesus calling the crowd to him for a special warning or explanation, or the crowd sitting round about him; and Mark thinks these details worth mentioning.

Usually Jesus took his patients away from the crowd to heal them, as is duly noted, but on one occasion the record describes the crowd's interest in the case. '*A good number of people*' was following Jesus, when a blind man, sitting begging at the roadside, called after him as the Son of David. Mark records his name, the crowd's fussy attempt to silence him, and the brief dialogue between Jesus, the crowd, and the man. 'Call him', says Jesus to the crowd. 'Cheer up. He is calling you', says the crowd to the man, and he 'throws away his cloak' in his eagerness, and 'jumps up', and is cured. The scene is ready for 'filming'. . . .

A good example of this 'moving picture' is the account of 'the great refusal' [Mark X. 17–22]. . . .

Luke has the section that occurs in Mark practically as it stands, but where he shortens it, he does so by leaving out just the graphic touches that belong to the *setting* of the story, the local colour and the drama. . . .

We have to thank Mark's Gospel for this vivid first-hand impression of Jesus the Man, his looks and gestures, his wonder, grief, and indignation, sitting in the boat teaching, asleep on a pillow in the ship's stern, walking round the Temple taking in the scene, watching the gifts dropping into the Temple box, taking up children in his arms. . . .

> P. C. Sands. *Literary Genius of the New Testament* (Oxford, Oxford University Press, 1932), pp. 14–18

Christian antiquity did not greatly prize the Gospel of Mark. Hippolytus described Mark as "stubfingered," a man whose fingers where thumbs. What he meant was that Mark, compared with Matthew, seemed clumsy and obscure. Augustine thought Mark a condensation of Matthew. . . .

It is as though Mark felt that he was in the presence of something too great for him to master or control, which he must simply record as faithfully as he might. This is why we get in Mark as in no other gospel this strange vague sense of great things close at hand—conflicts, insights, purposes, decision. It shows us Jesus not primarily as a teacher but as a man of action. He moves through the narrative with masterful vigor, finally even facing the nation's priesthood not with mere words but with bold acts of reformation. It is not without significance that in this earliest gospel we see Jesus as a man of action.

Indeed, the Gospel of Mark possesses the quality of action to a higher degree than any of the others. . . .

The three retreats of Jesus before his foes and then his turning against them and attacking them in their stronghold give Mark a dramatic quality peculiarly its own, and its thrilling account of the betrayal, arrest, trial, and death of Jesus makes it the supreme martyrdom. . . . From one point of view, indeed, Mark is a martyrdom, for the shadow of the cross already falls across the narrative from the beginning of the third chapter (3:6) on. It remained the pattern gospel to the end of the gospel-making age, and informal and unambitious as Mark's narrative is, no more convincing or dramatic account has ever been written of the sublime effort of Jesus to execute the greatest task ever conceived—to set up the Kingdom of God on earth.

> Edgar J. Goodspeed. *An Introduction to the New Testament* (Chicago, University of Chicago Press, 1937), pp. 145–147

I propose now that we should look at this short book (so far as possible) as if it were fresh from the press, and we had never read it before, and try to see what impression it makes.

The earlier chapters, I think, will appear rather scrappy. We are given a number of stories, some with an amount of picturesque detail, others brief and bald; but there is no very clear connection between them, and we are puzzled to know what is really happening. Bit by bit, however, these stories combine in our minds into a picture of Jesus of Nazareth at work in Galilee: his contacts with different types of people, and the opposition he aroused. We begin to suspect that the apparently artless story-telling has something in it of the art that conceals art, for the portrait of Jesus comes out unmistakably: his vivid and forceful speech, his poet's insight into nature and the human soul, his ready sympathy—but also on occasion his devastating severity—his integrity and strength of purpose, his power to command, and his tremendous energy. . . .

Presently the pace of the narrative gathers speed, and something like a plot begins to appear. The turning-point is at chapter viii. 27–38. Jesus, we learn, has retired beyond the frontier. Galilee has grown too hot to hold him. In his retirement he is enlisting volunteers for a dangerous enterprise. He leads them up to Jerusalem, rides into the city with a crowd at his back, clears the temple of the money-changers who do business in its courts, and challenges the ecclesiastical authorities on their own ground. They prepare to retaliate, and so we reach the final stage. With the beginning of chapter xiv the narrative takes on a fresh character. It becomes continuous, swift, and dramatic in the extreme. The loose ends of the earlier chapters are gathered up, and the reader is swept on irresistibly to the tragic climax.

It is the story of a great and good man, encircled by unscrupulous enemies, betrayed by a false friend, denied and deserted by his followers, trapped by scheming priests, condemned by a weak and vacillating judge, and put to death; but bearing himself all through with a strange dignity that wins the reluctant respect of his judge and his executioner. The story is told with extraordinary simplicity and force. There is no dwelling on grim details, and certainly no attempt to work on our feelings, yet no one with a scrap of imagination can read the story without being profoundly moved. . . .

But it is not all plain sailing. At a first reading the dramatic sweep of the narrative may carry us along, but on a second and more deliberate reading we shall certainly be held up by some perplexing passages; and the more realistic the story becomes to us as we study it, the more forcibly the difficulties will strike our minds. . . .

The total effect of these passages, and many others like them, is to suggest a mysterious undercurrent flowing beneath the ostensible stream of events. There is more here than appears on the surface. What appears to be—and indeed is, on its own level—a story of martyrdom is also the story of something deeper; something which cannot be defined in plain words, but must be hinted at in the exalted language of the imagination. . . .

Mark is perfectly aware of this under-current of mystery in his story. Indeed he draws attention to it. There are ten or a dozen places where he plainly indicates that the actors in the story were in the dark. . . .

C. H. Dodd. About the Gospels (Cambridge, Cambridge University Press, 1950), pp. 2–4, 6, 8–9

There is no doubt that the narratives of Mark are realistic. They are so realistic that as perceptive a modern literary critic as Erich Auerbach ascribes their realism to the personal reminiscence of an eyewitness and participant. . . .

This realism provides us with the first clue to the interpretation of Mark's gospel: the narratives are meant to be understood. The evangelist himself takes pains to help his readers by explaining the value of coins (12:42) and by giving the Roman equivalent for the name of a place (15:16). So we must welcome and utilize the patient work of historical scholarship that helps us understand the references and allusions in the narratives. . . .

A second clue lies in the fact that narrative functions in a certain way: it draws the reader into the story as a participant. The reader is *there* as the one who took up his cross challenges the disciples to be prepared to take up theirs (8:34), or as he who gave his life interprets the giving as a "ransom for many" (10:45). Similarly, the reader is caught up in the dark hours of the passion and hears Peter's protestations of loyalty (14:26–31), and so shares the catharsis of his breakdown in the courtyard (14:72). The natural function of narrative is to help the reader hear the voices, take part in the action, get involved in the plot. The effectiveness of the evangelist Mark as a preacher is that he has cast his message in a narrative rather than in the direct discourse of a letter or a homily. We appreciate once again the significance of the realism of Mark's narratives, for it enables the reader to be caught up into the narrative as a participant.

Norman Perrin. The New Testament: An Introduction (New York, Harcourt Brace Jovanovich, Inc., 1974), pp. 164–165

Considered from the viewpoint of dramatic composition, the *conclusion* of the Gospel at 16:8 is not only perfectly appropriate but also a stroke of genius. The Gospel ends even more abruptly than it begins, on a finale of poignant grandeur. The omission of postresurrection appearances is consistent with Mark's method of rigorous selection previously observed. He is an epitomizer. His method is to sketch and reduce rather than embellish. The comparative brevity of Mark cannot be explained merely in terms of the limited amount of sources available to him. The very diversity of the birth narratives, the genealogies, the resurrection appearances in Matthew and Luke attest to the richness of early tradition. But to begin his work, Mark chose to state in one line a powerful combination of the name "Jesus" with six Greek words summarizing what Matthew and Luke took several chapters to recount. The terse announcement of the entrance of the Christ, the Son of God, upon the scene of history suggests grandiose antecedents rendered even more momentous by the mystery surrounding them. Likewise for the temptation pericope, the omission of the elaborate threefold story for the simple statement that Jesus spent forty days in the wilderness in the presence of Satan, wild beasts, and angels conjures up visions of a gigantic epic on the cosmic scale of clashing spiritual powers. Suggestive epitome carries greater evocative power than detailed narration. It also requires more skill.

Similar comments could be made on almost every part of the Gospel. Even the passion story, which occupies one third of Mark's Gospel, reflects his tendency to mention only that which is suggestive and significant. . . .

The evocative simplicity of the narrative is even more apparent in its climactic conclusion. The "He has risen" constitutes the consummation that illumines retrospectively the whole Gospel. And yet, as the action of the Gospel unfolds, it anticipates, almost ordains, the resurrection. Consequently, once it takes place there is no need for proof or elaboration. Evidences for the resurrection abound sufficiently within the Gospel to make it complete once it is proclaimed at the very end that "He has risen." Of course the detailed narration of appearances is important. But it is the task of a chronicler, and Mark was no mere chronicler. By the sparseness of his style, by the careful balance of descriptive details, and even by his omissions Mark forced the sensitive reader to use his own imagination, to extrapolate and participate in the Gospel by making it come alive in his own mind. Further elaboration on the resurrection in the form of appearance narratives would have been superfluous and even detrimental to Mark's style. . . .

The dramatic power of the Gospel's ending is conveyed as much by what is left unsaid as by what is said regarding the resurrection. This method was not unknown to the ancient tragic poets. Some of their most profound works let the action continue beyond the last scene.

Gilbert Bilezikian. The Liberated Gospel (Grand Rapids,
Baker, 1977), pp. 134–135

In Mark certain aspects of the story are emphasized by repetition. This includes repetition of elements in a single scene (Peter denies Jesus three times), repetition of statements in a sequence of scenes (Jesus repeatedly announces his coming passion), and narration of similiar, though consecutive, events (Jesus feeds a multitude twice, followed in both cases by a boat scene which reveals the disciples' lack of understanding). The use of repetition for emphasis is clear from the fact that the most detailed and emphatic instance is placed last, that is, the series forms a climax. . . .

While any positive qualities of story characters will attract, a reader will identify most easily and immediately with characters who seem to share the reader's situation. Assuming that the majority of the first readers of the Gospel were Christians, they would relate most easily and immediately to characters in the story who respond positively to Jesus. The disciples, including the twelve, are the primary continuing characters who, at least at first, seem to respond in this way and so share this essential quality of the Christian reader's self-understanding. I believe that the author of Mark anticipated this response by his readers. He composed his story so as to make use of this initial tendency to identify with the disciples in order to speak indirectly to the reader through the disciples' story. In doing so, he first reinforces the positive view of the disciples which he anticipates from his readers, thus strengthening the tendency to identify with them. Then he reveals the inadequacy of the disciples' response to Jesus, presents the disciples in conflict with Jesus on important issues, and finally shows the disciples as disastrous failures. The surprisingly negative development of the disciples' story requires the reader to distance himself from them and their behavior. But something of the initial identification remains, for there are similarities between the problems of the disciples and problems which the first readers faced. This tension between identification and repulsion can lead the sensitive reader beyond a naively positive view of himself to self-criticism and repentance. The composition of Mark strongly suggests that the author, by the way in which he tells the disciples' story, intended to awaken his readers to their failures as disciples and call them to repentance. . . . The reader is left with a choice, a choice represented by the differing ways of Jesus and the disciples.

Robert C. Tannehill. *JR*. 57, 1977, pp. 390, 392–393

STYLE

Peter, whose personal account may be assumed to have been the basis of the story [of his denial], was a fisherman from Galilee, of humblest background and humblest education. The other participants in the night scene in the court of the High Priest's palace are servant girls and soldiers. From the humdrum existence of his daily life, Peter is called to the most tremendous role. Here, like everything else to do with Jesus' arrest, his appearance on the stage— viewed in the world-historical continuity of the Roman Empire—is nothing but a provincial incident, an insignificant local occurrence, noted by none but those directly involved. Yet how tremendous it is, viewed in relation to the life a fisherman from the Sea of Galilee normally lives. . . .

A tragic figure from such a background, a hero of such weakness, who yet derives the highest force from his very weakness, such a to and fro of the pendulum, is incompatible with the sublime style of classical antique literature. But the nature and the scene of the conflict also fall entirely outside the domain of classical antiquity. Viewed superficially, the thing is a police action and its consequences; it takes place entirely among everyday men and women of the common people; anything of the sort could be thought of in antique terms only as farce or comedy. . . .

What we see here is a world which on the one hand is entirely real, average, identifiable as to place, time, and circumstances, but which on the other hand is shaken in its very foundations, is transforming and renewing itself before our eyes. For the New Testament authors who are their contemporaries, these occurrences on the plane of everyday life assume the importance of world-revolutionary events, as later on they will for everyone. . . .

A scene like Peter's denial fits into no antique genre. It is too serious for comedy, too contemporary and everyday for tragedy, politically too insignificant for history—and the form which was given it is one of such immediacy that its like does not exist in the literature of antiquity. . . .

The story of Peter's denial, and generally almost the entire body of New Testament writings, is written from within the emergent growths and directly for everyman. Here we have neither survey and rational dispostition, nor artistic purpose. The visual and sensory as it appears here is no conscious imitation and hence is rarely completely realized. It appears because it is attached to the events which are to be related, because it is revealed in the demeanor and speech of profoundly stirred individuals and no effort need be devoted to the task of elaborating it. . . . Without any effort on [the author's] part, as it were, and purely through the inner movement of what he relates, the story becomes visually concrete. And the story speaks to everybody; everybody is urged and indeed required to take sides for or against it. Even ignoring it implies taking sides.

> Erich Auerbach. *Mimesis: The Representation of Reality in Western Literature*, trans. Willard R. Trask (Princeton, Princeton University Press, 1953), pp. 41–48

Even the superficial reader of the Gospel of Mark can easily discern in it the recurrence of many disturbing elements that cannot be said to have literary value. On the contrary, those irregular features of syntax and style characterize Mark's language as a very popular and colloquial brand of Greek. . . .

In contrast to the rather homely features . . . it is enhanced by delightful refinements and subtle artistic touches. The Gospel abounds in picturesque details and lifelike suggestions: an expressive gesture or impressive look caught by Mark's pen, or a mood described by a relevant verb, or details of setting given in passing. But the striking thing is that these features do not seem to result from strenuous efforts to produce a work of high literary quality; they appear suddenly and almost naturally, brought in by the narration itself. They are details that could almost be guessed. They seem to be brought into consciousness from a general background of many more motions and feelings. They reveal the art not of a story writer but of a narrator, a person who is interested primarily in recounting the most important facts, but who, in the course of his discourse, can stress a point with a motion, a silence, or an expressive look. It appears that these effects, proper to oral delivery, are deliberately integrated in the Gospel so that they can be renewed with each public reading. . . .

The indications of gesture, tone, and feeling are unusually vivid because they have a graphic quality. The narration seems to consist of a series of tableaux; the decor and surroundings are soberly suggested; the motions are described with one typical, almost theatrical gesture; the moods are reproduced by meaningful exclamations and conventional reflections. The ensemble results in a narration that is a spectacle of lifelike realism. Seven times Mark described Jesus looking around Him. Sometimes that look is charged with anger, sometimes with sorrow, sometimes with surprise. Twice the look penetrates right to the heart. Would it be possible to recite the passages describing the look of Jesus to an attentive audience without expressing its particular mood? Jesus is often said to take the hand of the sick as He heals them. Could these passages have been read to Roman Christians without at least a gesture of the hand expressing authority and sympathy at the same time?

> Gilbert Bilezikian. *The Liberated Gospel* (Grand Rapids, Baker, 1977), pp. 115–117

TRAGIC FORM

Study of the narrative of the gospel according to Mark, with particular reference to its plot and its chief character, Jesus, indicates that the Man of Nazareth is to be classed among the outstanding tragic figures of the race, an accompanying conclusion being that the Second Gospel comes under the classification of Greek tragedy. . . .

The Second Gospel must be regarded as a closet drama, that is, drama whose power is felt by the reader without stage presentation. For the gospel is not divided into acts and scenes, consists only in part of dialogue, has no stage directions, and lacks the "embellishment of song". . . . Yet within its prose narrative the Second Gospel has a well-constructed plot that corresponds to the demands of Greek dramatic criticism as shown in the following sketch of the story of Mark. . . .

The so-called Galilean ministry (up to 8:30) presents the rising action of the tragedy of Jesus. With the words, "And he began to teach them that the Son of man must suffer many things, and be rejected by the elders and the chief priests and the scribes, and be killed" (8:31), Mark introduces the "change of fortune" of his hero.

In order to appreciate the tragic significance of this reversal of fortune let it be recalled that for many decades the Jewish people had been expecting the advent of an outstanding person, who should be commissioned of God to lead his nation to victory and peace. A popular form of this expectation had it that a descendant of David was to occupy the throne and make of Isreal a great and enduring nation. . . . The answer of Peter at Caesarea Philippi, "Thou art Messiah," is the heart of the recognition scene, for as Mark delineates the action, Jesus had hitherto been known as "the carpenter" (6:3). From that moment indicated in 8:29 the carpenter became to the disciples the Messiah. . . .

The placing of the scene of transfiguration directly after that dialogue at Caesarea Philippi intensifies the recognition of Jesus as the Messiah. . . .

In dignity yet with falling fortunes the hero of the story took his way to Jerusalem. He frequently reminded his followers that he was facing an untimely fate. . . .

Events moved swiftly toward the tragic event. The triumphal procession, a remarkable combination of royal claim and show of humility, was but the forecast of the procession along the Via Dolorosa. . . . Every incident in those days was darkened by the shadow of the cross. . . . The tragic incident itself (*Poetics* xi. 6) was the crucifixion, following the arrest, trial, and condemnation. . . .

In further comment upon the story, attention should be called to the presence, here and there, of bystanders who function in the tragedy of Jesus as did the chorus in the classical plays. . . .

Does Jesus meet the requirements of an ideal tragic hero? . . .

Precisely the rigid adherence of Jesus to the program that he chose at the opening of his public ministry brought him to the judgment hall and to the cross. Coincident with the reversal of fortune, this hero foresaw the tragic outcome (8:31) and sent out a challenge to all who would ally themselves with him in devotement to the same program. . . .

Two objections may be urged against the inclusion of the resurrection story in the tragedy of Jesus. First, the resurrection forms the beginning of a new story. Second, if introduced, the resurrection offers an anticlimax to the story as the accepted text of Mark offers it. . . . The "end" of the action in Mark is the death and burial of the hero. Events continue to occur, but they belong to other stories.

Ernest W. Burch. JR. 11, 1931, pp. 346–347, 349–356

There is considerable similarity between the mood and structure of Mark's Gospel and the mood and structure of Greek tragic drama. A classical Greek tragedy concentrates upon a single theme. It has but one plot to unfold, one issue to resolve, one climax to achieve, one message to state. It moves relentlessly toward its culmination. One feels that the tragic end is inevitable, as everything is propelled by the unyielding hand of fate. The outcome is the necessary result of the premises introduced in the prologue and reveals the unwavering justice of the gods. From time to time during the play prophecies may be spoken by one who has divine knowledge, which give a forewarning of the outcome of the drama, so that the audience is continually reminded of what the end must be. Everything in a classic Greek drama is related to the outcome, and nothing is spoken which is not related, directly or indirectly, to that conclusion. . . .

It is not difficult to see the similarity between the structure of Mark's Gospel and the structure of *Agamemnon*. Like *Agamemnon*, Mark's Gospel begins with a prologue, in which Jesus' messianic role is introduced. From then on, everything that occurs in the Gospel is the outcome of the premises set forth in the prologue—an inevitable result of Jesus' messianic office.

Like *Agamemnon*, Mark's Gospel moves toward its end relentlessly. From the opening proclamation on, the unfolding of Mark's narrative is one straight line of action, culminating inevitably in the murder of Jesus. Hardly a word is spoken, hardly an incident is introduced, which does not bear, rather directly, on that culmination, or on the triumph which will follow.

As in *Agamemnon*, the tragedy in the Gospel is continually foreshadowed by prophecies of doom. . . .

Of course, one great difference between *Agamemnon* and Mark is that Mark does not end in tragedy. In the Easter story it ends on a note of joy. Through the unfolding of the drama it is continually asserted that Jesus' martyrdom will not be the end, that Jesus will come again in power to usher in God's Kingdom. Thus Mark has, running through the tragic action, the expectation of a joyful outcome, which does not take place within the drama itself, but is projected into the future.

There is no reason to suppose that Mark was familiar with classical Greek tragedy. Probably the similarity in structure and development is just a matter of good storytelling, rather than any specific dramatic tradition with which Mark was acquainted. However, the similarity is interesting. At least it shows that Mark was no mean writer, for his Gospel may be compared favorably in style and concept to the classic theater of the Graeco-Roman world.

> Curtis Beach. *The Gospel of Mark: Its Making and Meaning* (New York, Harper and Brothers, 1959), pp. 48–51

It has already been stated that Mark did not intend to write a Greek tragedy. His was the task of putting together a new form of literary composition that would promote the unique impact of a dynamic and effervescent religious experience. That in so doing, the availability of a compatible literary precedent in the rich heritage of his cultural milieu should have suggested itself to him is understandable, especially in view of the points of correspondence between Jesus in the Gospel and the hero in Greek tragedy. Points of the foregoing description of the tragic hero could equally apply to Jesus in the Gospel; He occupies the central place and the action is entirely dependent upon Him. . . . He moves in a threatening world fraught with contingencies. He is surrounded by unscrupulous and hypocritical faultfinders, boastful but cowardly followers, importunate and fickle crowds, derelicts ravaged in body and devastated in spirit. He Himself is sensitive to the pressure of circumstances. He grieves in empathy and in anger. He is overtaken by emotions and fatigue. He recoils from His tragic destiny and screams in anguish in the presence of death. But He is also "better than the ordinary man," as required of the tragic hero, not only because of His unique relation to God, not only because of His good, benevolent, and compassionate deeds. . . .

To some extent, the tragic hero is responsible for the vicissitudes that befall him. His heroic resolve reduces his options to those that entail suffering. This propensity for catastrophe is described by Aristotle as hamartia. . . .

This presence within the heroic character of a driving determination akin to obsession, often the result of predestination, also suggests some correspondence with the figure of Christ. Both in tragedy and in the Gospel, the fateful determination of the hero forces tragic confrontations with his environment. . . .

If Mark was acquainted with Greek drama, or at least with its Latin replica, he could hardly have failed to observe the frequent recurrence of a tragic character destined to suffer vicariously. As in many tragedies, the central figure of the Gospel fulfills a sacrificial role. In view of His foreknowledge of His own suffering and death, Jesus' refusal to escape His destiny, His aggressive challenge of the religious leaders and temple authorities, His self-incriminating answers to the high priest and to Pilate, His defenseless acceptance of violence against Himself—all point to deliberate self-sacrifice illumined by the declaration that He had come "to give his life as a ransom for many." Thus, to a narrator in search of a literary setting for the composition of a Gospel, the treatment of the hero in Greek tragedy would have presented sufficient points of correspondence to suggest itself as a valid precedent for depicting the hero of the Christian faith.

Gilbert Bilezikian. *The Liberated Gospel* (Grand Rapids, Baker, 1977), pp. 109–112

MATTHEW

STRUCTURE

Matthew's love of orderly arrangement is seen in his treatment of his sources. Mark's chronological and topographical statements are often omitted, and in Matthew iii-xii his order is drastically altered in the interests of a better topical arrangement. The material . . . is arranged in five main sections: the Sermon on the Mount (v-vii); the Mission Charge (x); the Parables of the Kingdom (xiii); sayings on Greatness and Forgiveness (xviii); and the Last Things (xxiv-xxv). There is also a tendency to arrange the material in groups of three, five, and seven.

> Vincent Taylor. *The Gospels: A Short Introduction* (London, The Epworth Press, 1930, 1945), p. 76

A too frequently neglected approach to Bible study is that which seeks to take in a book, or even all of Scripture, at a single glance. . . .

But how does one get a view-as-a-whole of a book of the Bible? More specifically, of the Gospel according to Matthew?

One of the simplest procedures is what might be called a beginning-end comparison. Set down in parallel columns a list of items summarizing points of likeness and of difference between the opening and the closing portions of the book. The results would soon start off somewhat as follows:

CHAPTER 1	CHAPTER 28
1. His coming to Earth	1. His departure to heaven near
2. Past promises fulfilled	2. Promise for future given
3. "God with us"	3. He is still with us
4. His birth (chapter 2 needed)	4. His death (chapter 27 needed)
5. Bethlehem	5. Jerusalem
6. A list of his ancestors	6. Are we in his posterity?
7. THE INCARNATION	7. THE RESURRECTION

Like two handles, you grasp the two ends of the book and then ask yourself the question: How does one get from here (the beginning) to there (the end)?

You are then ready to leaf through the pages of the book to trace the main steps of how the author unfolds the Life and Ministry, The Sufferings and Triumph of Jesus (Saviour), The Christ (Messiah), Son of Man, Son of God, and other aspects of our Lord's life and mission. . . .

But a more careful investigation of the whole seeks to determine *the main framework, the chief structural parts.* Fortunately, in Matthew we have a book that readily lends itself to structural analysis. Whether it was Matthew, the publican who wrote this book, assembling these materials as we now have them, no one may be able to say with finality. But this can be said: Whoever did write this book must have been an orderly sort of person—just like a good keeper of accounts who has everything well organized and grouped together. . . .

The student of Matthew's Gospel will not have to search long before he finds at 4:17 and 16:21 the major division points in this book. The literary formula, "From that time began Jesus to . . . ," gives them away. The three major divisions thus marked off are readily related to the composition as a whole. A common description of them . . . is: I. Preparation, 1:1 through 4:16; II. Proclamation, 4:17 through 16:20; III. Passion, 16:21 through 28:20. . . .

Another fruitful procedure . . . is *the application of the law of proportion.* An author often reveals his purpose by the relative amounts of time or space he gives to each portion of his narrative or argument.

Dean G. McKee. *Int.* 3, 1949, pp. 194–197

The strict unity which is so essential in the over-all development of an oral composition, is also necessary within the separate sections of such work. This necessity is in its origin a result of the conditions of performance in a strictly oral literature, where the reciter is forced to concentrate on one thing at a time. Because oral literature is directed to a listening audience, the composer has to choose a subject which is at once simple and attractive, omitting details and concentrating on a single mood or effect. He must avoid complication of any kind. He must be clear and keep strictly to the point, taking only one aspect of a situation and making the most of it. . . . The two methods most common in the Hebraic tradition are the habit of grouping like materials and the device of developing a leading idea by stressing certain key words. . . .

This habit of grouping together like materials is most obvious in Mt's collection of the sayings of the Lord into five extensive sermons, each marked by the same formula, "When Jesus had finished this discourse" (7, 28; 11, 1; 13, 53; 19, 1; 26, 1). It is very clear that these discourses have not simply grown; they have been built up by design, and stamped each with a character of its own, determined by its place in Mt's outline. . . .

The same desire to bring home a single point in each section of the Gospel can be found in Mt's groupings of narrative material. For example, in the collection of Jesus' "mighty works" (cc. 8–9), the central idea is the power of Jesus and the invitation to follow him. Its effectiveness is due primarily to the combination of scenes all of the same type, the miracle-stories of the tradition. . . . The section thus produces a single impression of Jesus' authority and attractiveness which can . . . be referred to again and again in the different contexts of the Gospel to bind together its parts and contribute to the imposition of a oneness of meaning on the whole. Similarly in the other narrative sections of the Gospel, the small, crystallized scenes of the tradition are combined according to their recurrent motifs, so that we are left with a single, clear impression after each section. In cc. 11–12 it is the rejection of Christ by "this generation," in cc. 14–17 the acknowlegement of him by the few, and in cc. 19–22 the Evangelist returns to the theme of authority. It is this grouping which illustrates perhaps best of all Mt's skill with the oral style.

The Gospel taken as a whole can be regarded as one great symmetrical structure. The division of the Gospel would appear as follows:

```
┌──── 1–   Narrative: Birth and beginnings
│      5–7  Sermon: Blessings, Entering Kingdom ──┐
│  ┌─ 8–9  Narrative: Authority and invitation    │
│  │  10    Sermon: Mission Discourse   ──┐        │
│ ┌│11–12 Narrative: Rejection by this generation │
│ ││ 13    Sermon: Parables of the Kingdom │       │
│ └│14–17 Narrative: Acknowledgment by disciples   │
│  │ 18    Sermon: Community Discourse ────┘        │
│  └─19–22 Narrative: Authority and invitation     │
│    23–25 Sermon: Woes, Coming of Kingdom ────────┘
└────26–28 Narrative: Death and rebirth
```

Seen thus, the balancing of the discourses is especially clear. The first and last discourses pair off: the blessings and the woes; entering the Kingdom and the coming of the Kingdom (5–7 and 23–25). The second and fourth can also be compared: the sending out of the apostles, and the receiving of the little ones (10 and 18). The great central discourse (13) on the nature of the Kingdom forms the high point of the Gospel. There is also a symmetry in the narrative sections. For example, there seems to be a comparison or contrast between the birth of Jesus at the beginning of the Gospel, and the resurrection (or rebirth) at the end; between Herod and Pilate; John the baptist and Judas; the baptism and the crucifixion; the triple temptation by the devil and the triple agony in the garden.

There are considerable advantages in regarding the structure of the Gospel in this way. It shows first of all the old question of the relation of the sermons to the narration to be a false problem. The Gospel cannot be divided into five books each of which is made up of sermon plus narrative, or vice versa, because whichever it is taken, there is one narrative section left over.

Charles H. Lohr. *CBQ*. 23, 1961, pp. 427–428

Mk's framework is extended backwards and forwards. Matthew places before the complex of stories about John the Baptist a prelude to the story of Jesus containing a genealogy (beginning with Abraham and leading up to Joseph: i. 2–17), a birth story (in which Joseph's fatherhood is expressly disputed: i. 18–25), the stories of the Wise Men from the East (ii. 1–12), the Flight into Egypt (ii. 13–15), the Masacre of the Innocents (ii. 16–18) and the return to Nazareth (ii. 19–23). From ch. iii onwards Matthew follows in essence the outline of Mk., apart from a few instances where the order and grouping are changed. The conclusion to the work—after the altered and expanded account of the Empty Tomb—is formed by the section about the appearance of the Risen Lord on the mountain in Galilee with the proclamation of his authority and the missionary command (xxviii. 16–20).

Even this outline is enough to show a certain "historicizing" tendency, for Matthew sets his "history" of Jesus in a vast context stretching from Abraham to the beginning of the Christian mission. That there are large gaps between the birth and public appearance of Jesus simply arises from the fact that the author had no material at his disposal, for at first the early Church was not interested in the biography of Jesus.

Within the framework we can trace a grouping of the material according to theme. We can see this on the one hand in the bringing together of miracle stories (viii-ix) which were scattered in Mk., and on the other hand in the formation of larger complexes of sayings: the Sermon on the Mount (v-vii), the Mission Charge (x), the discourse in parables (xiii), the Church's discipline (xviii), teaching against the Pharisees and about the *parousia* and the Last Judgement (xxiii-xxv). That we have in these instances a deliberate composition of units of teaching can be seen from the sterotype phrases at the end of each section: "And it came to pass, when Jesus ended these words. . . " (vii. 28; xi. 1; xiii. 53; xix. 1; xxvi. 1).

W. Marxsen *Introduction to the New Testament*, trans. G. Buswell (Philadlphia, Fortress Press, 1968), pp. 146–147

Of the three sections into which Matthew can be divided, the central section is by far the longest and most important. It has five parts, each of which contains both narrative and sayings material.

1. The Coming of Jesus as God's Messiah (1–2)
2. The Ministry of the Messiah and His Followers (3–25)
   a. Narrative: The Beginnings of the Ministry in Galilee (3:1–4:25)
   Discourse: The Sermon on the Mount (5:1–7:29)

b. Narrative: The Authority of Jesus' Ministry (8:1–9:35)
  Discourse: The Messianic Mission (9:36–10:42)
c. Narrative: The Kingdom and Its Coming (11:1–12:50)
  Discourse: The Parables of the Kingdom (13:1–52)
d. Narrative: The Life of the New Community (13:53–17:27)
  Discourse: Greatness and Responsibility (18:1–35)
e. Narrative: Conflict and Consummation (19:1–24:3)
  Discourse: Revelation of the End (24:4–25:46)
3. The Humiliation and Exaltation of the Messiah (26–28)

Each of the five parts of the second section concludes with a statement consisting in part of the words "when Jesus had finished . . ." (7:28; 11:1; 13:53; 19:1; 26:1). Transitions from narrative to discourse are marked off at 4:23 and 9:35 by summarizing statements about the healing ministry, but the pattern is not carried through consistently.

The five-part structure of the middle section is best explained as the result of a conscious imitation of the structure of the Torah, the first five books of the Old Testament, which are attributed by Jewish tradition to Moses.

> Howard Clark Kee. *Jesus in History: An Approach to the Study of the Gospels* (New York, Harcourt, Brace and World, 1970), pp. 151–152

The following is a general outline of The Gospel According to Matthew: (1) The infancy narratives (Matt. chs. 1;2); (2) The early ministry of Jesus (Matt. chs. 3;4); (3) The Sermon on the Mount (Matt. chs. 5 to 7); (4) The mighty acts of Jesus (Matt. chs. 8;9); (5) Discourse on the disciples' mission and martyrdom (Matt. 10:1 to 11:1); (6) Responses to Jesus' ministry (Matt. chs. 11; 12); (7) Discussion on the parables of the Kingdom (Matt. 13: 1–52); (8) Rejections and withdrawls with the disciples (Matt. 13:53 to 17:27); (9) Discourse on life in the Christian community (Matt., ch. 18); (10) The Jerusalem ministry (Matt., chs. 19 to 22); (11) Woes on the scribes and Pharisees and eschatological discourse (Matt. 23:1 to 26:2); and (12) The passion narrative and the resurrection appearances (Matt. 26:3 to 28:20).

> John H. Hayes. *Introduction to the Bible* (Philadelphia, Westminster Press, 1971), p. 425

Five times in Matthew (7:28; 11:1; 13:53; 19:1; 26:1) an expression something like "And when Jesus finished these sayings . . ." occurs, each time at the end of a collection of teachings composing a unified discourse. . . .

The center or substance of Matthew (3–25) is comprised of five books, each one containing a narrative and discourse section. The birth narrative (1–2) and passion (26–28), therefore, serve as prologue and epilogue. This fivefold structure reflects the Old Testament Pentateuch, and Matthew thus presents the Christian gospel as a new or revised law and Jesus as a new Moses or more authoritative law-giver.

Let me now present one set of criticisms of this view of Matthew and an alternative proposal regarding the governing structure of the Gospel. . . . 4:17 and 16:21 are parallel verses, no less striking as dividing marks than the five formula-statements noted above. Each verse contains the words "from then Jesus began" plus an infinitive and a summary of the content of the material to follow. This suggests that 1:1 is the introduction to 1:1–4:16, and Matthew is seen thus to have a fundamentally three-fold structure: (1) Jesus as Son of David and Son of Abraham (ideal Israelite) (1:1–4:16); (2) Jesus' proclamation of the Kingdom (4:17–16:20); (3) Jesus' proclamation of his death and resurrection (16:21–28:20). . . .

The three main sections deal with: (1) the person of Jesus Messiah; (2) the proclamation of Jesus Messiah; (3) the suffering, death, and resurrection of Jesus Messiah. The function of the structure is thus, not to present the gospel as law, but to set forth the claim of Jesus' person, ministry, and passion as ultimately significant. . . .

Any narrative may foreground certain elements and background others. The foreground pattern is likely to express a deviation from a norm and the background pattern, the norm which has been surpassed. . . .

Matthew foregrounds the three-fold Christological structure and backgrounds the five-fold legal one. The simultaneous juxtaposition of the two patterns has behind it and expresses a diachrony which is a part of Matthew's theological content. In the distant past God spoke in the prophets (1:22; 2:15, etc.) and law (5:21, etc.), but in the much more recent past the event promised by the prophets has been fulfilled (1:21–23; 2:14–15) and the real intention of the law has been brought to light (5:17; 5:21–26; etc.) in Jesus. . . .

The five-fold Pentateuchal demarcation is more evident than the three-fold Christological one. The relative strength of the legal structure vis-a-vis the Christological structure reflects what might be considered a theological problem in Matthew: Jesus fulfills and transcends the law of Moses but not law in principle.

> Dan O. Via, Jr. "Structure, Christology, and Ethics in Matthew," in *Orientation by Disorientation*, ed. Richard A. Spencer (Pittsburgh, Pickwick Press, 1980), pp. 199–201

It may be going too far to say that Matthew collected Jesus' teachings into five discourses because there were five books of Moses. Perhaps his organization was simply for convenient, ready reference as his book was used by teachers instructing new converts. . . .

Probably from the first century to the twentieth, students have memorized the outline of Matthew by counting off the five discourses on the fingers of one hand. (Jewish teachers were fond of numerical helps to the memory.) Between each of the following discourses, Matthew incorporated stories of

Jesus' life, taken mostly from Mark:

1) How are citizens of the kingdom to live? The Sermon on the Mount provided clear guidance, set in relationship to Jewish law, tradition, and practice (Matt. 5–7).

2) How are traveling preacher-disciples to conduct themselves on their evangelistic journeys? Jesus' words as he sent out the Twelve supplied the answers (Matt. 10).

3) What were those parables Jesus told? Matthew gathered seven and put them together for ready reference (Matt. 13).

4) How shall Christians conduct themselves toward each other and as they face persecution? Jesus' words about humility and sacrifice, as he journeyed toward Jerusalem and his own martyrdom, provided the answer (Matt. 18–20).

5) How will it all end? Matthew collected Jesus' eschatological sayings, predictions of the future and the end of the world, as a final discourse (Matt. 24–25).

Note how Matthew even marks each of these discourses with the phrase "When Jesus had finished these sayings" (Matt. 7:28; 11:1; 13:53; 19:1; and 26:1).

Add the stories of Jesus' birth and infancy at the beginnings and of his death and resurrection at the end, fill in between the discourses with miracle stories and stories of Jesus' growing conflicts with his enemies, and the student in the first century or the twentieth finds in Matthew an easily remembered manual for Christian faith and practice. . . .

The following outline, centered on what seems even more a major theme of the book, the promised king and his kingdom, will provide the framework around which [to] survey the Gospel.

Subject Matter	Chapters	Theme
Birth and Infancy	1–2	The King Is Born
Baptism and Temptation	3–4	The King Prepares
The Sermon on the Mount	5–7	The Kingdom Is Proclaimed
Miracle Stories, the Disciples, Opposition	8–15	Conflicting Responses to the King
The Great Confession	16–17	The King Is Recognized
Teachings on the Way to Jerusalem	18–20	The Cost of the King's Company
The Last Week and Easter	21–28	The King Is Crowned

William M. Ramsay. *The Layman's Guide to the New Testament* (Atlanta, John Knox Press, 1981), pp. 37–39

UNIFYING MOTIFS

The primary aim of S. Matthew was to prove to the Jews that Jesus Christ was their promised Messiah—that mysterious Person to Whom all the prophets gave witness, in Whom the spirit of prophecy found its highest and fullest expression. . . . It was calculated to claim their attention at once, when the Apostle made known the circumstances of Christ's Birth, all of which he pointed out were so ordered as to fulfill what was written, and even more, as he went on to show, that it was equally true at every stage of His life and work, in His rejection, His Death and Passion, and in His Resurrection. . . .

The character which laid the strongest hold upon the Jewish mind and affections was the Regal. Indeed at last the expectation of a mighty king, who should restore the independence of their nation, and make it once more a great material power, so fascinated them that every other aspect of Messianic hope was overshadowed. . . .

No wonder, then, that S. Matthew, himself a Jew, deeply conversant with his countrymen's aspirations, and realizing how far they had fallen short of the true ideal, should write his Gospel to show that Jesus Christ fulfilled all prophecy, and had set up such a spiritual kingdom as had been foretold, though their rulers and guides had lost sight of its true character.

While, however, S. Matthew's dominant aim is to exhibit the ideal King, he lays more stress than the other Evangelists do upon Christ as a Teacher fulfilling the Messianic gift of Prophecy. . . .

The Evangelist intended . . . to show at the very outset that the Messiah of Whom he wrote was not only of the chosen seed of Abraham, but heir of the kingdom, drawing His human descent from a line of kings which reaches back to the great king David.

His birth is followed by the visit of the Magi, whom tradition has clothed in all the emblems of royalty; and they made it known at once that the object of their quest across the trackless desert was to find Him Who was born "King of the Jews." Without any hesitation they prostrated themselves before the Infant Jesus, and presented the gold which betokened His Royalty. Here, too, we are told of the alarm of Herod at the birth of a rival king. . . .

Again S. Matthew puts the same fact more forcibly forward by a remarkable group of parables in the thirteenth chapter, all of which speak of the nature of His kingdom. . . . Further, in one of these parables the aim of S. Matthew is distinctly brought out through an important detail. Men have commonly identified the parable of the Marriage Feast of the King's son with that of the Great Supper; but there are many considerations connected with time and place which tend to distinguish them from each other. If we separate them, S. Matthew, the messenger of the kingdom, fulfills his purpose in selecting as most worthy of record that which is described as a Royal banquet.

Herbert Mortimer Luckock. *The Special Characteristics
of the Four Gospels* (London, Longmans, Green, and
Company, 1900), pp. 51–53, 55–57

A very notable characteristic of Matthew is his view of *the Christian Message
as the consummation of Old Testament religion*. This interest is shown by
his preoccupation with the ideas of Messiahship and the Kingdom, his description of Jesus as 'the son of David', and his evident pleasure in narrating
the story of the Triumphal Entry (xxi. 1–11). The Old Testament is freely
cited. . . .

One may dislike the phrase 'that it might be fulfilled', but its deeper
suggestion is that Christianity is not an accident, but a consummation. . . .

Matthew's *apocalyptic interests* are seen in his attitude to the Last Things
and the Return of Christ. These interests are evident in some of the parables
peculiar to Matthew: the Ten Virgins, which ends with the warning: 'Watch
therefore, for ye know not the day nor the hour' (xxv. 13); the Talents, where
the unprofitable servant is consigned to outer darkness and to 'weeping and
gnashing of teeth' (xxv. 30); the Sheep and the Goats, which portrays the
Son of man 'in his glory, and all the angels with him', and the separation to
the right hand and to the left (xxv. 31ff.). . . .

The *ecclesiastical interests* of Matthew appear in certain passages which
are peculiar to his Gospel.

Vincent Taylor. *The Gospels: A Short Introduction* (London, The Epworth Press, 1930, 1945), pp. 77–80

Mark seems to have addressed his Gospel to the Roman Gentiles and to have
aimed primarily at relating the deeds of Jesus. Addressing a different audience,
the Jews and Gentiles of Asia Minor, Matthew had other, more specific aims:
(1) to present a fuller biography of Jesus, beginning with his birth and ending
with his reappearance to the Disciples after his Resurrection; (2) to record
the *teachings* of Jesus, to a large extent ignored by Mark; (3) to convince the
Jewish people that Jesus was the Messiah descended from David and promised
by the prophets of the Old Testament, that Jesus had come to fulfill and
extend—not to overthrow—the ancient Jewish Law, . . . and (4) to persuade
the Gentiles that Jesus was the Messiah for all the peoples of the world.

Buckner B. Trawick. *The Bible as Literature: The New
Testament* (New York, Barnes and Noble, 1964, 1968),
p. 40

STORYTELLING TECHNIQUE

In many cases . . . a man's calling or occupation leaves its mark upon what
he writes, and that even though it be wholly unconnected with the subjects
in hand. Such traces . . . abound in the Gospel of S. Matthew. . . . Anything

connected with money would have a natural attraction for a publican; and in this Gospel there is more frequent mention of money than in the others, and not only so, but more and rarer coins are introduced.

In S. Mark's Gospel we read only of three coins and those the poorest; the mite, the farthing, and the penny. . . . S. Luke goes further, for he speaks even of pounds or minas. . . . But S. Matthew mentions more coins, and deals with those of the highest value current at the time, and not once only but again and again.

The difference is shown in a striking manner in the several records of our Lord's directions to the Apostles when He sent them out on their first mission. In S. Mark we read that He charged them "that they should take nothing for their journey . . . no money in their purse." . . . In S. Matthew, however, where in all probability we have the exact injunctions as they were given in detail, and fully appreciated by one who knew the whole monetary coinage of the country, "neither gold, nor silver, nor brass in your purses."

Again, it is in perfect harmony with the above distinction that the two parables of the talents should find a place in S. Matthew's Gospel, though neither of them receives any notice from the other Evangelists. A talent was worth some seventy times as much as "the pound" of S. Luke, or above eight thousand times more than "the penny" of S. Mark. The amount of the debt, viz., ten thousand talents, which was owed to the king by one of his servants, was quite within the grasp of a publican, who was responsible for enormous sums, but it made little or no impression upon the common mind.

Herbert Mortimer Luckock. *The Special Characteristics of the Four Gospels* (London, Longmans, Green, and Company, 1900), pp. 32–34

Matthew's penchant, in common with contemporary Jewish rabbis, was for arithmetical arrangements. He was particularly fond of grouping his material by three's. The following are some of the more obvious instances of this systematizing. There are three divisions in the genealogy of our Lord (1:1–17), three temptations (4:1–11), three illustrations of righteousness (6:1–18), three commands (7:7), three miracles of healing (8:1–15), three miracles of power (8:23–9:8), a threefold answer to the question regarding fasting (9:14–17), a threefold "fear not" (10:26, 28, 31), a threefold repetition of "he is not worthy of me" (10:37–38), three parables of sowing (13:1–32), three sayings concerning "the little ones" (18:6, 10, 14), three parables of warning (21:18–22:14), three questions by his adversaries (22:15–40), three prayers in Gethsemane (26:39–44), three denials by Peter (26:69–75), and three questions by Pilate (27:11–17). A sevenfold arrangement is represented, among other examples in Matthew, by the seven clauses in the Lord's prayer (6:9–13)—two more than in the Lukan version—seven demons (12:45), seven parables (ch. 13), seven loaves (15:34), seven baskets (15:37), forgiving not "seven times, but seventy times seven" (18:22), seven brothers (22:25), and seven "woes" (ch. 23).

Bruce M. Metzger. "The Language of the New Testament," *Interpreter's Bible*, Vol. 7 (Nashville, Abingdon Press, 1951), pp. 49–50

Among Matthew's merits as a writer are aptness in choice of words, and the use of balance, parallelism, contrast, and repetition. He gains a great deal from abundant use of dialogue and monologue, especially when he allows Jesus to speak for himself.

Other noteworthy features of his style and technique are (1) a fondness for the numbers 3, 5, and 7 (three appearances of the angel to Joseph, Peter's three denials of Jesus, division of teachings in five discourses, seven loaves of bread, seven woes [in Ch. 23], and so on); (2) the use of formulas and catchwords, such as "The Kingdom of Heaven is like . . ." and "that it might be fulfilled"; (3) the presence of a strong apocalyptic element, especially evident in the parables of the Ten Virgins and the Talents; and (4) ecclesiastical interest.

Buckner B. Trawick. *The Bible as Literature: The New Testament* (New York, Barnes and Noble, 1964, 1968), p. 41

St. Matthew retains all the Marchan parables, since he aims to write an expanded Mark; but his own parables are set in the world of men. Kings and nobles and their slaves, farmers and their workmen, housebuilders and fisherman, a father and his sons, wedding-guests and bridesmaids, a woman in the kitchen and children at play, a tenant-farmer, a merchant, and a burglar— these are the world of the Matthaean parables. Where he gives us a country parable his eye is on the people, and nature is in the background. . . .

Matthew is a lover of the grand scale. He (or his tradition) is the oriental story-teller so beloved by the commentators. . . . Mark's owner sends to the Wicked Husbandmen three servants in turn and then a number; Matthew's a group each time, and more the second than the first. His journeying householders are away for weeks, perhaps years: their servants know not the *day* nor the hour. . . . His shepherd has 100 sheep. The treasure in the field and the pearl exceed in value all that their discoverers possess. The very fall of the house on sand is great. . . . When it comes to money, Matthew moves among the millionaires. His householder entrusts nothing less than a talent to his servants, ten, twenty, fifty thousand *denarii*, a man's wage for 30, 60, 150 years. The Unmerciful Servant's debt is astronomical, the tribute of many provinces. . . .

His long parables are without exception black-and-white caricature contrasts: the Two Builders upon sand and rock, the man and his ememy sowing their Wheat and Tares, the Dragnet with the good fish in buckets and the bad thrown out, the ninety-nine safe sheep and the wanderer, the Merciful King and the Unmerciful Servant, the First Labourers in the Vineyard and the last, the obedient and disobedient sons, the invited and the chosen at the wedding feast, the faithful and the faithless servant in charge of the house, the wise and the foolish steward. Often the contrasts are laboured by repetitive language so that they shall not escape us, as with the Two Builders, the Unmerciful Servant, and the Talents especially. Usually the contrast is even: wheat with tares, five wise virgins and five foolish. It is the art of the author that he achieves just as black and white a contrast when he intrudes third and fourth parties. . . .

All thirteen of the long Matthaean parables are contrast-parables. . . .

In Matthew all is stylized. People are either good or bad, wise or foolish, obedient or disobedient, merciful or merciless. His Two Builders is typical: one is wise and one builds upon the sand. There are the same rain and the same rivers and the same winds, and the inevitable end. His Two Sons is more stark than most of his parables, but it reveals the essential Matthaean technique. The boys are stock figures, not human beings. Nine words apiece suffice to sketch in their characters. We can tell a Matthaean faithful or unfaithful servant as quickly as we can Colonel Blimp or the T.U.C. horse.

M. D. Goulder. JTS, n.s. 19, 1968, pp. 54, 56–57

The characters of the Gospel tend to play fixed roles. Angels are supernatural beings whose presence signals, or alludes to, the immediate or future inter-vention of God in human affairs, often on behalf of Jesus (cf. chaps. 1–2; 28). Satan is likewise a supernatural being, the transcendent adversary of Jesus. The disciples, upright persons such as "Joseph" (cf. 1:19), and people who approach Jesus in faith for healing are "allies" of Jesus. The Israelite crowds form the background for much of Jesus' activity in public, but they remain unbelieving and in the passion narrative join their leaders in con-demning Jesus to death. The Israelite leaders of whatever designation are the inveterate opponents of Jesus. Now since in Matthew's day Jesus is the Exhalted One whom his church confesses and worships, the reader of the Gospel is not invited to identify with him per se, but with the disciples and people who come to him in faith. In learning of Jesus, the reader learns of the basis of salvation. In experiencing with the disciples their moments both of "understanding" and of "little faith," the reader is taught either positively or by reverse example what it means to be a follower of Jesus in post-Easter times.

It would be too much to say that Matthew attributes special meaning to more than a handful of the settings in which Jesus is described as carrying out his ministry. But some of the settings do possess a significance beyond what is strictly literal. Thus, "Galilee" is the place where Jesus proffers

salvation to the Jews (4:12, 23) and where his church following easter begins
its mission of salvation to the gentiles (28:16–20). "Capernaum" and "Nazareth," the two cities in which Jesus is at home in Galilee (2:23; 4:13), are
symbols of the rejection of divine grace (11:23–24; 13:54–58). "Jerusalem"
is the place where Jesus must die (16:21). It is the "home" of such as are
his mortal enemies—Herod (chap. 2), Pilate (chap. 27), and the "chief priests
and the elders of the people" (cf., e.g., 2:4; 21:23; 26:3, 47; 27:1). The
"mountain" . . . is the place that alludes to Jesus as the Son of God. The
"temple," as the dwelling place of God, is depicted as superseded through
death and resurrection by the person of the Son of God (26:61; 27:51). And
the phrase "in those days" (3:1; chap 24) connotes . . . the "last times"
that will culminate in Jesus' visible return in glory for judgment.

> Jack Dean Kingsbury. *Matthew* (Philadelphia, Fortress
> Press, 1977), pp. 19–20

SERMON ON THE MOUNT

The literary form of this new constitution of the Kingdom of Heaven is
remarkable. Dean Charles R. Brown of Yale says: "In the Sermon on the
Mount, brief though it is, there are no less than fifty-six metaphors, which
are really word pictures. Salt, light, candle, bushel, treasure, moth, rust,
lilies, ravens, splinter, beam, bread, fish, scorpion—these are examples.
Fifty-six of them! The entire Sermon on the Mount can be read aloud in
fifteen minutes. These fifty-six metaphors mean, therefore, that in this particular utterance word-pictures came from his lips at the rate of more than
three per minute."

One can easily convince himself that this is very far removed from the
ordinary legal document by looking up the following forms: metaphors in
Matthew 5:13, 14; symbol in 5: 29; parable in 7: 24–27; hyperbole in 5: 39–
42. . . .

It has often been noted that Jesus used the proverbial form of speech so
characteristic of our book of Proverbs. The Sermon on the Mount is full of
these Wisdom sayings: "Ye are the salt of the earth," "Ye are the light of
the world."

> Herbert R. Purinton and Carl E. Purinton. *Literature of
> the New Testament* (New York, Charles Scribner's Sons,
> 1925), pp. 80–81

How full were the talks of Jesus of illustration by metaphor and simile, using
common concrete objects to make clear spiritual and moral ideas, will only
be grasped if we look closely at the Sermon on the Mount, in which illustration
follows hard on illustration. After the Beatitudes in Matt. v, Jesus commences

with common household objects, like *salt* and *lamps* and *corn measures*, to explain Christian influences. . . . *Parts of* the *body* are used next. *Hand* and *eye* are put for bad habits, Christian retaliation is to turn the other *cheek*, modesty is like one *hand* not knowing what the other does, hypocrisy is the same as not noticing a *beam* in your own *eye*. Then come objects of nature, to show worry unnecessary, *lilies, birds, grass put in the oven*, strengthened by an example from history, in the person of *Solomon*. Praying is like *knocking at a door*, or a son asking for a *helping at meal-times. Pearls* and *swine*, narrow *gates* and broad *roads*, *grapes* from *thorns* and *figs* from *thistles*— all these link the hearers' common everyday life with the moral life, and even Aesop's Fables are drawn upon for the hypocrisy of the *wolf in sheep's clothing*, while the talk closes with the fine illustration of sincerity taken from *housebuilding*. He *thought* in pictures.

> P. C. Sands. *Literary Genius of the New Testament* (Oxford, Oxford University Press, 1932), p. 76

The manner of the Sermon is, first of all, *poetical*. If we printed it in our Bible as it should be printed, we should have to deal in couplets and even stanzas. For much of the Sermon is Hebrew poetry. . . . Even in an English dress, we can detect in the Sermon not only that "parallelism" which is the chief formal feature of Semitic poetry but also clearly marked rhythm.

"Parallelism" is "a rhyming of thoughts"; the correspondence in sense of one line with another. . . .

Poetic forms occur in the Sermon on the Mount. Thus . . . Matt. 7:6 is a sample of "synonymous" parallelism. Matt. 7:17 is "antithetic". . . . But paralellism can be a matter not only of couplets like these but even of strophes, as in our Lord's words about prayer (Matt. 7:7f.).

Rhythm, the other main feature of Semitic poetry, is also found in the Sermon. . . . The best example is perhaps the Lord's Prayer in Matthew's version. . . .

The poetical symmetry [in the Lord's Prayer] is unmistakable. We have two stanzas, each of three lines, and each of the three lines has four beats. Anyone can see how such poetic form would conduce to easy memorizing. Are we to say that all this is merely accidental? Is it not rather the work of One who so framed his pattern Prayer that he might fix it surely in the memory of his disciples?. . . .

One of the secrets of the perennial freshness of the great Sermon is that it is radically *pictorial*. Not only does it employ parables, but it abounds in vivid, concrete speech and is illustrated direct from common life and nature.

We see the germ of the parable in such sayings as "A city that is set on an hill cannot be hid" or "The eye is the lamp of the body". . . .

We Occidentals moralize in abstract terms; Jesus deals in "things which you can touch and see". When we should say, "Charity should never be obtrusive", he says, "When you give alms, sound not a trumpet before you".

If we had to express the thought in Matt. 7:6, we should probably say, "Exercise reserve in your communication of religious truth". Jesus says, "Give not that which is holy unto the dogs". . . .

Akin to all this is the way the Sermon keeps close to human life and everyday reality for its illustrations. Think of the variety of "characters" who make their brief entrances in the sayings of the Sermon, conjured up for us sometimes by a single word. They range through all grades of society from "Solomon in all his glory" to the beggar by the roadside (5:42). . . . All these and many more serve to "illustrate" the Sermon: the village women heating their ovens with "the lilies of the fields" (6:30); their children clamouring for a piece of bread or a bit of fish (7:9f.); these, with all the sights and sounds of nature: sun and rain, wind and flood, thistle and thorn, vine and fig, with birds and moths, dogs and swine, sheep and wolves. . . .

The third feature of the Sermon's style worth noting is its *proverbial* nature.

Archibald M. Hunter. *A Pattern for Life* (Philadelphia, Westminster Press, 1965; orig. pub. London, SCM Press, 1965), pp. 18–22

. . . Jesus, using older materials, made his perfect Prayer [the Lord's Prayer].
  On the positive side, we may find the originality of the Prayer in:
  (a) its *brevity*. Here is no "much speaking"—no holy verbosity—but six short petitions that go arrow-like to the unseen world;
  (b) its *order*. The Prayer puts first things first, the heavenly things before the earthly; and
  (c) its *universality*. The Prayer is concerned wholly with the needs common to humanity, so that all men, whatever their class or colour, can make it their own. It is, as Helmut Thielicke puts it, "the Prayer that spans the World".
  The *plan*, or shape, of the Prayer is simplicity itself. After the Invocation—"our Father who art in heaven"—there follow six petitions. Three are for God's glory; three are for man's needs.

A. M. Hunter. *Bible and Gospel* (Philadelphia, West-minster Press, 1969), p. 68

The Sermon on the Mount (Matt. 5–7) has affinities to several literary forms. It is similar in tone to Old Testament wisdom literature, in which a wise authority figure sits in the middle of his disciples and instructs them. Much of the discourse is a satiric attack on religious abuses. In its composite picture of the Christian, the sermon resembles the genre known as "the character." The discourse is sometimes considered an example of utopian literature, an appropriate designation for the work because it outlines the general principles for the conduct of the perfect spiritual kingdom that Christ came to establish and of which this sermon is a kind of inaugural address.

The beatitudes that begin the discourse are one of the most famous passages in the literature of the world. They are one of the most patterned passages in the Bible. . . . Much of the memorable quality of the beatitudes, like that of the Ten Commandments, stems from the artistic form in which they are cast. The overall literary genre is the character, in this case a composite portrait of the blessed person. The various beatitudes are organized around a central theme—the qualities of character that make for blessedness. Recurrence underlies the whole series, with each beatitude following the same pattern, based on a balancing of blessing with the reason for blessing. The formula consists of three parts—an initial statement beginning with the clause "Blessed are," the naming of a character type, and a rationale for the pronouncement of blessing, starting with the statement "for they shall" or "for theirs is." this parallelism of expression, which comes straight from the Hebraic poetry with which Jesus was so familiar, lends an aphoristic quality to the individual beatitudes and links them with the proverbs of Hebrew wisdom literature. . . .

The next main section of the Sermon on the Mount, Jesus' discourse about the law (5:17–48), is mainly satiric in form. . . .

Satiric attack and positive advice continue in the next section (6:1–16), where Jesus takes up the topic of religious observances. In the areas of giving alms, prayer, and fasting, Jesus conducts a satiric attack on those who are ostentatious in their religious practices. . . .

The three pieces of advice on religious observances are balanced by a threefold exhortation on the theme of choosing heavenly or spiritual values over earthly values (6:19–24). Antithesis underlies the contrasts between earthly and heavenly treasures, light and darkness (or sound and unsound eyes), and the two masters, God and mammon. . . .

One of the most eloquent passages in the Sermon on the Mount is the section in which Jesus dispraises anxiety (6:25–34). The unit is structured like an argument, as Jesus gives reasons against being anxious. Like any good persuasive speech, it mingles evidence and direct appeal to the listener. . . .

The parallelism of the Hebraic poetry that Jesus knew and loved pervades the next section of His discourse (7:1–12). . . .

As He concludes His discourse (7:13–27), Jesus sharpens the issues and begins to force a response from His listeners. He leaves His audience with a challenge, urging them to make sure that they are members of God's kingdom. In order to make His point with impact, Jesus used three memorable contrasts—the narrow gate that leads to life vs. the wide gate that leads to destruction (vss. 13–14), true prophets vs. false prophets (vss. 15–23), and the wise man who builds his house on a rock vs. the foolish man who builds on the sand (vss. 24–27).

Leland Ryken. The Literature of the Bible (Grand Rapids, Zondervan, 1974), pp. 293–298

PARABLE
(See also separate entries on the following parables: *Good Samaritan, Prodigal Son, Sower.*)

They belong to the world's "little masterpieces of fiction." . . .

With wonderful economy of effort he sets his characters before us as living men and women. His device is not to describe, but to show them doing or speaking. . . . With the realistic exactness of one reporting an incident out of his own experience, he mentions now one, now another characteristic detail such as only a poetic imagination would emphasize. . . . Even in the brief mention of the woman making bread, he tells us she hid the leaven not simply in the meal, but in three measures of meal—and that makes the difference between a lay-figure and an actual housewife. It is just these apparently trivial touches that betray the born storyteller. . . .

Near to the folk also was his constant use of what our Latin grammar calls "direct discourse". . . . He reports the householder, which went out at different hours of the day to hire more laborers into his vineyard, as in actual conversation in the market-place; he does not tell us the Prodigal said he would arise and go to his father, but he lets us overhear the Prodigal's own spoken resolve.

Near to the folk, again, are his repetitions, like those familiar in Homer and in ballad poetry, found in the *Gospel* narratives about Jesus as well (e.g., *Luke* XIX, 31–34), and in all primitive recitals: as "Enter thou into the joy of thy Lord" in the parable of the Talents; and "I have sinned against heaven," etc., of the Prodigal Son. . . .

His characters belong to the literature of the world, even with the more developed creations of so-called secular letters. . . .

One might expect the realistic habit that adds so many little touches of accurate detail would have led him to locate, as is so common in folk-lore and legend, his stories in some appropriate place . . . ; but he is thus definite only in the story of the man who was going down to Jericho. Moreover, his characters are unnamed, save the beggar on Abraham's bosom. . . . And in this way his stories, with all their simple realism, acquire something of that remoteness and mystery characteristic of fairy tales, which usually tell of what happened somewhere, once upon a time, to some certain prince, or maiden, or forest child whose names we shall never know. . . .

But these stories exist not for themselves alone; like all great art, they have a meaning beyond themselves. Each exists for an idea; they all illustrate the ethical or religious principles that fired the imagination of the Poet of Galilee. . . .

The fitness of the stories as illustrations is quite independent of their excellence as narrative compositions.

They are a part of the glowing concreteness of a poet's thinking.

> William Ellery Leonard. *The Poet of Galilee* (New York,
> B. W. Huebsch, 1909), pp. 118–124, 126

The finished literary form of these stories may be appreciated more highly if we realize that they have been the standard for some of our best modern authors. In the introduction to the complete edition of his works, the famous American short-story writer, Bret Harte, declared it his rule to "conform to the rules laid down by a Great Poet who created the parable of the 'Prodigal Son' and the 'Good Samaritan,' whose works have lasted eighteen hundred years, and will remain when the present writer and his generation are forgotten." Bret Harte's two greatest short stories, *The Luck of Roaring Camp* and *The Outcasts of Poker Flat*, are strikingly similar to the *Prodigal Son* and the *Good Samaritan*.

> Herbert R. Purinton and Carl E. Purinton. *Literature of
> the New Testament* (New York, Charles Scribner's Sons,
> 1925), p. 108

The parables of Jesus are the work of an artist devoting himself to the answer of demands more humanly imperative than the call of beauty. They were his characteristic utterance because it was he who in one and the same intent called humanity to consider the lilies and himself undertook the conflict that led to the cross. . . .

In its most characteristic use the parable is a weapon of controversy, not shaped like a sonnet in undisturbed concentration, but improvised in conflict to meet an unpremeditated situation. . . . In its highest use it shows the imagination and sensitiveness of the poet, the penetration, rapidity and resourcefulness of the protagonist, and the courage that allows such a mind to work unimpeded by the turmoil and danger of mortal combat. . . .

While the parable's essential function is to evoke a judgment in one field and secure its application in another, it does not therefore follow that there is only one point of contact between the story of the parable and the other field to which we carry the judgment evoked by the story. Indeed, it is comparatively seldom that it is so. . . . This is clearly so in the case of the prodigal, where many things in the father and in the prodigal and in the elder brother are very suggestive of things in God, the sinner and the Pharisee, and where these similarities, because they do not spoil the naturalness and inward consistency of the story, make the transference of our judgment from it to the relations of God and man all the more emphatic and all the richer in content.

The resolution to find only one point of comparison between the parable and that to which it is applied has two unfortunate results. The judgment for which the parable asks is likely to be sought for in one element of it only and is thus unduly simplified; and all other elements of the parable are regarded as *mise en scène*. Hence the parable becomes a figuratively enjoined platitude obscured by unnecessary ornament. . . .

A parable is the work of a poor artist if the picture or story is a collection of items out of which we have to pick one and discard the rest. A good parable is an organic whole in which each part is vital to the rest; it is the story of a complex and sometimes unique situation or event, so told that the outstanding features of the story contribute to the indication and nature of its point. . . .

From these considerations we may get guidance in our attempt to understand the parables of Jesus. Where we have reliable indication of the parable's occasion we have to ask:

(1) What is the natural point of the picture or story?
(2) What is the outstanding interest of the occasion?
(3) What does the point of the story persuade us to think about the outstanding interest of the occasion?

. . . The parable elicits a judgment in one sphere in order to transfer it to another. Therefore in an effective parable the hearer passes judgment unhesitatingly on the situation depicted in the story.

> A. T. Cadoux. *The Parables of Jesus: Their Art and Use* (London, James Clarke and Company, 1930), pp. 12–13, 50–52, 54, 56

The style . . . follows the laws operating unconsciously in the art of popular story-telling. Thus, "epic repetition" is seen in the parable of the prodigal son, when the speech which the prodigal is to make to his father is given twice—when he is meditating in the fields and when he reaches home (Luke xv, 18 and 21). "Antithesis of types," frequent in all folk-tradition, is seen in the parables of the Pharisee and the Publican (Luke xviii, 9-14) and Dives and Lazarus (Luke xvi, 19–31). The "law of three-fold repetition," with stress upon the third instance, a law well known in fairy-tales, operates in the parable of the Good Samaritan, when the third passer-by is the true neighbour. In the same way, in the parable of the Talents, the third servant is the lazy one, and his case constitutes the point of the story (Matt. xxv, 14–39).

Martin Debelius. *A Fresh Approach to the New Testament and Early Christian Literature* (New York, Charles Scribner's Sons, 1936), pp. 30–31

While parables and similitudes display their affinity with proverb or simile, they also to a wide extent obey the "laws" of all popular, nonliterary, story-telling. . . . Repetition is the means whereby the story-teller elaborates and excites interest in his tale. The same incident is repeated—as a rule three times. . . . In the parables we have instances of such repetition in the visits of the employer to the market-place to hire labourers, and of the lord's slaves to the wicked husbandmen to collect the rent; in the interviews between the master and the slaves to whom he has entrusted monies and between the steward and his lord's debtors. . . . We have many examples of the rule of three: the three slaves of the parable of Entrusted Wealth, the three typical excuses of the Unwilling Guests, the three travellers of the parable of the Good Samaritan, the three missions of individual slaves in Mark's parable of the Wicked Husbandmen or of slaves, more slaves, son in Matthew's version, the three kinds of unfruitful soil and the three varieties of yield of the good soil in the parable of the Sower, the three stages of the seed's growth in the parable of the Patient Husbandman, the three enemies of the builder in Matthew's version of the parable of the Two Houses. On the other hand, there are never so many as three persons (or groups treated as individuals) taking an active part on the stage of the story at the same time: here the "rule of two" holds sway. . . . In the parable of the Prodigal Son we have successively the scenes between father and prodigal, father and household, elder son and slave, father and elder son. The "rule of contrast" refers to the dualism which is a frequent feature of the folk-tale—the contrast between virtue and vice, youth and age, strength and weakness and the like—and may be illustrated by the parables of Dives and Lazarus, the Pharisee and the Publican, the Ten Virgins, the Two Houses, the Faithful and Unfaithful Servants, and the Unwilling Guests. The "rule of end-stress", in accordance with which special importance attaches to the last of a series (the youngest son, the final adventure), finds illustration in the parables of the Sower (the fertile soil), Entrusted Wealth (the important figure is the servant who lets the money lie idle), the Wicked Husbandmen (the mission of the son), the Good Samaritan (the last of the travellers), and the Labourers in the Vineyard (the lesson of the parable turns upon those hired last). Finally, the "rule of the single theme" forbids the interweaving of two tales. . . .

To formulate these "laws" is but to call attention to the fact that the popular story-teller cannot attempt to portray complicated situations, and that the folk-tale must take on a certain simplicity and symmetry of form. . . .

The tendency towards "schematization" is accentuated, in the case of the parables of Christ and the Rabbis, by the Jewish love of parallelism and of formulas. The parable of the Two Houses, for example, has a definite pattern. . . .

Other characteristics of the popular and in particular of the vivid Oriental story are to be found in the use of . . . soliloquy, in the preciseness and concreteness of such detail as is given combined with the elimination of all that is not relevant to the point of the story, and in the portrayal of character, motives, feelings by deeds or words.

> B.T.D. Smith. *The Parables of the Synoptic Gospels* (Cambridge, Cambridge University Press, 1937), pp. 35–39

Parable is a form of teaching. "Almost all teaching," Dean Inge has said, "consists in comparing the unknown with the known, the strange with the familiar." It is a matter of everyday experience that you can hardly explain anything at all except by saying it is *like* something else, something more familiar. . . .

Combine, then, this mode of teaching by analogy with the Oriental's innate love of pictorial speech and every man's delight in a story, and you have most of the reasons why men took to using parable to communicate truth. . . .

Jesus' parables *obey the rules of popular storytelling*. Down the centuries men have found by experience that stories become more effective if you follow certain rough rules in telling them. "Repetition" in the "build-up" is a common one. Another is "the rule of contrast" whereby wisdom and folly, riches and poverty, etc., are set in contrast. Yet a third is the "the rule of three" whereby the story has three characters. . . . A fourth is the rule of "end stress" whereby the spotlight falls on the last in the series, whether it is the youngest son or the final adventure. . . .

Second, the Gospel parable is something *extemporised* in the living encounter with men rather than something lucubrated in study or cell. If the sonnet, for example, grows slowly in the soil of quiet—is essentially "emotion recollected in tranquility"—the parable is often improvised in the cut-and-thrust of conflict. For Jesus' parables, as we shall see, arise out of real situation and are often instruments of controversy in which he justifies his actions, confronts men with the will of God, or vindicates the gospel against its critics.

Third, every parable of Jesus was meant to evoke a response and to strike for a verdict. "What do you think?" he sometimes begins, and where the words are not found, the question is implied. There follows a true-to-life story or the description of a familiar happening; and the hearer is invited to transfer the judgment forward on the happening or the story to the urgent issues of the Kingdom of God, which is the theme of all his parables.

The Gospel parable is meant to make people *think*. It appeals to the intelligence through the imagination. And sometimes, like the smoked glass we use during an eclipse—it *conceals* in order to reveal. Seen thus, the parable is not so much a *crutch* for limping intellects as a *spur* to spiritual perception.

Where did Jesus get the Stuff of His Parables? Not from some "never-never land" but from the real world all around him. Everbody knows how many images and illustrations he took from the book of *nature*. . . .

Still larger in the parables bulks *the human scene* and the life of ordinary men and women in home or farm or market. . . .

But the realism of the parables goes even further; for many of them . . . must have been based on real happenings to real people. . . .

The parables are not fables. They hold the mirror up to life.

A. M. Hunter. Int. 14, 1960, pp. 71–76

Julicher's total rejection of allegory is an oversimplification. . . . There is no really sharp distinction between parable and allegory in the Semitic mind. In the OT, the apocrypha, and the rabbinic writings, *mashal* covers parable and allegory and a host of other literary devices (riddle, fable, proverb, etc.). Therefore, there is no reason to believe that Jesus of Nazareth . . . ever made a distinction between parable and allegory. He was a popular teacher and would naturally favor simple stories, so we need not look for the complicated allegories that the Fathers found. But simple allegory, and metaphors already familiar to his hearers from the OT—these lay within his illustrative range. In fact, turning the tables on the Julicher school, we may well ask would a popular teacher be able to disassociate himself completely from familiar metaphor and speak in pure parables? . . .

Certain of the parables cry out for an allegorical interpretation of their details. In the example of the Prodigal Son the common Jewish reference to God as Father would make an allegorical identification of the father in the parable perfectly intelligible. We may grant that, for the sake of the story, God is portrayed as an earthly father; but . . . this is so close to allegory as to make no difference.

Raymond E. Brown. NT. 5, 1962, pp. 37–38

The *conciseness* of the narrative is characteristic. Only the necessary *persons* appear. Thus in the story of the Prodigal Son there is no mother, or in the parable of the Importunate Friend no wife of the disturbed sleeper. There are never more than three chief characters, and for the most part only two. . . .

The law of stage duality is operative, i.e. only two persons speaking or acting come on at a time. If others are present, they remain in the background. If more than two have to speak or act, they have to do it in separate successive scenes. . . .

There is also the *law of the single perspective*, i.e. one is not asked to watch two different series of events happening at the same time. In the parable of the prodigal son the whole story is told from the point of view of the prodigal. How the father took his son's departure, and what he thought while he was absent is never stated. . . .

Only seldom are the *characters* portrayed by some attribute, like the judge who 'feared not God and regarded not man' (Lk. 18:2) or the ten virgins of whom five were wise and five foolish (Matt. 25:2). For the most part people are characterized by what they say or do, or how they behave, like the prodigal son and his loving father, or the magnanimous King and the merciless debtor. . . .

Feelings and motives are mentioned only when they are essential for the action or the point. . . . For the most part feelings are only portrayed indirectly or left to the hearer's own imagination. . . .

Other participants are described only in so far as it is necessary. In Lk. 10:30-55 there is no description of either the man who went down to Jericho or the innkeeper. . . .

Above everything else, there is complete lack of *motivation* in the exposition, for the simple reason that it is irrelevant to the point. Thus the request of the younger son for his share of the inheritance (Lk. 15:12f.) and his journey into a far country is quite unmotivated. Similarly we are not told why the employer in Matt. 20:1ff. needed so many labourers for his vineyard as to go out every three hours to take on more hands. . . .

There is similar economy governing the *description of events and acctions*. Anything unnecessary is omitted; e.g. we are not told how the steward dissipated his master's wealth. There is no description of how the widow besought the judge, but just a very brief indication that she did, etc. In understandable antithesis to this whatever is reported is described in very concrete terms. . . . The prodigal son becomes a swineherd; when he comes home the father clothes him with the best robe, adorns him with a ring, and kills the fatted calf for him. The luxury of the rich man and the lamentable state of poor Lazarus are vividly portrayed. . . . In all this there is a correspondence with the art of popular story telling.

There is another point of correspondence in the use of *direct speech and soliloquy*. . . .

We can find other elements of style typical of popular story telling, like the *law of repetition*. . . . There is also the law of *End-stress*, i.e. the most important thing is left to the end. The clearest example is Mk. 4:3ff.: the fruitful seed is mentioned last of all.

Rudolf Bultmann. *The History of the Synoptic Tradition*, trans. John Marsh (Oxford, Basil Blackwell, 1963), pp. 188–191

They are, indeed, a picture of the society of the time, possessing the variety and vividness of a small *Comédie Humaine*. Most of contemporary society is there. . . . All reveal an amazing power of observation and the activity of a live and continuously creative imagination. Hardly any of them have any religious content. . . . They make of the Synoptic Gospels extraordinarily vivid and convincing documents and, when compared with the rest of the New Testament, are surprising in their down-to-earth secularity.

The raw material, the stuff of the parables, is human life—human life as worked upon and shaped by the creative imagination. For it should not be forgotten that Jesus was not only a religious teacher but a creative artist of unusual skill and penetration, the author of some of the world's classics in short stories and fables, and one whose distinction in this field was as unique as the rest of his mission. . . .

Reference might be made, moreover, to a characteristic of parable . . . which has not received the consideration which it merits: the significance of improbable traits. . . .

A further characteristic of Jesus' parabolic method is the technique of obtaining the approving interest of the listener until the tables are turned on him. One example of this is . . . the parable of the Samaritan, which, like other exemplary stories, can be invoked to illustrate several things. All would approve of the action of the Samaritan, but the final injunction to do likewise would be unpalatable to those who resented Samaritans as such. . . .

As for the general characteristic of the parable: it is distinguished from mere metaphor by its narrative content, however simple. Thus the parables of the kingdom are usually similitudes involving some degree of action. . . .

The parables are more or less forms of narrative art. Whether they are wholly fictitious or not it is impossible to ascertain. . . .

The parables, then, are, in the main, very short stories, given point and pungency . . . by surprise and risk. The longest of them, such as those of the Talents, the Samaritan, and the Prodigal Son, are most conspicuous because of their form. Not only do they follow roughly the rule of three (three employees, plus the employer; two sons and the father; Levite, Priest, and Samaritan plus victim and innkeeper): they possess a structure and balance of narrative form which can scarcely be accidental. If they were flung off, as it were, in the heat of the moment as instruments of controversy or defence, they must have been conceived with a spontaneous artistry unique in the history of literature. . . .

The figures in the parable are anonymous. Only one of the parabolic characters is given a name: Lazarus, and commentators have wondered why. Yet the people in the Prodigal Son are not formal, desiccated types, though we have to use our imagination to re-create them to our own satisfaction. . . . Nowhere else in the world's literature has such immortality been conferred on anonymity. . . .

The characters, though nameless, are far from vague. Namelessness does not stand in the way of literary excellence or didactic persuasion for here the name is not necessary to the art. . . . Through this exercise of the creative imagination in the service of truth the parable, because it is art, however miniature its dimension, has imported the quality of time-and-place-transcendence to its characters which is typical of all great narrative creations. The persons have become representative; they exist by their own right; we refer to them, as we refer to Mr. Micawber and Falstaff and Don Quixote and Job *as if* they possessed the momentum of a historical existence of their own: as if their creator had liberated them into the universal consciousness of man.

> Geraint Vaughan Jones. *The Art and Truth of the Parables* (London, S.P.C.K., 1964), pp. 112–113, 116–120, 124–125

The familiar couched in the familiar is boring; the familiar and unfamiliar in juxtaposition are stimulating.

Parabolic imagery is vivid in just this way. Everydayness if framed by the ultimate. The commonplace is penetrated so that it becomes uncommonly significant. . . .

Vividness of this order, as Barfield also notes, requires that the strangeness produced by the superimposition shall have *interior* significance. It cannot be artificial, contrived, or merely eccentric. Vividness must inhere in the different thing that is said, not solely in the way that it is said. . . . The everyday imagery of the parable is vivid fundamentally, then, because it juxtaposes the common and the uncommon, the everyday and the ultimate, but only so that each has interior significance for the other. . . .

Closely related is what Dodd describes as the surprise element in many of the parables, i.e., an unusual action. . . .

Hyperbole and paradox, for this reason, are intrinsic to the parable. They are one means, among others, of indicating the "gappiness" of conventional existence. . . .

In sum, the parables as pieces of everydayness have an unexpected "turn" in them which looks through the commonplace to a new view of reality. This "turn" may be overt in the form of a surprising development in the narrative, an extravagant exaggeration, a paradox; or it may lurk below the surface in the so-called transference of judgment for which the parable calls. In either case the listener is led through the parable into a strange world where everything is familiar yet radically different.

This characterization of the parable also explains their argumentative or provocative character, why they demand a decision. They present a world the listener recognizes, acknowledges. Then he is caught up in the dilemma of the metaphor: it is not his world after all! Should he proceed on this venture into strangeness or draw back? He must choose to unfold with the story, be illuminated by the metaphor, or reject the call and abide with the conventional.

Robert W. Funk. *Language, Hermeneutic, and Word of God* (New York, Harper and Row, 1966; rpt. Polebridge Press), pp. 160–162

What we have in fact is a sliding scale of allegory-content which it is possible to represent mathematically. A parable consists of so many features, or points, and we can ask ourselves, 'Does this point have a hidden meaning for the evangelist, and this, and this?' If all the points correspond, we say the parable has an allegory-content of 1; if, say, three points out of ten correspond, we say the parable has an allegory-content of 0.3. If there are features in the story which are unreal and dictated by the meaning, we count these to the meaning and not to the story, and may end with an allegory content of more than 1. The method leaves something to the discretion of the exegete, but gives as objective a guide as we can have to the evangelist's understanding of his parable. . . . To take the Tares for an example, as the Interpretation is supplied, and exegesis is minimal: the householder is the Son of Man, the good seed the sons of the kingdom, the field the world, the enemy the devil, the tares his sons, growth is the advance of time, gathering is judgement, harvest the End, the reapers angels, the burning hell, the barn heaven; while the points of men sleeping, the servants asking the master for orders and the uprooting of the wheat are without allegorical meaning. Thus 11 points correspond out of 14, and the allegory-content is 0.79. . . .

The point is that a recognizable pattern emerges such as we should have suspected from a general acquaintance with the Gospels. . . . On a total count we should rate Mark's allegory-content 0.75. . . . His stories correspond fully with what he understood to be their meaning, and . . . on the average three points fit out of every four.

Matthew has a higher over-all allegory-content than Mark: 185 points corresponding out of 226 in all his parables, an average of 0.82. This is the more remarkable because Matthew contains a much higher proportion of long parables than Mark, with incidental details of no allegorical significance involved unless one is determined upon allegory pure. . . .

St. Luke's colorful tales, *per contra*, lead us to expect much less allegory, and this is in fact consistently the case. His over-all rating is 0.6 (152 correspondences out of 253).

M. D. Goulder. *JTS*, n.s. 19, 1968, pp. 59–60

In view of the fact that the basic speech mode in the Bible is the story—a narration of action in time—it is not surprising that in Jesus' narrative parables the plot, on the whole, is the controlling form to which all else is related. And I say "plot" purposely rather than simply "story." According to E. M.

Forster the story is a "narrative of events arranged in their time sequence," while plot preserves the time sequence but emphasizes the causality operating within the events. About a story we say, "and then," but of a plot we ask "why." In this light the narrative parables clearly have plot. . . .

The narrative parables, as fully realized artistic works, present a union of form and content so that meaning depends as much on form as on content. The content is composed of the episodes in the protagonist's fate—his actions or nonactions, his encounters, and his moments of recognition and understanding. The form is not the disposable container for these parts but is rather the arrangement and fusion of them. Form exerts a kind of pressure on the matter, or content, with the result that meaning is diffused throughout the texture of the parable. Meaning, then, is not found in any one isolable part or "point" but in the configuration of action and understanding as a whole. . . .

The narrative parables . . . characteristically have three episodes—a beginning, middle, and end—which cohere tightly with each other, and whose nature may be more closely and exactly defined. Some of the parables describe a *crisis, response, denouement* pattern, while others present *action, crisis, denouement*.

It may also be observed that there are two types of plot movement which may be comprehended by the terms "tragic" and "comic" as long as we understand that these two terms are being used in a broad way. In the tragic parables we have a plot falling toward catastrophe and the isolation of the protagonist from society, while in the comic parables we have an upward movement toward well-being and the inclusion of the protagonist in a new or joyous society. . . .

The narrative parables typically have a master, king, father figure who in a sense initiates the action and has the final power of disposal, and a servant, subject, son figure (or group) who is the focal interest and whose fate gives the narrative its formal shape. The latter is the protagonist and he is in the story from beginning to end. What finally happens in the denouement to the prodigal son or the one talent man, for example, is a consequence of what *he* did and thought in both of the previous episodes. There may be characters whose fates differ from that of the protagonist (the *five* and *two* talent men, the *wise* maidens), but such characters are clearly secondary while the protagonist is involved in all of the episodes and his fate is the unifying factor. . . .

In the narrative parables the characters whose fate informs the story undergo some kind of change of existence. . . . The characters are the same people at the end that they were at the beginning, though not quite, for possibilities have been actualized which were at first only potentialities. Within each pattern there is an openness to change, and among the parables of Jesus there are several different patterns.

Dan O. Via, Jr. Int. 25, 1971, pp. 172–175, 180–181

The simplest way to explore the dynamics of . . . parable is to ask what there is about it as "words" that would make it interesting to the hearer or hold his attention. (We can leave out here the identity of the speaker.) First, it is a story; it is a narrative with the world-old appeal of "what happened?" "what happened next?" "how did it turn out?" Second, it is a kind of riddle or teaser with the similiar appeal of "what does it mean?" "what is he getting at?" Third, it is a conventional or artistic form, which arouses expectation of special import as well as delight in felicitous speech. Fourth, it evokes familiar matters in wholly appropriate locutions and persuasiveness. An initiated audience delights in exact mimetic detail, in cogent actuality, just as its attention is forfeited by any lack of verisimilitude in this kind of narrative. Fifth, the aesthetic medium or genre-form lifts the diurnal level of the action into another context, with new overtones. . . .

In biblical anecdotes and fictions we find features common to story telling anywhere in the world. . . . As in folktales and children's stories we find brevity, unity of perspective, limitation of the number of figures or agents, use of direct discourse, serial development, the rule of three, repetition of elements and formulae, binary opposition, and resolution often by reversal. Or our analysis may cut another way in terms of recurrent plot-patterns or *topoi* or motifs. Human nature has always responded to stories about quests and adventures, ups and downs, rags to riches, lost and found, reversals and surprises; stories about tricksters and strategems; about duels and conflicts— between the good and the bad son or daughter, of Greek meeting Greek; stories of magical transformation and wonders. Biblical narratives rejoin universal story-telling in their repertoire of motifs: masters and servants, the wise and the foolish, rewards and penalties, success and failure. . . .

If one presses this matter of our responses to particular rhetorical features or signals in a story or text one comes to something still more fundamental. There is indeed something in us that answers to the kinds of patterns of speech and motifs suggested. But among these are some that go very deep into our emotion and imagination and motivation. . . . Psychology can speak of archetypes. The study of dreams and folklore, etc., can uncover recurrent structures of consciousness, scenarios of wish, anxiety and fulfilment. . . . Jesus could use . . . plot-patterns (such as lost and found) or role-situations (master and servant) which similarly engage our deepest apperceptions. The master-servant relation evokes the archetype of authority deeply buried in the human psyche, an archetype which is ambivalent and charged both with anxiety and the craving for security.

Amos N. Wilder. *Semeia*. 2, 1974, pp. 138–140

The parables are oral literature. They were apparently composed by Jesus on the spur of the moment. They were responses to an immediate situation and often arose out of some kind of conflict. . . .

Another characteristic of the parables is that they rely heavily on the technique of realism. They draw upon the familiar experience of the listeners. They are experiential, so simple in detail that a child can usually grasp them. Part of their realism is that they do not violate rules of plausibility. There is an absence of unreality, and we find no talking animals or marvelous adventures. . . .

The parables as a whole illustrate a wide range of literary sophistication. At their most rudimentary they are no more than a brief analogy between the topic Jesus is discussing and some object or event in the world of familiar experience. At its most refined, the parable is a short story with a skillfully designed plot, a somewhat detailed setting, dialogue, and careful characterization.

Some of the parables are satiric. Virtually all of them serve an obvious rhetorical purpose. They are addressed to a specific audience and are the means of persuasion used by Jesus to move His audience. In fact, the gospel accounts of the parables often give a description of the context that occasioned the parables. . . .

The parables show the interrelationship of this world and the spiritual realm. The experiences of life point to the other world. By the same token, the great spiritual truths of the Christian faith are domesticated and made commonplace, in the manner of the English poet George Herbert.

In one sense the parables are a very sophisticated literary form—they work by indirection instead of direct statement. They force people to make a judgment on some commonplace situation and then to transfer that judgment to a spiritual realm.

> Leland Ryken. *The Literature of the Bible* (Grand Rapids, Zondervan, 1974), pp. 302–303

Modern research on the parables of Jesus has established a number of points about them which may be stated in summary fashion.

(a) Jesus taught in parables, but the early church readily translated them into allegories. The difference is that a parable makes its point as a totality. Moreover, the point is never exhausted by any one apprehension of it, but can be apprehended afresh as the parable is retold in different situations. For that reason the message of the parable can never adequately be expressed except in the metaphorical language of the parable itself; it cannot be translated into a propositional statement. . . .

(b) Both the allegorizing of the parables and their present context and application in the gospels are the work of the church and the evangelists. To interpret a parable as a parable of Jesus, therefore, one must first reconstruct the original nonallegorical form of the parable and then interpret it as a parable in the context of the message of Jesus without reference to its content or function in the gospel narratives.

(c) The fundamental element in a parable is the element of metaphor. A is compared to B so that meaning may be carried over from B to A. Normally, A is the lesser known and B is the better known. . . .

(d) There is, therefore, in the parable a literal point, the meaning of the story or image, and also a metaphorical point, the meaning, the story or image as it is transferred to what it is intended to refer to.

(e) The purpose of the parable is normally pedagogical; Jewish rabbis used them extensively to illuminate, illustrate, and instruct. In the case of Jesus, however, this normal use of the literary form "parable" seems to have been subordinated to another and different one. In the hands of Jesus the parable is not only a means of instruction but also a form of proclamation.

Norman Perrin. *The New Testament: An Introduction* (New York, Harcourt Brace Jovanovich, 1974), pp. 291–292

From the standpoint of literary criticism the parable presents a particular problem: most of the work of modern literary criticism has been directed toward the novel or the poem, and the parable is neither. It is far more compressed than any novel; yet unlike a poem it is a narrative, and it does not have the high degree of formal control characteristic of poetry. The characters in the parables are not characters in the Aristotelian sense of having many stereotypical and developed attributes, but, rather, they are agents of action. In The Prodigal Son the only descriptive evidence we are given is that they are a father and two sons. We find out in the course of the story that the father has property, servants, robes, a ring, shoes, and a fatted calf. We are not told whether there is a mother, other children, where they live, what the father does for a living, what any of them look like, etc.—all elements we might expect in a novelistic or dramatic development of character, and all elements we might *need* if we intended to discuss each of the parable's "characters" as if they were living individuals. . . . In fact the parable appears to have a much closer relation to the simplest type of dream than it does to a novel or poem. . . . The characteristic narrative of a parable could easily be described as a condensed or compressed dramatization. Any work of art, of course, differs from a dream in that it demands a far greater amount of conscious control, thus allowing a greater amount of conscious complexity, than a dream does. Yet the simplest type of dream, the dream of undisguised wish-fulfillment characteristic of childhood, is fully available to consciousness without any need for distortion or displacement. The parable might be seen, then, as a conscious, more complex representation of a simple wish-fulfillment type of dream with its formal elements drawn from the processes of dream work.

Mary Ann Tolbert. *Semeia.* 9, 1977, pp. 6–7

Within the tradition of *mashal* in the Bible there are other, more complex forms than the simple proverb. Of special interest are sayings which take the form of brief stories with metaphoric dimensions. Such a *mashal* combines narrative and metaphoric elements, both of which must be recognized in interpretation.

Like all stories, a narrative *mashal* creates through language a self-contained little world. It has a clear beginning and an end which separates it from its surrounding literart context. The narrative elements in such a *mashal* may be analyzed in different ways. They reflect Axel Olrik's laws: repetition, often threefold; two people to a scene; flat characters; contrasts and polarized behavior; dialogue; action over feelings; and emphasis given to the end-position. Their plot structure may be classified as comic or tragic or some combination of the two in which one character moves tragically and another comically. In the interpretation of a *mashal* that tells a story, the narrative element must be given its full due.

Narrative analysis of such a *mashal* does not, however, tell all. Ostensibly such a *mashal* tells about conflicts among certain trees of the forest, or animals. Or they may tell about a man and his ewe lamb, a beloved with a vineyard, a vine's adventures with an eagle, or planting grain and harvesting. . . . The world presented in them is more or less tightly organized and circumscribed by the narrative form. And yet upon reading a *mashal* one has the impression, however it is caused, that the *mashal* is not really talking about what it is talking about. One has the impression that, as with metaphor, the explicit story line is hiding another level of significance.

The metaphoric dimension of *mashal* creates a tension with its narrative dimension. As narrative, a *mashal* presents a self-contained story. As metaphor, it presents something beyond that self-contained structure. . . . In contrast to metaphor, which presents on the primary level a logical absurdity, the primary story line of a *mashal* or parable is complete, and for the most part satisfying. . . .

The most profound irony of the parables lies in their transformation of the ongoing, unchanged world. . . . Parables speak of mundane activities, everyday events, and are rarely religious in nature. They tell of a world in which God rarely appears. Yet parable is the essential literary form for presenting the kingdom of God in the Gospels. The extraordinary is hidden in the ordinary. . . . Although the everyday world is not changed, it is not the same after reading the parables. They bring a new perception of ordinary life. . . .

Leonard L. Thompson. *Introducing Biblical Literature: A More Fantastic Country* (Englewood Cliffs, Prentice-Hall, 1978), pp. 252–253, 260–261

Jesus drew verbal pictures of the world around him by telling parables. By teaching in parables he depicted what was happening in real life. That is, he used a story, taken from daily life, using an accepted, familiar setting, to teach a new lesson. That lesson quite often came at the end of the story and had an impact that needed time for absorption and assimilation. When we hear a parable, we nod in agreement because the story is true to life and readily understood. . . . We see the story unfold before our eyes, but we do not perceive the significance of it. The truth remains hidden until our eyes are opened and we see clearly. Then the new lesson of the parable becomes meaningful. . . .

While reading the parables of Jesus, one wonders why many details which would be expected to be part of the stories have been left out. For example, . . . in the parable of the prodigal son, the father is a leading character, but not a word is said about the mother. The parable of the ten virgins introduces the bridegroom, but completely ignores the bride. These details, however, are not relevant to the general composition of the parables, especially if we understand the literary device of *triads* that is often used in Jesus' parables. In the parable of the friend at midnight, there are three characters: the traveler, the friend, and the neighbor. The prodigal son parable also contains three persons: the father, the younger son, and the older brother. And in the story of the ten virgins there are three elements: the five wise virgins, the five foolish virgins, and the bridegroom.

Moreover, in Jesus' parables it is not the beginning of the story but the end that is important. The accent falls on the last person mentioned, the last deed, or the last saying. The so-called "end-stress" in the parable is a deliberate design in its composition. It was not the priest or the Levite who alleviated the wounded man's pain, but the Samaritan. Even though the servant who gained five additional talents and the servant who presented two more talents to his master received praise and commendation, it was the servant's deed of burying his one talent in the ground that brought him scorn and condemnation. . . .

By means of his parables Jesus explained the great themes of his teaching: the kingdom of heaven; the love, grace, and mercy of God; the rule and return of the Son of God; and the being and destiny of man.

Simon J. Kistemaker. *The Parables of Jesus* (Grand Rapids: Baker, 1980), pp. xiii, xv–xvii

The one-point theory is the most influential and the most pernicious part of Jülicher's legacy to a century of interpretation. What every seminary graduate remembers about the parables is that allegorizing is wrong and that every parable makes one main point. But any informed student of literature knows nowadays that these options are ill-framed—that an extended analogy of Spenser, Shakespeare, or Milton, or a metaphysical conceit of Donne's, is neither an allegory to be interpreted down to the last minute detail nor a comparison limited to a single point of resemblance. Why insist that the celebrated compass analogy in John Donne's "Valediction Forbidding Mourning" makes only one point, not several? "The point is not that the husband and wife are one in two, not that the wife will miss her absent husband, not that she will be herself again when he has returned, and not that her constancy will inspire him to constancy, but only that he will certainly return?" That is exactly what Jülicher persuaded biblical scholars to do with the parables. No wonder there are six or eight one-point interpretations of the Sower currently put forth, each to the exclusion of the others! . . .

The history which Jülicher made is being repeated in our own time by New Testament scholars' ill-advised forays into literary theory. Neither Via nor Crossan takes note of analogy as the essence of a parable—though Jülicher himself got that far, simply by paying attention to the customary meaning of the Greek word *parabole*. And neither recognizes the obligations of literary history as they apply to the gospel narratives: Jesus is represented as a preacher and teacher, not as a poet and story-teller; the gospel parables are anecdotal figures in discourse (fragments of imaginative "story" and "poetry," to be sure) put to the service of discursive aims—and hence not to be left to the fancies of any interpreter's preoccupations, without regard for Jesus' normative intention. . . . The literary historian properly makes the most of the best available evidence, before proceeding to inferences and speculations extrapolated from it. In the case of the gospel parables, this means taking full account of the form and function of the parables in *their gospel form*, before concluding how the evangelists' particular purposes might have brought about alterations in Jesus' own words and intent. . . .

What biblical scholars do not need is large doses of literary theory. Those most deeply read in the theory of criticism seem to be the ones most inhibited, in practical criticism, about observing what is actually going on in a text. . . . In some cases, what biblical scholars need to hear most from literary critics is that old-fashioned critical concepts of plot, character, setting, point of view, and diction may be more useful than more glamorous and sophisticated theories.

John W. Sider. C & L. 32, no. 1, 1982, pp. 17–20

The two central features of a parabolic story are its realism and its strangeness. First of all, it is drawn from the details of a particular situation of real life at a given time and given place. Parables show us occasional, transitory, essentially fleeting snapshots of *petit-bourgeois* and peasant life in first century Palestine. Each perfectly pictures something that we can observe in our own world. Parables tell about people getting married, runaway sons, wedding receptions, farmers planting and harvesting, women cooking, kings going to war, migrant workers, widows on welfare, doctors and patients, embezzlers, merchants.

But there is more to a parable than realism. At its heart lies a metaphor. Frost said, "A parable is a story that mean what it says and something besides." It strikes a comparison between ordinary life and another reality. . . .

A parabolic story makes good sense in itself, but it will surprise you with a sudden turn, a deformation of the language used, a surrealistic or "absurd" part of the story. When confronted with ordinary life which at some point is strange, the mind is left in sufficient doubt to tease it into active thought. Thus, metaphors catch or shock the imagination. They kindle new insight; they communicate knowledge. . . .

Cracks in the realism of the stories come in many forms, such as exaggeration, hyperbole, and dislocation. Think of the refusal of all the worthy guests to come to the wedding feast; the father shocking us by *running* to the prodigal son rather than walking; the unheard-of yield of a hundred fold grain harvest; . . . the merchant who disposes of all his possessions to buy a single pearl; or the man who without any cause was completely absolved from a ten million dollar debt.

We do not see "the divine" directly in the stories at all. They contain no reference to God, salvation from sin, spiritual realities or Christ. In this way they, like Jesus's outward life and form, are truly incarnational. The shock or new insight of the parable comes through showing us an everyday familiar situation in a new way—for instance, the wedding feast and its guest list yields the picture of an invitation based not on merit but on grace. And from this we gain an insight into God's nature and the way his kingdom is populated by a gracious invitation.

Such insight is not a secondary way of knowing this reality, or a mere embellishment added to the truth which we can know in some other, more literal, way. The parable *is* the truth, not a mere ornament. We may call the parabolic, then, the indirect genre par excellence. . . .

The parables of Jesus are stories of radical reversal. They challenge the status quo, conventional world-view of the hearers. . . .

By introducing a "Samaritan" into his story at a crucial point, Jesus completely overthrows the expectations of his audience. If he wanted to teach love of neighbor in distress, it would have been sufficient to talk of one person, a second person, and a third person. If he wanted to add a jibe against the clerical circles in Jerusalem he could have mentioned priest, Levite, and Jewish layperson. If he wanted merely to inculcate love of one's enemies, then it would have been radical enough to have a Jewish person stop and assist a wounded Samaritan.

But the reversal of figures challenges the hearer to put together two impossible and contradictory words: "Samaritan" and "neighbor." This brings a moment of revelation, a moment of challenge and address, and things can never be quite the same again.

Alan Johnson. *Kodon*. 36, no. 2, 1982, pp. 11–12

PAUL AS LETTER WRITER
(See also *Corinthians, First,* **and** *Epistle as a Literary Form.*)

Paul was an orator. Oratory is only pleading, and in his letters Paul sees his correspondents present before him, and pleads with them. Then he is never dull. When he embarks upon the main topics of his letter, even if it is a purely Jewish argument, he has soon done to it what every good orator is supposed to do, 'elevated it', lifted it up, raised it above the particular or the commonplace, given it a wider significance. He also gives it point with quotations from many sources. He enriches it with illustrations, and coins many a fine saying on his way. . . .

What he dictates shows all the studied devices of trained oratory: the *simile* that makes the meaning clearer, the *metaphor* that does this more concisely; the *question* that arrests attention, the *exclamation* that invites the hearer to sympathize or admire; *repetition* to bring out salient points and help the hearer to keep the thread of the argument; *balance*, above all, of thought and phrase, since the human mind and ear love contrasts of feeling and sound; *exaggeration* and *paradox* to surprise and startle him into thinking; *epigrams*, or sentences with the ring of a proverb, that he can easily carry away with him; *perorations*, or powerful conclusions of extra pathos or vigour to round off the appeal.

The orator in his pleading has recourse also to *prayers, wishes,* and *adjuration* or *oaths*, to strengthen his case. His sentence constructions vary with his mood, a longer period and more measured style for quieter argument, staccato style in hurried or passionate appeals. His diction is often picturesque, often forcible.

Paul's style may be called 'rich' in virtue of the wealth of words at his command, the abundance of illustration, the wealth of apt quotation, the flow of ideas, and rapid suggestion of one topic by another. His speed, and perhaps the checks suffered in dictating, cause omissions in syntax, and faults of construction, and verbs are sometimes left to be supplied by the sense, but on the whole the style is well controlled and balanced. So is his main argument well developed, and if he leaves it for a space, he inevitably returns, and ends it with a suitable conclusion, or works up to a peroration. . . .

The diction of Paul is as striking as his force of epigram. It is continually enlivened by metaphor, '*glueing* yourselves to the good', '*boiling* with the spirit', '*buying up* the opportunity', 'let the love of Christ *make its home in you*', 'let the peace of Christ be *umpire* in your hearts', obviously the diction of an enthusiast using the strongest and liveliest expressions, and still more so, when he uses doublets: '*I maul and master my body*' (to keep it in subjection), '*rooted and founded* (A.V., grounded) in love', or, as in the striking phrase about waverers, '*tossed-to-and-fro* and *carried-round-and-round* by every *wind* of doctrine', like cockle shells on stormy water, the two Greek words giving both motions of the storm. . . .

He is Shakespearian in his bold creation of words, 'I *wild-beast-fought* at Ephesus', 'not with *eye-service* as *men-pleasers*', '*person-respecting*' (respect of persons), 'will-worship' (or 'self-imposed devotions', Moffat).

> P. C. Sands. *Literary Genius of the New Testament* (Oxford, Oxford University Press, 1932), pp. 133–135, 153–154

Between us and the real person we are seeking there stands also his literary form and method, inculcated by education and by his traditional points of view, through which he must pour out the contents of his personality.

1. *His Literary Directness*. . . . In the most personal and intimate parts of his letters we can find a rhetorical form-element . . . But the true artist shows just in this, that it is given to him to breathe a new life into the inherited form, which for a genuinely artistic reason is just what it is, and thus he is able to develop it further organically. Now it is in this respect that the individuality of Paul reveals itself; that he understands how to handle freely the forms with which he is familiar, and can play upon this instrument as he wills. . . .

2. *Epistolary Forms*. Among these fixed forms is, e.g., the epistolary introduction. Paul knows how to vary and enliven the beginning of his letters in various ways in order to avoid monotony and to awaken interest. . . .

3. *Extravagance of Style*. This leads us to consider the exaggerated manner of expression which is found in all the letters, the bulky individual hyperboles and the exalted expression of feeling as a whole. . . . Naturally he would not have been inclined to such a redundant style if he had not been outwardly a man of strong emotions: joy and sorrow, fear and hope alternate very frequently in him, and the heart-stirrings and the many tears (II Cor. 4:4) we must indeed believe and grant to him. Nevertheless, much of his language is still a habit of literary style, as is also his fondness for piling up synonyms where one word instead of two or three would suffice. . . . To all this we must add the stylistic tendency, partly inherited from Judaism and partly learned in Hellenistic schools, to enhance the expression through the method of parallelism of members, often with the same beginning and the same ending. . . .

4. *Homiletic Tone.* In such places it seems that the sermon tone strongly dominates the lesson taught. Almost everything is said in a far more intense and emphatic manner than one would expect to find in a quiet friendly conversation or monologue. In this way these 'letters' are distinctly marked off from the usual epistolary style. . . .

5. *Artistry of Expression.* We have not only to reckon in the letters of Paul with the speaking element, which, by the grace of God, is natural to the speaker, but also with an artistic method of expression which occasionally leads him far beyond the practical purpose which lies at hand, in the creation of pictures which have a meaning all their own, and like independent mosaics project themselves out of the context. . . .

6. *Antithesis* is perhaps the most distinctive characteristic of his style. We may say, perhaps with some exaggeration, that all his speaking and thinking has an antithetical rhythm in it. . . .

7. *His Versatility.* Paul the writer, whom, naturally, we are unable to picture completely without the help of the Greek, appears before us in varying aspects according to the subjects he is dealing with; indeed, it would seem that the various letters are written in very different ways.

> Johannes Weiss. *Earliest Christianity*, Vol. II, trans. Frederick C. Grant (New York, Harper and Brothers, 1937), pp. 399–406, 411, 416

Antithesis is perhaps the most distinctive characteristic of his style. We may say, perhaps with some exaggeration, that all his speaking and thinking has an antithetical rhythm in it. . . .

Paul's preference for antithesis is not to be explained only by reference to the general period of Hellenism. Later Judaism itself with its sharp dualism, clearly apparent in its belief in Satan (II Cor. 4:4), in its doctrine of the two ages and the new creation (II Cor. 5:17), in its conception of the immense gulf between the supernatural God of heaven and man . . . represents religious thinking based entirely upon antithesis. Paul was clearly accustomed to this habit of thought and has brought it with him. . . .

To all this must be added the influence of his own experience. The two parts of his life are sharply separated, one from the other, by his conversion; on the one side there is only error, sin, and flesh; on the other, life, spirit, truth, and righteousness. Finally one must call to mind the entirely individual predisposition of Paul. Does he not belong to those choleric natures for whom there is an 'either-or,' who always observe things in their sharpest and most exclusive aspects? So he appears to us in the letters—even the more so on account of his strongly dominant tendency to use sharp and exclusive antitheses. The stylistic peculiarity seems to be grounded in the soul of this personality and in its wholly peculiar history. . . .

The Pauline antithesis . . . is a richly varied form of expression and has become for him an excellent method of self-representation.

Those main, recurrent antitheses . . . are well known, and every chapter furnishes examples, e.g., that unforgettable passage I Cor. 15:42f. . . . Or compare Rom. 14:7ff; I Cor. 12:3; II Cor. 9:6; Gal. 6:7f; II Cor. 4:16ff. . . .

There is in the faith of Paul, and also in that of primitive Christianity, especially in the proclamations of Jesus, a deeply engrained paradoxical and antithetical element: e.g. the joyfully defiant 'although'—'nevertheless' which is perhaps the really essential and eternal element in our religion. . . . It appears so often and in so many different nuances in Paul that it must . . . be considered a fundamental element in his outlook upon life. One may call to mind the three following passages (not to mention I Cor. 4:12; Roman 5:3; and others): I Cor. 7:29f . . . ; II Cor. 4:8 . . . ; II Cor. 6:4–10.

> Johannes Weiss. *Earliest Christianity*, Vol. II, trans. Frederick C. Grant (New York, Harper and Brothers, 1937), pp. 411–416

We must beware of trying to understand Paul's message on either life on earth or future immortality without giving primary attention to his symbols. He is a visionary; his imagery is exact, his thought chaotic and paradoxical.

St. Paul is not aiming primarily at poetic power. He has a resplendent gift of phrase, but he does not set out to write poetry. His aim is to convince and convert, and next to organize the few forces whose future is in his charge. His theoretical arguments spring not from love of theory but from a burning desire to explain what to him is a patent fact: he is forced to fight theory with theory. Sometimes he is accused of falsely intellectualizing Christianity and taking us away from the purity of Jesus' teaching. Nothing could be more unjust: he writes hurriedly and anxiously, forced to oppose his pupils' pseudo-intellectualism by passionate reasoning; he is always practical, transfixing the heart of his subject and hurrying on without loss of time. There is nothing of the pedant in him: he writes from an imaginative centre and loathes the arbitrary rules which a theoretical religion or ethic imposes. All is subservient to his one burning faith in the living Christ. . . .

The finest passages in the Epistles burn with a white-gold brilliance of light and glory, housed in solid imagery, 'dazzling' like his own vision . . . His grandest statements, if gathered into an anthology, would lack variety, subtlety, colour; he is no master of light and shade. As he says himself, he preaches the Gospel 'with no fine rhetoric, lest the cross of Christ should lose its power' (*I Corinthians*, I. 17). And yet the power of that Cross carves out its own resplendent rhetoric: the Gospel so blazes in his heart that it makes of his eloquence a golden trumpet, the while his faith splashes the page with liquid flame. 'Power' and 'glory' are favourite words, and the power and glory he envisages are splendorously bright.

> G. Wilson Knight. *The Christian Renaissance* (London, Methuen and Company, 1962), pp. 140–142

The style of Paul betrays on every page the marks of oral expression: imagined dialogue, accusation and defense, queries, exclamations, oaths, and the challenge. . . . The letter, consequently, is an appropriate substitute for oral word—it is as near oral speech as possible—yet it provides a certain distance on the proclamation as event. . . .

The desire to keep the letter as near to oral speech as possible is inherent in the silent coercion to give presence to the Christ-event. The written word tends to degenerate into meaning which can be isolated from its intentionality; the oral word retains its character as eventful speech when it is understood as free, untrammeled, spontaneous word.

In this light it is possible to account for the "travelogue," as that which announces his imminent presence, as a constituent element in the Pauline letter. Paul resists the written word, the crystallization of speech, which tends to bring the proclamation to rest in creed. Owing to his longing to keep it in motion . . . he leaves traces of its oral character in form, style, and in the travelogue, which implies the promise of oral word. If the body of the letter is in danger of falling into written word, the travelogue announces the necessary correction.

The opening thanksgiving, a convention taken over by Paul and then Christianized and historicized, assembles the same elements, explicity or implicitly, noticed in connection with the polarity of his language. It thus reflects a similar movement of language under the aspect of prayer. Here Paul assembles himself, his readers, Christ and God: himself and his readers implicitly before Christ, the ground of faith, and explicit in the presence of God, to whom thanks are due. The thanksgiving looks back, so to speak, on the effects of grace already experienced, just as the body of the letter calls the readers again into the presence of Christ, that the word of the cross may take effect anew as grace.

Robert W. Funk. *Language, Hermeneutic, and Word of God* (New York, Harper and Row, 1966; rpt. Polebridge Press), pp. 248–249

Paul seems to have had a sense of freedom in literary matters corresponding to the freedom in theology that many commentators have noted. Instead of remaining tied to literary models, for instance, he combined non-Jewish Hellenistic customs with Hellenistic Jewish customs, and created a form which cannot be equated with either tradition. The most obvious place in the Pauline letters where this fusion can be identified is in the very first part of the typical Pauline letter, in the phrase "Grace to you and peace. . . ." This phrase includes a modification of the stereotyped "greetings!" of Hellenistic letters (*chairein* becomes *charis*, "grace") and the characteristic "peace" (*shalom*) of Jewish letters. . . .

Other . . . changes include: (a) closing: inclusion of a (liturgicallyformulated?) benediction, which functions as the Hellenistic farewell; (b) thanksgiving: this signals the reason for writing, and is not thanksgiving for rescue from danger but for the addressee's faithfulness; (c) body: adaptation of formulaic expressions for purposes of Pauline teaching and preaching. . . .

Since Deissmann wrote, New Testament scholars have come to realize that Paul's letters are by no means "private personal letters" in the usual sense of that term. Rather, they were written to communities of Christian believers for use in their common life, and they were written by Paul in his self-conscious capacity as an official representative of early Christianity (as an "apostle"). . . . References within the Pauline letters provide ample proof that the letters are more than semi-private personal letters (1 Thess. 5:27; Philemon v. 2b; 2 Thess. 3:14–15). . . .

Far from being casual letters of the type found predominantly in the papyri, Paul's letters were intended for public use within the religious gatherings. . . .

Having overcome Deissmann's restriction of the Pauline letters to private letters, we must not, of course, simply revert to the previous position which treated them as primarily dogmatic essays. Subsequent scholarship has reached something of a balance between treating Paul's letters as purely occasional, contextual writings, directed only to specific situations, and as attempts to express a Christian understanding of life which had ramifications for theological expression beyond the particular historical situation. . . .

Paul, insofar as he was not writing as a private person but as an apostle, and not primarily to individual persons but to churches, did indeed write letters which had a public intent, bringing them closer to the official pronouncement than to the private letter. He wrote to instruct, to give advice, to encourage or reprimand; he taught, preached, and exhorted in the letters. But he . . . did not step out of the immediate epistolary situation to write treatises with only an epistolary flavoring. . . .

The contemporary emphasis on the formal nature of Paul's letters is an important corrective to two older viewpoints: the first . . . suggested that Paul's material was mostly Jewish in origins, but it was simply cast into Greek form. The other viewpoint is best exemplified by Deissmann, who gave us a view of a harried Paul who dictated letters in spurts. . . .

We have begun to appreciate the fact that Paul did have a clear sense of the form of what he wanted to write. To speak of "Pauline letter form" is to speak of a normal progression of elements. . . . Reference to this probable outline does not mean that we assume that when Paul was writing or paused in his dictation, he thought, "Well, now, I've finished part 3.a—on to 3.b." Nor are we to assume that Paul decided which itemized sections taken together should comprise a letter to a particular situation, and then set about meeting such criteria. Rather, as Robert W. Funk noted . . . , "It is simply the way Paul writes letters."

William G. Doty. *Letters in Primitive Christianity* (Philadelphia, Fortress Press, 1973), pp. 22, 25–28

Once the letter-writing conventions which Paul used are understood, the alert reader will also find clues to Paul's intent in his creative use of conventions as well.

The discussion below will treat both the form and the function of main elements in the Pauline letter. . . .

1. The Salutation

The salutation is one of the most stable elements in the ancient letter. The form is rather precise. Unlike our modern letter, the salutation includes the names of both sender and recipient, as well as a greeting. In spite of the highly stereotyped nature of the letter opening, it remained pliable in the hands of Paul. In Philemon, Romans, and Galatians Paul molds the salutation to his purposes in the letter as a whole. . . .

2. The Thanksgiving

The thanksgiving is a formal element of most Pauline letters and . . . terminates the letter opening, signals the basic intent of the letter, and may serve as an outline of the major topics to be considered.

Coming immediately after the salutation, the thanksgiving appears in all of Paul's letters except Galatians. In each case Paul brings into view the situation of the recipients. . . . In his thanksgivings Paul is not mechanically following a fixed epistolary form. Rather, the apostle has grafted onto this traditional epistolary form materials from liturgical tradition. Thus he has created a hybrid form. . . .

3. The Body of the Letter

After passing through the thanksgiving the reader enters a vast and varied conversational world. The landscape is as broad as Paul's theological understanding and as diverse as the needs of the churches. But in spite of the range and variety in the body of the letters, there is a pattern that repeatedly occurs. A request or disclosure formula ("I beseech you . . . ," or "I would not have you ignorant . . .") serves as the threshold of the body, while the end is marked by an announcement of Paul's travel plans. Usually these plans include a contemplated visit by the apostle himself. . . .

Others have noted an autobiographical section, or a report by Paul on his activity, near the beginning of the body in most letters. . . . In each case this autobiographical note is fully integrated into his theological argument. The report on his situation is made to impinge directly on the situation of his readers. By reciting the demands made on him as an apostle of Christ, Paul is apprising his hearers that like demands may be made on them. . . .

4. Paraenesis (ethical instruction and exhortation)

At least three different types of ethical instruction are found in Paul's letters. First there is the cluster of unrelated moral maxims, strung together like beads on a string. Often there is little to hold them together except their similarity of form, or perhaps a catchword carried over from one to another. . . .

Second, scattered throughout Paul's letters we find lists of virtues and vices in which both Jewish and Hellenistic traditions have merged. These lists, like the unrelated injunctions above, have only the most casual relationship to each other. In Galatians 5:19–23 we find such a catalogue. . . .

The third type of paraenitic material is a prolonged exhortation or homily on a particular topic. Strongly reminiscent of an oral situation, these materials are highly personal and supportive. . . . Pastoral in tone, such exhortations appear frequently throughout Paul's letters. The bulk of 1 Corinthians (chs. 5–15) probably belongs to this type of material. . . .

5. Conclusion of the Letter

. . . Like the letter opening, the conclusion is a stable element in the epistolary structure. We usually find there a peace wish, greetings, and a benediction (or grace). Occasionally, we see an apostolic pronouncement. And generally, all of this is preceded by a battery of last-minute instructions. Bridging the gap between the instruction cluster and the conclusion is the peace wish. Once Paul crosses this threshold with his readers he has committed himself to parting and he soon brings the conversation to a close. . . .

The benediction, "the grace of our Lord Jesus Christ be with you," is the most stable of the concluding elements. Appearing in every complete letter, this closing formula varies little.

> Calvin J. Roetzel. *The Letters of Paul: Conversations in Context* (Atlanta, John Knox Press, 1975, 1982), pp. 18–26

That "oral" style of Paul may first appear as "impulsive improvisation," but first appearances yield to a recognition of artistry in his expression. Much of Paul's language contains poetic elements: repetition, thought-rhythm, sense-lines, and different kinds of parallelism. Careful attention must be paid to what is repeated, how it is repeated, and how it is linked to new words and phrases (cf. Rom. 14:7–9).

Antithetical parallelism is a stylistic device especially determinative for the development of Paul's thought. A statement evokes its opposite: "I have often intended to come to you/ But thus far have been prevented" (Rom. 1:13). A reference to life calls for a discussion of death (Rom. 14:7); Jews call for Gentiles (Gal. 2:14); curses, blessings (Gal. 2:13–14); the flesh, the spirit (Gal. 4:29); works, grace (Rom. 6:14); and law, Christ (Gal. 2:21). If there is one, then there is its opposite (I Cor. 15:44). Antithesis is at work not only in Paul's choice of words, phrases, and sentences, but also in the very structure of . . . sections of the epistles. . . .

In part, the occurrence of antithesis reflects a propensity in Paul's particular way of expressing himself. That does not, however, totally explain it. Paul works in binary opposition because he is reflecting upon the Christian proclamation which has at its center the antithesis, crucifixion/resurrection. Viewing the world as Paul does from the vantage point of that crucifixion/resurrection, all is seen in relation to its structures: then/now; old/new; man prior to faith/man of faith; flesh/spirit. Paul thus sets up the indirections of New Testament rhetoric in antitheses: typologies with the Old Testament are viewed as the old/the new; irony as appearance/reality (e.g., though weak . . . yet strong); and typology with the eschaton as now/then; now/not yet; or possession/as if not.

Leonard L. Thompson. *Introducing Biblical Literature: A More Fantastic Country* (Englewood Cliffs, Prentice-Hall, 1978), pp. 285–286

POETRY
(See also: *Hymn; Jesus as Poet; Luke, Gospel of, Nativity Hymns.*)

The use of Synonymous Parallelism by our Lord is confined, for the most part, to single couplets, or . . . to couplets combined with Synthetic or Antithetic couplets. . . .

The following are examples of Synonymous parallelism: Luke 6:27, 28 = Matt. 5:44; Matt. 5:45; Luke 12:22, 23 = Matt. 6:25; Matt. 7:1, 8 = Luke 11:9, 10. . . .

Antithetic Parallelism. Our Lord's teaching, like the gnomic teaching of the O.T. authors of the Wisdom-literature, tended to express itself in sharply marked antitheses; and these antitheses are commonly expressed in balancing couplets. The antithesis is very often produced by the use of opposites, e.g.,: Matt. 7:17; John 3:6. . . . Occasionally, though somewhat rarely, it takes the form of contrast between positive and negative in identical terms. Thus: Matt. 6:14, 15; John 3:18; Matt. 15:11; John 8:35.

A very striking form of antithesis is one in which the contrast is obtained by simple inversion of terms in the parallel clauses. Of this nature are: Matt. 10:39; Matt. 20:16; Matt. 23:12. . . .

In Synthetic or Constructive parallelism . . . the second line of a couplet neither repeats nor contrasts with the sense of the first, but the sense flows on continuously, much as in prose. There is, however, a correspondence between line and line of the couplet which marks them as the parts of a whole. This appears both in *sense*, the second line completing or supplementing the first, and also in *form*, the two lines balancing one another, and being commonly marked by identity of *rhythm*. . . . A few examples: Matt. 23:5–10; Luke 12:49–51; John 8:44.

We may give the name of Step-parallelism to a form of parallelism somewhat freely used by our Lord, in which a second line takes up a thought contained in the first line, and, repeating it, makes it as it were a step upwards for the development of a further thought, which is commonly the climax of the whole. Thus the parallelism is neither wholly Synonymous nor wholly Synthetic, but is partly Synonymous (or rather Identical) and partly Synthetic.

This form of parallelism, while occurring fairly often in the Synoptists, is especially frequent in the Fourth Gospel . . . : Mark 9:37 = Matt. 18:5 = Luke 9:48; Matt. 10:46; Luke 10:16; John 13:20.

C. F. Burney. The Poetry of Our Lord (Oxford, Oxford University Press, 1925), pp. 63, 67, 71–73, 89–91

Since . . . the writings of the ancient Greek fathers and the techniques of the scribes who in ancient times copied the Greek New Testament give no evidence that the early Christians regarded any of the New Testament books or any substantial portions of them to be poetry, we are forced to ask whether we have the right to call that poetry which early Greek-speaking readers did not suspect to be such. Our question is: What parts of the New Testament were meant to be and were taken to be poetry at the time they were written and made public?

When this approach has been accepted, one sweeping conclusion immediately follows. With the exception of such rare snatches as the quotations in Acts 17:18 and Titus 1:12, the New Testament contains nothing which would have been considered poetry by those familar with the standards of Greek verse. The New Testament is in Greek, but it contains only the briefest echoes of Greek poetry or poetry patterns.

If, then, there is original poetry in the New Testament, it must be found by relating the material to Semitic poetic patterns. . . .

The conclusion suggested by the foregoing discussion is that New Testament scholars have been much too ready to speak of Aramaic poetry behind our Greek documents. An unassailable basis for such utterances has yet to be built.

Even if there were Aramaic poems behind some of our New Testament materials, the Greek could be a prose translation of the poetic original. We therefore ask what signs of poetry the Greek document show. The few ancient Fathers who discuss the poetry of the Old Testament offer no hint that they consider the New Testament books or substantial portions of them to be poetry. This is significant; if scholars whose native language was Greek failed to sense poetry, it creates a strong presupposition that it is not there. . . .

There is no agreement as to the extent and identity of poetic passages in the New Testament. We have no adequate materials and criteria with which to study and define Aramaic poetry. We therefore are not justified in making . . . sweeping statements about poetry in the New Testament. . . .

Floyd V. Filson. JBL. 67, 1948, pp. 126, 130, 134

There is relatively little poetry in the New Testament and what we do find is usually excerpted from the Old Testament to establish the continuum of history. For instance, Matthew in his account of the visit of the Magi and of the flight into Egypt (2:13–18) inserts four lines from Micah (5:1) and five lines from Jeremiah (35:15), recalling earlier prophecies. The entire Gospel contains numerous such insertions. Mark uses fewer poetic sections but does open his Gospel with five poetic lines; he uses four lines from Isaiah when speaking of the traditions of the Pharisees (7:7); he quotes from Psalm 118:22–23 in 12:11 and from Psalm 110:1 in 12:11, 36. Luke, too interweaves poetry through his prose, and John's "Prologue" assumes poetic form in some modern versions. In fact, in several of the new translations about one-third of John's account is printed in poetic form. And even Paul, whose *forte* was clear and logical prose, uses poetry when he wishes to appeal to the emotions.

Charlotte I. Lee. Oral Reading of the Scriptures (Boston, Houghton Mifflin, 1974), pp. 142–143

PARABLE OF THE PRODIGAL SON

The perfection lies, in the first place, in the complete avoidance of superfluous detail. In twenty-one verses enough is related to suggest to any listener with imagination the experiences of several years of the Prodigal Son's life. There is no moralising, no attempt to drive home the lesson. The details which are given are all suggestive. What a background is filled in by the imagination as we read of the younger son's demand for his inheritance; of the quiet acquiescence of the father, who accedes to the request; of the son's immediate departure to a far country and his wasting of 'his substance with riotous living.' The high lights are picked out, and without further emphasis, make one conscious of the depths and shadows.

In the next stage of the story we are not told directly of the younger son's misery, but we are given two concrete facts: 'He would fain have been filled with the husks that the swine did eat'; he was in absolute destitution. 'And no man gave unto him'; he was shut off in a strange land from all human sympathy. . . . Contrasts throughout the story heighten the effects. He comes to offer himself as a hired servant. His father greets him not merely as a son, but as a son to be specially honoured. He realises that one who was, as it were, dead, and lost spiritually as well as physically is alive again in a twofold sense. The servants, and the elder brother, have not the same spiritual perception, and the elder brother's very human—if somewhat self-righteous—complaint shows this. The restrained reproof of the father, and the repetition of the same phrase, 'was dead and is alive again, was lost and is found,' close the parable with its objects attained.

Kathleen E. Innes, The Bible as Literature (London, Jonathan Cape, 1930), pp. 211–212

To the question why the parables make such a universal appeal, the answer will be best seen from the longest of them, the Prodigal Son. We are dealing with its literary beauties; its other beauties have been the subject of thousands of addresses.

First, its *rapid movement* as a story keeps the interest at full pitch. The downfall of the young man is told in two phases, 'he wasted his substance in riotous living, and when he had spent all . . .'; his return in one sentence, 'he arose and came to his Father', while the father's only reply to his son's confession is an order to the servants to do him honour.

Secondly, it is 'things' that make stories go well, not emotions and abstractions. One of the secrets of the story's appeal to all ages and intelligences is its *concreteness*. Everything in it is concrete and vigorous. Everything is described in solid terms. . . .

The story is one of great moral issues, repentance, forgiveness, jealousy, but it is all expressed in incident and action. The younger son's feelings take concrete form: he 'comes to himself', he 'will go back and say "I have sinned"'. . . . The brother's jealousy takes a concrete form: 'Thou gavest me no *kid*.' The father's welcome takes a concrete form, he 'falls on his neck and kisses him tenderly'. So does his joy: 'Bring forth the best *robe*, a *ring*, and *shoes* (to show recovered sonship, for slaves went barefoot), and *kill*, *eat*, and be merry' (start *dancing* and *music*, ver. 25). His son's sin was a concrete thing to him, 'he was *dead*, and is *alive*'. The feelings and emotions are not analysed, they are instantly turned into action.

The vivid *dialogue*, as usual, and the use of direct speech, keep the story lively and quick. Even in such a small detail as the informing of the elder brother, the brother calls a servant and receives the news in direct speech.

The *diction* is simple in the extreme. . . .

As in the Old Testament stories, *repetition* is purposely used to bring out the main points of the story: e.g. in vv.18 and 21: 'Father, I have sinned . . .'; and in vv.24 and 32: 'for this my son was dead and is alive again. . . .'

P. C. Sands. *Literary Genius of the New Testament* (Oxford, Oxford University Press, 1932), pp. 86–88

The effort to divide the parable into two at v. 25 seems unnecessary and impossible. The place of the older son in the narrative is secured by the references in vs. 11–13. There would be no point in this if the older son were to play no part in the story. The elder disappears temporarily from the account when interest is focused on the adventures of the absent brother and then on the father, but he reappears when needed to create the climax which provides the real point of the parable. . . .

The story of the "prodigal's" adventures are so well drawn and are so sound psychologically that much exposition has centered about them, to the neglect of the central point. . . . The crux of the story lies in the activity of the father—not merely in his going to meet his son while "yet afar off." The father's preparedness, which is implied in "While he was yet afar off" he "saw him," his compelling compassion, his running, his embrace, and his disregard of his son's prepared speech, are all summed up and far exceeded by his instructions to the servants. These mean that the returned wanderer is not only treated as an honored guest but reinstated into the family circle, a son still. . . .

The elder's rather frigid dignity is well portrayed when he sends for a servant to explain the situation instead of making a personal investigation. The same concern shown for the younger son is shown by the father toward his other son in going out to plead with him. There is no reason to question the son's statements concerning his length of service or obedience, nor, on the whole, the contrast he draws. The point indeed rests on the acceptance of these things. His designation of the prodigal as "this thy son," which is a refusal to accord him the name of brother, is the core of his objection, for it refuses the penitent a place in the same family with himself. His loyalty and diligence are not in debate, but his proud exclusiveness must be weighed against them.

The story in its entirety calls for an opinion. Which attitude toward the prodigal is to be commended and endorsed? The contrast drawn requires the hearer to choose between father and older brother. And to the question the detail and progress of the story, with its power to move and enlist sympathy, permits only one answer. Every instinct of the human heart draws it one way. . . . The older brother wants to reverse the order. The parable is addressed to fathers in the audience—and to prodigals or outcasts. . . .

It will be observed that many of the details are so apt that, once the central point is grasped, many applications may be made and deductions drawn. The treatment of vs. 14–20a as an anatomy of repentance, while not the principal interest or purpose of the story, reveals how suitably and skillfully the details are selected and used. . . .

By the use of a truly human comparison it escapes from the captivity of time. It is as relevant now as then, and in exactly the same manner.

> Charles W. F. Smith. *The Jesus of the Parables* (Philadelphia, Westminster Press, 1948; rpt. Pilgrim Press, 1975), pp. 110–114

The third in the series of the Lost, The Prodigal Son, is, by common consent, the paragon of all. . . .

How consummately the tale is told! No wonder Robert Bridges, a fastidious critic, pronounced it "an absolutely flawless piece of work." Yet its artistry should not make us forget that it originated in Jesus' "warfare" with the Pharisees. But if it is polemic, it is polemic at its finest, polemic armed with the gentleness of love.

The story, with its deep psychological insights and its wonderful "anatomy of repentance," is too lifelike to be called an allegory. Yet, beyond doubt, in the mind of Jesus the father stood for God, the elder brother for the Scribes and Pharisees, and the prodigal for publicans and sinners.

It is important to realize that this is one of his two-pointed parables. We should therefore reject all suggestions that it might have ended at verse 24 (''For this my son was dead etc.''). The second half of the story is not an appendix which we may include or omit at will. It makes a point at least as important as the first half. Indeed, we may say that the contrast on which the whole parable hinges is that of the attitudes of the father and of the elder brother to the prodigal.

Observe how masterfully Jesus works it out. First, he forces his hearers to pronounce a judgment on the way in which the prodigal is treated, first by the father, and then by his brother. He compels them to admit that the father's way is as wholly right as the brother's is wrong. . . .

In the parable, then, Jesus does two things. To begin with, he justifies his own mission in the teeth of his critics: ''God is like the father of my story. This is his way with sinners, and therefore it is my way.'' But secondly, he rebukes the Scribes and Pharisees: ''You represent the elder brother in my story, because your way of treating sinners is his. But it is the wrong way, because it is not God's way.''

A. M. Hunter. Int. 14, 1960, pp. 182–184

The Prodigal Son . . . stands alone among the parables in its artistic perfection. . . .

Indeed, the end is not an appendix but a necessary chapter. There is no stylistic or structural or any other reason for regarding it as an appendix, for it continues the narrative after a sectional pause. The *two* sons, including the elder, are mentioned at the very start in that most famous opening; we await therefore with eagerness the appearance of the second, and so far there is no indication of what he is like or of what he will do. . . .

The parable, moreover, is satisfying, for it is told in such a manner as to make us feel that it is complete, leaving no more to be said. There are stages in the progress of the action. . . .

It is partly through the representative and paradigmatic character which it has achieved through familiarity that it makes its impact on the mind, and it is art in that it is not a propositional statement about how one should behave or how God acts: it shows the characters in action without any comment by the narrator. Through its impact as a story the Prodigal Son has become one of those ''primordial images'' of which Karl Mannheim wrote and whose possibilities are never exhausted. For it is not philosophy but parable; indeed it is significant that the biblical thought-world, when dealing with creation and fall, with man's existence ''in-the-world,'' does not make metaphysical statements but uses myth, that is to say, fictitious narrative. Man the eternal prodigal is both Adam and the Lost Boy. Only myth or parable can describe the ''existential'' truth about him. . . .

Right from the start its artistic authenticity is made clear, for its author, like many other authors, struck the decisive note in framing the first sentence.

Indeed, artists in words have exercised great care in choosing their opening words, so that they carry us onwards from the first sentence to the heart and the conclusion of the story. There are many famous first sentences. . . .

So it is with the parable of the Prodigal Son. "A certain man had two sons"—perhaps the briefest of all opening sentences, belonging to the memorable moments of great literature. . . .

We do not know the name of the father in the parable . . . ; indeed, it does not matter whether we do or not; but we know enough about him when we have read the story. . . . We know enough, too, about the two sons. Anything more would be superfluous. . . .

We infer that the father is old, that one son is young and silly, and that the other is more solid, more sensible, and less enterprising. He is as Esau is to Jacob. We know just as much as it is necessary for us to know, because the consummate artistry of the parable provides all that is necessary. . . .

What, then, does this parable say about the human condition? Without reading into it more than it can bear, we can at least perceive that the story which it unfolds combines into a succinct pattern such themes as Freedom and Responsibility, Estrangement, the Personalness of Life, Longing and Return, Grace, Anguish, and Reconciliation. The parable exposes certain universal characteristics of life and describes basic human needs. To exclude these in the interest of obedience to a principle of interpretation limited to the immediate setting would be to rob it of most of its richness and to impoverish it beyond measure; for such is its greatness that it does not cease to be recreative and reproductive. . . . It is not the context alone which confers immortality on the parable of the Prodigal Son (or the Lost Boy) but the form, the pressure of its style, the vigour of its imaginative conception, its delineation of character, and its exposure of motives and attitudes. It is a piece of life transfigured and given meaning by vision, and has become an archetypal pattern of human existence.

> Geraint Vaughan Jones. *The Art and Truth of the Parables* (London, S.P.C.K., 1964), pp. 120–125, 174–175

It has often been claimed that the father is the central figure in the parable and even that this is true to such an extent that it should be called The Father's Love. But it may be rejoined that the instinct of the Christian and Western tradition has been right in calling it The Prodigal Son, for it is the son's story. His experience gives the plot its formal shape. . . .

We see in The Prodigal Son a plot structure of interlocking parts moving finally upward from decision, through dissolution, to well-being and restoration. If the comic and hopeful may be lost in tragedy . . . , it is also possible for the tragic to be overcome by comedy (The Prodigal Son).

Frye has pointed out that the form of comedy may be developed in two ways: (a) The main emphasis may be placed on blocking characters, characters who resist the comic movement of the hero's story. (b) The accent may be caused to fall on scenes of discovery and reconciliation. The blocking character is typically made absurd by attributing to him some ruling passion. The plot movement is usually from a society controlled by habit, bondage, or law—a society typical of the blocking character—to a society marked by freedom.

The Prodigal Son reflects . . . characteristic features of comedy. . . . The elder brother—the blocking character—is given a certain stress by the fact that the section dealing with him comes last; nevertheless, the discovery and reconciliation of the prodigal son are more fully and powerfully developed than is the elder brother's story. . . .

The Prodigal Son is a comedy which includes and overcomes tragedy; therefore, the recognition scene follows the downfall as the most appropriate transition to the comic rescue of the tragic. In the comic ending the recognition scene is taken up again and transcended. That is, the prodigal acknowledged to his father, as he had acknowledged to himself, the forfeiture of his sonship, but the father took him back as son. . . .

In the recognition scene the prodigal is seen to be aware of his physical destitution and also of his having sinned against God and his father. . . .

The prodigal is able not only to recognize that something is wrong but to resolve to do something about it. The total movement of the story reveals, however, that more can be done about it than he can imagine. The final help comes from beyond him and far exceeds his expectations. He is incapable of knowing what possibilities for good might come to him until they do come. . . .

The ending of the prodigal's story restores the father-son relationship and is truly a new beginning, a new beginning based on the surprising generosity of the father rather than on the merits of the son. The acceptance is not based on any conditions, probation, or proofs of repentance. In fact repentance finally turns out to be the capacity to forego pride and accept graciousness. It should be noticed that the father not only goes out to the prodigal son; he also goes out to the elder brother. . . .

The comic movement of The Prodigal Son is from well-being, through fall, back to well-being, and this is also true for the total sweep of the Bible—from Genesis to Revelation. But if this movement is referred to as cyclical, it should not be thought that either the Bible in general or The Prodigal Son in particular envisions a literal cyclical return to the same beginning. . . . At the end he was the same person that he was at the beginning, and yet not quite. Throughout his story possibilities became actualized which had been only potentialities.

Dan Otto Via, Jr. *The Parables: Their Literary and Existential Dimension* (Philadelphia, Fortress Press, 1967), pp. 164–169, 174–175

God's love for sinners and outsiders is a major theme of Luke's. So is joy. Here the two come together, joined by another of Luke's themes: repentance, meaning a change or turning of mind and heart. This is tacked on to the two little pictures, but it is bound into the story of the Prodigal Son and so made more explicit.

Verse 1 sets the scene. It is triangular: Jesus, sinners, Pharisees. In the light of the gospel the opposite of goodness is not the sinner but the self-righteous and resentful 'good man'. . . .

Like the other long story of the Good Samaritan it bears many of Luke's trade-marks: a secular story without religious trappings, the well-to-do setting (people of property, with servants), journeying, the moment when dereliction turns to comfort, reference to the moral outer-fringes and the Old Testament.

There is a certain allegorical aspect to the story. The father's gifts in verse 22 have their meanings: a robe was honorific (in Heaven God's people would be given new robes—Revelation 6.11), the ring signified authority, and shoes were for freemen. Further than that, verses 1 and 2 suggest that there may well be something in the old interpretation which sees the father as God, the elder son as orthodox pharisaical Judaism, the younger son as the unrespectable kind of Jew who became a Christian (N.B. he is *not* a Gentile).

But the main interest of the story will always be its insight into the workings of the human heart and portrayal of contrasted characters. The father is the original good parent who, for all his fondness for him, lets his child go without question and, for all the distress he has caused, receives him back without recrimination. The younger son is a figure of youth with its ambiguous thirst for experience. His grief at the failure of his schemes does not deprive him of the mental resilience to see sense (very Lucan) and get out of it. The elder son is middle-aged in mentality if not years, a righteous and dutiful type who resents the fact that neither his father nor the way of the world is as morally tidy as he has made his own existence. His character is reminiscent of Jonah. The two brothers are thus played off against one another, but it is not a plain contrast of virtue and nastiness. Each misbehaves in his characteristic fashion. The goodness is with the uncondemning and deeply generous father. . . . Luke prefers to finish the tale with the triumphant joy which he can best express in the Christian terms of resurrection from the dead.

John Drury. *Luke* (New York, Macmillan Publishing
Company, 1973), pp. 155–157

The parable of the forgiving father (Luke 15:11–32), popularly known by the somewhat misleading title of the parable of the prodigal son, represents the technique of the parable at its most sophisticated and intricate. It is a fairly long story with complication of action and subtlety of characterization. The three-phase story emphasizes differentiation of characters and the relationships among them, with particular attention given to child rebellion, parental love, and sibling rivalry. The story also draws upon several archetypal plot patterns, including the journey (here a circular withdrawal-return journey, common in literature), the death-rebirth motif, and the initiation motif (initiation into sin and its consequences, into adulthood, into the hardships and suffering of life). The prodigal or wastrel is an archetypal character type. The story is constructed around the emotional climax of the reconciliation of father and son, and there is effective use of dialogue and realistic detail to evoke an explicit picture of what takes place. . . .

The picture of the prodigal son wasting his money in immoral indulgence (vs. 13) is told with stark simplicity. . . . As in many another work of literature, it is human suffering that contributes to the character development of the son (vs. 14). A few vivid details portray the depths to which the son falls as he is initiated into the world of adulthood and moral consequences (vss. 15–16). . . .

The turning point in the son's development comes when he reaches moral perception. His recognition of his moral failing to date is conveyed by the statement that "when he came to himself" he decided to return to his father (Luke 15:17). The son's reasoning that many of his father's "hired servants have bread enough and to spare" (vs. 17) must be understood in terms of the three kinds of employees in the Jewish culture of the day. Hired servants were the lowest of three categories of servants. The categories were bondmen (slaves with good family standing), servants (subordinates of the slaves), and hired servants (hired for the occasion). . . .

In the second phase of the action, the character of the father becomes the focus of interest. The father reverses our expectations of disapproval by having compassion on his returning son and embracing him (vs. 20). The father also rejects the son's offer to be accepted as a hired servant and instead commands, "Bring quickly the best robe, and put it on him; and put a ring on his hand, and shoes on his feet; and bring the fatted calf and kill it, and let us eat and make merry" (vss. 22–23). The command communicates its meaning through symbols. The robe would symbolize the honor with which the son was being received into family fellowship. The ring, if it was a signet ring, would signify great status for the son, who was being granted the rights and authority of a member of the ruling family instead of being subordinated as a slave. The shoes would also represent his status as a son, since slaves went barefoot. Yet another index to the exalted nature of the son's reception is the fatted calf, which in biblical times was reserved for occasions when a host entertained a special guest. . . .

In the third act of the drama, Jesus turns the story into a satiric attack on the scribes and Pharisees. The stimulus to the parable, we must remember, had been the complaint of the scribes and Pharisees that Jesus associated with sinners. This attitude is embodied in the elder son of the parable. As a literary character the elder son belongs to the familiar archetype of the refuser of festivities.

Leland Ryken. *The Literature of the Bible* (Grand Rapids, Zondervan, 1974), pp. 311–313

The introductory sentence and the younger son's request set the stage for the action of the story. After the younger son's request divides the unit, the story falls into two main sections, the younger son's experience with the father and the elder son's experience with the father. These two sections are paralleled to an amazing degree. . . . Both the younger son and the elder son travel to the house from a distance away; both are met outside by the father; both state their intentions to him outside; and with both the father has the final word. . . . The two sections of the parable are deeply intertwined, carefully paralleled, thematically and structurally, to bring the listener or reader to the father's proclamation of his intimate, though different, bonds with both of his sons which he expresses in his final speech in 15:31–32. . . . The parable as a whole . . . is expressing the longing of the human heart for wholeness, for a re-integration of the conflicting elements of life. . . .

The parable presents us with three characters, an adult and two children. The adult must mediate between the two children; he goes out of the house to talk with them, to restore them to himself (15:20 and 15:28). One of the sons has wasted himself on a dissipated life, "devoured your living with harlots" (15:30). The other son is rigid, judgmental and unforgiving. These three elements are present in the psyche of every individual. The voice inside us which demands the fulfilling of every desire, the breaking of every taboo is pitted against the often equally strong voice of harsh judgment on those desires. . . .

The prodigal is clearly connected in the story with sexual excess. He satisfies all his desires in the most direct way possible without regard for religious or moral taboos. Yet he is welcomed back into the family with rejoicing and feasting. . . . The father welcomes his prodigal son with an embrace and a kiss; he requires no change in his son's status or attitude before he offers his wholehearted compassion. . . . The younger son's desire for feasting and pleasure are still supplied in the unity of the family by the father's orders, but now the desire for pleasure is more restrained and controlled, still satisfied but not at the expense of life itself. . . .

The elder son's anger comes from his feeling of being treated unfairly by his father. . . . He is angry, not because his wild-living brother has been returned to the family, but because he never got the kind of feast his brother is getting. To the degree that he represents the views of established religion and morality, as many commentators have observed, his presentation in the story and stated motivations show the underside of such a rigid morality: childish selfishness. . . .

The father is both the unifying center of the parable and its most vacillating figure. He gives in to the request of the younger son and allows him to leave; he runs out to meet first one son and then the other; he does not order his elder son into the house or attempt to force either son to bend to his will; in fact, it is he who bends to the demands of his sons. In the history of the interpretation of this parable some scholars have suggested that it be titled The Father's Love rather than The Prodigal Son. Indeed one perceives something centrally important to the story in the action of the father, but at the same time there is something strangely weak in his depiction; the characters of the sons are far more strongly drawn. Yet in the course of interpreting the parable one begins to realize that in the father's weakness is his ultimate strength: because he bends to the demands of his sons, he can unite them in himself.

Mary Ann Tolbert. *Semeia*. 9, 1977, pp. 10–12, 14–15, 18–19

PROVERB AS A LITERARY FORM
(See also *Jesus as Poet.*)

Epigrams are continually coming in [Paul's] letters, to add force to an argument or close it summarily. Paul has a genius for coining a phrase, and giving it the ring of a proverb, and the truth of an axiom. They are another source of the richness and exuberance of Paul's style. In the Greek these epigrams are still more compact than in English, for Paul often omits the verb 'to be' and whatever else can be understood without saying.

'*None of us lives unto himself*' is a great enough saying, of wide bearing on life, simple and compact—yet it only comes out of a discussion about eating particular foods and keeping certain days. . . . '*For the wages of sin is death*' will be found a particularly interesting case of the forceful epigram concluding the argument, when you look at its setting. . . .

'*The love of money is the root of all evil*' ends a few remarks upon riches. In fact Paul rarely leaves an argument without saying something better than all that has gone before it. Even the passage on 'Love' is greatest in the close: 'And now abide faith, hope, love, these three, but the greatest of these is love'. . . .

Even in familiar talk, as with his great friends the Philippians, about whether he will be released to see them, he coins the memorable epigram that sums up his outlook on life and death: 'To me to live is Christ, and to die is gain.' Here as often the epigram is the kernel of the talk, the great saying that slips out all unpremeditated, a polished coin ready for currency, and on he goes with his argument. . . .

> P. C. Sands. *Literary Genius of the New Testament* (Oxford, Oxford University Press, 1932), pp. 148–150

In the NT we face two distinct bodies of Wisdom literature. The one centers around Jesus. The other is in the Epistle of James. The Wisdom literature having Jesus as a center can be divided into three groups: Wisdom parables of Jesus; proverb sayings of Jesus; and Wisdom material having Jesus as a subject.

295

The parables of Jesus represent the method of teaching most popularly associated with him. He used parables often and effectively. Such use is characteristic of prophetic teaching. But it is also a part of Wisdom teaching. . . . The sixteen Wisdom parables include the good Samaritan (Lk. 10:30–36), the Pharisee and the Publican (Lk. 18:10–14), and others whose intent is to point home a moral truth. . . .

The proverb sayings of Jesus emphasize the fact that Jewish Wisdom literature is, in the NT, reverting to older forms of expression. Wisdom is personified by Jesus only twice (Lk. 7:35 and Lk. 11:49), and both times the personification is casual. This abandoning of the newer personification technique and the frequent use of proverbs and parables indicates two general facts about Jesus' Wisdom teaching: a. It is not a literary effort. Literary Wisdom productions had come to place their proverbs in a setting of personification. b. It is, nevertheless, a conscious art-form or/and education technique. One or two well phrased proverbs might spring spontaneously into an inspired utterance, but the consistent recurrence of proverbs . . . indicates conscious craftsmanship.

But if Jesus was a conscious craftsman of proverbs and Wisdom parables, he was a sage. Let us, therefore, consider him in this light. In the first place, he taught in the manner of a sage. . . . The sage taught under intimate circumstances—in his own house (Mk. 2:1–12) or while eating (Mk. 2:15–22), or at the home of friends (Lk. 11:37–52). And, in the second place, Jesus was a sage in that he taught the same universally applicable moral truths which the sages of the ages had taught.

One example of his continuity with the most ancient teachings of the sages may be noted in Lk. 14:11. Here Jesus says, "Everyone who exalts himself will be humbled, but he who humbles himself will be exalted." Some hundreds of years before, the Jewish sages had a proverb saying, "A man's pride shall bring him low, but the humble in spirit will attain to honor." (Prov. 18:12). . . .

Jesus, then, used Wisdom techniques (proverbs and parables) when he taught. He taught what the sages had taught. And he taught in the manner of a sage.

Terence Y. Mullins. JBL. 68, 1949, pp. 335–337

Christ's continual battle for the minds of those about Him required the use of a wide variety of weapons. In His arsenal were expressions of proverbial wisdom, which people would recognize and respect, as well as new epigrams and parables based upon the common life of the common people. It is not known to us, and it is not important that it be known, how many of these expressions were wholly or partly proverbial. It was not necessary for His purpose that all that He said should be original. That it was *not* all original is shown by the well-known quotations from the Hebrew Scriptures and His adaptation of the words of John. . . .

Whether His epigrams were original or not is immaterial, because, in the latter case, He was demonstrating His ability to take the commonplace and to give it added currency, while, in the former, His original sayings were *becoming* maxims. "A maxim is," as Coleridge said, "a conclusion upon observation of matters of fact." The clearest example of Christ's use of a maxim, in the strategy of intellectual battle, is that to the effect that a prophet is honored in all countries except his own (Mark 6:4, Matt. 13:57, Luke 4:24). This, which represents the distillation of wisdom from observed experience, may be very old indeed, and may be a quotation. . . . Genius lies in keeping a maxim from becoming a platitude. It is almost certain to undergo this fate unless there is a humorous twist.

> Elton Trueblood. *The Humor of Christ* (New York, Harper and Row, 1964), pp. 69–70

In itself the proverb is a form of folk or popular literature. It is prediscursive rather than antidiscursive, though its appropriateness as a vehicle of modern rebellion is anticipated by its long-continuing life beside the more coherent and abstract forms of discursive thought. The proverb grasps a particular kind of situation; it expresses a flash of insight which sees the "order" in a certain kind of happening. Proverbs deal predominantly with the world of man, though what we abstract as "nature" is not excluded.

The most basic form of the proverb is the statement; the proverb declares the "shape" of some sort of situation or occurrence: "A prophet is not without honor, except in his own country." . . . But the proverb's function is not simply declarative; its compressed form compels insight. There is an implied challenge to see it this way. Similarly, the question, the interrogative form, arises naturally in the proverb as a part of its function of compelling or challenging insight: "Which of you be being anxious can add one cubit to his span of life?" . . .

In the ancient setting the proverb represented an ordering of a particular bit of experience. It is a tract of experience which can be repeated. That is the whole point of the proverb, which by its nature cannot deal with a unique situation. And it is an orderly tract of experience; that is the reason for the declarative form. Things are that way. . . .

In the ancient Near East, the proverb was not merely a popular form, but it was also, and is best known to us as, a form used by a scholarly or teaching class, the wise men or sages. The proverb was not their only form of speech, but it was their typical form, and the proverb as it comes into the New Testament, and in particular into the synoptic Gospels where it most frequently occurs, has not only the functions of the popular proverb, but at least some of the functions imposed by this scholarly class as well. . . .

It is in this focus on daily interpersonal relationships, on how a man gets on with his neighbor, his child, his enemy, that brought the proverbial form into the proclamation of Jesus and into early Christian preaching. The overall framework, both of Jesus' message and of that of the early church, was quite different from the world of the proverb, either in its general popular use or in its moral-religious setting in Jewish wisdom. But a concern with the daily life of man in his responsibilities to his fellows gives the proverb a prominent place in the speech of Jesus and of the early church and gives both Jesus and the early Christian proclamation a point of contact with secular wisdom as well as with moral religious wisdom.

William A. Beardslee. *Literary Criticism of the New Testament* (Philadelphia, Fortress Press, 1970), pp. 31–34

Though there are in Mark and Q (and in material peculiar to Luke and Matthew) examples of proverbs which express a rather general folk wisdom, with its rather relaxed and sometimes even resigned attitude toward the making of choices, it is evident that in the most characteristic Synoptic sayings this wisdom is immensely concentrated and intensified. The primary means of intensification are paradox and hyperbole.

Paradox is related to the antithetical formulations which are so widespread in proverbial literature. . . . The kind of antithesis which provides the background for the Synoptic paradox is the antithesis which expresses a reversal of situation. The story which lies behind the proverb is a story of reversal of fortune. This is also a very ancient proverbial form. Probably its original form, and certainly a very ancient widespread usage, was the function of expressing the disastrous consequence of exceeding one's role. "He that exalts himself shall be humbled," in common sense wisdom is a warning against what the Greeks called *hybris*. . . . These proverbs presuppose an order, and warn against transgressing it. Of this type we may cite such Synoptic proverbs as [Luke 14:11; Mark 10:31; Mark 8:36; Mark 10: 43–44]. Now we come to a saying which I classify as a paradox rather than an antithesis: Whoever loses his life will preserve it (Luke 17: 33; cf. Mark 8: 35 par.; John 12:25). . . .

Here the reversal situation is so sharp that the imagination is jolted out of its vision of a continuous connection between one situation and the other. . . .

For the purpose of classifying proverbial sayings, we have defined paradox in a very specific way, as an intensification of the "reversal of status" type of antithesis which is widely known in proverbial literature. We could define paradox more broadly, but instead choose for our broader term, "hyperbole." Here we can include a wide range of intensified or exaggerated language. . . .

In the Synoptics, hyperbole is used, like paradox, to jolt the hearer out of the project of making a continuity of his life. "Love your enemies" illustrated this. . . .

For the modern interpreter, the prominent place of the proverb in the Synoptic Gospels, and presumably in the speech of Jesus himself, is important from several points of view. As noted above, even the somewhat everyday and conventional proverbs are important, as reminding the reader of the everyday field of concern to which faith and action must relate. The characteristic thrust of the Synoptic proverbs, however, is not the cautious and balanced judgment so typical of much proverbial literature. Such middle-of-the-road style has as its presupposition the project of making a continuous whole out of one's existence. The intensification of the proverb in paradox and hyperbole functions precisely to call this project into question, to jolt the hearer out of the effort, and into a new judgment about his own existence.

William A. Beardslee. *Int.* 24, 1970, pp. 66–69, 71

The essence of a proverbial saying is that it is based on observation of how things are in the world. It is a flash of insight into the repeatable situations of life in the world, and its aphoristic form not only represents insight but also compels it. "A prophet is not without honor, except in his own country" (Mark 6:4). The proverb readily becomes imperatival, basing instruction on common-sense observation. "Do not throw your pearls before swine, lest they trample them underfoot" (Matt 7:6). The proverb can also be expressed in interrogative form, again compelling insight. "Which of you be being anxious can add one cubit to his span of life?" (Matt 6:27). Naturally, in the context of a firm belief in God, the proverb comes to express insight into the way things are, or should be, in the world ordered by God and a challenge to behavior that God will reward.

Norman Perrin. *The New Testament: An Introduction* (New York, Harcourt Brace Jovanovich, Inc., 1974), p. 296

The language of logic and clear definition has greater efficiency and precision, but it abstracts from the rich significance of man's encounters with reality. . . . Depth language seeks to respond more adequately to the richness of reality.

In this search "tensive language" is an important part of the poet's strategy. . . . Ordinary language used in ordinary ways reveals only the superficialities of ordinary experience. . . . If he is to escape the tyranny of the superficial, the poet must combine words in strange ways. He must engage in meaningful distortion of his raw material. He must place his work in tension with the old perspective which obscures our vision. His words will show this tension. In the synoptic sayings also we will find reflections in form and language of the necessary fight with the old perspective in order to found the new. . . .

I hope that the reader has come to share with me an interest in the possibility that features of texts which have consciously or unconsciously been dismissed as "merely rhetorical," i.e., unimportant decoration for theological ideas or historical facts, are important after all. They may be indications of a desire to speak with sufficient imaginative force to touch those fundamental images, those prerational visions of self and world, which determine how we think and what we are. Such force, in spite of some clear tendencies toward hyperbole in the Gospels, is not just a matter of shouting loudly and going to extremes. By a variety of means the Gospels speak with strong personal impact, challenging fundamental assumptions, thereby requiring the imagination to awake from its slumbers and interpret the world anew. That is why it is appropriate to speak of *forceful* and *imaginative* language. . . .

We can now understand what is lost when we reduce the sayings of Jesus to "plain speech." Plain speech is good for communication within established interpretations of the world but it bypasses the imagination and so has little power to change these fundamental interpretations. Therefore it has little power to change men. The communication of plain speech will be accepted as an "idea" and placed in the pigeonhole where it will least disturb our basic vision of self and world. Or it will be accepted as a rule of behavior without affecting the basic orientation of the self. . . .

Pattern and tension are major ways in which these little sayings gain the imaginative force necessary for their task. Through pattern the text gains unity and particularity. Pattern heightens the interaction of the parts, enforcing, contrasting, and enriching. The pattern of these sayings contribute especially to tension, which is strong and pervasive. This tension is the formal reflection of the text's desire to challenge prevailing structures of the personal world and to grant a new vision of some region of existence. . . .

Within the synoptic Gospels the "Kingdom of God" is the symbolic name for the reality beyond ourselves which is the cause and justification of this tension. The Kingdom of God is the (often uncited) basis for the challenge to the old perspective and is the reality which grants us a right to the new vision to which the sayings point. These sayings show us how things look from the viewpoint of the Kingdom. Futhermore, because they resist our attempts to digest them within the perspective of the old world, these sayings preserve the Kingdom's newness, its reality as *God's* Kingdom, which cannot be assimilated to the old world. . . . God's Kingdom is the basis for the new vision of the sayings, but these sayings themselves, along with the parables and stories of the Gospels, are the gate through which we must pass if we are to discover the reality which is their basis.

> Robert C. Tannehill. *The Sword of His Mouth* (Missoula,
> Scholar's Press, 1975), pp. 13–14, 26–27, 55–57

It is important to note how pervasive the view is in the primitive church that Jesus spoke in proverbial wisdom. . . . My very rough and inexact count gives 102 sayings in the Synoptics which could be considered wisdom-sayings, a very substantial percentage of the whole. When one notes as well that these sayings are included in all the synoptic sources and that they deal with a most varied kind of subject matter, the simplest and by far the most plausible interpretation of this phenomenon is that some of them must be authentic, that the form and content of Jesus' message at the outset invited an interpretation in wisdom categories by the earliest church. . . .

The appropriateness of the proverbs Jesus actually used . . . is by no means restricted to rural Palestine. The Q saying, "For nothing is covered (up) that will not be revealed, or hidden that will not be known" (Matt 10:26 = Luke 12:20) is not really much different from Thales's "Time brings all things to light" or Publilius Syrus's "Time conceals the reprobate and time reveals him. . . ."

That life should be lived one day at a time (Matt 6:34) is an astonishingly widespread notion in the ancient world, and so are weather proverbs like the one lying behind Matt 16:2–3 = Luke 12:54–55. Aesop's fable of the Dog in the Manger undoubtedly lies behind Matt 23:13. And proverbial wisdom is surely reflected in Jesus' insistence that the laborer deserves his food (Matt 10:10 = Luke 10:7). . . .

But, it may be objected, this is at best a half truth; Jesus' teaching differs in its use of hyperbole, its paradoxical formulations, its extremism, its demand for bold action, and perhaps above all in its eschatological conditioning. . . .

I freely concede that differences, in some cases substantial and significant differences, do exist between many of the above sayings and those ascribed to Jesus. But we must be very careful not to overstate what those differences are. If Jesus knows that the way to destruction is wide (Matt 7:13), so does Bion of Borysthenes, four centuries earlier. Menander, like Jesus, insists that life must be lived for others. Paradoxical formulations, especially about death, are commonplace in the Greco-Roman world, and the paradoxical notion that the mighty should be humble is known in fable, tale, and proverbial exhortation. . . .

Even this limited study has made clear some degree of similarity between Jesus' sententious sayings and similar material in the larger Greco-Roman world. So if the arguments given are supported by the evidence adduced, a number of conclusions ought to follow.

We might well stop concentrating so one-sidely on the unique and distinctive in Jesus' message. While such unique elements are undoubtedly important, an outlook which ignores universal elements as well can only prejudice us at the outset against wisdom-motifs in his teaching which probably cannot be eliminated without violence. . . .

Christian exegetes will have to become somewhat more open to the creative possibilities of the universally human elements in Jesus' life and teaching. Continuity will have to take its place alongside discontinuity as a basic category for understanding the significance of Jesus.

Charles E. Carlston. JBL. 99, 1980, pp. 91, 99–100, 102–105

REVELATION

GENRE

Modern writers taking the word *apocalypse* in its generic sense have applied the adjective *apocalyptic* to all writing whether Jewish or Christian which possess in common certain characteristic forms appearing in the Apocalypse of John and which contain an unveiling, a revelation, real or fictitious, of events and doctrines of the Last Things. . . .

There are . . . characteristics of . . . external and formal kind, the recognition of which will not only define the class more clearly, but will also serve to prevent the misinterpretation of many passages found in literature of this nature.

(1) *Visions and raptures.* The highly elaborated vision, or similar mode of revelation, is the most distinctive feature in the *form* of apocalyptic literature. . . . The vision or rapture is a literary form wrought out with great fullness of details, often with strange symbolism and with fantastic imagery. . . . It is this fundamental place of the vision, or similar mode of *unveiling* hidden things (*apocalypse*) in these writings, that has given them the *name* apocalyptic.

(2) *Mysteriousness.* It is characteristic of these writings that the revelations, or half revelations, are often given strange, unintelligible forms. The symbolic beasts are unimaginable monsters with their many heads and horns springing out and warring one with another; inanimate objects are represented with attributes of men and animals; the extraordinary and unnatural are preferred to the ordinary and natural. Hence a standing feature is the *interpreter* explaining the visions, allegories, and symbols; sometimes this is God himself, but commonly an angel. . . . It is not unlikely that even the writer himself, in order to give his picture fullness and power, or mysteriousness, sometimes introduced touches to which he did not attach a separate meaning in themselves. A specific meaning in every detail can no more be sought in an elaborate vision than in the parables of our Lord, or in the ornate picture of a Homeric simile. The significance of the representations is contained in the leading factors, while details are often designed only to give life and color.

(3) *Literary Dependence*. . . . The apocalyptist is not essentially an orig-
inator; he adopts, transforms, interprets apocalyptic matter already at hand.
The prophecies of the Old Testament writers, their visions, imagery and
symbolism, entered largely into these compositions, as did also popular traditions and conceptions in which were enshrined as in folk-lore, myths and
fancies belonging to the Hebrews and other orientals in common. The apocalypses do not spring from the professional scribes or the official class; they
are for the most part folk-literature. . . . Each writer borrows from his pred-
ecessor and from common tradition. Examples of such dependence are . . .
the dragon-form of the arch-enemy; portents in the heavens and the earth; the
emergence of the apocalyptic beasts from the sea; the trumpet-call ushering
in the great day. . . .

While the work in its fundamental conceptions must belong to his memory
of his visions, yet much also both in the framework and the details must be
due to his conscious effort as a literary artist struggling to give in familiar
apocalyptic form and manner a presentation of the truths revealed in his
ecstatic experiences. The plan, minutely organized with the sturcture of an
elaborate outline, with intricately interwoven threads, bears frequent traces
of a prophet who is working consciously to embody truth seized in an ecstacy
rather than to describe symbols actually seen.

> Isbon T. Beckwith. *The Apocalypse of John* (New York,
> Macmillan, 1922), pp. 168–172, 175

He casts his message in the old Jewish apocalyptic type, thus veiling his
meaning from matter-of-fact Roman minds by picturing empires and monarchs
under the form of beasts and monsters. The art of the apocalyptic literature . . . was the art of the grotesque, symbolizing dynasties, reigns, and
forces by weird creatures of fancy grouped in mystic numbers, especially in
sevens.

So commanding is this feature of the book that learning has almost completely ignored other traits no less important: the influence of the collected
letters of Paul and of Greek dramatic art. The portal of the Revelation is
formed by something entirely foreign to the apocalyptic type—a corpus of
letters to Christian churches, seven in number, preceded by a general message,
chapter 1, to all seven. . . .

The elaborate system of solos, antiphonies, choruses, and orchestration—
harps, trumpets, earthquakes, thunders, mighty waters, and hail—points just
as unmistakably to the influence of the contemporary Greek drama, with its
chorus of twenty-four. The whole structure of the Revelation is highly dramatic.

> Edgar J. Goodspeed. *An Introduction to the New Tes-
> tament* (Chicago, University of Chicago Press, 1937),
> pp. 243–244

He writes in the cryptic language of apocalyptic, which made his book a code message to those familiar with the vocabulary and imagery of such visions, while it would remain meaningless to the uninitiated Roman official who might chance to read it. But to its Christian readers it offered a great moral reinforcement of indomitable hope in the final triumph of their cause.

Strangely enough, although the book is an apocalypse, or revelation, . . . what we may call the portal of The Revelation of John is formed by a group of eight letters, a general one to the seven churches of the Roman province of Asia—Ephesus, Smyrna, Pergamum, Thyatira, Sardis, Philadelphia, and Laodicea—followed by short messages hardly two hundred words long to each of the seven, calling upon them to withstand the persecution that was threatening them. . . .

It is clear, however, that the letters are not sent singly, but all together, as a group, accompanied by the general letter to all seven, ch. 1. Each church is to read all the letters. Indeed, they are evidently written as a part of the Revelation, and included in its publication. . . . It is impossible to think such a collection of letters, to Christian churches, seven in number, prefaced with a general letter to all seven, was not influenced by the recent appearance of just such a collection of Paul's letters, to Christian churches, seven in number, accompanied by a general letter to Christians everywhere. Revelation is, in fact, the first book to show the influence of the collected and published letters of Paul.

Following this group of letters, which serve as introduction to the book, the main body of Revelation consists of three great visions, 4:1 to 22:5.

They are cast in the grotesque imagery and mysterious vocabulary of the old apocalyptic, as it was found in Dan., chs. 7 to 12. . . . But the influence of contemporary Greek drama is also to be seen in the Revelation, for it has its arias and antiphonies, its choruses of saints and elders, 4:4, 10; 14:3, and its prodigious orchestration, for its accompaniments are not only harps and trumpets, 5:8; 14:2, chs. 8; 9, but earthquakes, thunders, and the noise of mighty waters.

> Edgar J. Goodspeed. *How to Read the Bible* (Philadelphia, Universal Book and Bible House, 1946), pp. 200–201

John intentionally constructed it, in my judgment, on two literary models— *first*, as a *drama* of an original pattern (Seven Acts each consisting of Seven Scenes), but with certain features suggestive of the current Greek and Latin dramatic art with which his Christian readers in Asia Minor were familiar; and *secondly*, as a *letter* to the churches in that area, inasmuch as John could neither hope nor desire to see his drama enacted upon the stage of the Greek or Roman theatre. . . .

After the manner of the Greek and Latin dramatists from Euripides and

Plautus onward, as well as some of the Hebrew prophetic rhapsodies, one would anticipate—if the dramatic structure is maintained throughout—discovering both a Prologue and an Epilogue to John's drama.

Finally, bearing in mind the current method of presenting a drama in the Greek and Roman theatres to which many of John's erstwhile pagan readers will have been accustomed, one would expect that he would suggest the proper stage setting or stage props appropriate to the cosmic stage on which he conceived his drama as being enacted. This would, of course, lend a certain verisimilitude to the work as a whole. . . .

Once we have become convinced of the seven-times-seven-fold dramatic structure of this Apocalypse with its characteristic Prologue and Epilogue to match, it becomes intriguing to enquire whether other features of the book are in any way related to the requirements of the Graeco-Roman stage. And we are at once reminded of certain features of the book which have appeared to scholars to disrupt or disturb the sevenfold (or seven-times-seven-fold) character of the Apocalypse's structure. Such materials are found, indeed, *between every one of the Acts* as now outlined (i.e. at 1:9–20; 4:1–5:14; 8:3–5; 11:19; 15:5–8; 17:1,2; and 20:4–6) *and nowhere else!* . . .

John conceives of the cosmic stage on which is enacted the drama of the Christian theology of history (or the gospel) as assuming in general the sort of setup with which his readers would long have been familiar. For it is certainly highly significant both that these "extra" passages occurring between the Acts as now constructed contain *scenic data* all of which are taken from the furnishings of the Temple at Jerusalem and that these furnishings serve admirably to condition a stage after the Graeco-Roman pattern. . . .

John probably did not contemplate the enactment of his drama upon the stage at any time. It is not suggested here that this was his intention. Rather, our thought is that the Graeco-Roman stage suggested to him a new dramatic form in which to cast the gospel message which it was his wish to present. Bearing this consideration in mind, then, it is to be observed that John was forced, by the limitations of the literary artistry which he essayed, to develop through the single medium of descriptive phrases what on the actual stage could have been protrayed at a glance by means of scenic effects.

John Wick Bowman. Int. 9, 1955, pp. 440, 445, 448–
450

The impasse in our assessment of biblical apocalyptic . . . points to the wisdom of placing our topic in a wider context. We should study analogous texts of any period including our own and look for tools, approaches, and methods that may be carried over from contemporary literary criticism toward the illumination of the older writings. . . . Modern investigation of similar writings has refined its own sophistications, such as those bearing on the psychology of authorship, the social psychology of millenarian and utopian vision and fantasy, the phenomenology of genres in relation to views of time, and all such matters as symbol, myth, and archetype. . . .

Thus a kind of archetypal idiom is required in such a crisis of meaning. But this idiom and imagery cannot be wholly discontinuous with older categories of language and imagination. In Jewish apocalyptic we can recognize a falling back, indeed, upon pre-Israelite motifs and a generic mythology of chaos and order. But this is filtered through Israel's own archetypal mythology. . . .

The centrality of the category of "revelation" in the sense of ecstatic disclosure is evident in the term "apocalyptic". . . . All apocalyptic moves toward . . . cosmic scope and repertoire. Not only are non-human realities evoked but human issues are inseparably linked with these. . . .

The archaic and acultural character of the rhetorics is especially clear in the large role played by the nonhuman world, the imagery drawn from the inanimate order: stone, mountain, tree, fire, celestial bodies, meteorology; as well as from mythical theriology: dragon, beasts, insects. Associations with the sea, the clouds, earthquakes, eclipse, storm, and whirlwind are typical. It is in the nature of the case that cosmic transaction takes precedence over the political-historical, or that the latter is extrapolated into the former. Under various images the transaction moves through death to life, through chaos to order, and the recurrent pattern is that of war and victory, though more human models may shape the vision such as those of childbirth or of harvest.

If we have the appearance of a human figure it is in conjunction with the clouds of heaven, and this goes back to some primordial hierophany of enthronement conveying the miraculum of cosmic reversal and deliverance. . . . It would be another task to show how such utterance becomes culturized and diversified. . . . Here would be the place to discriminate the various genres and styles that have seemed especially predestined to serve this task. I would identify three language modes particularly: the vision, the dialogue, and the narrative. . . .

The dramatized vision carries over the original trans-historical and trans-subjective encounter. Angelic instruction or dream interpretation now include aspects of wisdom, mandate, paraenesis, and consolation—still in dynamic and mythological tenor—which carry the potency of the original event.

The dialogue mode, again, so recurrent a feature in our literature, dialogue between the revealer and the human medium or between cosmic powers, is again a mutation from the original encounter. In that situation there is no dialogue, only immediacy. When dialogue appears in apocalyptic writings it differs from that in prophecy. Dialogue in the Book of Revelation, for example, is different from that in the Gospel of John. The latter dialogue with all its antinomies and ironies is not charged with the same kind of numinous tension associated with the cosmic theater and the praeternatural voices and cries of the Apocalypse.

Amos N. Wilder. *Int*. 25, 1971, pp. 438, 441–442, 448–449

The unique character of the work is indisputable, but it is a mistake to consider it to be without analogy. Within the first five verses of the prologue John employs three different categories of composition in referring to his work. The first word he pens is the term 'revelation', the Greek word for which is *apocalypsis*, and this self-description of the book has given the name to the whole class of writing with which it is mostly related, namely the 'apocalypses'. In verse 3 John speaks of his work as a 'prophecy', and in verse 4 he proceeds as though he were writing an 'epistle', or letter of instruction (cf. also v. 11). John's book takes its unusual character from its combination in a unique fashion of all three of these forms. . . .

The *letter* as a form of instruction became established in Greek literature before Christian times. . . . The New Testament letters were intended to be read during services of worship (cf. Col. 4:16). The same is true of the Book of Revelation, as is evident from its introduction (1:3) and conclusion (22:6ff.), the letters to the seven churches (chs. 2–3), the hymns and songs scattered through the book, and the nature of the work as a whole.

An important corollary of this feature of the work is the relation which the book was intended to have to a group of Christian people in a known area of the world at a particular time in history. . . .

Apocalypse means revelation. . . .

As in prophecy, the great theme of apocalyptic writings was the coming of the day of the Lord and the kingdom of God. . . . Unlike prophecy, apocalyptic was literary rather than oral, composed in longer prose episodes rather than in short poetic oracles. . . .

John's adoption of the style of an apocalyptist in no way hinders him from thinking as a prophet. This appears with all clarity in the letters to the seven churches, which in content (and even style) are extraordinarily reminiscent of the prophetic oracles of the Old Testament. The doom song of chapter 18 could have been lifted out of an Old Testament prophetic writing, and indeed has been written in conscious reminiscence of similar Old Testament compositions. Apart from such obvious examples of prophetic writing, it is perhaps not unworthy of note that most of John's work, even in its highly apocalyptic passages, consists of series of prophetic-like oracles, strung together. This is immediately apparent from chapter 14, which is a group of seven little oracles, giving almost an independent view of the end of the age.

G. R. Beasley-Murray. *The Book of Revelation* (London, Marshall, Morgan & Scott, 1974), pp. 12–14, 22

The book of Revelation belongs to a category of literature known as apocalyptic writing. This genre has a number of identifying characteristics. The world of an apocalyptic work is dualistic in the sense of being clearly divided into good and evil. Apocalyptic writing is also eschatological, being primarily concerned with future events. Pseudonymity is a frequent trait, as is the presence of visions as a means of expressing the content of the work. Biblical apocalypse tends to be messianic, centering in the appearance and work of a divine Messiah. Spiritism, in the form of angels and demons, is prevalent. There is also animal symbolism and numerology (the recurrent use of certain numbers, sometimes with symbolic intent). Apocalyptic writing also tends to be judgmental, with the writer predicting woes.

> Leland Ryken, *The Literature of the Bible* (Grand Rapids, Zondervan, 1974), p. 339.

Not only may apocalyptic be distinguished by certain motifs which combine to form its general outlook, but also by several distinctive literary characteristics. Russell identifies apocalyptic as "esoteric in character, literary in form, symbolic in language and pseudonymous in authorship." . . . The content of apocalyptic normally comes to the author by means of a drama or vision in which he is translated into heavenly realms where he is privileged to see revealed the eternal secrets of God's purpose. Often an angelic interpreter is present to guide him on his heavenly journey and disclose the meaning of the extraordinary things he is seeing. . . .

Symbolism plays a major role in apocalyptic. In giving free rein to the imagination, symbols of the most bizarre sort become the norm. . . .

The book of Revelation is regularly regarded as belonging to that literary genre we have described as apocalyptic. It is the NT counterpart to the OT apocalyptic book of Daniel. There are good reasons to support this classification. The extensive use of symbolism, the vison as a major instrument of revelation, concentration on the close of this age and the dramatic inauguration of the age to come, the unveiling of spiritual order lying behind and determining the course of events in history, the use of common apocalyptic motifs—all combine to justify the application of the term apocalyptic to the book of Revelation.

> Robert H. Mounce. *The Book of Revelation* (Grand Rapids, William B. Eerdmans, 1977), pp. 20–21, 23

The term "apocalypse" is simply the Greek word for revelation. However, it is commonly used in a more restricted sense, derived from the opening verse of the book of Revelation (The Apocalypse of John) in the NT, to refer to "literary compositions which resemble the book of Revelation, i.e., secret divine disclosures about the end of the world and the heavenly state" (Koch). . . .

There is always a narrative framework in which the manner of revelation is described. This always involves an otherworldly mediator and a human recipient. . . . The content always involves both an eschatological salvation which is temporally future and present otherworldly realities. The eschatological salvation is always definitive in character and is marked by some form of personal afterlife. . . . This is seldom the only aspect of eschatological salvation: cosmic transformation is very frequently involved. . . . The spatial, otherworldly realities always involve the activity of otherworldly, angelic or demonic beings. Heavenly geography is described in detail in many apocalypses. The existence of another world beyond what is accessible to humanity by natural means is a constant element in all the apocalypses.

This common core of constant elements permits us, then, to formulate a comprehensive definition of the genre: "Apocalypse" is a genre of revelatory literature with a narrative framework, in which a revelation is mediated by an otherworldly being to a human recipient, disclosing a transcendent reality which is both temporal, insofar as it envisages eschatological salvation, and spatial insofar as it involves another, supernatural world. . . .

The key word in the definition is transcendence. The manner of revelation requires the mediation of an otherworldly being: i.e., it is not given directly to the human recipient and does not fall within the compass of human knowledge. The manner of revelation then already asserts the reality of another work, superior to our own in knowledge, even in the knowledge of human affairs and destiny. The reality of this other world is further affirmed by reference to angelic and demonic beings, and by the descriptions of heavenly geography. Human life is set in a context which is shaped by this otherworldly, supernatural dimension. Finally, the transcendent nature of apocalyptic eschatology looks beyond this world to another. The forms of salvation are diverse, exaltation to the heavens or renewal of the earth, but in all cases they involve a radically different type of human existence, in which all the constraints of the human condition, including death, are transcended.

John J. Collins. Semeia. 14, 1979, pp. 2, 9–10, 12

STRUCTURE

In modern literature we are accustomed to look for some climax or catastrophe coming near the end of a poem. In a broader survey of literature, and especially in the Bible, there is another type of poetic movement, which has its turning point in the very center of the poem. This type of poetic movement has been beautifully compared to the figure of an arch. . . . Moreover, the principle of symmetry comes in: for everything we find on the one side of the turning point, we may expect a point of correspondence on the other side. . . . In the present case, traditional interpretation, with its prepossession for revelation of the future, concentrates attention on the concluding chapters of Revelation as a storehouse of eschatological secrets. Meanwhile the real climax of the poem, to which all the rest is only accessory, it has passed over as a detail at the center.

The literary form, then, of the book may be thus summed up. Between a Prologue of the Words to the Seven Churches, and an Epilogue of the Seven Last Words, we have a succession of Seven Visions passing like dissolving views before the imagination; these Visions are built up of symbols, all echoing the symbolism of the Old Testament; and the master thought which binds the whole into a unity is to be looked for at the center and not at the close.

As we pass from the Prologue to the First Vision, heaven opens. . . . What Ezekiel had seen as a vision of movement is here beheld in the eternal splendor of repose: the Throne of Deity. . . .

But the vision becomes modified to . . . a Book sealed with Seven Seals. . . . When to the Lamb is transferred the Book of mystery, all heaven's adoration is transferred with it. . . . As . . . incense rises and fills the whole scene, the First Vision . . . dissolves away; leaving on the memory two thoughts— the Book sealed with Seven Seals, and the Lamb standing as though it had been slain. . . .

And now the Second Vision begins to loom upon the eye of the imagination, and we reach the idea of Judgment. . . . But the second vision is Judgment Potential: powers of judgment pass before us, but are not yet seen in their sphere of operation. . . .

The Third Vision breaks, and judgment begins to move forward. But at every point it is checked: this Third Vision is Judgment Imperfect. The symoblism is that of the Seven Angels with their trumpets: mystic trumpets . . . open a prophetic Day of Judgment. . . .

We thus reach the Central Vision, the keystone of the arch. As a Vision of Salvation it towers above the other Visions of Judgment. And its theme is, the Kingdom of the World becoming the Kingdom of Christ. . . .

But all that is left imperfect must be brought to completion, now that the key to all mystery has been unveiled. There is a Fifth Vision that balances the Third. The Third Vision had been Judgment Imperfect; the Fifth Vision is Judgment Consummated. For symbolism the Third Vision had the Seven Angels with their trumpets; in the Fifth Vision we have Seven Angels with their golden Bowls. . . . The Sixth Vision supplements the Second: that was Judgment Potential, this is Judgment Enthroned. . . .

The first Vision had given us the eternal repose of Deity, before the slightest ripple of mystery—mystery that craves solution—had come to disturb. The Seventh Vision gives us the peace that is on the other side of judgment. We see a new heaven and a new earth; a New Jerusalem adorned as a bride.

Richard G. Moulton. *The Bible at a Single View* (New York, Macmillan Company, 1918), pp. 62–69, 73–76

We must approach the Revelation . . . as a mighty super-opera, with three great acts, each broken into scenes of agony or beauty, and with mighty choruses and terrific bursts of the cosmic orchestra punctuating its action.

The three visions are:

I. The Roll of Destiny, chs. 4 to 11. John finds himself caught up into the presence of God, and sees him seated on his throne, holding out a scroll full of writing but tightly sealed from end to end. No one dares to approach and take the scroll from God's hands, but at length a lamb that has been slain appears and, taking the scroll, begins to break its seals. Dreadful portents attend the breaking of the seals, the angels of invasion, war, famine, and death appear, the martyrs cry to God to deliver them and there is a great earthquake. At the seventh seal, seven angels with trumpets appear, and as each one blows his blast, some fresh calamity develops. When the seventh trumpet is blown, "Loud voices were heard in heaven, saying, 'The sovereignty of the world has passed into the possession of our Lord and of his Christ, and he will reign forever and ever.' "

So the first great act in the drama ends with Christ triumphant.

II. The Dragon War, 12:1 to 19:10. In this second act, in the war between Michael and Satan, Satan has been cast down to the earth, where the conflict is renewed. The prophet looking seaward sees an animal symbolizing the empire come up out of the sea. Then as he looks toward the land he sees another animal coming down from the interior. . . . Rome appears as an adulterous woman, seated on seven hills which are also seven kings. . . . The vision ends with the renewed prediction of the triumph of the Kingdom of God. . . .

III. The New Jerusalem, 19:11 to 22:5. Mounted on a white horse, the leader of the heavenly armies, the Word of God, rides forth to victory over the empire. Satan is cast into the abyss, and the martyrs reign with Christ a thousand years. In a final battle God's people triumph, and the great spectacle of the judgment ensues. After it came the new heaven and the earth, with the New Jerusalem. God's dwelling would be with men, and he would wipe all tears from their eyes. They would live in the city of unspeakable splendor, with its street of gold, its foundations of precious stones, and its gates of pearls. A river flowed through the city, and on its banks grew the tree of life. In the city God's people would worship him, and they would see his face.

Edgar J. Goodspeed. *How to Read the Bible* (Philadelphia, Universal Book and Bible House, 1946), pp. 201–203

Certain themes emerge distinctly for the modern reader's profit:

1. The absolute sovereignty of God, and His ultimate purpose to destroy all forms of evil.

2. The inevitable judgments of God upon evil, upon the worship of false gods, which include riches, power, and success.

3. The necessity for patient endurance, the ultimate security being the knowledge that God is in control of history.

4. The existence of reality, represented here under such symbols as the New Jerusalem, apart and secure from the battles and tribulations of earthly life, promises complete spiritual security to those who are faithful to God and His Christ.

5. The glimpses of worship and adoration, constantly offered to God and the Lamb, are a kind of pattern of man's ultimate acknowledgment of the Character of God when he sees Him as He is.

> J. B. Phillips. *The Book of Revelation* (New York, Macmillan Company, 1957), p. 2

St. John follows the convention of vision; his story is presented in 'stills', thrown one after another on the screen. Not absolute 'stills'—there is some simple movement within each visionary episode; but there is no continuous flow of movement from one to another. The gaps have to be filled by an appreciation of what the transition means. . . .

We will mention one more formal procedure of St. John's—the cyclic, or repetitive. We are not told that the bowl-plagues repeat the trumpets with significant variations; we are surely meant to observe it.

> Austin Farrer. *The Revelation of St. John the Divine* (Oxford, Oxford University Press, 1964), pp. 56, 58

Though it owes little or nothing to Greek drama, the book is powerfully dramatic. The basic compositional device is simple repetition—one vision set after another. It was noted above how effective this additive method is in the Gospels in leading us to the climax of the book. The same repetitive method is used in Revelation, so much so that some readers find it tedious. It is more correct to see the interwoven repetitions as building the inexorable and rapid pace of the narrative. The method of repetition, however, has been modified in two very important respects. In the first place, a common stock of symbols links the separate visions, and the repeated appearance of these symbols gives both unity and cumulative effect to the whole. "Fire," "smoke," "incense," "star," "crown," and "white" are among the basic symbols which hold these separate units together and give cumulative force as they are used in one context after another. The interweaving of different episodes through the use of a group of symbols running through them is a distinctive trait of this book. . . .

The other technique by which the author achieves an interwoven texture is his use of numerical structure. Seven, the symbol of divine perfection, is the basic and recurring number. Numerous outlines have tried to show that the book is built on an outline of seven seven's. . . . In the outworking of the book's pattern, different numerical combinations interweave and overlap in such a way that no one outline can be taken as final.

The interweaving of visions in this numerical way, especially in the first half of the book, has the effect of combining a cyclic sense of repetition with a powerful forward thrust. The book is strongly end-oriented rather than encyclopedic in its mode of apocalyptic narrative, yet the repetitive structure enables it to communicate the same sense of involvement with the total human reality that the encyclopedic mode also tries to communicate.

The forward thrust of the narrative is counterbalanced in another way. From time to time, the historical-cosmic struggle is set aside by an "interlude," a vision of perfection beyond struggle (initially, and therefore not strictly as an interlude, in chapters 4–5, then in 7:1–17; 10:1–11; 14:1–5; 15:2–4; 19:1–10). By thus repeatedly breaking through his successive cycles of struggle, the author suggests that, for the believer, the passage of time may be momentarily stopped, as he participates in advance in the total presence toward which the action moves. This double pattern of forward movement and of anticipatory penetration beyond the forward movement, is a structural expression of the tension between longing for the future and a sense of the presence of Christ and the Spirit now newly known.

William A. Beardslee. *Literary Criticism of the New Testament* (Philadelphia, Fortress Press, 1970), pp. 59–61

The book of Revelation is the most carefully structured long work in the Bible. It does not have a unified narrative structure. In fact, as a story it is one of the most disjointed works in the Bible. The main element of structure is the vast system of contrasts that underlies the whole work. The overriding conflict is a spiritual struggle between good and evil. This results in character conflicts, scenic conflicts, and contrasting actions. . . .

A second structual principle is the recurrent use of the number seven. There are so many details in Revelation that we might well despair of finding unity and of being able to keep it in our mind as a single entity. Upon close study, however, the work turns out to have a simple and very manageable sequential structure. There is a prologue, a series of six sevenfold units, and an epilogue. . . .

The third element of structure is simply the linear sequence of visions, images, and events. There are few works of literature that have such a strong onward pressure, with the reader being propelled ever forward. The linear movement is not a smooth narrative flow from one event to the next. Instead, the sequential structure is exactly like that of modern cinema—a kaleidoscopic sequence of visions, pictures, sounds, images, and events, ever shifting and never in focus for very long. . . . Although the book as a whole lacks the

sustained movement of a single narrative, each small unit will be most easily
grasped if it is approached with the usual narrative questions as follows: (1)
What is the setting? (2) Who are the characters? (3) What action occurs? (4)
What are the consequences?

Leland Ryken. *The Literature of the Bible* (Grand Rapids, Zondervan, 1974), pp. 335–337

The book commences with a brief prologue, stating its origin and conveying
the writer's customary greeting, together with a doxology to Christ and two
prophetic sayings which announce the theme of the book. This is followed
by an account of John's vision of the risen Christ on Patmos. The passage
recalls and invites comparison with narratives in the Old Testament wherein
the prophets recount their experiences of a call to the prophetic ministry.
Characteristically the object of a prophet's vision in the new age is the risen
Christ, not God in his solitary glory. . . .

The letters to seven churches in proconsular Asia follow in chapters 2–
3. These letters are set in every case in relation to the vision described in
chapter 1, to the situation of the church addressed, and to the closing vision
of the kingdom of Christ and the city of God in chapters 20–22. . . .

As the vision of the risen Lord in chapter 1 leads into the seven letters
and is related to them, so in chapters 4–5 a vision of heaven is given which
introduces the main body of the Revelation. This vision of God and the
Lamb . . . occupies a key position in the structure of the book. It initiates
the process of events leading to the unveiling of the final kingdom (chs. 6–
19), and at the same time by the symbolism determines the series of messianic
judgments which immediately follows (the seven seals which open the book
of destiny, 6:1–8:5).

At this point a decision has to be made on how the remainder of the book
is to be construed. Are chapters 6–19 to be viewed as a continuous narration
of events leading to the parousia? Or are we to regard the three series of
messianic judgments, set forth under the symbolism of the seals, trumpets,
and cups of wrath, as parallel? The present writer is persuaded that the latter
interpretation alone accords with the evidence. . . .

The three series of judgments . . . describe under different images a single
short period in history, namely, the time of the end which precedes the coming
of Christ's kingdom. . . .

The descriptions of judgments however are themselves not allowed to
proceed without interruption. They are interspersed with episodes of varying
length, the chief intention of which is to shed light on what happens to the
Church and on the nature of her task during the great distress. . . . The longest
interruption in the flow of the visions occurs in chapters 12–14. It sets the
conflict between the Church and the state on the background of the agelong

conflict between the powers of darkness and the God of heaven, and draws a vivid picture of the kind of pressure to which the Church is subject when Caesar demands what belongs to God. . . . At last the revelation of Christ is portrayed, and all that is bound up with it in relation to his kingdom—the last judgment, the new creation, and the city of God (chs. 19–22).

An epilogue, summing up and pressing home the lessons of the book, brings the whole to a conclusion (22:6–25).

G. R. Beasley-Murray. *The Book of Revelation* (London, Marshall, Morgan & Scott, 1974), pp. 29–32

SYMBOLISM

Apocalyptic writings are characterized by the use of symbols and highly figurative language. Among writers of this type of literature there was developed an elaborate system of cryptic symbols and figures of speech for the expression of spiritual ideas. An empire was symbolized by a wild beast, as in the prophecies of Daniel, an angel by a star; men were spoken of under the figure of animals. . . .

There is a difference between picture writing and symbolic writing. . . . Symbolic writing . . . does not paint pictures. It is not pictographic but ideographic. The Indian sign of the arrow dipped in blood was not a picture but a symbol of war, just as three arrows in a tree was the symbol of an enemy. The skull and crossbones on the bottle of medicine is a symbol of poison, not a picture. . . . The fish, the lamb, and the lion are all symbols of Christ, but never to be taken as pictures of Him. In other words, the symbol is a code word and does not paint a picture. One must understand the code in order to read the symbolic writing. Jesus frequently spoke in pictures. . . .

The book of Revelation has very few pictures, but it is full of symbols. In the first chapter we have a symbolic presentation of the Church and of Jesus. . . . Here each part of the symbolism has a very definite meaning, but a picture of Christ as thus presented would be grotesque and meaningless. Throughout the book there are symbolic presentations, which even a cubist of the postimpressionistic school of art could not picture on canvas. A beautifully expressive symbol is that of a lamb sitting on a throne. As a mere picture it would be ludicrous, but as a symbol we have the grace and gentleness and tenderness of the lamb and the power and dominion of a great throne. In the twelfth chapter we read of a great red dragon, having seven heads and ten horns, and upon his head seven diadems. . . . It is not a pictorial but a symbolic description of the Devil. And so in chapter twelve the sun-clothed, star-crowned woman is not a picture but a symbol of the Church. For the most part the symbolism of the book is non-picturable. . . . The meaning of the greater part of the symbolism of Revelation is quite clear to the modern reader. . . .

Donald W. Richardson. *The Revelation of Jesus Christ: An Interpretation* (Richmond, John Knox Press, 1939, 1964), pp. 15–18

When we try strenuously to visualize the scene described by John we find many details in it which are intellectually but not pictorially comprehensible. For example, it is obvious that the living Creatures are meant to convey amongst other things the idea of God's omniscience: but it is impossible to visualize 'eyes inside and out,' or to reconstruct a Creature with a face like a man, and yet with eyes all over. Or, to take another example, one of many: much arid speculation has been lavished on such questions as the distribution of the Lamb's seven horns and seven eyes. But were they ever visualized? Did John see some weird original of that scene which the van Eycks have made immortal? One may doubt it: for how, let us ask, did a *Lamb* grasp the sealed scroll of the last days, and how did a *Lamb* break the seals which no other could break? . . . It is in fact quite impossible to visualize, and we must therefore take it that John is using a metaphor so familiar that its pictorial quality does not appear. That is by no means true of all the scenes in John's book. . . . But it is true of many; and it will be found that the quality of dreamlike inconsequence which is often attributed to Revelation, in order to explain *pictorial* inconsistencies or contradictions, is in reality an illusion of its later readers. For John uses symbols for their immediate intellectual appeal; and when their immediate lesson has been delivered they vanish, or are subtly changed to present a new aspect of what the seer has understood about heavenly mysteries.

Martin Kiddle. *The Revelation of St. John* (New York, Harper and Brothers, 1940), pp. 70–71

We are concerned not only with the form, but with the *kind* of literature in the book. It is, of course, known as apocalyptic—the revealing of things hidden. Various writers have explained the weird symbols and the use of mysterious numbers by the simple statement that it is a book of poetry. This is naive simplification. Isaiah and the Psalms are pure poetry and lovely poetry at that, but for the most part easy to understand. This book contains a very different kind of poetry. We might cull a contemporary term and call it *underground* literature. These obscure and indirect symbols were necessary for the safety both of writer and readers at a time when the church was driven underground by the Roman Gestapo. All underground literature uses this *double-entendre* method. Thus, when Sienkiewicz, in his novel, *Quo Vadis*, pictures the vices of the tyrant Rome, all Poland knew he was satirizing the tyranny of the Russian Czars, who then dominated that unhappy land. So, when this book denounces Babylon, it would not be hard for the harried Christian to understand that the author meant Rome. The present writer has been told that when the Nazis occupied Paris, one of the theaters made a smash hit by reviving the old Greek drama in which Aristophanes satirized the tyrant Cleon. While the Nazi officers sat dumbly in the boxes, the audience roared its applause, as night after night the Greek patriots hurled defiance at the tyrant. So, the terrific invective against Babylon in the eighteenth chapter of the Revelation would be read and understood as God's judgment on a tyrant Caesar.

In this system of code symbols, we would expect to find, and do find, the use of code numbers. Probably only the contemporary reader could know the full significance of numbers in the Revelation. It seems quite obvious and extremely crucial for interpreters that these numbers were not mathematical but symbolical; that they were not measures of quantity or duration, but of quality and of ideas. . . . Some of these symbolical meanings are obvious enough. Three and seven and ten and twelve—and their multiples—were good numbers signifying in general, perfection, completeness, fulfillment, victory. Six apparently paralleled our superstitious modern use of thirteen. It was a sinister number. It corresponded to the New Testament word for sin, *hamartia*—"missing the mark." It approaches seven, but falls fatally short. What of three and one-half? We have seen that the turning point and climax of the seven visions was at three and one-half. "Time and times and half a time" equal three and a half. The two witnesses preached three and a half years. The outer courts of the church were trampled by the ungodly three and a half years. The saints were persecuted forty-two months—three and a half years. The church was in the wilderness twelve hundred and sixty days— three and a half years. Apparently the number stood for incompleteness, for the temporary reign of evil, but always with the assurance that it was *only temporary*.

Charles F. Wishart. *Int.* 1, 1947, pp. 459–460

[In the vision of Christ in Chapter 1], we may substitute for the white hair the terms: venerable age, dignity, purity, holiness. Or we may say that the flashing eyes express divine omniscience. There is genuine danger of distortion, however, in turning picture-language into more abstract concepts. . . .

Dangers of another sort may be seen in the famous block prints of Revelation made by A. Durer. . . . With great care for detail, Durer presents in this picture the Christ whom John describes. The face literally shines with rays like the sun, the hand holds seven stars, and the sword is emerging from the mouth. Yet Durer's effort to visualize a single figure with all the details mentioned by the prophet adds up to a bizarre ensemble indeed. One must say that, when John's description is turned into a visual replica, it shatters into fragments. The picture conveys neither the prophet's feelings nor his concerns. We can safely assert that John did not intend that his readers try to transfer his words into a single visual collage. . . .

The whole of John's book consists of visions of "heavenly things." In each of the visions he tells of seeing a series of events taking place in heaven. Everything which transpires on earth is first seen as happening in heaven. But the locale of the action does not affect the integrity of the vision or the reality of the event. He does not shuttle back and forth between an imagined heaven and a real earth, but everything he says is equally real and equally vsionary. He remains consistent in maintaining the integrity of the visions as visions. . . .

It would be wrong, therefore, to attribute a non-visionary substantiality to the various objects which John saw in heaven. When he speaks of the first heaven and earth he is not . . . writing as a historian or a sociologist, let alone an astronomer or a physicist. Nor does he do so when he tells of the descent of the new heaven and earth, for these two "creations" were interacting aspects of the same vision. Yet if we can analyze the interior logic of that vision, we may be able to make more sense of his treatment of those phenomena which we call space and time.

Paul S. Minear. *I Saw a New Earth* (Washington, Corpus Books, 1968), pp. 30–31, 270

The closest modern parallel to this mode of communication is the political cartoon, which has gained an established place in the popular press all over the world. The purpose of a cartoon is to embody a message relating to a contemporary situation, whether it be of local, national, or international import. Many of the symbols employed by cartoonists are stereotyped. Some of their representative figures are human (like John Bull and Uncle Sam), others are animal (e.g., the lion for Britain, the bear for Russia, the eagle for USA), and occasionally the animals are given human faces, identifying leaders of the nations in their representative actions. Frequently the situations depicted are deliberately exaggerated, and even made grotesque, in order that the message may be made plain. But no one complains of that. . . . Now it would be overpressing the parallel to suggest that the apocalyptists were religious cartoonists, for much of their writing is not in picture form. But it would not be misleading to compare their works with writings frequently illustrated by drawings, and at times containing whole chapters of strip cartoon. . . .

It is important to observe that the symbols by which the contemporary political forces and the spiritual powers of heaven and hell are portrayed were as traditional as Britannia and the British lion, the Russian bear, and the Chinese dragon. . . . The earliest readers of the book will have recognized the caricature immediately, and approved of the judgment thereby implied as to the nature of the tyrannical empire of their day and its impending doom from the God of heaven. This is the source of the portrayals of the antichristian empire and ruler in the book of Revelation.

> G. R. Beasley-Murray. *The Book of Revelation* (London, Marshall, Morgan & Scott, 1974), pp. 16–17

The book of Revelation is the most archetypal piece of literature in the Bible. One notices at once the presence of terms and images that name the elemental, universal aspects of human experience—life, death, blood, lamb, dragon, beast, light, darkness, earth, heaven, water, sea, sun, war, harvest, white, scarlet, bride, throne, jewels, and gold. There are many references to rising, usually associated with spiritual goodness, and falling, associated with spiritual evil. Heaven is high and light, while the bottomless pit is low and dark. There are also several archetypal plot patterns. The last half of the book (chapters 12–22) is a spiritualized version of several common fairy tale motifs, including a lady in distress who is marvelously delivered, a hero who kills a dragon, a wicked witch who is finally exposed, the marriage of the triumphant hero to his bride, the celebration of the wedding with a feast, and the description of a palace glittering with jewels in which the hero and his bride live happily ever after. . . .

The work also makes use of two timeless and popular literary devices—animal characters and color symbolism. The first convention is readily apparent in the presence of "living creatures" around the throne in heaven, the divine Lamb, horses of various colors, locusts, a dragon, and terrifying "beasts" from the sea and earth. Color symbolism is less prevalent but still noteworthy. The color white is associated with Christ (1:14), the saints of God (3:18; 4:4; 7:9; 14; 19:8), the armies of heaven (19:14), and God's throne of judgment (20:11). Red, by contrast, appears in contexts of evil—warfare (6:4), the appearance of the satanic dragon (12:3), and the whore of Babylon and her beast (17:3–4).

> Leland Ryken, *The Literature of the Bible* (Grand Rapids, Zondervan, 1974), pp. 338–339

The portrait [in chapter 1], obviously of Jesus Christ, is the first of four major portraits of Christ in Revelation which, augmented by numerous allusions, especially in the songs throughout the narrative, will produce for us a very full portrait by the end of the book. This first portrait . . . emphasizes Christ's hair, eyes, feet, and voice. The hair, he tells us, is white as wool, white as snow. The connotations we have for whiteness, presumably shared by John, help characterize Christ—he is pure, innocent, perhaps old in some sense. . . . John has noted his details carefully. Our initial impressions of the figure before him involve whiteness and redness, snow and fire. We recognize the paradoxical nature of the figure—he seems innocent (white), yet passionate (red), cool (snow), yet hot (fire). . . . His feet, John tells us, are like burnished

bronze. Several details might spark our imaginations. We may think of feet
trampling on something, as Christ will soon trample on the dragon and the
beast and the false prophet. . . . More striking about the description as a
whole is the fact that what seem to be carefully stated details are not specific
at all. The figure before John cannot, finally, be described except in a series
of similes: he is *like* a son of man, his hair is white *as* wool and snow, his
eyes flame *like* fire, his feet are *like* burnished bronze, his voice is *like* the
sound of many waters. John *sees* and *hears* someone, but language can only
approximate his appearance. The sight is inexpressible, as the New Jerusalem
at the end of Revelation will be inexpressible.

> Kenneth R. R. Gros Louis. *Literary Interpretations of
> Biblical Narratives* (Nashville, Abingdon Press, 1974),
> pp. 333–335

STYLE

When one considers these descriptions of Heaven and of the Almighty carefully and tries to visualize what is described, one sees that there is no real
hold on concrete and present fact: all that most touches one's imagination
resolves itself into a vague blaze of glory which defies every effort to distinguish its outlines. Even the great Italian painters failed when they put such
descriptions as these into visual form. . . . Though the descriptions seem so
specific, yet it is impossible to visualize them. The picture of the New Jerusalem, which is seemingly phrased in terms of sight, cannot be put together. . . . No effort to make a mental picture of these splendors will leave
any definite impression: the effect is only of an overwhelming glory and of
a blessedness which passes man's understanding. In spite of the fact that the
imagery is material, the effect is wholly immaterial and ideal.

In this power of the prophecies and the apocalypse to communicate the
sense of glories which are real, and yet impalpable, to give us a fleeting
glimpse of unseen realities beyond the apprehension of our present faculties,
we come, I think, to the inner essence and power of this biblical literature
of which the prophecy and the apocalypse are the most typical portion. When
one thinks of the serenity of the Greek representations of the gods beside
these visions of the Hebrew and Christian seers, the latter at first may seem
confused and turgid. Then as one thinks it over the very clarity and definiteness
of outline in those wonderful marbles stand out as a limitation: in comparison
with these vague and mystical imaginings of the Christian seers the representations of Greek art are impotent. In the end the Greek statue of a god,
for all its gracious beauty, is only a glorified and idealized man. The visions
of the apocalypse, on the other hand, transcend once for all the limitations
of human nature. . . . Thus even in literature one feels that the prohibition,
''Thou shalt not make unto thee any graven image, or any likeness of anything

that is in heaven above or that is in the earth beneath, or that is in the water under the earth,'' produced unique results; for the Jewish mind and the Christian mind have never limited the godhead to visible form.

J. H. Gardiner. The Bible as English Literature (New York, Charles Scribner's Sons, 1906), pp. 270–273

The content of the book is found to be a succession of visions which pass like dissolving views before the eye of the imagination. Our imagination must fully grasp these visions before the work of the interpreter can begin. . . .

Here we have an elaborate poem built up out of symbolic details. On examination, no one of these symbolic details is new; they are all echoes of Old Testament symbolism. We recognize the important principle of literary echoing, which pervaded poetry from the age of Homer to the age of Milton. . . . The reader . . . must turn to the Old Testament, and be prepared to see an old thought in a new adaptation.

Richard G. Moulton. The Bible at a Single View (New York, Macmillan Company, 1918), pp. 60–62

Of the New Testament there is very little equal to the Old in literary value; indeed, I should recommend the reading only of the closing book—the book called the Revelation, or the Apocalypse, from which we have derived a literary adjective ''apocalyptic,'' to describe something at once very terrible and very grand. Whether one understands the meaning of this mysterious text makes very little difference; the sonority and the beauty of its sentences, together with the tremendous character of its imagery, can not but powerfully influence mind and ear, and thus stimulate literary taste. At least two of the great prose writers of the nineteenth century, Carlyle and Ruskin, have been vividly influenced by the book of Revelation.

Lafcadio Hearn. Books and Habits (New York, Dodd, Mead and Company, 1921), p. 105

A 'mystery' was once something which was intended to proclaim a meaning beyond the power of literal expression: to-day, a mystery is something which withholds its meaning. Now, John actually *thought* in pictures. It was not that he conceived an idea as an abstraction, and then sought a convenient and traditional symbol to render it more vivid. It was probably in the shape of a symbol that an idea came into his mind, and it was certainly in this way that he was able to communicate it to his fellows. . . . His visionary mind moved about in regions where *omnipotence* was recognized in a throne, where *omniscience* was indicated by innumerable eyes, where the very impulse to worship and pray found emblems in harps and bowls of incense. We find such a manner of thinking and speaking magnificent but sometimes obscure.

Martin Kiddle. The Revelation of St. John (New York, Harper and Brothers, 1940), pp. 68–69

Apart from the direct religious value of the Scriptures, they may also enter into the category of books which, by their literary greatness, profoundly modify a writer's mind, or style, or both. And by "literary greatness" I mean not simply beauty of external form, but the whole content and soul of the book, approached from the literary rather than the moral and dogmatic side. In the one case you read to be taught, in the other you are taught, often insensibly, through the book's appeal to the sensitive side of your nature. . . . As a child I read [the Bible], but for its historical interest. Nevertheless, even then I was greatly, though vaguely, impressed by the mysterious imagery, the cloudy grandeurs, of the *Apocalypse*. Deeply uncomprehended, it was, of course, the pageantry of an appalling dream: insurgent darkness, with wild lights flashing through it; terrible phantasms, insupportably revealed against profound light, and in a moment no more; on the earth hurryings to and fro, like insects of the hearth at a sudden candle; unknown voices uttering out of darkness darkened and disastrous speech; and all this in motion and turmoil like the sands of a fretted pool. Such is the *Apocalypse* as it inscribes itself on the verges of my childish memories. In early youth it again drew me to itself, giving to my mind a permanent and shaping direction.

Francis Thompson. *Literary Criticisms* (New York, E.P. Dutton, 1948), pp. 542–543

The differences of style and composition between the various books of the New Testament are completely hidden for most English readers by the overall majesty of the King James Version. . . . But when one is confronted with the language of Revelation it is no mere difference of style which makes one gasp, but crudities, grammatical errors, and a quite extraordinary juxtaposition of words. . . . Revelation piles word upon word remorselessly, mixes cases and tenses without apparent scruple, and shows at times a complete disregard for normal syntax and grammar. . . .

The tumultuous assault of words is not without its effect upon the mind. . . . The inspired words seem to me to pour forth in a stream both uninhibited and uncorrected, and I therefore find it impossible to agree with those who say that this work is either a revision of an earlier one or a combination of several such works. The writer's mind was plainly steeped in the spirit and in the knowledge of Jewish apocalyptic. There is hardly a single direct quotation form the Old Testament, but there are scores of parallels, echoes, and recollections of it. . . . I make therefore this bold suggestion: the writer, who had a genuine ecstatic experience, wrote down what he saw *during the visions*. The intense emotion of being, as it were, "in the heavenlies," the excitement of seeing what is normally invisible to human eyes, and the frustration of having to use human words to describe what is beyond human expression would, it seems to me, fully account for the incoherence, the strange formation of sentences, the repetition, and the odd juxtaposition of words. If we suppose this to be true, and if we suppose also that the writer were wholly convinced that what he had written was in fact written while "in the spirit," then we can reasonably imagine that he would shrink from correction or revision lest he distort or modify the revelation he had been given.

I feel I must record that, once one has absorbed the initial shock of the peculiar Greek, the effect of the language of this book is most powerful. The crowns, the thrones, the gold, the jewels, the colors, the trumpets, the violence of action and the impact of incredible numbers and awe-inspiring size—all these images stir that threshold of the brain where monsters lurk and supernatural glories blaze. John is stirring with a kind of surrealistic artistry the vastnesses of our unconscious minds. The book is probably an impossibility for the pictorial illustrator, but the figures created in the mind are vivid and powerful enough to transport us to another spiritual dimension. . . . The poetic impact of the book carries us away to a realm where the pedestrian rules of grammar no longer apply—we are dealing with celestial poetry and not with earthly prose. To be literal-minded and studiously analytical in such a work is to kill its poetic truth. Dissection is not infrequently the death of beauty.

> J. B. Phillips. *The Book of Revelation* (New York, Macmillan Company, 1957), pp. x–xiii

Revelation is a superb piece of literature. The pictorial imagination of its author is unsurpassed even by that of Isaiah, Dante, or Blake. Its careful construction—shown especially in its three series of "woes," each followed by a brief passage of rejoicing—prove its author a master of architectonics. It never lags, but builds to a resounding climax in Chapters 12–14, and ends in a triumphant denouement. Its ability to inspire other creators of literature and the arts is attested by such works as Dante's *Divine Comedy*, Milton's *Paradise Lost*, Bunyan's *Pilgrim's Progress*, Van Eyck's "Adoration of the Lamb," Michelangelo's "Last Judgment," Tintoretto's "Paradiso," and Holman Hunt's "Light of the World." It is not too enthusiastic to say that the book of Revelation is the imaginative masterpiece of the New Testament.

> Buckner B. Trawick. *The Bible as Literature: The New Testament* (New York, Barnes and Noble, 1964, 1968), p. 147

The methods of the writer owe little to the literary techniques of sophisticated Hellenistic culture. The book is consciously Hebraic in style. . . . The Old Testament is the great source of the author's symbolism, though he combines and revises the Old Testament symbols with so great a freedom that he almost never quotes it directly. The "invented" nature of the literary pattern is also shown by the character of the language. In general the New Testament is not favourable to a special religious language, a "sacred language." The Book of Revelation, however, approximates such a special diction, a special artistic language. It does so by imposing Hebrew or Aramaic language patterns on Greek in such a way as to produce what has been called the most sustained body of violation of the rules of Greek grammar that exists anywhere. These are not mere violations of ignorance, although it is a difficult question how much ignorance is involved. The intention, brilliantly successful, is to produce a hieratic speech, a language appropriate to a renewal of prophecy.

William A. Beardslee. *Literary Criticism of the New Testament* (Philadelphia, Fortress Press, 1970), pp. 58–59

NEW JERUSALEM AND FINAL VISIONS

The end reproduces the beginning: as at the startingpoint "he that overcometh" was the only hero, so he alone reappears at the goal. At the outset, however, temptation after temptation, snare after snare, each having special features, was enumerated: and one soldier and servant was summoned to face, despise, triumph over one form of evil; whilst another was summoned to oppose and conquer a diverse foe. . . . Now on the contrary at the beatific consummation when the King deigns to be glorified in His saints and admired in all them that believe, "he that overcometh" is rewarded without measure: he inherits not one thing, not many things, but even "all things." . . .

As from Pisgah Moses beheld the Holy Land, so now from this mountain St. John the Holy City. . . . The unearthly mountain of vision becomes as a watch-tower of hope, a threshold of possession, because the holy city descends to appease desire. . . .

"The Bride" appears not under the semblance of a woman, but as a "great city" beautiful for situation, the joy of the whole earth, the city of the Great King: thus repelling mortal frailty from any sensual, equivocal, unworthy image of transcendent spiritual truths which demand purged hearts for their contemplation, purged lips for their utterance.

Not Holy Jerusalem but obscene Babylon flaunts forth under the figure of a woman. . . .

That New Jerusalem has a wall expresses to me a local, distinct, defined heaven . . . ; not indiscriminate as were the waters before the formation of a firmament, nor without form like void chaos; but a genuine home, with recognizable features and amiabilities of a home meet for those who have weaned themselves from earth on the promise and faith of heaven. . . .

Indeed all through the Book of Revelation lessons enforcing what we must or must not do or be, are as clear and as definite as in the rest of Holy Writ. . . .

To study the Apocalypse out of idle curiosity would turn it, so far as the student's self were concerned, into a branch of the Tree of the Knowledge of Good and Evil. . . .

Every ending includes a solemn element: the ending of God's Revelation to humankind is solemn indeed. Every ending, winding up, cutting short, foreshadows the ending, winding up, cutting short of life and of probation.

The reiterations of the Apocalypse emphasize this finality, this note of preparation.

Christina G. Rossetti. *The Face of the Deep* (London, S.P.C.K., 1893), pp. 491–492, 496–498, 531, 534

Hints for the description are taken from some verses of real poetry in Isiah, and from the last eight chapters of Ezekiel. Three tedious chapters of measurements of Ezekiel are condensed to three verses in Revelation. The kernel is extracted, and the chief idea seized, which is that the city *has perfect proportions*, 'lieth *foursquare*'. The city must also have *perfect safety*, so we have the symbol of the *high wall*. It must be *easily approached* from all parts, and this is symbolized by the three gates on each side, always open. . . . The city must also have *beauty*. So its foundations are *jewels*, its gates *pearl*, and its streets *gold*, for the Oriental loves precious stones and is sensitive to colour.

But, as always, *light* is the highest possible symbol of the divine and spiritual, for light is life. So the city is to be one of radiant light, filled with the presence and glory of God. No temple is required, because the whole city is a temple, God everywhere, not localized.

P. C. Sands. *Literary Genius of the New Testament* (Oxford, Oxford University Press, 1932), pp. 200–201

In this closing vision we have set before us the Church Triumphant, perfected, glorified, and the new heaven and the new earth that follow. . . . Here we have the final issue of the conflict; and here we pass from time into eternity. . . .

First John sees a new heaven and a new earth. . . .

The beauty and wonder of John's words fall upon our ears like soft and entrancing music from some faraway glory world (21:1–4). . . . When we are told that there shall be no more sea, of course the words are intended to be interpreted symbolically; for there could be no fruitful and beautiful earth without the sea. The sea is the symbol of separation, of isolation, and of unrest. The sea represents the stormy and turbulent realm out of which the terrible persecuting beast rose. . . . It was that which Matthew Arnold visioned as "the unplumbed, salt, estranging sea." . . .

In that new world God dwells with men in the holy city. . . .

In the verses that follow, 21:9–22:5, we have the symbolic description of the Holy City. . . .

The security of the city is symbolized by the wall, great and high, which surrounds it: it is a strong city, spacious, beautiful, and glorious. An easy entrance into it is provided by the twelve gates, three on each side. Twelve

angels stand as guardians of the gates, but not to bar the way as in Eden. . . .
The measurement of the city was a guarantee of its preservation; and no
significance is to be attached to the literal numbers of its dimensions. In form
it was a perfect cube, expressive of symmetry and harmony. To the ancient
mind the cube suggested perfection. The precious stones and gold of verses
eighteen to twenty-one suggest the ideas of beauty and richness and splendor,
and stand of course for spiritual realities. . . .

In the final section of this vision (22:1–5) John turns our thoughts from
the wonderful structure of the city to the blessedness of the life of its inhab-
itants. In the book of Genesis we have Paradise Lost; and here at the close
of the Bible we have a picture of Paradise Regained. The first paradise was
the garden of Eden; and here in the final paradise we have the picture of a
garden in a city. The heavenly world is pictured as a city because redeemed
humanity will constitute a community, a society, a Church. All that man
lost—and more—will be completely regained in the paradise which John
saw. . . .

The occupation of the citizens of the Holy City is sketched in a final word
(22:3–5). Service is the highest type and condition of life, either here or
hereafter; and the life of heaven will be a life of service. Heaven is not a
silent place, but a place of song. It is not an idle place of placid repose, but
a place of service. . . .

Revelation begins with the power and glory of God. It carries us in parallel
visions through the sin and sorrow, the death and darkness, of many inter-
vening centuries; and brings us out at last into the radiance of the eternal
morning of the new world: and there shall be no night there.

Donald W. Richardson. *The Revelation of Jesus Christ:
An Introduction* (Richmond, John Knox Press, 1939,
1964), pp. 130–140

It is not easy to speak of these ultimate things. They are almost beyond human
imagination, as they are beyond human experience. . . . John's attempt to
depict the new order is, however, extremely successful. He does not, on the
one hand, prsent us with a mere list of abstractions; his symbols give the
imagination something to grasp and treasure. And on the other hand, the
abstraction embodied in the symbol is conveyed with striking clarity. . . .

It is not only by the absence of grief and pain and death that John sketches
the blessings of the reign of God; the absence of accursed things is matched
by a glorious fulfilment of everything that is good in human life, a positive
bliss symbolized in the appearance of the holy City, the new Jerusalem, all
ready like a bride arrayed for her husband. Both of these metaphors, that of
the Bride and that of the City represent the company of the loyal in their final
state of bliss. . . .

His vision is of the City, the holy Jerusalem—a city which comes from

God out of heaven; a city which wears a brightness of a different sort from that of earthly cities, no reflected brilliance, but the very glory of God. From the first we perceive that John wishes to describe the intangible rather than the tangible; the glory of God is more than a pictorial term; it is an indication of God's active and indwelling presence, something to do with the very intensity of His being. . . .

Much is obviously symbolical; but the interpretations put on John's symbols are sometimes over-ingenious or eccentric. Yet other features seem to win their place for their poetical effect. Others, again, it is often said, are included out of regard for tradition. . . .

The wall is a *sign* written in visionary skies . . . , standing principally for limits within which the believer will be eternally safe. . . .

The measurement of the City is more obviously symbolical than some of the incidental details. . . . First, the City is foursquare. The square was a Hellenic symbol of perfection; but we have only to recall Ezekiel's picture of the holy City to understand how John had merely to utter these words, the City lies foursquare to convey the notion of divinely wrought perfection. Hellenic and Semitic symbols here tell the sme story. . . .

The City reaches heaven. The new heaven and the new earth are one. God does not dwell apart in heaven, but among men; so that the distinction between heaven and earth has lost its point. The height of the City is not a matter of elevated buildings, but of the marriage of earth and heaven, of God and man, of the new order on earth with hosts of heaven. . . .

The precious stones and gold, clear as crystal, out of which the City is composed are obviously intended to convey the splendour of the new order, to fashion out a picture of sparkling beauty, emblematic of a perfection beyond the power of thought. . . .

The materials of the new Jerusalem, like its measurements, form a picture of a place of transcendent beauty, an absolute beauty, which nothing can rival. It is a place which will form a fitting dwelling for God; or rather, less a place than a community amongst which God may fitly dwell. . . . John claims for the whole of the new Jerusalem that absolute holiness which the temple represented. God dwells among men.

Martin Kiddle. *The Revelation of St. John* (New York, Harper and Brothers, 1940), pp. 412–413, 424, 427–429, 431, 435–436

Throughout the New Testament, there is a vision of the conclusion of all history. . . .

This confident expectation pervades the New Testament, and may be seen repeatedly in its various books. It reaches its final expression at the end of the last New Testament book, the Apocalypse, or Book of Revelation. . . . Here we see the burning lake of perdition, a description which is drawn directly from the garbage pit in the Valley of Hinnom or Gehenna where the city of Jerusalem burned its refuse and useless waste. The symbolism is apt and easily understood: sin and evil will be as utterly destroyed as refuse. This, we are told, is "the second death." Then above the starkly described smoking dump in the valley is a great and high mountain—an obvious allusion to the Mount Zion where Jerusalem stood above the valley of Hinnom. But what appears now is not the old Jerusalem, with its many defections, but "the holy Jerusalem descending out of heaven from God." Continuity is observed in the relationships, but a radically new community is now called into being. Here in the final culmination, man and society are perfectly established in community with and under God. This perfection is conveyed through rich and luxuriant symbols of dimensions, design, and decoration. We are not much accustomed, in the twentieth century, to such symbolic opulence, and it may strike some readers at first as too "oriental" or even baroque, but it is utterly magnificent. The quality of its richness is set in sharp contrast—and I think purposely so—with the stark simplicity of the opening verses of the Bible. The purpose of the contrast is to indicate that here men will find completion in the most ultimate sense of which their imagination is now capable and of which their purified personalities will eventually become capable. With this vision of the establishment of faithful men within a community of the life everlasting under God, the Biblical epic comes to its incomparable close.

> Roland M. Frye. "Introduction," *The Bible: Selections from the King James Version for Study as Literature* (Boston, Houghton Mifflin, 1965; rpt. Princeton University Press, 1977), pp. xxiv–xxv

As we have come to expect from the Bible, terrors and conflicts do not have the last word. Conflict comes to a conclusion in the visions of 19:11–20:15. . . .

That consummation brings to an end biblical narrative, which began in the freshly created Garden of Eden. Viewed as a diachronic line, the biblical story takes a circuitous route from the Garden in Genesis to the descent of the heavenly Jerusalem, passing through various mythic patterns and modulating through different keys: cosmogonies, heroic quests and ordeals, tribal epics, theophanic encounters, rites of passage, royal/messianic births, Savior mythology, and apocalyptic visions. From another point of view, the narrative line in the Bible is repetitive, with different people walking in the footsteps of those who went before. From that point of view the end in Revelation is familiar to us. We have met it many times before: in the Garden, at Sinai, at Jerusalem, and in crucifixion/resurrection of Jesus. We are led once again, for the last time, to the center.

> Leonard L. Thompson. *Introducing Biblical Literature: A More Fantastic Country* (Englewood Cliffs, Prentice-Hall, 1978), pp. 303–304

SATIRE

No one questions that Jesus was a master of ironical speech. "Many good works have I showed you from my Father; for which of these do you stone me?" he asks of his enemies. "When thou doest thine alms, do not sound a trumpet before thee, as the hypocrites do in the synagogues and in the streets," he admonishes his disciples. Though the scholars tell us that there is no proof that the Pharisees ever did such a ludicrous thing, yet the spirit of it endures to our time, and derision is the only effective method of discouraging it. The parable of the unjust steward is a masterpiece of satire. When Jesus compares his generation to children playing feast and funeral, and complaining of one another, "We have piped unto you, and ye have not danced; we have mourned unto you, and ye have not wept," his criticism must have brought a smile to the faces of those who heard him.

George P. Eckman. *The Literary Primacy of the Bible* (New York, Methodist Book Concern, 1915), pp. 117–118

[In Luke 11:33–44 Luke uses] anti-Pharisaical material from Matthew 23. In verses 37 and 38 he characteristically provides a setting in life to relieve the long stretch of teaching with a touch of narrative. It is one of his favourite scenes, the dinner table. He adapts Matthew's version to make it clearer that the outside and inside of human life is the issue here rather than matters of ritual. God is concerned with content. . . .

The rest of the passage is in the form of three curses on the Pharisees which, together with the subsequent three curses on the lawyers, are adapted from Matthew's seven curses in chapter 23. The first attacks their obsession with detail to the exclusion of what really matters; *justice* and (Luke's addition) *the love of God*. The second is aimed at their ridiculous self-importance and hunger for popular recognition, a perennial ecclesiastical vice. The third brings in a macabre note: having to do with such people is like walking over an unmarked grave, coming near death and defilement without knowing it. . . .

[In Luke 11:45–54] the moral authorities and guardians come in for three curses, none of which is out of date. The rigorousness which comes easily to the respectable and timid but falls hard on the others, the reverence paid by the establishment to characters it would never have tolerated in their lifetime, the dog-in-the-manger attitude of those who have excluded themselves from real life: all these are familiar enough.

John Drury. Luke (New York, Macmillan Publishing
Company, 1973), pp. 129–131

The satiric discourses of Jesus illustrate both the sophisticated and informal kinds of satire. The sophisticated satire appears in Jesus' satiric parables. Here we find a carefully designed story, presumably fictional, in which the satiric attack is embodied. The satirist is not only the one who denounces but also the one who makes a literary object.

In the parable of the rich fool (Luke 12:13–21), for example, Jesus tells a fictional story about a farmer to make an attack on a generalized moral category—covetous greed for material things. . . .

The parable of the rich man and Lazarus (Luke 16:19–31) is occasional in nature. After Jesus had warned that people "cannot serve God and mammon" (vs. 13), the Pharisees, "who were lovers of money, heard all this, and they scoffed at him" (vs. 14). In reply, Jesus attacked their love of money in a satiric parable involving two characters. . . .

The parable of the Pharisee and tax collector (Luke 18:9–14) is another attack on a historical particular, this time the self-righteousness of the Pharisees. Jesus repeats the technique of using a story involving two characters, one a satiric norm and the other a villain. . . .

For an example of Christ's use of informal satire, the best known passage is Matthew 23, a discourse in which Jesus lashes out against the Pharisees. . . . The object of attack is the gap between the Pharisees' doctrine and practice, as Jesus makes clear at the outset (vss. 2–3). What follows is a very loosely structured series of attacks on the practices of the Pharisees. There is no carefully designed literary object, as in the parables. In verses 5–7 Jesus simply narrates or describes customary vices of the Pharisees, following His narrative with an explanation of the norm by which their actions are blameworthy (vss. 8–11). Beginning with verse 13, Jesus pronounces a series of woes against the Pharisees. The "woe formula" is a standard device in informal satire. Jesus uses satiric exaggeration, as when He pictures the Pharisees "straining out a gnat and swallowing a camel" (Matt. 23:24). He also uses vivid metaphor, claiming that the Pharisees "are like whitewashed tombs, which outwardly appear beautiful, but within they are full of dead men's bones and all uncleanness" (vs. 27). Elsewhere Christ uses direct personal attack: "You serpents, you brood of vipers, how are you to escape being sentenced to hell?" (vs. 33). Corresponding to this random sequence of satiric devices is the constantly shifting objects of attack, which include the Pharisees' religious ostentatiousness (vss. 5–7), unbiblical distinctions regarding oaths (vss. 16–19), neglect of the important moral issues (vss. 23–24), hypocrisy (throughout the discourse), and hostility to God's prophets (vss. 29–36).

Leland Ryken. *The Literature of the Bible* (Grand Rapids, Zondervan, 1974), pp. 263–265

There are . . . a number of helpful ways to approach the Jesus-Pharisees controversy; one such approach is to study part of the polemic as satire. . . . Among the elements of satire are the following: satire exposes and points out foible or error or incongruity; it does so in a playful, witty, or humorous manner; it often involves ridicule of the "target"; it makes use of a number of techniques, of which irony and exaggeration are the most common; it aims at the correction of mankind. Satire may either encompass a complete work, such as Voltaire's *Candide*, or it may be an occasional aspect of a work, as in Dickens' novels. . . .

I have limited my analysis to Matthew, but much of the analysis can be applied to the other gospels as well. . . .

At least one expression for Jesus seems to shade from irony into sarcasm. In castigating them for not discerning true prophets, Jesus links the Pharisees with those forefathers who murdered the prophets and then adds sardonically: "Fill up, then, the measure of your fathers," that is, "Go ahead, and do them one better" (23:33).

The satirist sometimes makes a point simply by placing two items next to each other to demonstrate an incongruity. . . . Incongruity is accentuated in 23:23, where mint, dill, and cumin are placed next to law, justice, mercy and faith. Here again, the juxtaposing of the minute and the awesome, the trivia and the abiding principle, is intended to exhibit the ludicrousness of the Pharisees' preoccupation.

Some commentators see the dill and cumin comments as one example of the unfairness of Jesus' portrayal of the Pharisees, since they did not really tithe these herbs. . . . But if one discerns Jesus' polemic as partly satiric, then unfair is not the most appropriate designation. Satire nearly always exaggerates by highlighting certain features or by speaking in hyperbole, and the satirist is usually aware of his exaggeration. Thus "satiric hyperbole for polemic effect" would be a more appropriate evaluation.

Another example of hyperbole is the "sounding of the trumpet" to announce almsgiving (6:2); certainly one need not ferret a citation out of Rabbinic literature to see if this were actual practice! The Pharisees traversing land and sea to gain a convert (23:15) is in the same mode. The superb "straining out a gnat and swallowing a camel" (23:24) is, of course, the best known and most effective piece of hyperbole, and, one expects, provoked chuckles in the audience. . . .

Ch. 23, the culmination of the denunciation of the Pharisees, has a number of metaphorical expressions aimed at exposing the Pharisees. They are charged with placing heavy burdens on men's shoulders (4), or being blind guides and fools (16, 17, 19, 24), whitewashed tombs (27), and a brood of vipers (33). And the literal cleaning of cup and plate is transmuted into a metaphor for human rectitude. . . .

We find Jesus' parables an effective satiric device. A series of linked parables all serve as indictments of the Jewish leaders. The parable of the two sons (22:28–32) appears directed against the chief priests and elders. The double parable of the vineyard and tenants and of the rejected stone (21:33–42) is specifically aimed at the chief priest and Pharisees. . . . So, too, the succeeding parable of the marriage feast (22:1–14) is followed by the Pharisees' attempt to ensnare Jesus. . . .

If one end of the satiric spectrum presents gentle irony, then the other end is invective and name-calling. The "blind guides" and "blind fools" of Ch. 23 are probably in this category, and even more so the "brood of vipers" (also in 12:34) and the "whited sepulchres." . . . The repeated use of the epithet "hypocrite" is also invective.

Harry Boonstra. C & L. 29, no. 4, 1980, pp. 32, 38–42

PARABLE OF THE SOWER

The parable describes the results of any sowing. Some of the seed falls on the hard field-path and is eaten by birds. Some falls on places, characteristic of the cornlands of Galilee, where rock lies near the surface, and here it germinates rapidly in the shallow soil only to be scorched up at once by the sun. And because however carefully the farmer may clean his land, seeds and roots will remain in the earth, some falls among "thorns"—the prickly, thorny weeds of Palestine—to grow indeed, but only to be choked eventually by its more vigorous neighbours. Such losses are incidental to every sowing. There is always the other seed . . . which falls on fertile ground and yields a harvest which makes all talk of loss in sowing meaningless. It will be noted that three degrees of fertility are named, corresponding to the three kinds of unfertile soil.

Mark has probably added the concluding call to attention, "Who hath ears to hear, let him hear", in order to suggest that the parable has a hidden significance and to prepare the way for the following section. . . .

The parable . . . closes on the note not of loss but of gain. . . . "Sowing" is a natural and widely used figure for "teaching". . . .

If we look for the application of the parable of the Sower along these lines, it will illustrate the truth that the spoken word can only bear fruit when its hearers are receptive. But, though in the interpretation of the parable interest is concentrated upon the wasted seed, in the parable the stress appears to be laid upon the rich harvest that is reaped from fertile soil. The parable, therefore, is more likely to have been employed by Christ as an encouragement to his disciples to believe that the preaching of the Kingdom would prove fruitful, than as a warning to his hearer comparable to the parable of the Two Houses.

B. T. D. Smith. *The Parables of the Synoptic Gospels* (Cambridge, Cambridge University Press, 1937), pp. 124–126

If we look at the fourth and final section of the parable we note that it is not concerned with the hour of the harvest or with harvesting but with the seed which bears abundant fruit. These images contrast with what is depicted in the previous sections, seed which did not come to fruition. . . . The three first moments of the parable are certainly not imaginative pictures of the obstacles and difficulties that can face the sower; the factors in the parable which affect the fate of the seed have been chosen in accordance with a certain system. In all four cases the type of ground is the primary factor (the sowing takes place on the path, on the stony ground, among thorns and on good ground). Secondary factors (birds, heat of the sun, the thorns which spring up) have therefore only a destructive effect. . . .

The order in which the unsuccessful sowings are placed should be noted. That failures should precede successes is a common idea and a frequently employed device in folk tales (the 'law of the final climax'). . . .

We have here an important insight into the mental process which lay behind the creation of a parable. The composer of the parable of the sower wanted to express the complex idea which we could formulate in a rather abstract and schematic way as follows: When God's word is now spoken to the people of his covenant, it comes in vain to those who do not love God with their whole heart, their whole soul and their whole might, but it bears rich fruit in those who fulfil the fundamental demand of the covenant. This can be expressed in simple, concrete ('unveiled') words: we find such in the interpretation. But this teaching is given in the first place in the form of a parable. In other words, the parable of the sower does not instruct openly, its theme is presented in veiled form. . . . Its presentation is a peculiar middle stage between clarity and incomprehensibility. We can furthermore state that this parable is not intended to put over only one point, but to convey a complex—though concentrated—didache. Every element is carefully thought out; the four stages can be interpreted individually as long as the main theme controlling the parable as a whole is not lost sight of.

To say this of the nature, contents and construction of the parable is to say that it was created to be *memorized* and *meditated upon* (as well as to be expounded and put into practice). . . .

The parble and the interpretation fit each other as hand fits glove. If the parable—in the only form we know it—is from Jesus, then so is the interpretation. . . .

Only detailed studies can determine how far the parable of the sower is to be equated with the other gospel parables. . . . But we make an important step towards understanding the nature of parables if we can get an idea of the 'fundamental-parable' of the gospels. . . . To a certain extent it can be understood immediately because of its use of traditional metapors, particularly those belonging to known or relevant passages of the scriptures. . . . The imagery used predisposes an exposition which will incorporate simliar themes from the scriptures and from the established traditions.

Birger Gerhardsson. *NTS*. 14, 1967–68, pp. 186–188, 192–193

We . . . note the "rule of three" thrice instanced: three types of loss, three verbs of bringing forth (growing up, increasing, yielding), the three degrees of increment (thirtyfold, sixtyfold, one hundredfold). We also observe the feature of reversal and surprise, the fourth case against the first three. But this denouement or resolution is also marked by at least rhetorical hyperbole.

There is, indeed, a question as to whether the yield, thirtyfold, sixtyfold, one hundredfold, represents an extraordinary outcome. (It refers not to the whole sowing but to the seed sown on the good soil.) . . . Two considerations argue for taking the yield as hyperbolic and a departure from realism. (1) The ascending serial enumeration in the context of the art-form intensifies the feature of surprise and disproportion. The imagination is pointed even beyond the hundredfold. Thus at least rhetorical hyperbole. (2) The motif of disproportion is paralleled by other parables like that of the leaven and another parable of growth, that of the mustard seed. . . .

In the case of the parable of the Sower I see two deep sounding boards that lend power to the communication and which enter into its proper inter-pretation. . . . For one thing, man's relation to the earth and its processes is primordial and full of mystery. Folklore, mythology and the "savage mind" see tilling and planting as transaction with powers, . . . and harvest as having the character of miracle. Our parable as an art-form identifies itself with this naive depth. In contrast perhaps with the parable of the mustard seed this one . . . involves the husbandman. It has to do with culture and not with wild nature alone. The enigmatic vicissitudes of loss and gain involve man's place in creation and its exuberance, the primordial wonder that existence emerges out of and prevails over nothingness. If one speaks of "structure" here it would refer to an internalized pattern in the psyche which dictates such universal motifs as those of the garden, Paradise, etc., in dreams and human fabulation.

A second sounding-board evoked in the parable goes even deeper. It relates to man's ultimate *conatus* or striving or going out from himself in search of fulfilment. Our very being and security in existence are strangely poised between trust and untrust. . . . The parable speaks out of and to this dynamic turmoil by assurance not only of the trustworthiness of existence but of its plenitude and excess.

Our parable speaks to this particular sounding-board or register in the hearer in terms of sower, seed, soils and harvest. What is here presented in the language-analogue of the husbandman or the archetype of the garden could equally well be dramatized or storied in some other metphor of human activity. The basic paradigm of man's initiative vis-à-vis his world and its sequel could employ other types of venture: not only sowing but fishing, and also hunting, digging, mining, risking, investing, gambling.

Amos N. Wilder. *Semeia*. 2, 1974, pp. 139–142

Jesus' parable of the sower (Matt. 13:1–9, 18–23), more accurately called the parable of the soils, is typical of many of the parables. The story draws upon a rural situation and no doubt struck a responsive note in the lives of Christ's audience. In this respect it illustrates the realism of the parables. On the narrative level there are three main ingredients in the parable—a sower, seed, and soil. The action of the plot is negligible: a farmer sows seed in four kinds of soil, only one of which proves productive. This means that of the three elements in the story, the sower and seed are constant, while the types of soil are variable. Despite the paucity of action, the plot does contain conflict. A certain amount of struggle is conveyed by the description of how the birds "devoured" the seeds (Matt. 13:4) and how the thorns "choked" them (vs. 7), as well as by the statement that the sun "scorched" some of the shoots (vs. 6).

The story becomes a parable when Jesus allegorizes the event of the sower and his seed (Matt. 13:18–23). The seed is God's message of salvation and righteous living. The sower is the evangelist, or even Christ Himself. The kinds of soil are the responses of hearers to the Word of God. Since it is the kinds of soil that are variable, this is where the emphasis of the parable falls. . . .

What application might this classification of responses to the Gospel have had in Christ's day? . . .

Most interpreters of the parable believe that Jesus intended it as an encouragement to His disillusioned disciples. When the disciples saw the resistance that Jesus encountered, this theory states, they became discouraged and doubtful. Jesus told a parable that had the concept of fruitfulness and success as its climax in order to counteract their disillusionment.

This emphasis is somewhat misleading. Matthew 13:2 makes it clear that Jesus was speaking to a huge crowd of people, not simply to His disciples. The parable, moreover, concentrates on the kinds of soil, not the sower. The whole interest is with the soil, that is, the hearers of the Gospel. It would appear that the parable was a challenge to those who were listening to the claims of the Gospel. Jesus delineates three inadequate reponses to His message of the kingdom. It is a warning to His listeners to avoid these errors. The fourth response provides the opportunity to choose a better way. Even here there are varieties of fruitfulness, thereby providing a challenge to the listeners to be as responsive as they possibly could. To sum up, the parable of the sower stresses human responsiveness to God's message of salvation. It sets up options from which the listener must choose.

Leland Ryken. *The Literature of the Bible* (Grand Rapids, Zondervan, 1974), pp. 303–304

The parable is an allegory, an extended metaphor in narrative form. Regardless of what its original setting and meaning may have been, that it always had both a literal and a metaphorical level of meaning is certain. . . .

In [Mark 4:1–9], the parable of the sower begins "Listen!" (vs. 3). . . . In Mark the word warns the hearer to be attentive both because what follows is of great import, and because it will be conveyed indirectly in a parable. The point is reiterated in the conclusion: "He who has ears to hear, let him hear" (vs. 9). . . .

On the literal level, the parable tells the story of a sower scattering seed, some of which falls on poor soil and dies, some of which falls on good soil and lives and grows and bears fruit. On the metaphorical level, according to Mark's Gospel, it exhorts the hearer to receive in faith and keep with steadfastness the word that is disseminated. As it stands in the Gospel, of course, the parable has two historical settings. Mark tells of Jesus' preaching to a Jewish audience, and so the "word" is Jesus' proclamation of the coming kingdom (cf. 2:2); but Mark himself is addressing his own readers, and so the "word" is also the Church's proclamation of the Christian message. . . .

The parable of the sower and its explanation stress the need for man to respond to the proclamation of the kingdom. The success of the proclamation depends as much on the hearer as on the speaker. It is incumbent on man to resist the attacks of Satan, "tribulation or persecution," "the cares of the world, and the delight in riches, and the desire for other things"; and to "hear the word and accept it and bear fruit" (vss. 15–20). . . .

The sower is placed at the beginning of this collection because it is the most important parable in the Gospel. That is because it is the key to understanding all the other parables. It is basic because the seed that is sown is the word spoken by Jesus; but it is only in parables that Jesus spoke the word (vss. 11, 33–34); then, in a sense, the seed stands for the parables. Thus it is a parable on the right hearing of parables. That is why Jesus says to his disciples, "Do you not understand this parable? How then will you understand all the parables?" (vs. 13). The very question, it should be noted, shows the understanding of parables to be a possibility. . . .

The Markan interpretation gives a very natural rendering of the parable, one which fits it perfectly. The hearer would have to be told that the parable as a whole has to do with hearing the word; but once so informed, he would have little difficulty in apprehending many of its constituent meanings. That the scattering of seed stands for the dissemination of the word; the ground for those among whom the word is broadcast; the poor and rich soil for those respectively who fail and who succeed in receiving and keeping the word; and the final yield of grain for righteousness—these are meanings that are derived quite naturally from the story. There is nothing in the broad lines of this interpretation that strains the sense of the reference in the parable itself. Even a simple, uneducated hearer of the kind that must have largely made up the audiences of Jesus would have been able to supply these constituent meanings, once he had perceived the whole meaning to be about the word. . . .

What the author of the interpretation (whoever he may have been) has done with the parable . . . is by no means a falsification of its meaning. With artful skill, he has delineated the psychological dispositions of various hearers who by their states of mind are led to one or another kind of action of a moral order. This the author has done in such a way that the description of each kind of hearer in the interpretation is quite suited to the description of each kind of soil in the parable.

Madeleine Boucher. *The Mysterious Parable: A Literary Study* (Washington, D. C., Catholic Biblical Association of America, 1977), pp. 45–46, 49–50

The narrative is so structured as to contrast loss and gain. First it talks about seed that yields nothing because it is devoured or scorched or choked. Then it tells of seeds that yield thirty-, sixty-, even a hundred fold. Most attention is given to the seed falling upon rocky ground, but the end position of emphasis describes success, underscoring the fertiity of the seed, the extravagance of the harvest. . . .

Immediately after the opening line, the story is told from the point of view of the seeds. That gives to the familiar world of sowing a certain strangeness through dislocation. In any case, for agricultural procedures the story is disappointing, if not misleading. After reading or hearing it, no one learns much about sowing.

Among the elements in the story there are no surprises, no end reversals, and no contradictions. Indeed one of its striking characteristics is its blandness. Through the stylized "some seed," "other seed," "other seeds," all elements are leveled out to the same intensity. It is that very blandness and vagueness which calls for a reading on a secondary level.

Leonard L. Thompson. *Introducing Biblical Literature: A More Fantastic Country* (Englewood Cliffs, Prentice-Hall, 1978), pp. 257–258

COPYRIGHT ACKNOWLEDGMENTS

ABINGDON PRESS. For permission to quote excerpts from the following books: *An Introduction to New Testament Literature* by Donald Juel. Copyright © 1978 by Donald Juel. Used by permission of the publisher, Abingdon Press. *The Interpreter's Bible, Vol. 7.* Copyright renewal © 1980 by Abingdon Press. *Literary Interpretations of Biblical Narratives* by Kenneth Gros Louis. Copyright © 1974 by Abingdon Press. Used by permission.

THE ASSOCIATION OF BAPTIST PROFESSORS OF RELIGION. For permission to quote excerpts from *Perspectives on Luke-Acts*, ed. Charles H. Talbert (1978).

BAKER BOOK HOUSE. For permission to quote excerpts from the following books: Gilbert Bilezikian, *The Liberated Gospel* (1977); and Simon J. Kistemaker, *The Parables of Jesus* (1980). Copyright by Baker Book House and used by permission.

BETHANY PRESS. For permission to quote an excerpt from Gary Webster, *Laughter in the Bible* (1960).

BIBLIOTHECA SACRA. For permission to quote an excerpt from Merrill C. Tenney, "The Imagery of John," 121 (1960).

BASIL BLACKWELL PUBLISHER. For permission to quote excerpts from Rudolf Bultmann, *History of the Synoptic Tradition*, trans. John Marsh (1963). Used by permission.

BODLEY HEAD PRESS. For permission to quote an excerpt from G. K. Chesterton, *Orthodoxy* (1909).

CAMBRIDGE UNIVERSITY PRESS. For permission to quote excerpts from the following books: Gerald H. Rendall, *The Epistle of St. James and Judaic Christianity* (1927); B. T. D. Smith, *The Parables of the Synoptic Gospels* (1937); C. H. Dodd, *About the Gospels* (1950); C. H. Dodd, *The Interpretation of the Fourth Gospel* (1953); E. J. Tinsley, *The Gospel According to Luke* (1965); J. H. Davies, *A Letter to Hebrews* (1967); Allison A. Trites, *The New Testament Concept of Witness* (1977). All used by permission of Cambridge University Press.

340 ACKNOWLEDGMENTS

JONATHAN CAPE LTD. For permission to quote excerpts from Kathleen E. Innes, *The Bible as Literature* (1930).

CATHOLIC BIBLICAL ASSOCIATION OF AMERICA. For permission to quote excerpts from Madeleine Boucher, *The Mysterious Parable: A Literary Study* (1977).

CATHOLIC BIBLICAL QUARTERLY. For permission to quote excerpts form Charles H. Lohr, "Oral Techniques in the Gospel of Matthew," 23 (1961); and Willim G. Doty, "The Classification of Epistolary Literature," 31 (1969).

CHRISTIANITY AND LITERATURE. For permission to quote excerpts from Harry Boonstra, "Satire in Matthew," 29, no. 4 (1980); and John W. Sider, "Nurturing Our Nurse: Literary Scholars and Biblical Exegesis," 32, no. 1 (1980).

JAMES CLARK AND COMPANY LTD. Forpermission to quote excerpts from A.T. Cadoux, *The Parables of Jesus: Their Art and Use* (1930).

T & T. CLARK. For permission to quote excerpts from E.F. Scott, *The Fourth Gospel: Its Purpose and Theology* (1906, 1908).

DODD, MEAD, AND COMPANY. For permission to quote an excerpt from Lafcadio Hearn, *Books and Habits* (1921).

WILLIAM B. EERDMANS PUBLISHING COMPANY. For permission to quote excerpts from George Eldon Ladd, *The New Testament and Criticism* (1967); and Robert H. Mounce, *The Book of Revelation* (1977). Used by permission.

E. P. DUTTON AND COMPANY, INC. For permission to quote an excerpt from *Literary Criticism by Francis Thompson* by Rev. Terence L. Connolly, S.J. Ph.D. Copyright 1948 by E. P. Dutton and Company, Inc. Reprinted by permission of the publisher, E. P. Dutton, Inc.

EPWORTH PRESS. For permission to quote excerpts from Vincent Taylor, *The Gospels: A Short Introduction* (1930, 1945).

FARRER. TRUSTEES OF KATHARINE DOROTHY For permission to quote exerpts from *A Study in St Mark* by Austin Farrer (London: Dacre Press, 1951).

FORTRESS PRESS. For permission to quote excerpts from the following books: W. Marxsen, *Introduction to the New Testament* (1964, 1968); Dan Otto Via, Jr., *The Parables: Their Literary and Existential Dimension* (1967); William A. Beardslee, *Literary Criticism of the New Testament* (1970); Clyde Weber Votaw, *The Gospels and Contemporary Biographies in the Greco-Roman World* (1970; originally published 1915); Theodore J. Weeden, *Mark—Traditions in Conflict* (1971); William G. Doty, *Letters in Primitive Christianity* (1973); Dan Otto Via, Jr., *Kerygma and Comedy in the New Testament*

(1975); Birger Gerhardsson, *The Origins of the Gospel Tradition* (1977); Jack Dean Kingsbury, *Matthew* (1977), *Luther's Works*, Volume 35, pp. 117–121. Copyright (c) 1960 by Fortress Press. Reprinted by permission of Fortress Press.

ROLAND M. FRYE. For permission to quote excerpts from *The Bible: Selections from the King James Version for Study as Literature* (Boston: Houghton Mifflin Company, 1965; rpt. Princeton University Press, 1977). Copyright by Roland M. Frye and used by permission.

ROBERT W. FUNK. For permission to quote excerpts from *Language, Hermeneutic, and Word of God* (New York: Harper and Row, 1966; rpt. Polebridge Press).

HARCOURT BRACE JOVANOVICH, INC. For permission to quote excerpts from *Jesus in History: An Approach to the Study of the Gospels* by Howard Clark Kee, copyright © 1970 by Harcourt Brace Jovanovich, Inc. Reprinted by permission of the publisher. Excerpts from *The New Testament: An Introduction* by Norman Perrin, copyright © 1974 by Harcourt Brace Jovanovich, Inc. Reprinted by permission of the publisher. Excerpts from *The Great Code: The Bible and Literature* copyright © 1982, 1981 by Northrop Frye. Reprinted by permission of Harcourt Brace Jovanovich, Inc.

HARPER AND ROW PUBLISHERS, INC. For permission to quote excerpts from the following books: Pages 37–45, 46–48, 48–51 from *The Gospel of Mark: Its Making and Meaning* by Curtis Beach. Copyright © 1959 by Curtis Beach. Pages 9, 19–21, 41–44, 46–49, 50–51, 55, 57–59, 63–64, 69–70 from *The Humor of Christ* by Elton Trueblood. Copyright © 1964 by Elton Trueblood. Pages 40, 41, 52–53, 70, 71, 99–100, 139–140, 147 from *The Bible as Literature: The New Testament* by Buckner B. Trawick; Copyright © 1964, 1968 by Harper and Row Publishers, Inc. Excerpt from *Telling the Truth: The Gospel as Tragedy, Comedy, and Fairy Tale* by Frederick Buechner. Copyright © 1977 by Frederick Buechner. All reprinted by permission of Harper and Row Publishers, Inc.

HODDER AND STOUGHTON. For permission to quote excerpts from the following books: Adolf Diessmann, *Light from the Ancient East* (1923, 1927); R. H. Strachan, *The Fourth Evangelist: Dramatist or Historian?* (1925); Robert H. Lightfoot, *Locality and Doctrine in the Gospels* (1938); Martin Kiddle, *The Revelation of St. John* (1940). All reprinted by permission of Hodder and Stoughton Limited.

HOUGHTON MIFFLIN COMPANY. For permission to quote an excerpt from Charlotte I. Lee, *Oral Reading of the Scriptures* (1974).

INTERPRETATION. For permission to quote excerpts from the following articles: Charles F. Wishart, "Patmos in the Pulpit: A Meditation on Apocalyptic," 1 (1947); Dean G. McKee, "The Gospel According to Matthew,"

3 (1949); James L. Price, "The Gospel According to Luke," 7 (1953); John Wick Bowman, "The Revelation to John: Its Dramatic Structure and Message," 9 (1955); Albert C. Winn, "Elusive Mystery: The Purpose of Acts," 13 (1959); A. M. Hunter, "Interpreting the Parables," 14 (1960); William A. Beardslee, "Uses of the Proverb in the Synoptic Gospels," 24 (1970); Dan. O. Via, Jr., "The Relationship of Form to Content in the Parables: The Wedding Feast," 25 (1971); Amos N. Wilder, "The Rhetoric of Ancient and Modern Apocalyptic," 25 (1971); Paul J. Achtemeier, "The Ministry of Jesus in the Synoptic Gospels," 35 (1981).

INTER VARSITY PRESS. For permission to quote excerpts from F. F. Bruce, *The Speeches in the Acts of the Apostles* (1942).

WILSON G. KNIGHT and THE UNIVERSITY PRESS OF AMERICA. For permission to quote excerpts from *The Christian Renaissance* (London: Methuen and Company, 1962; rpt. University Press of America).

JOHN KNOX PRESS. For permission to quote excerpts from the following books: *The Revelation of Jesus Christ: An Interpretation* by Donald W. Richardson. Original Edition, copyright 1939 by John Knox Press. Aletheia Edition, copyright 1964 by M. E. Bratcher. Published by John Knox Press. Used by permission. *Letters of Paul: Conversations in Context* by Calvin J. Roetzel. Copyright John Knox Press 1975, second edition 1982. Published by John Knox Press. Used by permission. *The Layman's Guide to the New Testament* by William M. Ramsay. Copyright John Knox Press 1981. Published by John Knox Press. Used by permission.

THE JOURNAL OF BIBLICAL LITERATURE. For permission to quote from the following articles: Clayton R. Bowen, "The Fourth Gospel as Dramatic Material," 49 (1930); C. Milo Connick, "The Dramatic Character of the Fourth Gospel," 67 (1948); Floyd V. Filson, "How Much of the New Testament Is Poetry?" 67 (1948); Terence Y. Mullins, "Jewish Wisdom Literature in the New Testament," 68 (1949); Massey H. Shepherd, Jr., "The Epistle of James and the Gospel of Matthew," 75 (1956); Joseph B. Tyson, "The Blindness of the Disciples in Mark," 80 (1961); Paul Schubert, "The Final Cycle of Speeches in the Book of Acts," 87 (1968); William G. Johnsson, "The Pilgrimage Motif in the Book of Hebrews," 97 (1978); Charles E. Carlston, "Proverbs, Maxims, and the Historical Jesus," 99 (1980).

JOURNAL OF THE EVANGELICAL THEOLOGICAL SOCIETY. For permission to quote excerpts from the following articles: Robert A. Guelich, "The Gospels: Portraits of Jesus and His Ministry," 24 (1981); Donald A. Hagner, "Interpreting the Gospels: The Landscape and the Quest," 24 (1981); Simon J. Kistemaker, "The Structure of Luke's Gospel," 25 (1982); Ronald Russell, "Pauline Letter Structure in Philippians," 25 (1982).

JOURNAL OF RELIGION. For permission to quote excerpts from the following articles: Ernest W. Burch, "Tragic Action in the Second Gospel," 12 (1931); and Robert C. Tannehill, "The Disciples in Mark," 57 (1977).

JOURNAL OF THEOLOGICAL STUDIES. For permission to quote excerpts from M.D. Goulder, "Characteristics of the Parables in the Several Gospels," 19, n.s. (1968). Reprinted from the *Journal of Theological Studies* (Oxford University Press) by permission of the editors.

KODON. For permission to quote an excerpt from Alan Johnson, "Jesus and Imagination," 36, no. 2 (1982). Reprinted by permission from *Kodon* © 1982.

MACMILLAN PUBLISHING COMPANY. For permission to quote excerpts from the following books: *The Gospel of Luke* by John Drury. Reprinted with permission of Macmillan Publishing Company. Copyright © 1973 by John Drury. *The Book of Revelation*, translated and with an introduction by J. B. Phillips. Reprinted with permission of Macmillan Publishing Company. © Macmillan Publishing Company, Inc., 1957. *The Bible and the Common Reader* by Mary Ellen Chase. Reprinted with permission of Macmillan Publishing Company. Copyright 1944, and renewed 1972, by Mary Ellen Chase. Richard G. Moulton, *The Bible at a Single View* (1918). Reprinted with permission of Macmillan Publishing Company.

MARSHALL, MORGAN & SCOTT. For permission to quote excerpts from G. R. Beasley-Murray, *The Book of Revelation* (1974); and Ralph P. Martin, *Worship in the Early Church* (1964; rpt. William B. Eerdmans, 1974).

PAUL S. MINEAR. For permission to quote excerpts from *I Saw a New Earth* (Washington, D.C.: Corpus Books, 1968).

NEW TESTAMENT STUDIES. For permission to quote excerpts from the following articles: Birger Gerhardsson, "The Parable of the Sower and Its Interpretation," 14 (1967–68); Nigel Turner, "The Literary Character of New Testament Greek," 20 (1973–74); W. S. Vorster, "Kerygma/History and the Gospel Genre," 29 (1983). Reprinted with permission of Cambridge University Press.

NOVUM TESTAMENTUM. For permission to quote excerpts from the following articles: Raymond E. Brown, "Parable and Allegory Reconsidered," 5 (1962); and Allison A. Trites, "The Importance of Legal Scenes and Language in the Book of Acts," 16 (1974). Reprinted with permission of E. J. Brill.

OXFORD UNIVERSITY PRESS. For permission to quote excerpts from the following books: P. C. Sands, *Literary Genius of the New Testament* (1932); Wilbur Owen Sypherd, *The Literature of the English Bible* (1938); William A. Curtis, *Jesus Christ the Teacher* (1943); Austin Farrer, *The Revelation of St. John the Divine* (1964); *The Notebooks and Papers of Gerard Manley*

Hopkins, edited by Humphrey House (1939) by permission of Oxford University Press on behalf of the Society of Jesus.

PATERNOSTER PRESS, LTD. For permission to quote excerpts from *New Testament Interpretation*, edited by I. Howard Marshall (1977).

PICKWICK PRESS. For permission to quote excerpts from the following books: *From Faith to Faith*, ed. D. Y. Hadidian (1979); and *Orientation by Disorientation*, ed. Richard A. Spencer (1980).

PITTSBURGH THEOLOGICAL SEMINARY. For permission to quote an excerpt from *Jesus and Man's Hope*, Volume 2. Edited by Donald G. Miller and Dikran Y. Hadidian. Pittsburgh Theological Seminary, 1971, pp. 207, 209–212. Used by permission.

PRENTICE-HALL, INC. For permission to quote excerpts from Leonard L. Thompson, *Introducing Biblical Literature: A More Fantastic Country*, © 1978. Reprinted by permission of Prentice-Hall, Inc., Englewood Cliffs, N.J.

PRINCETON UNIVERSITY PRESS. For permission to quote excerpts from the following books: Northrop Frye, *Anatomy of Criticism* (1957). Copyright © 1957 by Princeton University Press. Erich Auerbach, *Mimesis: The Representation of Reality in Western Literature*, trans. Willard R. Trask. Copyright 1953 by Princeton University Press, copyright © renewed 1981 by Princeton University Press.

REVIEW AND EXPOSITOR. For permission to quote excerpts from the following articles: William E. Hull, "A Structural Analysis of the Gospel of Luke," 64 (1967); and Harold S. Songer, "Luke's Portrayal of the Origins of Jesus," 64 (1967).

SCM PRESS. For permission to quote an excerpt from R. V. G. Tasker, *The Nature and Purpose of the Gospels* (1944); and A. M. Hunter, *Design for Life* (1953; published in USA by Westminster Press, 1965, under the title *A Pattern for Life*).

CHARLES SCRIBNER'S SONS. For permission to quote excerpts from *A Critical and Exegetical Commentary on the Epistle of St. James* by James Hardy Ropes, reprinted with the permission of Charles Scribner's Sons. Copyright 1916 Charles Scribner's Sons; copyright renewed 1944; and from *Literature of the New Testament* by Herbert R. Purinton and Carl E. Purinton, copyright 1925 by Charles Scribner's Sons and reprinted by permission of the publisher.

SOCIETY OF AUTHORS. For granting permission, as the literary representatives of the Estate of J. Middleton Murry, to quote excerpts from *The Problem of Style*, by J. Middleton Murry (Oxford: Oxford University Press, 1922).

THE SOCIETY OF BIBLICAL LITERATURE. For permission to quote excerpts from Robert C. Tannehill, *The Sword of His Mouth* (1975) and from the following articles that appeared in *Semeia*: John Dominic Crossan, "The Good Samaritan: Towards a Generic Definition of Parable," 2 (1974); Amos N. Wilder, "The Parable of the Sower: Naivete and Method of Interpretation," 2 (1974); Mary Ann Tolbert, "The Prodigal Son: An Essay in Literary Criticism from a Psychoanalytic Perspective," 9 (1977); Norman R. Peterson, "Point of View in Mark's Narrative," 12 (1978); John J. Collins, "Towards the Morphology of a Genre," 14 (1979); Jean Calloud, "Toward a Structural Analysis of the Gospel of Mark," 16 (1979); Werner H. Kelber, "Mark and Oral Tradition," 16 (1979); Robert C, Tannehill, "The Gospel of Mark as Narrative Christology," 16 (1979).

CHARLES W. F. SMITH. For permission to quote excerpts from *The Jesus of the Parables* (Philadelphia, Westminster Press, 1948; rpt. Pilgrim Press, 1975).

SOCIETY FOR PROMOTING CHRISTIAN KNOWLEDGE. For permission to quote excerpts from the following books: S. C. Carpenter, *Christianity According to S. Luke* (1919); C. K. Barrett, *The Gospel According to St. John* (1955); J. D. Goulder, *Type and History in Acts* (1964); Geraint Vaughan Jones, *The Art and Truth of the Parables* (1964); J. C. O'Neill, *The Theology of Acts in Its Historical Setting* (1970).

UNIVERSITY OF CHICAGO PRESS. For permission to quote excerpts from the following sources: Edgar J. Goodspeed, *An Introduction to the New Testament* (1937); Ernest W. Burch, "Tragic Action in the Second Gospel," *Journal of Religion*, 12 (1931); Robert C. Tannehill, "The Disciples in Mark," *Journal of Religion*, 57 (1977).

NELVIN VOS. For permission to quote an excerpt from *The Drama of Comedy: Victim and Victor* (Richmond: John Knox Press, 1966).

WESTMINSTER PRESS. For permission to quote from the following books: *The Unity of the Bible* by H. H. Rowley. First Published and Printed, 1953, in Great Britain by The Carey Kingsgate Press Limited. Used by permission of The Westminster Press, Philadelphia, Pennsylvania. *Westminster Introductions to the Books of the Bible*. © MCMXLVIII, MCMLVII, by W. L. Jenkins. Used by permission of The Westminster Press, Philadelphia, Pennsylvania. *Bible and Gospel* by A. M. Hunter. © SCM Press Ltd. 1969. Published in the USA by The Westminster Press and used by permission. *The Acts of the Apostles* by Ernst Haenchen. © in this translation Basil Blackwell 1971. Published in the U.S.A. by The Westminster Press. Used by permission. *Introduction to the Bible* by John H. Hayes. Copyright © MCMLXXI The Westminster Press. Used by permission.

THE ESTATE OF MRS. RUFUS ROCKWELL WILSON. For permission to quote excerpts from Johannes Weiss, *Earliest Christianity*, Vol. II, trans. Frederick C. Grant (New York: Harper and Row, 1937).

THE YALE REVIEW. For permission to quote an excerpt from Roger L. Cox, "Tragedy and the Gospel Narratives," 59 (1968).

ZONDERVAN PUBLISHING CORPORATION. For permission to quote excerpts from Leland Ryken, *The Literature of the Bible*. Copyright © 1974 by the Zondervan Corporation.

INDEX TO CRITICS